2021 AP EXAM FORMAT INFORMATION

The COVID-19 pandemic affected the administration of AP exams in both 2020 and 2021. Although things remain subject to change at any time, it appears we are now on our way back to the traditional AP track. College Board continues to make decisions based on the health and safety of students and educators across the country, so it's a good idea to stay informed of the latest changes to your AP course and exam as the school year progresses.

<u>The big news for the 2021 tests was the introduction of varied testing date and format options.</u> Rather than offering the traditional single test approach, AP exams were administered three times—in early May, late May, and early June—with some subjects having been administered in a digital format in addition to the traditional paper format. Several exams offered different formats for paper- and digital-based exams, and the differences varied by subject. **All exams, however, were full length and covered the full scope of content for each AP course.**

AP English Literature exam followed the following format:

- Exams were offered on paper in early May, and as a digital exam in late May and early June
- Both the paper and digital versions contained the traditional multiple-choice and free-response sections
- There was no difference in format between the exams

Is this *5 Steps* guide relevant and up-to-date?

Yes! Everything in this book is reflective of the current course and exam as it was originally designed. The *5 Steps* team strives to keep all information relevant and as up-to-date as possible, both in print and online.

What will happen in May 2022?

Your guess is as good as ours. Whether the AP exams return fully to their original paper format, continue in the 2021 hybrid (paper and online) models, or morph into something entirely new – remains uncertain. However, no matter what College Board will decide for next year - we have you covered! We'll be updating our materials whenever any new information becomes available, and will make every effort to revise our digital resources as quickly as possible.

So, whatever this AP school year may bring, please continue to check in to your *5 Steps* Cross-Platform course at **mheducation.com/5stepslit**. We will make every effort to keep the practice tests on the platform reflective of what you'll see on test day.

Most importantly, look for regular updates on the College Board website for the latest information on your course at **apcentral.collegeboard.org**. This will be your best resource for the most up-to-date information on all AP courses.

5 STEPS TO A 5™

AP English Literature

2022

ELITE STUDENT EDITION

5 STEPS TO A 5

AP English Literature

2022

Barbara L. Murphy
Estelle M. Rankin

McGraw Hill

New York   Chicago   San Francisco   Athens   London   Madrid
Mexico City   Milan   New Delhi   Singapore   Sydney   Toronto

1 2 3 4 5 6 7 8 9   LHS   26 25 24 23 22 21   (Cross-Platform Prep Course only)
1 2 3 4 5 6 7 8 9   LHS   26 25 24 23 22 21   (Elite Student Edition)

ISBN   978-1-264-26777-4   (Cross-Platform Prep Course only)
MHID   1-264-26777-0

e-ISBN   978-1-264-26778-1   (Cross-Platform Prep Course only)
e-MHID   1-264-26778-9

ISBN   978-1-264-26779-8   (Elite Student Edition)
MHID   1-264-26779-7

e-ISBN   978-1-264-26780-4   (Elite Student Edition)
e-MHID   1-264-26780-0

Trademarks: McGraw Hill, the McGraw Hill logo, *5 Steps to a 5*, and related trade dress are trademarks or registered trademarks of McGraw Hill and/or its affiliates in the United States and other countries and may not be used without written permission. All other trademarks are the property of their respective owners. McGraw Hill is not associated with any product or vendor mentioned in this book.

AP, Advanced Placement Program, and *College Board* are registered trademarks of the College Board, which was not involved in the production of, and does not endorse, this product.

McGraw Hill products are available at special quantity discounts to use as premiums and sales promotions or for use in corporate training programs. To contact a representative, please visit the Contact Us pages at www.mhprofessional.com.

CONTENTS

ELITE
STUDENT
EDITION

5 Minutes to a 5

Appendixes

PREFACE

Welcome to our latest revised AP Literature class. As we said in the earlier versions of this book, we are first and foremost teachers who have taught Advanced Placement to literally thousands of students who successfully took the AP exam. With this guide, we hope to share with you what we know as well as what we have learned from our own students.

We see you as a student in our class—only quieter! Our philosophy has always been NOT to teach only for the AP test. Instead, our goal has always been to develop those insights, appreciations, and skills that lead to advanced levels of facility with literature and composition. These are the very same skills which will enable you to do well on the AP Literature exam. Our aim is to remove your anxiety and to improve your comfort level with the test. We believe that you are already motivated to succeed; otherwise, you would not have come this far. And, obviously, you would not have purchased this prep book.

Since you are already in an English class, this book is going to supplement your literature course readings, analysis, and writing. We are going to give you the opportunity to practice processes and techniques that we know from experience REALLY WORK! If you apply the techniques and processes presented in this book, we are confident you can succeed in both the course and on the exam.

We have listened to comments and suggestions from both instructors and students of AP English Literature, and keeping their thoughts in mind, this revised text has more interactive activities and practice to help hone those skills needed to do well in class and on the AP Literature exam. In addition, there are special review questions and activities related to specific chapters that McGraw Hill has available on its website devoted to the *5 Steps* series. There you can test how well you have internalized the material in the chapter.

Let's begin.

ACKNOWLEDGMENTS

Our love and appreciation to Allan and to Leah for their constant support and encouragement. Our very special thanks to our professional mentors who have guided us throughout our careers: Steven Piorkowski and Howard Damon. To the following for their support and suggestions: Diane Antonucci, Richard Andres, Mary Moran, Mike Thier, Mark Misthal, Dave Martin, Edward Stern, Christine Scarf, John Smales, and Michael Hartnett—thank you.

The authors wish to acknowledge the participation, insights, and feedback provided us by the following colleagues and students:

Islip High School:
  Teacher: Marge Grossgold
  Students: Caitlin Rizzo and Katelyn Zawyrucha

Jericho High School:
  Teachers: Diane Antonucci, Michael Hartnett
  Students: Tara Arschin, Samantha Brody, Jenna Butner, Julie Ivans, Grace Kwak, Ari Weiss, Erica Ross, David Swidler, and Sherli Yeroushalmi

Massapequa High School:
  Teachers: Sue Bruno and Rosemary Verade
  Student: Margaretta Dimos

Solomon Schechter School:
  Teachers: Dennis Young and Miriam Fischer
  Students: Yadin Duckstein, Ari Lucas, and Jonathan Kotter

Wantagh High School:
  Teachers: Sherry Skolnick and Pat Castellano
  Student: Lauren Manning

Also, our thanks to Danielle Tumminio and Andrew Brotman.

Barbara L. Murphy taught AP Language and other college-level courses at Jericho High School for over 26 years. She is a long-time reader of the AP English Language exam and is a consultant for the College Board's AP Language and Composition and Building for Success divisions, for which she has conducted workshops, conferences, and Summer Institutes.

After earning her BA from Duquesne University and her MA from the University of Pittsburgh, Ms. Murphy did her doctoral course work at Columbia University. She also holds professional certifications in still photography and motion picture production and is one of the founding members of the women's film company Ishtar Films.

Estelle M. Rankin taught AP Literature at Jericho High School for over 25 years. She was honored with the AP Literature Teacher of the Year award by the College Board in 1996. She also received the Long Island Teacher of the Year award in 1990. She was the recipient of the Cornell University Presidential Scholars' Award and has been recognized by the C.W. Post Master Teachers Program.

Ms. Rankin earned her BA from Adelphi University and her MA from Hofstra University. She pursued further graduate work in the field of creative studies at Queens College and Brooklyn College.

Ms. Rankin did extensive work in the research and development of the film, drama, and creative writing curriculum, SAT prep, the new NYS Regents AP Literature conferences, and workshops. She was a College Board consultant for pre-AP and AP English. Her finest teachers were her parents, Edward and Sylvia Stern.

Ms. Murphy and Ms. Rankin are also the coauthors of McGraw Hill's *5 Steps to a 5: AP English Language, Writing the AP English Essay,* and *Writing an Outstanding College Application Essay.*

Michael Hartnett has been a high school AP Literature teacher and college professor for more than 30 years. He received his PhD in Literature from the State University of New York at Stony Brook. He is the author of five published novels, the latest being *Blue Gowanus* (Black Rose Writing, 2020), and he has also worked as an editor for the literary magazine *Confrontation*. Michael is the coauthor of the *5 Minutes to a 5* section of *5 Steps to a 5: AP English Literature*, Elite Edition.

INTRODUCTION: THE FIVE-STEP PROGRAM

Some Basics

Consider this section as a map of the new territory you are going to explore. We will provide the general directions, and you can decide when, where, and how you will follow this map.

Reading

We believe that reading should be an exciting interaction between you and the writer. You have to bring your own context to the experience, and you must feel comfortable reaching for and exploring ideas. You are an adventurer on a journey of exploration, and we will act as your guides. We will set the itinerary, but you will set your own pace. You can feel free to "stop and smell the roses" or to explore new territory.

The Journey

On any journey, each traveler sees something different on new horizons. So, too, each student is free to personalize his or her own literary experience, provided he or she tries at all times to strive for excellence and accuracy.

Critical Thinking

There are no tricks to critical thinking. Those who claim to guarantee you a score of 5 with gimmicks are doing you a disservice. No one can guarantee a 5; however, the reading and writing skills you will review, practice, and master will give you the very best chance to do your very best. You will have the opportunity to learn, to practice, and to master the critical thinking processes that can empower you to achieve your highest score.

The Beginning

It is our belief that if you focus on the beginning, the rest will fall into place. Once you purchase this book and decide to work your way through it, you are beginning your journey to the AP Literature exam. We will be with you every step of the way.

Why This Book?

We believe we have something unique to offer you. For over 25 years we have addressed the needs of AP students just like you. And we've been fortunate to learn from these students. Therefore, the content of this book reflects genuine student concerns and needs. **This is a student-oriented book**. We will not overwhelm you with pompous language, mislead you with inaccurate information and tasks, or lull you into a false sense of confidence with easy shortcuts. We stand behind every suggestion, process, and question we present. There is no "busywork" in this book.

We know you will not do every activity. Therefore, think of this book as a resource and guide to accompany you on your AP Literature journey to the exam. This book is designed to serve many purposes. It will:

- Clarify requirements for the AP English Literature exam.
- Provide you with test practice.
- Show you rubrics (grading standards) on which you can model and evaluate your own work.
- Anticipate and answer your questions.
- Enrich your understanding and appreciation of literature.
- Help you pace yourself.
- Make you aware of the Five Steps to Mastering the AP English Literature exam.

Organization of the Book

We know that your primary concern is to obtain information about the AP Literature exam. So, we begin at the beginning with an overview of the AP exam in general. We then introduce you to our Diagnostic/Master exam, which we use throughout the book to show you the ins and outs of an AP Literature test. In separate chapters you will become familiar with both sections of the exam. We will lead you through the multiple-choice questions and explain how you should answer them. Then we will take you through the essay questions and discuss approaches to writing these essays.

Because you must be fluent in the language and processes of literary analysis and composition, we provide a Comprehensive Review section in both prose and poetry. This review is not a mere listing of terms and concepts. Rather, it is a series of practices that will hone your analytical and writing skills. But, do not fear. You will find terms and concepts clearly delineated within their contexts. We also provide annotated suggestions for high-interest prose and poetry readings.

A separate section of the book contains practice exams. Here is where you will test your skills and knowledge. You may be sure that the prose and poetry selections included in each exam are on the AP level. The multiple-choice questions provide you with practice in responding to typical types of questions asked in past AP exams. The essay questions are designed to cover the techniques and terms required by the AP exam. The free-response essays are both challenging and specific, yet they are broad enough to suit all curricula. After taking each test, you can check yourself against the explanations of every multiple-choice question and the ratings of the sample student essays.

The final section is one that you should not pass over. It presents a Suggested Reading Guide, a General Bibliography, a Glossary of Terms that may be of importance to you, and a list of websites related to the AP Literature exam.

Introduction to the Five-Step Preparation Program

The **Five-Step Program** is a powerful program designed to provide you with the best possible skills, strategies, and practice to help lead you to that perfect 5 on the Advanced Placement English Literature exam that is administered each May to more than 350,000 high school students. Each of the five steps will provide you with the opportunity to get closer and closer to the 5, which is the gold medal to all AP students.

Step 1: Set Up Your Study Program

- Useful information about the Advanced Placement program and exams
- Three alternative study schedules and advice for determining which is best for you

Step 2: Determine Your Test Readiness

- A first look at the overall exam, to be repeated in greater detail later

Step 3: Develop Strategies for Success

- Learn about the test itself
- Learn to read multiple-choice questions
- Learn how to answer multiple-choice questions, including whether or not to guess
- Learn how to deconstruct the essay prompts
- Learn how to plan the essay

Step 4: Review the Knowledge You Need to Score High

- Practice activities that will hone your skills in close reading
- Practice activities in critical thinking
- Practice activities in critical/analytical writing

Step 5: Build Your Test-Taking Confidence

- Two practice exams that test how well honed your skills are
- Rubrics for self-evaluation

Finally, at the back of the book you'll find additional resources to aid your preparation. These include:

- A comprehensive review of literary analysis
- A glossary of terms
- A bibliography for further reading
- A list of websites related to the AP English Literature exam

The Graphics Used in This Book

To emphasize particular skills and strategies, we use several icons throughout this book. An icon in the margin will alert you that you should pay particular attention to the accompanying text. We use three icons:

 This icon points out a very important concept or fact that you should not pass over.

 This icon calls your attention to a problem-solving strategy that you may want to try.

 This icon indicates a tip that you might find useful.

Boldfaced and *italicized* words indicate important terms as well as those that are included in the Glossary at the back of the book.

Throughout the book you will find margin notes and boxes. We want you to pay close attention to these areas because they can provide tips, hints, strategies, and explanations that will help you reach your full potential.

5 STEPS TO A 5™

AP English Literature

2022

STEP 1

Set Up Your Study Program

CHAPTER 1

What You Should Know About the AP Literature Exam

IN THIS CHAPTER

Summary: Information about the AP English Literature and Composition exam and its scoring

Key Ideas
✪ Learn answers to frequently asked questions
✪ Learn how your final score is calculated
✪ Learn tips for successfully taking the exam

The College Board has introduced changes that will be reflected in the AP English Literature exam.

You should be aware of the following:

The rating of the exam will remain 1, 2, 3, 4, 5.

Multiple choice will comprise 45% of the final score, with the essay section of the exam comprising 55%.

- There are **no changes** to MC questions.
- There are **no changes** to the types of prompts (FRQ): poetry + prose + free response
- There is **renewed emphasis** on skills development in consideration of prose + poetry + longer works

> - The <u>**MAJOR CHANGE**</u> is in the method of rating essays
>   - From holistic to analytic
> - **From 9 points to 6 points**
>   - 6 points
>   - ✓ 1 point for thesis/claim
>   - ✓ 4 points for appropriate evidence and commentary
>   - ✓ 1 point for syntax, diction, and/or complexity

Background on the Advanced Placement Exam

"AP" does not stand for "Always Puzzling." The following should help lift the veil of mystery associated with the AP exam.

What Is the Advanced Placement Program?

The Advanced Placement program was begun by the College Board in 1955 to construct standard achievement exams that would allow highly motivated high school students the opportunity to be awarded advanced placement as freshmen in colleges and universities in the United States. Today, there are more than 39 courses and exams with over 2.7 million students from every state in the nation, and from foreign countries, taking the annual exams in May.

As is obvious, the AP programs are designed for high school students who wish to take college-level courses. The AP Literature course and exam are designed to involve high school students in college-level English studies in both literature and composition.

Who Writes the AP Literature Exam?

According to the folks at the College Board, the AP Literature exam is created by college and high school English instructors called the AP Development Committee. The committee's job is to ensure that the annual AP Literature exam reflects what is being taught and studied in college-level English classes in high schools.

This committee writes a large number of multiple-choice questions that are pretested and evaluated for clarity, appropriateness, and a range of possible answers. The committee also generates a pool of essay questions, pretests them, and chooses those questions that best represent the full range of the scoring scale to allow the AP readers to evaluate the essays fairly.

It is important to remember that the AP Literature exam is thoroughly evaluated after it is administered each year. This way, the College Board can use the results to make course suggestions and to plan future tests.

What Are the Advanced Placement Scores, and Who Receives Them?

Once you have taken the exam and it has been scored, your test will be assigned one of five numbers by the College Board:

- 5 indicates you are extremely well qualified.
- 4 indicates you are well qualified.
- 3 indicates you are qualified.
- 2 indicates you are possibly qualified.
- 1 indicates you are not qualified to receive college credit.

A score of 5, 4, 3, 2, or 1 will be reported to your college or university first, to your high school second, and to you third. All this reporting is usually completed by the middle to end of July.

Reasons for Taking the Advanced Placement Exam

At some point during the year, every AP student asks the ultimate question: Why am I taking this exam?

Good question. Why put yourself through a year of intensive study, pressure, stress, and preparation? To be honest, only you can answer that question. Over the years, our students have indicated to us that there are several prime reasons why they were willing to take the risk and to put in the effort:

- For personal satisfaction
- To compare themselves with other students across the nation
- Because colleges look favorably on the applications of students who elect to enroll in AP courses
- To receive college credit or advanced standing at their colleges or universities
- Because they love the subject
- So that their families will really be proud of them

There are plenty of other reasons, but no matter what the other reasons might be, the top reason for your enrolling in the AP Lit course and taking the exam in May should be to feel good about yourself and the challenges you have met.

What You Need to Know About the AP Lit Exam

Let's answer a few of the nitty-gritty questions about the exam and its scoring.

If I Don't Take an AP Lit Course, Can I Still Take the AP Lit Exam?

Yes. Even though the AP Lit exam is designed for the student who has had a year's course in AP Literature, there are high schools that do not offer this type of course, yet there are students in these high schools who have also done well on the exam. However, if your high school does offer an AP Lit course, by all means take advantage of it and the structured background it will provide you.

How Is the Advanced Placement Literature Exam Organized?

The exam has two parts and is scheduled to last 3 hours. The first section is a set of multiple-choice questions based on a series of prose passages and poems. You will have 1 hour to complete this part of the test. The second section of the exam is a 2-hour essay-writing segment consisting of three different essays: one on prose, one on poetry, and one free-response based on a major work of literary complexity.

After you complete the multiple-choice section and hand in your test booklet and scan sheet, you will be given a brief break. Note that you will not be able to return to the multiple-choice questions when you return to the examination room.

Must I Check the Box at the End of the Essay Booklet That Allows the AP People to Use My Essays as Samples for Research?

No. This is simply a way for the College Board to make certain that it has your permission if it decides to use one or more of your essays as a model. Checking the box will not affect your grade.

How Is My AP Lit Exam Scored?

Let's look at the basics first. The multiple-choice section counts for 45 percent of your total score, and the essay section counts for 55 percent. Next comes a four-part calculation: the raw scoring of the multiple-choice section, the raw scoring of the essay section, the calculation of the composite score, and the conversion of the composite score into the AP grade of 5, 4, 3, 2, or 1.

How Is the Multiple-Choice Section Scored?

The scan sheet with your answers is run through a computer that counts the number of correct answers. Questions left blank and questions answered incorrectly are treated the same and get no points. There is no "guessing penalty," which would involve the deduction of a fraction of a point for answering a question but getting it wrong.

How Is My Essay Section Scored?

Each of your essays is read by a different, trained AP reader. The AP/College Board people have developed a highly successful training program for these readers. This factor, together with many opportunities for checks and double checks of essays, ensures a fair and equitable reading of each essay.

The scoring guides are carefully developed by a chief faculty consultant, a question leader, table leaders, and content experts. All faculty consultants are then trained to read and score just *one* essay question on the exam. They actually become experts in that one essay question. No one knows the identity of any writer. The identification numbers and names are covered, and the exam booklets are randomly distributed to the readers in packets of 25 randomly chosen essays. Table leaders and the question leader review samples of each reader's scores to ensure that quality standards are consistent.

Each essay is scored as 6, 5, 4, 3, 2, 1, plus 0, with 6 the highest possible score. Once your essay is given a number from 6 to 1, the next set of calculations is completed using a formula developed to account for the score of each essay. This is the raw score for the essay section of the exam.

$$(\text{pts.} \times 3.055) + (\text{pts.} \times 3.055) + (\text{pts.} \times 3.055) = \text{essay raw score}$$
$$\text{Essay 1} \qquad \text{Essay 2} \qquad \text{Essay 3}$$

How Is My Composite Score Calculated?

The total composite score for the AP Lit test is 150. Of this score, 55 percent is the essay section; that equals 82.5 points. The multiple-choice section is 45 percent of the composite score, which equals 67.5 points. Each of your three essays is graded on a 6-point scale; therefore, each point is worth 4.58. Divide the number of multiple-choice questions by 67.5.

If you add together the raw scores of each of the two sections, you will have a composite score.

How Is My Composite Data Turned into the Score That Is Reported to My College?

Keep in mind that the total composite scores needed to earn a 5, 4, 3, 2, or 1 are different each year. This is determined by a committee of AP/College Board/Educational Testing Service directors, experts, and statisticians. The score is based on items such as:

- AP distribution over the past three years
- Comparability studies
- Observations of the chief faculty consultant
- Frequency distributions of scores on each section and the essays
- Average scores on each exam section and essays

However, over the years a trend is apparent which indicates the number of points required to achieve a specific score:

- 150–100 points = 5
- 99–86 = 4
- 85–67 = 3

Scores of 2 and 1 fall below this range. You do not want to go there.

What Should I Bring to the Exam?

You should bring:

- Several pencils with erasers
- Several *black* pens (black ink is easier to read than other colors)
- A watch
- Something to drink—water is best
- A quiet snack
- Tissues

Is There Anything Else I Should Be Aware Of?

You should be aware of the following:

- Allow plenty of time to get to the test site.
- Wear comfortable clothing.
- Eat a light breakfast or lunch.
- Remind yourself that you are well prepared and that the test is an enjoyable challenge and a chance to share your knowledge. Be proud of yourself! You worked hard all year. Now is your time to shine.

Is There Anything Special I Should Do the Night Before the Exam?

We certainly don't advocate last-minute cramming. If you've been following the guidelines, you won't have to cram. But there may be a slight value to some last-minute review. Spend the night before the exam relaxing with family or friends. Watch a movie; play a game; gab on the phone, blog, or Twitter. Then find a quiet spot. While you're unwinding, flip through your own notebook and review sheets. Recall some details from the full-length works you've prepared and think of your favorite scenes. By now, you're bound to be ready to drift off. Pleasant dreams.

How to Plan Your Time

IN THIS CHAPTER

Summary: Assess your own study patterns and preparation plans.

Key Ideas
- ✪ Explore three approaches
- ✪ Choose a calendar that works for you

Three Approaches to Preparing for the AP Literature Exam

No one knows your study habits, likes, and dislikes better than you do. So you are the only one who can decide which approach you want and/or need to adopt to prepare for the Advanced Placement Literature exam. Look at the brief profiles below. These may help you to place yourself in a particular prep mode.

You're a full-year prep student (Approach A) **if:**

1. You're the kind of person who likes to plan for a vacation or the prom a year in advance.

2. You'd never think of missing a practice session, whether it's your favorite sport, musical instrument, or activity.

3. You like detailed planning and everything in its place.

4. You feel you must be thoroughly prepared.

5. You hate surprises.

6. You're always early for appointments.

You're a one-semester prep student (Approach B) **if:**

1. You begin to plan for your vacation or the prom 4–5 months before the event.

2. You are willing to plan ahead so that you will feel comfortable in stressful situations, but you are okay with skipping some details.

3. You feel more comfortable when you know what to expect, but a surprise or two does not floor you.

4. You're always on time for appointments.

You're a 4–6 week prep student (Approach C) **if:**

1. You accept or find a date for the prom a week before the big day.

2. You work best under pressure and tight deadlines.

3. You feel very confident with the skills and background you've gained in your AP Literature class.

4. You decided late in the year to take the exam.

5. You like surprises.

6. You feel okay if you arrive 10–15 minutes late for an appointment.

CALENDARS FOR PREPARING
FOR THE AP LITERATURE EXAM

This is a personal journey, and each of you will have particular time constraints. Choose the calendar that will work best for you.

Calendar for Approach A:
Yearlong Preparation for the AP Literature Exam

Although its primary purpose is to prepare you for the AP Literature exam you will take in May, this book can enrich your study of literature, your analytical skills, and your writing skills.

SEPTEMBER–OCTOBER (Check off the activities as you complete them.)

_____ Determine the student mode into which you place yourself.

_____ Carefully read Chapters 1 and 2.

_____ Pay close attention to the walk through the Diagnostic/Master exam.

_____ Take a close look at the AP Central website(s).

_____ Skim the Comprehensive Review section.

_____ Buy a highlighter.

_____ Flip through the entire book. Break in the book. Write in it. Highlight it.

_____ Get a clear picture of what your own school's AP Literature curriculum is.

_____ Review the Bibliography and establish a pattern of outside reading in the literary genres (pp. 221–223).

_____ Begin to use the book as a resource.

NOVEMBER (The first 10 weeks have elapsed.)

_____ Write the free-response essay in the Diagnostic/Master exam.

_____ Compare your essay with the sample student essays.

_____ Refer to the section on the free-response essay.

_____ Take five of our prompts and write solid opening paragraphs.

DECEMBER

_____ Maintain notes on literary works you studied in and out of class.

_____ Refine your analytical skills.

_____ Write the prose passage or poetry essay in the Diagnostic/Master exam. (This will depend on the organization of your own curriculum.)

_____ Compare your essay with sample student essays.

JANUARY (20 weeks have elapsed.)

_____ Write the third essay in the Diagnostic/Master exam. (This will depend on the one you did previously.)

_____ Compare your essay with sample student essays.

FEBRUARY

_____ Take the multiple-choice section of the Diagnostic/Master exam.

_____ Carefully go over the explanations of the answers to the questions.

_____ Score yourself honestly.

_____ Make a note of terms, concepts, and types of questions that give you difficulty.

_____ Review troublesome terms in the Glossary.

MARCH (30 weeks have elapsed.)

_____ Form a study group.
_____ Outline or create a chart for full-length works that would be appropriate for the free-response essay.
_____ Choose a favorite poem and create an essay question to go with it, or use one of our suggested prompts.
_____ Choose a prose passage or essay and create an essay question to go with it, or choose one of our suggested prompts.
_____ Write the poetry essay.
_____ Write the prose essay.
_____ Compare essays and rate them with your study group. (Use our rubrics.)

APRIL

_____ Take Practice Test 1 in the first week of April.
_____ Evaluate your strengths and weaknesses.
_____ Study appropriate chapters to correct your weaknesses.

_____ Practice creating multiple-choice questions of different types with your study group.
_____ Develop and review worksheets for and with your study group.

MAY—First 2 Weeks (THIS IS IT!)

_____ Highlight only those things in the Glossary you are still unsure of. Ask your teacher for clarification. Study!
_____ Thoroughly prepare three to five complete, full-length works; include several quotations that you can work into various responses.
_____ Write at least three times a week under timed conditions.
_____ Take Practice Test 2.
_____ Score yourself.
_____ Give yourself a pat on the back for how much you have learned and improved over the past 9 months.
_____ Go to the movies. Call a friend.
_____ Get a good night's sleep. Fall asleep knowing you are well prepared.

GOOD LUCK ON THE TEST.

KEY IDEA Make certain you become familiar with and make good use of AP Central's APCLASSROOM site at https://myap.collegeboard.org/login?.

Calendar for Approach B:
Semester-Long Preparation for the AP Literature Exam

Working under the assumption that you've completed one semester of literature studies, apply those skills you've learned to prepare for the May exam.

You have plenty of time to supplement your course work by taking our study recommendations, maintaining literary notations, doing outside readings, and so on.

We divide the next 16 weeks into a workable program of preparation for you.

JANUARY–FEBRUARY (Check off the activities as you complete them.)

_____ Carefully read Chapters 1 and 2.

_____ Write the three essays in the Diagnostic/Master exam.

_____ Compare your essays with the sample student essays.

_____ Complete the multiple-choice section of the Diagnostic/Master exam.

_____ Carefully go over the answers and explanations of the answers.

_____ Take a close look at the Bibliography for suggestions on possible outside readings.

MARCH (10 weeks to go.)

_____ Form a study group.

_____ Outline or create a chart for full-length works that would be appropriate for the free-response essay.

_____ Choose a favorite poem and create an essay question to go with it, or use one of our suggested prompts.

_____ Choose a prose passage or essay and create an essay question to go with it, or choose one of our suggested prompts.

_____ Write the poetry essay.

_____ Write the prose essay.

_____ Compare essays and rate them with your study group. (Use our rubrics.)

APRIL

_____ Take Practice Test 1 in the first week of April.

_____ Evaluate your strengths and weaknesses.

_____ Study appropriate chapters to correct your weaknesses.

_____ Practice creating multiple-choice questions of different types with your study group.

_____ Develop and review worksheets for and with your study group.

MAY First 2 Weeks (THIS IS IT!)

_____ Highlight only those things in the Glossary you are still unsure of. Ask your teacher for clarification. Study!

_____ Thoroughly prepare at least three to five complete, full-length works; include several quotations that you can work into various questions.

_____ Write at least three times a week under timed conditions.

_____ Take Practice Test 2.

_____ Score yourself.

_____ Give yourself a pat on the back for how much you have learned and improved over the past 9 months.

_____ Go to the movies. Call a friend.

_____ Get a good night's sleep. Fall asleep knowing you are well prepared.

GOOD LUCK ON THE TEST.

 **KEY IDEA**

Make certain you become familiar with and make good use of AP Central's APCLASSROOM site at https://myap.collegeboard.org/login?.

"One of the first steps to success on the AP exam is knowing your own study habits."
—Margaret R.
  AP English
  teacher

Calendar for Approach C:
4–6 Week Preparation for the AP Literature Exam

At this point, we are going to assume that you have been developing your literary, analytical, and writing skills in your English class for more than 6 months. You will, therefore, use this book primarily as a specific guide to the AP Literature exam.

Remember, there is a solid review section in this text to which you should refer.

Given the time constraints, now is not the time to try to expand your AP Literature background. Rather, it is the time to limit and refine what you already know.

APRIL

_____ Skim through Chapters 1 and 2.
_____ Carefully go over the "rapid reviews."
_____ Strengthen, clarify, and correct areas you are weak in after taking the Diagnostic/Master exam.
_____ Write a minimum of three sample opening paragraphs for each of the three types of essays.
_____ Write a minimum of two timed essays for each type of essay on the exam.
_____ Complete Practice Test 1.
_____ Score yourself and analyze your errors.
_____ Refer to appropriate chapters to correct your weaknesses.
_____ Refer to the Bibliography.
_____ If you feel unfamiliar with specific poetic forms, refer to the list of suggested, appropriate works.

_____ Create review sheets for three to five solid, full-length works.
_____ Skim and highlight the Glossary.
_____ Develop a weekly study group to hear each other's essays and to discuss literature.

MAY—First 2 Weeks (THIS IS IT!)

_____ Complete Practice Test 2.
_____ Score yourself and analyze your errors.
_____ Refer to appropriate chapters to correct your weaknesses.
_____ Go to the movies. Call a friend.
_____ Get a good night's sleep. Fall asleep knowing you are well prepared.

GOOD LUCK ON THE TEST.

KEY IDEA

Make certain you **become familiar** with and make good use of AP Central's APCLASSROOM site at https://myap.collegeboard.org/login?.

STEP 2

Determine Your Test Readiness

CHAPTER 3 The Diagnostic/Master Exam

CHAPTER 3

The Diagnostic/Master Exam

IN THIS CHAPTER

Summary: Put yourself to the test with the diagnostic exam.

Key Ideas
❂ Peruse the multiple-choice section in Section I of the exam
❂ Familiarize yourself with the essays in Section II

A Walk Through the Diagnostic/Master Exam

"You know, from my experience with AP exams, I've learned never to assume anything."
—Jeremy G.
  AP student

This chapter presents our version of an Advanced Placement Literature and Composition exam which we use throughout this book to demonstrate processes, examples, terms, and so on. We call this the Diagnostic/Master exam. You will not be taking this exam at this point, but we would like you to "walk through" the exam with us now.

The first part of this 3-hour exam is always the multiple-choice section, which lasts 1 hour. It is related to both prose passages and poetry. The multiple-choice section of the Diagnostic/Master exam contains two prose passages from different time periods and of different styles. It also has two poems from different time periods and of different forms. The multiple-choice questions for each selection were developed to provide you with a wide range of question types and terminology that have been used in the actual AP Lit exams over the years.

To begin to know what the exam looks like, take some time to look through the multiple-choice section of the Diagnostic/Master exam. Do not try to answer the questions; just peruse the types of passages and questions.

• Take a turn through all of the pages of the test and familiarize yourself with the format.
• See where the longer and shorter readings are.
• See how many prose and poetry passages there are.

- Check the total number of questions and know what you are facing.
- Check out the essay prompts.

A Word About Our Sample Student Essays

We field-tested each of the essay questions in a variety of high schools, both public and private. We could have chosen to present essays that would have "knocked your socks off," but we chose to present samples that are truly representative of the essays usually written within the time constraints of the exam.

These essays are indicative of a wide range of styles and levels of acceptability. We want you to recognize that there is not one model to which all essays must conform.

"To Thine Own Self Be True" (Polonius—*Hamlet*)

"Be true to yourself" is always the best advice and is especially appropriate for a writer. Listen to your teacher's advice; listen to our advice; **listen to your own voice**. Yours is the voice we want to "hear" in your writing. Use natural vocabulary and present honest observations. It is wonderful to read professional criticism, but you cannot adopt someone else's ideas and remain true to your own thoughts. Trust your brain—if you've prepared well, you'll do well.

DIAGNOSTIC/MASTER EXAM

Advanced Placement Literature and Composition

Section I

Total time—1 hour

Carefully read the following passages and answer the questions that come after them.
Questions 1–10 are based on the next passage.

Now Goes Under . . .
by Edna St. Vincent Millay

Now goes under, and I watch it go under, the sun
    That will not rise again.
Today has seen the setting, in your eyes cold
    and senseless as the sea,
Of friendship better than bread, and of bright charity   5
That lifts a man a little above the beasts that run.

That this could be!
That I should live to see
Most vulgar Pride, that stale obstreperous clown,
So fitted out with purple robe and crown   10
To stand among his betters! Face to face
With outraged me in this once holy place,
Where Wisdom was a favoured guest and hunted
Truth was harboured out of danger,
He bulks enthroned, a lewd, and insupportable stranger!   15

I would have sworn, indeed I swore it:
The hills may shift, the waters may decline,
Winter may twist the stem from the twig that bore it,
But never your love from me, your hand from mine.

Now goes under the sun, and I watch it go under.   20
Farewell, sweet light, great wonder!
You, too, farewell—but fare not well enough to dream
You have done wisely to invite the night before the darkness came.

1. The poem is an example of a(n)
   A. sonnet
   B. lyric
   C. ode
   D. ballad
   E. dramatic monologue

2. The setting of the sun is a symbol for
   A. the beginning of winter
   B. encountering danger
   C. the end of a relationship
   D. facing death
   E. the onset of night

3. The second stanza is developed primarily by
   A. metaphor
   B. simile
   C. personification
   D. hyperbole
   E. allusion

4. "He" in line 15 refers to
   A. Wisdom
   B. Truth
   C. I
   D. Pride
   E. charity

5. According to the speaker, what separates man from beast?
   A. love
   B. friendship
   C. charity
   D. truth
   E. wisdom

6. For the speaker, the relationship has been all of the following *except*
   A. honest
   B. dangerous
   C. spiritual
   D. ephemeral
   E. nourishing

7. The reader can infer from the play on words in the last stanza that the speaker is
   A. dying
   B. frantic
   C. wistful
   D. bitter
   E. capricious

8. "This once holy place" (line 12) refers to
   A. the sunset
   B. the relationship
   C. the sea
   D. the circus
   E. the Church

9. The cause of the relationship's situation is
   A. a stranger coming between them
   B. the lover not taking the relationship seriously
   C. the lover feeling intellectually superior
   D. the lover's pride coming between them
   E. the lover being insensitive

10. The speaker acknowledges the finality of the relationship in line(s)
    A. 1–2
    B. 7
    C. 8
    D. 16
    E. 18–19

Questions 11–23 are based on the following passage from *The Heart of Darkness* by Joseph Conrad, 1902.

The sea-reach of the Thames stretched before us like the beginning of an
interminable waterway. The air was dark above Gravesend, and farther back still
seemed condensed into a mournful gloom, brooding motionless over the biggest and
the greatest town on earth.
   "I was thinking of very old times, when the Romans first came here, nineteen   5
hundred years ago—the other day . . . Light came out of this river since—you say knights?
Yes; but it is like a running blaze on a plain, like a flash of lightning in the clouds. We live
in the flicker—may it last as long as the old earth keeps rolling! But darkness was here
yesterday. Imagine the feelings of a commander of a fine—what d'ye call 'em?—trireme
in the Mediterranean, ordered suddenly to the north; run overland across the Gauls in a   10
hurry; put in charge of one of these craft the legionnaires—a wonderful lot of handy men
they must have been, too—used to build, apparently by the hundred, in a month or two, if
we may believe what we read. Imagine him here—the very end of the world, a sea the color
of lead, a sky the color of smoke, a kind of ship about as rigid as a concertina—and going
up this river with stores, or orders, or what you like. Sandbanks, marshes, forests, savages—   15
precious little to eat for a civilized man, nothing but Thames water to drink. No Falernian

wine here, no going ashore. Here and there a military camp lost in a wilderness, like a
needle in a bundle of hay—cold, fog, tempests, disease, exile, and death—death skulking
in the air, in the water, in the bush. They must have been dying like flies here. Oh yes—he
did it. Did it very well, too, no doubt, and without thinking much about it either, except   20
afterwards to brag of what he had gone through in his time, perhaps. They were men enough
to face darkness. And perhaps he was cheered by keeping his eye on a chance of promotion
to the fleet at Ravenna by and by, if he had good friends in Rome and survived the awful
climate. Or think of a decent young citizen in a toga—perhaps too much dice, you know—
coming out here in the train of some prefect, or tax-gatherer, or trader even, to mend his   25
fortunes. Land in a swamp, march through the woods, and in some inland post feel the
savagery, the utter savagery, had closed round him—all that mysterious life of the wilderness
that stirs in the forest, in the jungles, in the hearts of wild men. There's no initiation either
into such mysteries. He has to live in the midst of the incomprehensible, which is also
detestable. And it has a fascination, too, that goes to work upon him. The fascination of the   30
abomination—you know, imagine the growing regrets, the longing to escape, the powerless
disgust, the surrender, the hate."
    He paused.
    "Mind," he began again, lifting one arm from the elbow, the palm of the hand
outwards, so that, with his legs folded before him, he had the pose of a Buddha preaching in   35
European clothes and without a lotus flower—"Mind, none of us would feel exactly like this.
What saves us is efficiency—the devotion to efficiency. But these chaps were not much
account, really. They were no colonists; their administration was merely a squeeze, and
nothing more, I suspect. They were conquerors, and for that you want only brute force—
nothing to boast of, when you have it, since your strength is just an accident arising from the   40
weakness of others. They grabbed what they could get for the sake of what was to be got. It
was just robbery with violence, aggravated murder on a great scale, and men going at it blind—
as is very proper for those who tackle a darkness. The conquest of the earth, which mostly
means taking it away from those who have a different complexion or slightly flatter noses
than ourselves, is not a pretty thing when you look at it too much. What redeems it is the idea   45
only. An idea at the back of it; not a sentimental pretense but an idea; and an unselfish belief
in the idea—something you can set up, and bow down before, and offer a sacrifice to . . . "

11. In the passage, *darkness* implies all of the following *except*
  A. the unknown
  B. savagery
  C. ignorance
  D. death
  E. exploration

12. The setting of the passage is
  A. Africa
  B. Ancient Rome
  C. the Thames River
  D. the Mediterranean
  E. Italy

13. The tone of the passage is
  A. condescending
  B. indignant
  C. scornful
  D. pensive
  E. laudatory

14. Later events may be foreshadowed by all of the following phrases *except*
  A. "Imagine the feelings of a commander . . . "
  B. ". . . live in the midst of the incomprehensible . . . "
  C. ". . . in some inland post feel the savagery . . . "
  D. "They must have been dying like flies here."
  E. ". . . the very end of the world . . . "

15. The narrator draws a parallel between
    A. light and dark
    B. past and present
    C. life and death
    D. fascination and abomination
    E. decency and savagery

16. In this passage, "We live in the flicker . . ." (lines 7–8) may be interpreted to mean *ALL* of the following *EXCEPT*
    A. In the history of the world, humanity's span on earth is brief.
    B. Future civilizations will learn from only a portion of the past.
    C. Periods of enlightenment and vision appear only briefly.
    D. The river has been the source of life throughout the ages.
    E. A moment of present-day insight about conquest.

17. One may conclude from the passage that the speaker
    A. admires adventurers
    B. longs to be a crusader
    C. is a former military officer
    D. recognizes and accepts the presence of evil in human experience
    E. is prejudiced

18. In the context of the passage, which of the following phrases presents a paradox?
    A. "The fascination of the abomination . . ."
    B. ". . . in the hearts of wild men"
    C. "There's no initiation . . . into such mysteries"
    D. ". . . a flash of lightning in the clouds"
    E. ". . . death skulking in the air . . . "

19. The lines "Imagine him here . . . concertina . . . " (lines 13–14) contain examples of
    A. hyperbole and personification
    B. irony and metaphor
    C. alliteration and personification
    D. parallel structure and simile
    E. allusion and simile

20. According to the speaker, the one trait which saves Europeans from savagery is
    A. sentiment
    B. a sense of mystery
    C. brute force
    D. religious zeal
    E. efficiency

21. According to the speaker, the only justification for conquest is
    A. the "weakness of others"
    B. it's being "proper for those who tackle a darkness . . . "
    C. their grabbing "what they could get for the sake of what was to be got"
    D. ". . . an unselfish belief in the idea . . . "
    E. "The fascination of the abomination"

22. In the statement by the speaker, "Mind, none of us would feel exactly like this" (line 36), "this" refers to
    A. ". . . a Buddha preaching in European clothes . . . " (lines 35–36)
    B. ". . . imagine the growing regrets . . . the hate." (lines 31–32)
    C. "What redeems it is the idea only." (lines 45–46)
    D. ". . . think of a decent young citizen in a toga . . . " (line 24)
    E. "I was thinking of very old times . . . " (line 5)

23. The speaker presents all of the following reasons for exploration and conquest *except*
    A. military expeditions
    B. ". . . a chance of promotion"
    C. ". . . to mend his fortunes . . . "
    D. religious commitment
    E. punishment for a crime

Questions 24–35 are based on the following poem by William Shakespeare.

> That time of year thou mayst in me behold
> When yellow leaves, or none, or few, do hang
> Upon those boughs which shake against the cold,
> Bare ruin'd choirs, where late the sweet birds sang.
> In me thou see'st the twilight of such day   5
> As after sunset fadeth in the west;
> Which by and by black night doth take away,
> Death's second self, that seals up all in rest.
> In me thou see'st the glowing of such fire,
> That on the ashes of his youth doth lie,   10
> As the deathbed whereon it must expire,
> Consum'd with that which it was nourish'd by.
> This thou perceiv'st, which makes thy love more strong,
> To love that well which thou must leave ere long.

24. "That time of year" (line 1) refers to
   A. youth
   B. old age
   C. childhood
   D. senility
   E. maturity

25. "Death's second self" (line 8) refers to
   A. "That time of year"
   B. "sunset fadeth"
   C. "the west"
   D. "ruin'd choirs"
   E. "black night"

26. Line 12 is an example of
   A. paradox
   B. caesura
   C. parable
   D. hyperbole
   E. metonymy

27. "Twilight of such day" (line 5) is supported by all of the following images *except*
   A. "sunset fadeth"
   B. "the glowing of such fire"
   C. "west"
   D. "Death's second self"
   E. "ashes of his youth"

28. "This thou perceiv'st" (line 13) refers to
   A. the beloved's deathbed
   B. the sorrow of unrequited love
   C. the passion of youth expiring
   D. the beloved's acknowledgment of the speaker's mortality
   E. the speaker sending the lover away

29. The poem is an example of a(n)
   A. elegy
   B. Spenserian sonnet
   C. Petrarchan sonnet
   D. Shakespearean sonnet
   E. sestina

30. The poem is primarily developed by means of
   A. metaphor
   B. argument
   C. synecdoche
   D. alternative choices
   E. contradiction

31. The irony of the poem is best expressed in line
   A. 5
   B. 7
   C. 10
   D. 11
   E. 12

32. "It" in line 12 can best be interpreted to mean
  A. a funeral pyre
  B. spent youth
  C. the intensity of the speaker's love
  D. the impending departure of his beloved
  E. the immortality of the relationship

33. An apt title for the poem could be
  A. Love Me or Leave Me
  B. Death Be Not Proud
  C. The End Justifies the Means
  D. Love's Fall
  E. Grow Old Along with Me

34. The tone of the poem can best be described as
  A. contemplative
  B. defiant
  C. submissive
  D. arbitrary
  E. complaining

35. The speaker most likely is
  A. jealous of the beloved's youth
  B. pleased that the lover will leave
  C. unable to keep up with the young lover
  D. unwilling to face his own mortality
  E. responsive to the beloved's constancy

Questions 36–47 are based on a careful reading of the following excerpt from the first chapter of the 2001 novel *White Teeth* by Zadie Smith that centers on two families who live in North London.

Archie's marriage felt like buying a pair of shoes, taking them home and finding they don't fit. For the sake of appearances, he put up with them. And then, all of a sudden and after thirty years, the shoes picked themselves up and walked out of the house. She left. Thirty years.

As far as he remembered, just like everybody else they began well. The first spring of 1946, he had stumbled out of the darkness of war and into a Florentine coffee house, where he was served by a waitress truly like the sun: Ophelia Diagilo, dressed all in yellow, spreading warmth and the promise of sex as she passed him a frothy cappuccino. They walked into it blinkered as horses. She was not to know that women never stayed as daylight in Archie's life; that somewhere in him he didn't like them, he didn't trust them, and he was able to love them only if they wore haloes. No one told Archie that lurking in the Diagilo family tree were two hysteric aunts, an uncle who talked to aubergines[1] and a cousin who wore his clothes back to front. So they got married and returned to England, where she realized very quickly her mistake, he drove her very quickly mad, and the halo was packed off to the attic to collect dust with the rest of the bric-a-brac[2] and broken kitchen appliances that Archie promised one day to repair. Amongst that bric-a-brac was a Hoover.

On Boxing Day[3] morning, six days before he parked outside Mo's halal[4] butchers, Archie had returned to their semi-detached in Hendon[5] in search of that Hoover. It was his fourth trip to the attic in so many days, ferrying out the odds and ends of a marriage to his new flat, and the Hoover was amongst the very last items he reclaimed—one of the most broken things, most ugly things, the things you demand out of sheer bloody-mindedness because you have lost the house. This is what divorce is: taking things you no longer want from people you no longer love.

"So you again," said the Spanish home-help at the door, Santa-Maria or Maria-Santa or something. "Meester Jones, what now? Kitchen sink, si?"

"Hoover," said Archie, grimly. "Vacuum."

She cut her eyes at him and spat on the doormat inches from his shoes. "Welcome, señor."

The place had become a haven for people who hated him. Apart from the home-help, he had to contend with Ophelia's extended Italian family, her mental-health nurse, the woman from the council,[6] and of course Ophelia herself, who was to be found in the kernel of this nuthouse, curled up in a fetal ball on the sofa, making lowing sounds into a bottle of Bailey's.[7] It took him an hour and a quarter just to get through enemy lines—and for what? A perverse Hoover, discarded months earlier because it was determined to perform the opposite of every vacuum's objective: spewing out dust instead of sucking it in.

"Meester Jones, why do you come here when it make you so unhappy? Be reasonable. What can you want with it?" The home-help was following him up the attic stairs, armed with some kind of cleaning fluid: "It's broken. You don't need this. See? See?" She plugged it into a socket and demonstrated the dead switch. Archie took the plug out and silently wound the cord round the Hoover. If it was broken, it was coming with him. All broken things were coming with him. He was going to fix every damn broken thing in this house, if only to show that he was good for something.

"You good for nothing!" Santa whoever chased him back down the stairs. "Your wife is ill in her head, and this is all you can do!"

Archie hugged the Hoover to his chest and took it into the crowded living room, where, under several pairs of reproachful eyes, he got out his toolbox and started work on it.

"Look at him," said one of the Italian grandmothers, the more glamorous one with the big scarves and fewer moles, "he take everything, capisce?[8] He take-a her mind, he take-a the blender, he take-a the old stereo—he take-a everything except the floorboards. It make-a you sick . . ."

The woman from the council, who even on dry days resembled a long-haired cat soaked to the skin, shook her skinny head in agreement. "It's disgusting, you don't have to tell me, it's disgusting . . . and naturally, we're the ones left to sort out the mess; it's muggins[9] here who has to—"

Which was overlapped by the nurse: "She can't stay here alone, can she . . . now he's buggered off, poor woman . . . she needs a proper home, she needs . . ."

I'm here, Archie felt like saying, I'm right here you know, I'm bloody right here. And it was my blender.

But he wasn't one for confrontation, Archie. He listened to them all for another fifteen minutes, mute as he tested the Hoover's suction against pieces of newspaper, until he was overcome by the sensation that Life was an enormous rucksack[10] so impossibly heavy that, even though it meant losing everything, it was infinitely easier to leave all baggage here on the roadside and walk on into the blackness. You don't need the blender, Archie-boy, you don't need the Hoover. This stuff's all dead weight. Just lay down the rucksack, Arch, and join the happy campers in the sky. Was that wrong? To Archie—ex-wife and ex-wife's relatives in one ear, spluttering vacuum in the other—it just seemed that The End was unavoidably nigh. Nothing personal to God or whatever. It just felt like the end of the world. And he was going to need more than poor whisky, novelty crackers and a paltry box of Quality Street[11]—all the strawberry ones already scoffed—to justify entering another annum.

Patiently he fixed the Hoover, and vacuumed the living room with a strange methodical finality, shoving the nozzle into the most difficult corners. Solemnly he flipped a coin (heads, life, tails, death) and felt nothing in particular when he found himself staring at the dancing lion.[12] Quietly he detached the Hoover tube, put it in a suitcase, and left the house for the last time.

---

[1]**aubergines:** eggplants
[2]**bric-a-brac:** odds and ends, objects of little value
[3]**Boxing Day:** The British celebration of the day after Christmas
[4]**halal:** food prepared according to Muslim law
[5]**Hendon:** a suburb of London
[6]**council:** a type of elected British advisory or legislative body
[7]**Bailey's:** a brand of whiskey
[8]**capisce:** Italian for *understand*
[9]**muggins:** a foolish, gullible person
[10]**rucksack:** backpack
[11]**Quality Street:** a brand of candy
[12]**dancing lion:** reverse side of a twenty-pence coin

36. The function of the first paragraph can best be described as
   A. a diatribe against marriage
   B. an introduction to the setting
   C. an introduction to the central plot
   D. an introduction to Archie's attitude toward his former wife and their marriage
   E. an introduction to Ophelia

37. After reading the second paragraph, one can infer all of the following *except*
   A. Archie and Ophelia's love was based on passion.
   B. Archie was self-motivated.
   C. Archie wanted to be able to place his wife on a pedestal.
   D. Ophelia and Ophelia were quick to make important decisions.
   E. Archie was unsure and suspicious of women.

38. The metaphor of the halo in the second paragraph serves mainly to emphasize
   A. the beauty and innocence of Ophelia
   B. the religion of both Ophelia and Archie
   C. the inevitability of future events
   D. the hastiness of Archie and Ophelia's marriage
   E. an unrealistic desire for the perfect love

39. In line 7, *it* is referring to
   A. pledge of love
   B. move to England
   C. marriage
   D. divorce
   E. sexual relationship

40. The response of "Santa-Maria or Maria-Santa" (23–26) to Archie's arrival can best be described as
   A. hostile and denigrating
   B. suspicious and cowering
   C. warm and welcoming
   D. condescending and dismissive
   E. curious and insecure

41. Paragraph 7, lines 27–33, progresses from a primarily third-person, objective narrator to
   A. stream-of-consciousness
   B. interior monologue
   C. first-person narrator
   D. third-person subjective
   E. third-person omniscient

42. Lines 39–40, reveal that Archie
   A. believes he is capable of fixing broken appliances
   B. wants to prove that he is not a failure
   C. feels he has been taken advantage of
   D. is basically selfish
   E. wants to show the help that he is in charge

43. For Archie, the Hoover vacuum symbolizes each of the following *except*
   A. ownership
   B. potential to redeem himself
   C. failure of his life so far
   D. his love for Ophelia
   E. control

44. As a way to characterize Archie's perceived burden, the author uses the image of
   A. pair of shoes (first paragraph)
   B. halo (second paragraph)
   C. Hoover vacuum (throughout passage)
   D. the blender (lines 47 and 56)
   E. rucksack (next-to-last paragraph)

45. The author uses dialect with the home-help's dialogue primarily
   A. to add a sense of realism to the narrative
   B. to indicate the class differences between Archie and the home-help
   C. to make a point about the working conditions of the working class
   D. to add a bit of humor to the passage
   E. to gain more sympathy for Archie

46. Archie's behavior in the last two paragraphs suggests he
   A. wants to move on
   B. believes it's possible to help Ophelia
   C. is beginning to feel hopeless
   D. wonders why he bothered fixing the Hoover
   E. wants to get back at the home-help and Ophelia's relatives

47. Which of the following best describes the effect of the last paragraph?
   A. hopeful
   B. looking for redemption
   C. impending doom
   D. loss of control
   E. anger at the world

Questions 48–55 are based on a careful reading of the 2002 poem "Litany" by Billy Collins.

Litany[1]

You are the bread and the knife,
The crystal goblet and the wine . . .
—Jacques Crickillon

You are the bread and the knife,
the crystal goblet and the wine.   5
You are the dew on the morning grass
and the burning wheel of the sun.
You are the white apron of the baker,
and the marsh birds suddenly in flight.

However, you are not the wind in the orchard,   10
the plums on the counter,
or the house of cards.
And you are certainly not the pine-scented air.
There is just no way that you are the pine-scented air.

It is possible that you are the fish under the bridge   15
maybe even the pigeon on the general's head,
but you are not even close
to being the field of cornflowers at dusk.

And a quick look in the mirror will show
that you are neither the boots in the corner   20
nor the boat asleep in its boathouse.
It might interest you to know,
speaking of the plentiful imagery of the world,
that I am the sound of rain on the roof.

I also happen to be the shooting star,   25
the evening paper blowing down an alley
and the basket of chestnuts on the kitchen table.

I am also the moon in the trees
and the blind woman's tea cup.

But don't worry, I'm not the bread and the knife.
You are still the bread and the knife.
You will always be the bread and the knife,
not to mention the crystal goblet and—somehow—the wine.

30

---

[1]**litany**: (secondary meaning) a recital or a repetitive series of phrases with a type of call-and-response

48. This poem is an example of
   A. blank verse
   B. rhymed verse
   C. metered verse
   D. free verse
   E. rhymed, metered verse

49. The tone of the poem can best be described as
   A. formal and critical
   B. uncaring and suspicious
   C. informal and indifferent
   D. brusque and patronizing
   E. casual and playful

50. Line 9, "and the marsh birds suddenly in flight"
   A. hints at an element of uncertainty
   B. sums up the preceding five lines
   C. indicates the speaker's fear
   D. introduces a new setting
   E. suggests the speaker's fascination with nature

51. As the poem progresses, it becomes clear that this poem is
   A. an elegy for a deceased loved one
   B. a description of the depth of the speaker's love
   C. an ode to love
   D. an apology to the speaker's loved one
   E. a tribute to the speaker's beloved

52. The turning point in the poem occurs in stanza
   A. 1
   B. 2
   C. 5
   D. 6
   E. 7

53. All of the following literary devices are used in the poem *except*
   A. rhyme
   B. metaphor
   C. alliteration
   D. simile
   E. repetition

54. Elements of humor in the poem are created by using
   A. improbable circumstances
   B. counterbalance and exaggeration
   C. gentle criticism and apologies
   D. slapstick put-downs
   E. satirical comments

55. The repetition in the last four lines of the poem can best be interpreted to mean
   A. the speaker will always be the opposite of the beloved
   B. the beloved holds the key to the speaker's life and always will
   C. both the speaker and the beloved will remain in separate worlds
   D. the speaker will always accept the beloved's point of view
   E. the speaker cannot imagine living without the beloved

END OF SECTION I

The second part of the test is the 2-hour essay-writing section. You take this part of the exam after the break following your completion of the multiple-choice section. You will be required to write three different essays. In all likelihood, one of the questions will be based on a prose passage, one on a poem or two, and one will be what is called the free-response essay.

Do not write any essays at this time. Just take a careful look at each of the questions to get an idea of the types of writing assignments you are expected to be able to handle. Essay questions are called "prompts" by the AP.

Section II

Total time—2 hours

Question 1

(Suggested time 40 minutes. This question counts as one-third of the total score for Section II.)

In the following passage from the 1914 short story "The Dead," James Joyce presents an insight into the character of Gabriel. Carefully read the passage. Then, in a well-written essay analyze how Joyce uses literary strategies and techniques to reveal various aspects of Gabriel's complex character to the reader and to Gabriel himself.

In your response you should do the following:

- Respond to the prompt with a thesis that presents an assertion that requires defense and support.
- Select and use evidence to support your line of reasoning.
- Explain how the evidence supports your line of reasoning.
- Use appropriate grammar and punctuation in communicating your argument.

The Dead

She was fast asleep.

Gabriel, leaning on his elbow, looked for a few moments
unresentfully on her tangled hair and half-open mouth, listening to her
deep-drawn breath. So she had had that romance in her life: a man had
died for her sake. It hardly pained him now to think how poor a part   5
he, her husband, had played in her life. He watched her while she slept
as though he and she had never lived together as man and wife. His
curious eyes rested long upon her face and on her hair and, as he thought
of what she must have been then, in that time of her first girlish beauty,
a strange friendly pity for her entered his soul. He did not like to say   10
even to himself that her face was no longer beautiful but he knew that it
was no longer the face for which Michael Furey had braved death.

Perhaps she had not told him all the story. His eyes moved to the
chair over which she had thrown some of her clothes. A petticoat string
dangled to the floor. One boot stood upright, its limp upper fallen down: 15
the fellow of it lay upon its side. He wondered at his riot of emotions of
an hour before. From what had it proceeded? From his aunt's supper,
from his own foolish speech, from the wine and dancing, the merry-making
when saying good-night in the hall, the pleasure of the walk along the river
in the snow. Poor Aunt Julia! She, too, would soon be a shade with the   20

shade of Patrick Morkan and his horse. He had caught that haggard look
upon her face for a moment when she was singing *Arrayed for the Bridal*.
Soon, perhaps, he would be sitting in the same drawing-room dressed in
black, his silk hat on his knees. The blinds would be drawn down and
Aunt Kate would be sitting beside him, crying and blowing her nose and   25
telling him how Julia had died. He would cast about in his mind for some
words that might console her, and would find only lame and useless ones.
Yes, yes: that would happen very soon.

Question 2

(Suggested time 40 minutes. This question counts as one-third of the total score for Section II.)

In "On the Subway," Sharon Olds brings two worlds into close proximity. Carefully read the poem. Then, in
a well-written essay analyze how Olds uses poetic elements and techniques to develop the complex contrasts
and insights presented in the poem.

In your response you should do the following:

- Respond to the prompt with a thesis that presents an assertion that requires defense and support.
- Select and use evidence to support your line of reasoning.
- Explain how the evidence supports your line of reasoning.
- Use appropriate grammar and punctuation in communicating your argument.

On the Subway
by Sharon Olds

The boy and I face each other
His feet are huge, in black sneakers
laced with white in a complex pattern like a
set of intentional scars. We are stuck on
opposite sides of the car, a couple of   5
molecules stuck in a rod of light
rapidly moving through darkness.
He has the casual cold look of a mugger,
alert under hooded lids. He is wearing
red, like the inside of the body   10
exposed. I am wearing dark fur, the
whole skin of an animal taken and
used. I look at his raw face,
he looks at my fur coat, and I don't
know if I am in his power—   15
he could take my coat so easily, my
briefcase, my life—
or if he is in my power, the way I am
living off his life, eating the steak
he does not eat, as if I am taking   20
the food from his mouth. And he is black
and I am white, and without meaning or
trying to I must profit from his darkness,
the way he absorbs the murderous beams of the

nation's heart, as black cotton   25
absorbs the heat of the sun and holds it. There is
no way to know how easy this
white skin makes my life, this
life he could take so easily and
break across his knee like a stick the way his   30
own back is being broken, the
rod of his soul that at birth was dark and
fluid and rich as the heart of a seedling
ready to thrust up into any available light

Question 3

(Suggested time 40 minutes. This question counts as one-third of the total score for Section II.)

Often in literature, a literal or figurative journey is a significant factor in the development of a character or the meaning of the work as a whole. Either from your own reading or from the list below, choose a work of fiction that illustrates this idea. Then, in a well-written essay analyze how the journey contributes to the character's complex development or the work's meaning as a whole. Do not merely summarize.

In your response you should do the following:

- Respond to the prompt with a thesis that presents an assertion that requires defense and support.
- Select and use evidence to support your line of reasoning.
- Explain how the evidence supports your line of reasoning.
- Use appropriate grammar and punctuation in communicating your argument.

As I Lay Dying	*Tom Jones*
Jane Eyre	*Heart of Darkness*
The Odyssey	*Moby Dick*
Don Quixote	*The Sun Also Rises*
Candide	*The Grapes of Wrath*
A Streetcar Named Desire	*The Stranger*
A Passage to India	*Ulysses*
Gulliver's Travels	*Their Eyes Were Watching God*
No Exit	*Obasan*
The Kite Runner	*Twelfth Night*

END OF SECTION II

Afterword

So that's what the Advanced Placement Literature and Composition exam looks like. If you're being honest with yourself, you're probably feeling a bit overwhelmed at this point. Good! This is primarily why we are going to deconstruct this entire Diagnostic/Master exam for you and with you throughout this book. By the time you reach Practice Exams 1 and 2, you should be feeling much more confident and comfortable about doing well on the AP Literature exam.

As you progress through this book, you will:

- Take each section of the Diagnostic/Master exam.
- Read the explanations for the answers to the multiple-choice questions.
- Read sample student essays written in response to each of the three prompts.
- Read the rubrics and ratings of the student essays.
- Evaluate your own performance in light of this information.

Develop Strategies for Success

CHAPTER 4

Section I of the Exam: The Multiple-Choice Questions

IN THIS CHAPTER

Summary: Become comfortable with the multiple-choice section of the exam. If you know what to expect, you can prepare.

Key Ideas
- ✪ Review the types of multiple-choice questions asked on the exam
- ✪ Learn strategies for approaching the multiple-choice questions
- ✪ Prepare yourself for the multiple-choice section of the exam
- ✪ Take the multiple-choice section of the exam
- ✪ Score yourself by checking the answer key and explanations for the multiple-choice section of the Diagnostic/Master exam

Introduction to the Multiple-Choice Section of the Exam

Multiple choice? Multiple guess? Multiple anxiety? The day after the exam, students often bemoan the difficulties and uncertainties of Section I of the AP Literature exam.

"It's unfair."

"It's crazy."

"Was that in English?"

"Did you get four Ds in a row for the second poem?"

"I just closed my eyes and pointed."

Is it really possible to avoid these and other exam woes? We hope that by following along with us in this chapter, you will begin to feel a bit more familiar with the world of multiple-choice questions and, thus, become a little more comfortable with the multiple-choice section of the exam.

What Is It About the Multiple-Choice Questions That Causes Such Anxiety?

Basically, a multiple-choice literature question demands that you concentrate on items that are incorrect before you can choose what is correct. We know, however, that complex literature has a richness that allows for ambiguity. When you are taking the exam, you are expected to match someone else's take on a work with the answers you choose. This is what often causes the student to feel intimidated. However, the test is designed to allow you to shine, *not* to be humiliated. To that end, you will not find "cutesy" questions, and the test writers will not play games with you. What they will do is present several valid options as a response to a challenging and appropriate question. These questions are designed to separate the perceptive and thoughtful reader from the superficial and impulsive one.

This said, it's wise to develop a strategy for success. Practice is the key to this success. You've been confronted with all types of multiple-choice questions during your career as a student. The test-taking skills you have learned in your social studies, math, and science classes may also apply to the AP Literature exam.

What Should I Expect in Section I Multiple Choice?

For this first section of the AP Literature exam, you are allotted 1 hour to answer 55 objective questions on four or five prose and poetry selections. The prose passage will comprise works of fiction or drama. The multiple-choice section will contain 4–5 texts with at least two prose passages and two poetry passages. Each text will have 8–13 questions. You can expect the poems to be complete and from different time periods and of different styles and forms with an emphasis on contemporary works and those of the twentieth century. In other words, you will not find two Shakespearean sonnets on the same exam.

These are *not* easy readings. They are representative of the college-level work you have been doing throughout the year. You will be expected to

- Follow sophisticated syntax
- Respond to diction
- Be comfortable with upper-level vocabulary
- Be familiar with literary terminology
- Make inferences
- Be sensitive to irony and tone
- Recognize components of style

With these skills in mind, the multiple-choice section will ask you to consider the following functions within each of the five texts:

- Character
- Setting
- Plot and structure
- Narrator or speaker
- Diction
- Imagery
- Symbols
- Comparison

You will also be asked to consider interpretations supported by the text.

> ## Areas of Multiple-Choice Questions
> **Short Fiction:** 42–49 percent of the questions
> **Poetry:** 36–45 percent of the questions
> **Longer Works:** 15–18 percent of the questions

The good news is that the selection is self-contained. This means that if it is about the Irish Potato Famine, you will not be at a disadvantage if you know nothing about it prior to the exam. Frequently there will be biblical references in a selection. This is especially true of works from an earlier time period. You are expected to be aware of basic allusions to biblical and mythological works often found in literature, but the passage will never require you to have any specific religious background.

Do not let the subject matter of a passage throw you. Strong analytical skills will work on any passage.

How Should I Begin to Work with Section I?

Take no more than a minute and thumb through the exam, looking for the following:

- The length of the selections
- The time periods or writing styles, if you can recognize them
- The number of questions asked
- A quick idea of the type of questions

This brief skimming of the test will put your mind into gear because you will be aware of what is expected of you.

How Should I Proceed Through This Section of the Exam?

"Creating my own multiple-choice questions was a terrific help to me when it came to doing close readings and correctly answering multiple-choice questions on the exam."
—Bill N.
   AP student

Timing is important. Always maintain an awareness of the time. Wear a watch. (Some students like to put it directly in front of them on the desk.) Remember, this will not be your first encounter with the multiple-choice section of the test. You've probably been practicing timed exams in class; in addition, this book provides you with three timed experiences. We're sure you will notice improvements as you progress through the timed practice activities.

Depending on the given selections, you may take less or more time on a particular passage, but you must know when to move on. The test *does not* become more difficult as it progresses. So, you will want to give yourself adequate opportunity to answer each set of questions.

Work at a pace of about one question per minute. Every question is worth the same number of points, so don't get bogged down on those that involve multiple tasks. Don't panic if a question is beyond you. Remember, it will probably be beyond a great number of other students as well. There has to be a bar that determines the 5's and 4's for this exam. Just do your best.

Reading the text carefully is a must. Begin at the beginning and work your way through. Do not waste time reading questions before you read the selection.

Most people read just with their eyes. We want you to slow down and read with your senses of sight, sound, and touch.

- Underline, circle, bracket, or highlight the text.
- Read closely, paying attention to punctuation and rhythms of the lines or sentences.
- Read as if you were reading the passage aloud to an audience, emphasizing meaning and intent.

- As corny as it may seem, hear those words in your head.
- This technique may seem childish, but it works. Using your finger as a pointer, underscore the line as you are reading it aloud in your head. This forces you to slow down and to really notice the text. This will be helpful when you have to refer to the passage.
- Use all the information given to you about the passage, such as title, author, date of publication, and footnotes.
- Be aware of foreshadowing.
- Be aware of thematic lines and be sensitive to details that **will obviously** be material for multiple-choice questions.
- When reading poetry, pay particular attention to enjambment and end-stopped lines because they carry meaning.
- With poetry, it's often helpful to paraphrase a stanza, especially if the order of the lines has been inverted.

You can practice these techniques any time. Take any work and read it aloud. Time yourself. A good rate is about 1½ minutes per page.

Types of Multiple-Choice Questions

Multiple-choice questions are not written randomly. There are certain formats you will encounter. The answers to the following questions should clarify some of the patterns.

Is the Structure the Same for All of the Multiple-Choice Questions?

No. Here are several basic patterns that the AP test makers often employ:

1. **The straightforward question,** such as:
   - The poem is an example of a
     C. lyric
   - The word "smooth" refers to
     B. his skin

2. **The question that refers you to specific lines and asks you to draw a conclusion or to interpret.**
   - Lines 52–57 serve to
     A. reinforce the author's thesis

3. **The "all . . . except" question** requires extra time because it demands that you consider every possibility.
   - The AP Literature exam is all of the following *except*:
     A. It is given in May of each year.
     B. It is open to high school seniors.
     C It is published in the *New York Times*.
     D. It is used as a qualifier for college credit.
     E. It is a 3-hour test.

Note: There are fewer and fewer of this type of question on the exam.

4. **The question that asks you to make an inference or to abstract a concept that is not directly stated in the passage.**
   - In the poem "My Last Duchess," the reader can infer that the speaker is
     E. arrogant

The infamous Roman Numeral question has been eliminated from the exam.

What Kinds of Questions Should I Expect on the Exam?

The 55 multiple-choice questions center around:

- the function of character, setting, plot, structure, narrator/speaker, diction, imagery, symbols, comparison;
- the interpretation of a text.

The test makers want to assess your understanding of the meaning of the selection as well as your ability to draw inferences and perceive implications based on it. They also want to know whether you understand *how* a writer develops his or her ideas.

One way of thinking about these multiple-choice questions is to categorize them as factual, technical, analytical, or inferential. Remember that this is merely a way of approaching a multiple-choice question, but it can prove to be helpful in both reading the question and determining the best answer. The two tables that follow illustrate the types of key words and phrases in these four categories that you can expect to find in questions for both the prose and the poetry selections.

Note: Do not memorize these tables. Also, do not panic if a word or phrase is unfamiliar to you. You may or may not encounter any or all of these words or phrases on any given exam. You can, however, count on meeting up with many of these in the practice exams in this book.

Prose: Key Words and Phrases Found in Multiple-Choice Questions

FACTUAL	TECHNICAL	ANALYTICAL	INFERENTIAL
words refer to	sentence structure	rhetorical strategy	effect of diction
allusions	style	shift in development	tone
antecedents	grammatical purpose	rhetorical stance	inferences
pronoun referents	dominant technique	style	effect of last paragraph
genre	imagery	metaphor	effect on reader
setting	point of view	contrast	narrator's attitude
	organization of passage	comparison	image suggests
	narrative progress of passage	cause/effect	effect of detail
	conflict	argument	author implies
	irony	description	author most concerned with
	function of	narration	
		specific-general	symbol
		how something is characterized	
		imagery	
		passage is primarily concerned with	
		function of	

Poetry: Key Words and Phrases Found in Multiple-Choice Questions

FACTUAL	TECHNICAL	ANALYTICAL	INFERENTIAL
all except	imagery	character portrayal	mood
definition	literary devices	imagery	attitude of
thesis	paradox	literary devices	poet's attitude
sequence of events	organizational pattern	paradox	purpose of
the object of ____ is ____	syntax	purpose of	tone of the poem
allusion	metrics	rhetorical shifts	theme of the poem
the subject of dramatic situation	parallel structure	ironies presented	reader may infer
	rhetorical shifts	least important	best interpreted as
paraphrasing	ironies presented	most important	effect of diction
subject	function of diction		speaker implies
references	dramatic moment		____ is associated with ____
	meaning conveyed by		context
			symbol

A word about jargon. Jargon refers to words that are unique to a specific subject. A common language is important for communication, and there must be agreement on the basic meanings of terms. Even though it is important to know the universal language of a subject, it is also important that you *not* limit the scope of your thinking to a brief definition. All the terms used in the tables are interwoven in literature. They are categorized only for easy reference. They also work in many other contexts. *In other words, think beyond the box.*

Scoring the Multiple-Choice Section

How Does the Scoring of the Multiple-Choice Section Work?

The College Board has implemented a new scoring process for the multiple-choice section of the AP English Literature and Composition exam. No longer are points deducted for incorrect responses, so there is no longer a penalty for guessing incorrectly. Therefore, it is to your advantage to answer ALL of the multiple-choice questions. Your chances of guessing the correct answer improve if you skillfully apply the process of elimination to narrow the choices.

Multiple-choice scores are based solely on the number of questions answered correctly. If you answered 36 questions correctly, then your raw score is 36. This raw score, which is 45 percent of the total, is combined with that of the essay section to make up a composite score. This is then manipulated to form a scale on which the final AP grade is based.

Strategies for Answering the Multiple-Choice Questions

You've been answering multiple-choice questions most of your academic life, and you've probably figured out ways to deal with them. However, there may be some points you have not considered that will be helpful for this particular exam.

General Guidelines

- Work in order. This is a good approach for several reasons:
  - It's clear.
  - You will not lose your place on the scan sheet.
  - There may be a logic to working sequentially that will help you answer previous questions. But, this is your call. If you are more comfortable moving around the exam, do so.
- Write on the exam booklet. Mark it up. Make it yours. Interact with the test.
- Do not spend too much time on any one question.
- Focus on your strengths. If you are more comfortable working with poetry, answer the poetry questions first.
- Don't be misled by the length or appearance of a selection. There is no correlation between length or appearance and the difficulty of the questions.
- Don't fight the question or the passage. You may know other information about the subject of the text or a question. It's irrelevant. Work within the given context.
- Consider all the choices in a given question. This will keep you from jumping to a false conclusion. It helps you to slow down and to really look at each possibility. You may find that your first choice is not the best or most appropriate one.
- Maintain an open mind as you answer subsequent questions in a series. Sometimes the answer to a later question will contradict your answer to a previous one. Reconsider both answers. Also, the phrasing of a question may point to an answer in a previous question.
- Remember that all parts of an answer must be correct.
- When in doubt, go to the text.

Specific Techniques

- **Process of elimination:** This is your primary tool, except for direct knowledge of the answer.
  1. Read the five choices.
  2. If no choice immediately strikes you as correct, you can
     - Eliminate those choices that are obviously wrong
     - Eliminate those choices that are too narrow or too broad
     - Eliminate illogical choices
     - Eliminate answers that are synonymous
     - Eliminate answers that cancel each other out

   3. If two answers are close, do one *or* the other of the following:
   - Find the one that is general enough to cover all aspects of the question
   - Find the one that is limited enough to be the detail the question is looking for

- **Substitution/fill in the blank**
   1. Rephrase the question, leaving a blank where the answer should go.

   2. Use each of the choices to fill in the blank until you find the one that is the best fit.

- **Using context**
   1. Consider the context when the question directs you to specific lines, words, or phrases.

   2. Locate the given word, phrase, sentence, or poetic line and read the sentence or line before and after the section of the text to which the question refers. Often this provides the information or clues you need to make your choice.

- **Anticipation:** As you read the passage for the first time, mark any details and ideas that you would ask a question about. You may be able to anticipate the test makers this way.
- **Intuition or the educated guess:** You have a wealth of skills and knowledge in your literary subconscious. A question or a choice may trigger a "remembrance of things past." This can be the basis for your educated guess. Have the confidence to use the educated guess as a valid technique. Trust your own resources.

> ## Survival Plan
>
> If time is running out and you haven't finished the fourth selection:
>
>   1. Scan the remaining questions and look for:
>   - The shortest questions
>   - The questions that direct you to a specific line.
>
>   2. Look for specific detail/definition questions.
>
>   3. Look for self-contained questions. For example: "The sea slid silently from the shore" is an example of C. alliteration. You do not have to go to the passage to answer this question.

If I Don't Know an Answer, Should I Guess?

You can't be seriously hurt by making *educated guesses* based on a careful reading of the selection. Be smart. Understand that you need to come to this exam well prepared. You must have a foundation of knowledge and skills. You cannot guess through the entire exam and expect to do well.

This is not Lotto. This book is **not** about how to "beat the exam." We want to maximize the skills you already have. There is an inherent integrity in this exam and your participation in it. With this in mind, when there is no other direction open to you, it is perfectly fine to make an educated guess.

Is There Anything Special I Should Know About Preparing for the Prose Multiple-Choice Questions?

After you have finished with the Diagnostic/Master exam, you will be familiar with the format and types of questions asked on the AP Lit exam. However, just practicing answering multiple-choice questions on specific works will not give you a complete understanding of this questioning process. We suggest the following to help you hone your multiple-choice answering skills with prose multiple-choice questions:

- Choose a challenging passage from a full-length prose work.
- Read the selection a couple of times and create several multiple-choice questions about specific sections of the selection.
- Make certain the section is self-contained and complex.
- Choose a dialogue, monologue, introductory setting, set description, stage directions, philosophical passage, significant event, or moment of conflict.
- Create a variety of question types based on the previous chart.
- Refer to the prose table given earlier in this chapter for suggested language and type.
- Administer your mini-quiz to a classmate, study group, or class.
- Evaluate your results.
- Repeat this process through several different full-length works during your preparation for the exam. The works can certainly come from those you are studying in class.

"One of my biggest challenges in preparing for the exam was to learn not to jump to conclusions when I was doing the multiple-choice questions."
—Samantha S.
   AP student

Here's what should happen as a result of your using this process:

- Your expectation level for the selections in the actual test will be more realistic.
- You will become familiar with the language of multiple-choice questions.
- Your understanding of the process of choosing answers will be heightened.
- Questions you write that you find less than satisfactory will trigger your analytical skills as you attempt to figure out "what went wrong."
- Terminology will become more accurate.
- *Bonus:* If you continue to do this work throughout your preparation for the AP exam, you will have created a mental storehouse of literary information. So when you are presented with a prose or free-response essay in Section II, you will have an extra resource at your disposal.

Your Turn

To Do:

1. Circle/highlight/underline the words and/or phrases that appear to be important for the meaning of the excerpt.

2. Carefully consider each of the given sample questions.

3. Construct your own question that is an example of the specific type.

from Mark Twain's *Huckleberry Finn*

Sometimes we'd have the whole river all to ourselves for the longest time. Yonder was the banks and the islands, across the water; and maybe a spark—which was a candle in a cabin window—and sometimes on the water you could see a spark or two—on a raft or a scow, you know; and maybe you could hear a fiddle or a song coming over from one of them crafts. It's lovely to live on a raft. We had the sky, up there, all speckled with stars, and we used to lay on our backs and look up at

5

them, and discuss about whether they was made, or only just happened—Jim he allowed they was made, but I allowed they happened; I judged it would have took too long to make so many. Jim said the moon could a laid them; well, that looked kind of reasonable, so I didn't say nothing against it, because I've seen a frog lay most as many, so of course it could be done. We used to watch the stars that fell, too, and see them streak down. Jim allowed they'd got spoiled and was hove out of the nest.   10

Title: *Huckleberry Finn*
Author: Mark Twain
Type of passage: Narrative description

Sample <u>Factual</u> Question: In lines 10–11, "I've seen a frog lay most as many" refers to

<u>Answer:</u> stars

<u>Rationale:</u> The implied comparison has Huck inferring that the number of stars in the sky is similar to the number of eggs a frog lays.

Your <u>Factual</u> Question:

<u>Answer:</u>   <u>Rationale:</u>

Sample <u>Technical</u> Question: A primary function of the sentence "It's lovely to live on a raft" is

<u>Answer:</u> to contrast with the lyrical description in the passage

<u>Rationale:</u> The straightforward break in the middle of the passage emphasizes the key point of the description.

Your <u>Technical</u> Question:

<u>Answer:</u>   <u>Rationale:</u>

Sample <u>Analytical</u> Question: The primary purpose of using dialect is most likely to

<u>Answer:</u> reinforce the innocence and natural state of Huck and Jim

<u>Rationale:</u> The regional dialect illustrates the lack of the stereotypical education and background of the period.

Your <u>Analytical</u> Question:

<u>Answer:</u>   <u>Rationale:</u>

Sample <u>Inferential</u> Question: The tone of the passage can best be described as

<u>Answer:</u> nostalgic and philosophical

<u>Rationale:</u> The diction supports their reverie and their curiosity about their place in the universe.

Your <u>Inferential</u> Question:

<u>Answer:</u>   <u>Rationale:</u>

Is There Anything Special I Should Do to Prepare for the Poetry Questions?

The points made about prose hold true for the poetry multiple-choice questions as well. But there are a few specific pointers that may prove helpful:

- Choose thoughtful and interesting poems of some length. (See our suggested reading list.)
- Read the poems several times. Practice reading the poems aloud.
- The greatest benefit will be that as you read any poem, you will automatically begin to respond to areas of the poem that would lend themselves to a multiple-choice question.

- Here is a list of representative poets you may want to read.

    - Shakespeare
    - John Donne
    - Philip Larkin
    - Emily Dickinson
    - Sylvia Plath
    - Dylan Thomas
    - May Swenson
    - Theodore Roethke
    - Sharon Olds
    - Billy Collins
    - Pablo Neruda

    - Richard Wilbur
    - Adrienne Rich
    - Edmund Spenser
    - W. H. Auden
    - W. B. Yeats
    - Gwendolyn Brooks
    - Elizabeth Bishop
    - Langston Hughes
    - Galway Kinnell
    - Marianne Moore
    - May Sarton

> You might want to utilize this process throughout the year with major works studied in and out of class and keep track of your progress. See the Bibliography of this book.

Your Turn

To Do:

1. Circle/highlight/underline the words and/or phrases that appear to be important for the meaning of the poem.

2. Carefully consider each of the given sample questions.

3. Construct your own question that is an example of the specific type.

It Sifts from Leaden Sieves
By Emily Dickinson

It sifts from leaden sieves,
It powders all the wood,
It fills with alabaster wool
The wrinkles of the road.

It makes an even face   5
Of mountain and of plain, –
Unbroken forehead from the east
Unto the east again.

It reaches to the fence,
It wraps it, rail by rail,   10
Till it is lost in fleeces,
It flings a crystal veil

On stump and stack and stem, –
The summer's empty room,
Acres of seams where harvests were,   15
Recordless, but for them.

It ruffles wrists of posts,
As ankles of a queen, –
Then stills its artisans like ghosts,
Denying they have been.   20

Title: "It Sifts from Leaden Sieves"
Poet: Emily Dickinson

Sample <u>Factual</u> Question: The subject of the poem's dramatic situation is

<u>Answer:</u> the falling snow   <u>Rationale:</u> The images all support the snow
                                                                                        metaphor.

Your <u>Factual</u> Question:

<u>Answer:</u>   <u>Rationale:</u>

Sample <u>Technical</u> Question: The primary literary device used in the poem is

<u>Answer:</u> metaphor   <u>Rationale:</u> Metaphor is used in every stanza.

Your <u>Technical</u> Question:

<u>Answer:</u>   <u>Rationale:</u>

Sample <u>Analytical</u> Question: Paradox is most readily seen in

<u>Answer:</u> the softness imagery vs. the last two lines of the poem

<u>Rationale:</u> There is a shift from description to the effect of the cold in the last two lines.

Your <u>Analytical</u> Question:

<u>Answer:</u>   <u>Rationale:</u>

Sample <u>Inferential</u> Question: Based on the poem, the reader could infer that

<u>Answer:</u> the power of nature is all-encompassing

<u>Rationale:</u> Nothing in the poem is excluded from the power of the snow.

Your <u>Inferential</u> Question:

<u>Answer:</u>   <u>Rationale:</u>

The Time Is at Hand

It is now time to try the Diagnostic/Master exam, Section I. Do this section in *one* sitting. Time yourself! Be honest with yourself when you score your answers.

Note: If the 1 hour passes before you finish all the questions, stop where you are and score what you have done up to this point. Afterwards, answer the remaining questions, but do not count the answers as part of your score.

When you have completed all the multiple-choice questions in this Diagnostic/Master exam, carefully read the explanations of the answers. Spend time here and assess which types of questions give you trouble. Use this book to learn from your mistakes.

ANSWER SHEET FOR DIAGNOSTIC MULTIPLE-CHOICE QUESTIONS

1. _____   15. _____   29. _____   43. _____

2. _____   16. _____   30. _____   44. _____

3. _____   17. _____   31. _____   45. _____

4. _____   18. _____   32. _____   46. _____

5. _____   19. _____   33. _____   47. _____

6. _____   20. _____   34. _____   48. _____

7. _____   21. _____   35. _____   49. _____

8. _____   22. _____   36. _____   50. _____

9. _____   23. _____   37. _____   51. _____

10. _____   24. _____   38. _____   52. _____

11. _____   25. _____   39. _____   53. _____

12. _____   26. _____   40. _____   54. _____

13. _____   27. _____   41. _____   55. _____

14. _____   28. _____   42. _____

I _____ did _____ did not finish all the questions in the allotted 1 hour.

I had _____ correct answers. I had _____ incorrect answers. I left _____ questions blank.

I have carefully reviewed the explanations of the answers, and I think I need to work on the following types of questions:

THE MULTIPLE-CHOICE SECTION OF THE DIAGNOSTIC/MASTER EXAM

The multiple-choice section of the Diagnostic/Master exam follows. You have seen the questions in the "walk through" in Chapter 3.

Advanced Placement Literature and Composition

Section 1

Total time—1 hour

Carefully read the following passages and answer the accompanying questions. Questions 1–10 are based on the following poem.

Now Goes Under . . .
by Edna St. Vincent Millay

Now goes under, and I watch it go under, the sun
    That will not rise again.
Today has seen the setting, in your eyes cold
    and senseless as the sea,
Of friendship better than bread, and of bright charity   *allit.*   5
That lifts a man a little above the beasts that run.

That this could be!
That I should live to see
Most vulgar Pride, that stale obstreperous clown,   *person.*
So fitted out with purple robe and crown   10
To stand among his betters! Face to face
With outraged me in this once holy place,
Where Wisdom was a favoured guest and hunted
Truth was harboured out of danger,
He bulks enthroned, a lewd, and insupportable stranger!   15

I would have sworn, indeed I swore it:
The hills may shift, the waters may decline,
Winter may twist the stem from the twig that bore it,
But never your love from me, your hand from mine.

Now goes under the sun, and I watch it go under.   20
Farewell, sweet light, great wonder!
You, too, farewell—but fare not well enough to dream
You have done wisely to invite the night before the darkness came.

1. The poem is an example of a(n)
   A. sonnet
   B. lyric
   C. ode
   D. ballad
   E. dramatic monologue

2. The setting of the sun is a symbol for
   A. the beginning of winter
   B. encountering danger
   C. the end of a relationship
   D. facing death
   E. the onset of night

3. The second stanza is developed primarily by
   A. metaphor
   B. simile
   C. personification
   D. hyperbole
   E. allusion

4. "He" in line 15 refers to
   A. Wisdom
   B. Truth
   C. I
   D. Pride
   E. charity

5. According to the speaker, what separates man from beast?
   A. love
   B. friendship
   C. charity
   D. truth
   E. wisdom

6. For the speaker, the relationship has been all of the following *except*
   A. honest
   B. dangerous
   C. spiritual
   D. ephemeral
   E. nourishing

7. The reader can infer from the play on words in the last stanza that the speaker is
   A. dying
   B. frantic
   C. wistful
   D. bitter
   E. capricious

8. "This once holy place" (line 12) refers to
   A. the sunset
   B. the relationship
   C. the sea
   D. the circus
   E. the Church

9. The cause of the relationship's situation is
   A. a stranger coming between them
   B. the lover not taking the relationship seriously
   C. the lover feeling intellectually superior
   D. the lover's pride coming between them
   E. the lover being insensitive

10. The speaker acknowledges the finality of the relationship in line(s)
    A. 1–2
    B. 7
    C. 8
    D. 16
    E. 18–19

6/10

Questions 11–23 are based on the following passage from *The Heart of Darkness* by Joseph Conrad, 1902.

The sea-reach of the Thames stretched before us like the beginning of an
interminable waterway. The air was dark above Gravesend, and farther back still
seemed condensed into a mournful gloom, brooding motionless over the biggest and
the greatest town on earth.

"I was thinking of very old times, when the Romans first came here, nineteen   5
hundred years ago—the other day . . . Light came out of this river since—you say knights?
Yes; but it is like a running blaze on a plain, like a flash of lightning in the clouds. We live
in the flicker—may it last as long as the old earth keeps rolling! But darkness was here
yesterday. Imagine the feelings of a commander of a fine—what d'ye call 'em?—trireme
in the Mediterranean, ordered suddenly to the north; run overland across the Gauls in a   10

hurry; put in charge of one of these craft the legionnaires—a wonderful lot of handy men they must have been, too—used to build, apparently by the hundred, in a month or two, if we may believe what we read. Imagine him here—the very end of the world, a sea the color of lead, a sky the color of smoke, a kind of ship about as rigid as a concertina—and going up this river with stores, or orders, or what you like. Sandbanks, marshes, forests, savages— 15 precious little to eat for a civilized man, nothing but Thames water to drink. No Falernian wine here, no going ashore. Here and there a military camp lost in a wilderness, like a needle in a bundle of hay—cold, fog, tempests, disease, exile, and death—death skulking in the air, in the water, in the bush. They must have been dying like flies here. Oh yes—he did it. Did it very well, too, no doubt, and without thinking much about it either, except 20 afterwards to brag of what he had gone through in his time, perhaps. They were men enough to face darkness. And perhaps he was cheered by keeping his eye on a chance of promotion to the fleet at Ravenna by and by, if he had good friends in Rome and survived the awful climate. Or think of a decent young citizen in a toga—perhaps too much dice, you know— coming out here in the train of some prefect, or tax-gatherer, or trader even, to mend his 25 fortunes. Land in a swamp, march through the woods, and in some inland post feel the savagery, the utter savagery, had closed round him—all that mysterious life of the wilderness that stirs in the forest, in the jungles, in the hearts of wild men. There's no initiation either into such mysteries. He has to live in the midst of the incomprehensible, which is also detestable. And it has a fascination, too, that goes to work upon him. The fascination of the 30 abomination—you know, imagine the growing regrets, the longing to escape, the powerless disgust, the surrender, the hate."

He paused.

"Mind," he began again, lifting one arm from the elbow, the palm of the hand outwards, so that, with his legs folded before him, he had the pose of a Buddha preaching in 35 European clothes and without a lotus flower—"Mind, none of us would feel exactly like this. What saves us is efficiency—the devotion to efficiency. But these chaps were not much account, really. They were no colonists; their administration was merely a squeeze, and nothing more, I suspect. They were conquerors, and for that you want only brute force— nothing to boast of, when you have it, since your strength is just an accident arising from the 40 weakness of others. They grabbed what they could get for the sake of what was to be got. It was just robbery with violence, aggravated murder on a great scale, and men going at it blind— as is very proper for those who tackle a darkness. The conquest of the earth, which mostly means taking it away from those who have a different complexion or slightly flatter noses than ourselves, is not a pretty thing when you look at it too much. What redeems it is the idea 45 only. An idea at the back of it; not a sentimental pretense but an idea; and an unselfish belief in the idea—something you can set up, and bow down before, and offer a sacrifice to . . . "

11. In the passage, *darkness* implies all of the following *except*
A. the unknown
B. savagery
C. ignorance
D. death
E. exploration

12. The setting of the passage is
A. Africa
B. Ancient Rome
C. the Thames River
D. the Mediterranean
E. Italy

13. The tone of the passage is
   A. condescending
   B. indignant
   C. scornful
   D. pensive
   E. laudatory

14. Later events may be foreshadowed by all of the following phrases *except*
   A. "Imagine the feelings of a commander . . . "
   B. " . . . live in the midst of the incomprehensible . . . "
   C. " . . . in some inland post feel the savagery . . . "
   D. "They must have been dying like flies here."
   E. " . . . the very end of the world . . . "

15. The narrator draws a parallel between
   A. light and dark
   B. past and present
   C. life and death
   D. fascination and abomination
   E. decency and savagery

16. In this passage, "We live in the flicker..." (lines 7–8) may be interpreted to mean *ALL* of the following *EXCEPT*
   A. In the history of the world, humanity's span on earth is brief.
   B. Future civilizations will learn from only a portion of the past.
   C. Periods of enlightenment and vision appear only briefly.
   D. The river has been the source of life throughout the ages.
   E. A moment of present-day insight about conquest.

17. One may conclude from the passage that the speaker
   A. admires adventurers
   B. longs to be a crusader
   C. is a former military officer
   D. recognizes and accepts the presence of evil in human experience
   E. is prejudiced

18. In the context of the passage, which of the following phrases presents a paradox?
   A. "The fascination of the abomination . . . "
   B. " . . . in the hearts of wild men"
   C. "There's no initiation . . . into such mysteries"
   D. " . . . a flash of lightning in the clouds"
   E. " . . . death skulking in the air . . . "

19. The lines "Imagine him here . . . concertina . . . " (lines 13–14) contain examples of
   A. hyperbole and personification
   B. irony and metaphor
   C. alliteration and personification
   D. parallel structure and simile
   E. allusion and simile

20. According to the speaker, the one trait which saves Europeans from savagery is
   A. sentiment
   B. a sense of mystery
   C. brute force
   D. religious zeal
   E. efficiency

21. According to the speaker, the only justification for conquest is
   A. the "weakness of others"
   B. it's being "proper for those who tackle a darkness . . . "
   C. their grabbing "what they could get for the sake of what was to be got"
   D. " . . . an unselfish belief in the idea . . . "
   E. "The fascination of the abomination . . . "

22. In the statement by the speaker, "Mind, none of us would feel exactly like this" (line 36), "this" refers to
   A. " . . . a Buddha preaching in European clothes . . . " (lines 35–36)
   B. " . . . imagine the growing regrets . . . the hate." (lines 31–32)
   C. "What redeems it is the idea only." (lines 45–46)
   D. " . . . think of a decent young citizen in a toga . . . " (line 24)
   E. "I was thinking of very old times . . . " (line 5)

23. The speaker presents all of the following
reasons for exploration and conquest *except*
   A. military expeditions
   B. " . . . a chance of promotion"
   C. " . . . to mend his fortunes"
   D. religious commitment
   E. punishment for a crime

Questions 24–35 are based on the following poem by William Shakespeare.

> That time of year thou mayst in me behold
> When yellow leaves, or none, or few, do hang
> Upon those boughs which shake against the cold,
> Bare ruin'd choirs, where late the sweet birds sang.
> In me thou see'st the twilight of such day   5
> As after sunset fadeth in the west;
> Which by and by black night doth take away,
> Death's second self, that seals up all in rest.
> In me thou see'st the glowing of such fire,
> That on the ashes of his youth doth lie,   10
> As the deathbed whereon it must expire,
> Consum'd with that which it was nourish'd by.
> This thou perceiv'st, which makes thy love more strong,
> To love that well which thou must leave ere long.

24. "That time of year" (line 1) refers to
   A. youth
   B. old age
   C. childhood
   D. senility
   E. maturity

25. "Death's second self" (line 8) refers to
   A. "That time of year"
   B. "sunset fadeth"
   C. "the west"
   D. "ruin'd choirs"
   E. "black night"

26. Line 12 is an example of
   A. paradox
   B. caesura
   C. parable
   D. hyperbole
   E. metonymy

27. "Twilight of such day" (line 5) is supported by
all of the following images *except*
   A. "sunset fadeth"
   B. "the glowing of such fire"
   C. "west"
   D. "Death's second self"
   E. "ashes of his youth"

28. "This thou perceiv'st" (line 13) refers to
   A. the beloved's deathbed
   B. the sorrow of unrequited love
   C. the passion of youth expiring
   D. the beloved's acknowledgment of the
      speaker's mortality
   E. the speaker sending the lover away

29. The poem is an example of a(n)
   A. elegy
   B. Spenserian sonnet
   C. Petrarchan sonnet
   D. Shakespearean sonnet
   E. sestina

30. The poem is primarily developed by
A. metaphor
B. argument
C. synecdoche
D. alternative choices
E. contradiction

31. The irony of the poem is best expressed in line
A. 5
B. 7
C. 10
D. 11
E. 14

32. "It" in line 12 can best be interpreted to mean
A. a funeral pyre
B. spent youth
C. the intensity of the speaker's love
D. the impending departure of his beloved
E. the immortality of the relationship

33. An apt title for the poem could be
A. Love Me or Leave Me
B. Death Be Not Proud
C. The End Justifies the Means
D. Love's Fall
E. Grow Old Along with Me

34. The tone of the poem can best be described as
A. contemplative
B. defiant
C. submissive
D. arbitrary
E. complaining

35. The speaker most likely is
A. jealous of the beloved's youth
B. pleased that the lover will leave
C. unable to keep up with the young lover
D. unwilling to face his own mortality
E. responsive to the beloved's constancy

Questions 36–47 are based on a careful reading of the following excerpt from the first chapter of the 2001 novel *White Teeth* by Zadie Smith that centers on two families who live in North London.

Archie's marriage felt like buying a pair of shoes, taking them home and finding they don't fit. For the sake of appearances, he put up with them. And then, all of a sudden and after thirty years, the shoes picked themselves up and walked out of the house. She left. Thirty years.

As far as he remembered, just like everybody else they began well. The first spring of 1946, he had stumbled out of the darkness of war and into a Florentine coffee house, where he [5] was served by a waitress truly like the sun: Ophelia Diagilo, dressed all in yellow, spreading warmth and the promise of sex as she passed him a frothy cappuccino. They walked into it blinkered as horses. She was not to know that women never stayed as daylight in Archie's life; that somewhere in him he didn't like them, he didn't trust them, and he was able to love them only if they wore haloes. No one told Archie that lurking in the Diagilo family tree were two [10] hysteric aunts, an uncle who talked to aubergines[1] and a cousin who wore his clothes back to front. So they got married and returned to England, where she realized very quickly her mistake, he drove her very quickly mad, and the halo was packed off to the attic to collect dust with the rest of the bric-a-brac[2] and broken kitchen appliances that Archie promised one day to repair. Amongst that bric-a-brac was a Hoover. [15]

On Boxing Day[3] morning, six days before he parked outside Mo's halal[4] butchers, Archie had returned to their semi-detached in Hendon[5] in search of that Hoover. It was his fourth trip to the attic in so many days, ferrying out the odds and ends of a marriage to his new flat, and the Hoover was amongst the very last items he reclaimed—one of the most broken things, most ugly things, the things you demand out of sheer bloody-mindedness because you have [20] lost the house. This is what divorce is: taking things you no longer want from people you no longer love.

"So you again," said the Spanish home-help at the door, Santa-Maria or Maria-Santa or something. "Meester Jones, what now? Kitchen sink, si?"

"Hoover," said Archie, grimly. "Vacuum." [25]

She cut her eyes at him and spat on the doormat inches from his shoes. "Welcome, señor."

The place had become a haven for people who hated him. Apart from the home-help, he had to contend with Ophelia's extended Italian family, her mental-health nurse, the woman from the council,[6] and of course Ophelia herself, who was to be found in the kernel of this nuthouse, curled up in a fetal ball on the sofa, making lowing sounds into a bottle of Bailey's.[7] It took him an hour and a quarter just to get through enemy lines—and for what? A perverse Hoover, discarded months earlier because it was determined to perform the opposite of every vacuum's objective: spewing out dust instead of sucking it in.

"Meester Jones, why do you come here when it make you so unhappy? Be reasonable. What can you want with it?" The home-help was following him up the attic stairs, armed with some kind of cleaning fluid: "It's broken. You don't need this. See? See?" She plugged it into a socket and demonstrated the dead switch. Archie took the plug out and silently wound the cord round the Hoover. If it was broken, it was coming with him. All broken things were coming with him. He was going to fix every damn broken thing in this house, if only to show that he was good for something.

"You good for nothing!" Santa whoever chased him back down the stairs. "Your wife is ill in her head, and this is all you can do!"

Archie hugged the Hoover to his chest and took it into the crowded living room, where, under several pairs of reproachful eyes, he got out his toolbox and started work on it.

"Look at him," said one of the Italian grandmothers, the more glamorous one with the big scarves and fewer moles, "he take everything, capisce?[8] He take-a her mind, he take-a the blender, he take-a the old stereo—he take-a everything except the floorboards. It make-a you sick . . ."

The woman from the council, who even on dry days resembled a long-haired cat soaked to the skin, shook her skinny head in agreement. "It's disgusting, you don't have to tell me, it's disgusting . . . and naturally, we're the ones left to sort out the mess; it's muggins[9] here who has to—"

Which was overlapped by the nurse: "She can't stay here alone, can she . . . now he's buggered off, poor woman . . . she needs a proper home, she needs . . ."

I'm here, Archie felt like saying, I'm right here you know, I'm bloody right here. And it was my blender.

But he wasn't one for confrontation, Archie. He listened to them all for another fifteen minutes, mute as he tested the Hoover's suction against pieces of newspaper, until he was overcome by the sensation that Life was an enormous rucksack[10] so impossibly heavy that, even though it meant losing everything, it was infinitely easier to leave all baggage here on the roadside and walk on into the blackness. You don't need the blender, Archie-boy, you don't need the Hoover. This stuff's all dead weight. Just lay down the rucksack, Arch, and join the happy campers in the sky. Was that wrong? To Archie—ex-wife and ex-wife's relatives in one ear, spluttering vacuum in the other—it just seemed that The End was unavoidably nigh. Nothing personal to God or whatever. It just felt like the end of the world. And he was going to need more than poor whisky, novelty crackers and a paltry box of Quality Street[11]—all the strawberry ones already scoffed—to justify entering another annum.

Patiently he fixed the Hoover, and vacuumed the living room with a strange methodical finality, shoving the nozzle into the most difficult corners. Solemnly he flipped a coin (heads, life, tails, death) and felt nothing in particular when he found himself staring at the dancing lion.[12] Quietly he detached the Hoover tube, put it in a suitcase, and left the house for the last time.

---

[1]**aubergines:** eggplants
[2]**bric-a-brac:** odds and ends, objects of little value
[3]**Boxing Day:** The British celebration of the day after Christmas

[4]**halal:** food prepared according to Muslim law
[5]**Hendon:** a suburb of London
[6]**council:** a type of elected British advisory or legislative body
[7]**Bailey's:** a brand of whiskey
[8]**capisce:** Italian for *understand*
[9]**muggins:** a foolish, gullible person
[10]**rucksack:** backpack
[11]**Quality Street:** a brand of candy
[12]**dancing lion:** reverse side of a twenty-pence coin

36. The function of the first paragraph can best be described as
   A. a diatribe against marriage
   B. an introduction to the setting
   C. an introduction to the central plot
   D. an introduction to Archie's attitude toward his former wife and their marriage
   E. an introduction to Ophelia

37. After reading the second paragraph, one can infer all of the following *except*
   A. Archie and Ophelia's love was based on passion.
   B. Archie was self-motivated.
   C. Archie wanted to be able to place his wife on a pedestal.
   D. Ophelia and Ophelia were quick to make important decisions.
   E. Archie was unsure and suspicious of women.

38. The metaphor of the halo in the second paragraph serves mainly to emphasize
   A. the beauty and innocence of Ophelia
   B. the religion of both Ophelia and Archie
   C. the inevitability of future events
   D. the hastiness of Archie and Ophelia's marriage
   E. an unrealistic desire for the perfect love

39. In line 7, *it* is referring to
   A. pledge of love
   B. move to England
   C. marriage
   D. divorce
   E. sexual relationship

40. The response of "Santa-Maria or Maria-Santa" (23–26) to Archie's arrival can best be described as
   A. hostile and denigrating
   B. suspicious and cowering
   C. warm and welcoming
   D. condescending and dismissive
   E. curious and insecure

41. Paragraph 7, lines 27–33, progresses from a primarily third-person, objective narrator to
   A. stream-of-consciousness
   B. interior monologue
   C. first-person narrator
   D. third-person subjective
   E. third-person omniscient

42. Lines 39–40, reveal that Archie
   A. believes he is capable of fixing broken appliances
   B. wants to prove that he is not a failure
   C. feels he has been taken advantage of
   D. is basically selfish
   E. wants to show the help that he is in charge

43. For Archie, the Hoover vacuum symbolizes each of the following *except*
   A. ownership
   B. potential to redeem himself
   C. failure of his life so far
   D. his love for Ophelia
   E. control

44. As a way to characterize Archie's perceived burden, the author uses the image of
   A. pair of shoes (first paragraph)
   B. halo (second paragraph)
   C. Hoover vacuum (throughout passage)
   D. the blender (lines 47 and 56)
   E. rucksack (next-to-last paragraph)

45. The author uses dialect with the home-help's dialogue primarily
  A. to add a sense of realism to the narrative
  B. to indicate the class differences between Archie and the home-help
  C. to make a point about the working conditions of the working class
  D. to add a bit of humor to the passage
  E. to gain more sympathy for Archie

46. Archie's behavior in the last two paragraphs suggests he
  A. wants to move on
  B. believes it's possible to help Ophelia
  C. is beginning to feel hopeless
  D. wonders why he bothered fixing the Hoover
  E. wants to get back at the home-help and Ophelia's relatives

47. Which of the following best describes the effect of the last paragraph?
  A. hopeful
  B. looking for redemption
  C. impending doom
  D. loss of control
  E. anger at the world

Questions 48–55 are based on a careful reading of the 2002 poem "Litany" by Billy Collins.

Litany[1]

You are the bread and the knife,
The crystal goblet and the wine . . .
—Jacques Crickillon

You are the bread and the knife,
the crystal goblet and the wine.   5
You are the dew on the morning grass
and the burning wheel of the sun.
You are the white apron of the baker,
and the marsh birds suddenly in flight.

However, you are not the wind in the orchard,   10
the plums on the counter,
or the house of cards.
And you are certainly not the pine-scented air.
There is just no way that you are the pine-scented air.

It is possible that you are the fish under the bridge   15
maybe even the pigeon on the general's head,
but you are not even close
to being the field of cornflowers at dusk.

And a quick look in the mirror will show
that you are neither the boots in the corner   20
nor the boat asleep in its boathouse.

It might interest you to know,
speaking of the plentiful imagery of the world,
that I am the sound of rain on the roof.

I also happen to be the shooting star,   25
the evening paper blowing down an alley
and the basket of chestnuts on the kitchen table.

I am also the moon in the trees
and the blind woman's tea cup.
But don't worry, I'm not the bread and the knife.   30
You are still the bread and the knife.
You will always be the bread and the knife,
not to mention the crystal goblet and–somehow–the wine.

---

[1]**litany:** (secondary meaning) a recital or a repetitive series of phrases with a type of call-and-response

48. This poem is an example of
A. blank verse
B. rhymed verse
C. metered verse
D. free verse
E. rhymed, metered verse

49. The tone of the poem can best be described as
A. formal and critical
B. uncaring and suspicious
C. informal and indifferent
D. brusque and patronizing
E. casual and playful

50. Line 9, "and the marsh birds suddenly in flight"
A. hints at an element of uncertainty
B. sums up the preceding five lines
C. indicates the speaker's fear
D. introduces a new setting
E. suggests the speaker's fascination with nature

51. As the poem progresses, it becomes clear that this poem is
A. an elegy for a deceased loved one
B. a description of the depth of the speaker's love
C. an ode to love
D. an apology to the speaker's loved one
E. a tribute to the speaker's beloved

52. The turning point in the poem occurs in stanza
A. 1
B. 2
C. 5
D. 6
E. 7

53. All of the following literary devices are used in the poem *except*
A. rhyme
B. metaphor
C. alliteration
D. simile
E. repetition

54. Elements of humor in the poem are created by using
A. improbable circumstances
B. counterbalance and exaggeration
C. gentle criticism and apologies
D. slapstick put-downs
E. satirical comments

55. The repetition in the last four lines of the poem
can best be interpreted to mean
  A. the speaker will always be the opposite of
     the beloved
  B. the beloved holds the key to the speaker's
     life and always will
  C. both the speaker and the beloved will
     remain in separate worlds
  D. the speaker will always accept the beloved's
     point of view
  E. the speaker cannot imagine living without
     the beloved

STOP.

THIS IS THE END OF THE MULTIPLE-CHOICE SECTION OF THE DIAGNOSTIC/MASTER EXAM

ANSWERS TO MULTIPLE-CHOICE QUESTIONS

Answer Key

1. B	20. E	39. C
2. C	21. D	40. A
3. C	22. B	41. D
4. D	23. E	42. B
5. C	24. B	43. D
6. B	25. E	44. E
7. D	26. A	45. A
8. B	27. B	46. C
9. D	28. D	47. C
10. A	29. D	48. D
11. E	30. A	49. E
12. C	31. E	50. A
13. D	32. C	51. E
14. A	33. D	52. C
15. B	34. A	53. D
16. B	35. E	54. B
17. D	36. D	55. B
18. A	37. B	
19. D	38. E	

Answers and Explanations

Now Goes Under . . .
by Edna St. Vincent Millay

1. **B.** This question requires the student to know the characteristics of various poetic forms. (See Chapter 9.) Using the process of elimination, the correct answer B is readily confirmed. Lyric poetry is emotional and personal.

2. **C.** Although the setting sun is often associated with winter, death, and darkness, these answers are not symbolic of the literal topic of the poem—the end of the love relationship.

3. **C.** The poet uses personification in lines 9–15: "vulgar Pride," "Where Wisdom was a favoured guest," "hunted Truth" as characters to develop the conflicts apparent in the poem. [TIP: Capitalization of nouns often indicates personification.]

4. **D.** This is an antecedent question. The student must retrace the reference "He" back to its origins to locate the correct answer. Try asking "who is enthroned, lewd and unsupportable?" Since truth, charity, and wisdom are described positively, only *vulgar* pride qualifies as the answer.

5. **C.** This question requires you to find the antecedent. Ask yourself, "Who or what lifts man?" The answer, *charity*, should be obvious.

6. **B.** Sometimes you can find information from a previous question. In question 2, "danger" was eliminated as a choice; therefore, it probably wouldn't be suitable for this question either. Try finding proof of the others. Truth = honest; holy = spiritual; bread = nourishment. Therefore, *dangerous* has to be the answer.

7. **D.** This is a tone question based on a repetitive contradictory phrase. She does *not* wish him well; therefore, she is bitter and resigned. There is nothing playful, wistful, or frantic in the conclusion.

8. **B.** This is a relationship question. You should realize this by the intensity of the opposing lewd force, pride, which destroyed the sanctity of the love. (If you see this, you could validate your answer to question 9.)

9. **D.** The cause is developed in the longest stanza, lines 7–15. Find the proof for your answer in lines 7–12.

10. **A.** Interestingly enough, the speaker reveals the conclusion in the first two lines of the poem. "The sun that will not rise again" establishes the totality of the circumstances.

Heart of Darkness
by Joseph Conrad

11. **E.** Here's an easy question to start you off. For years you heard your English teachers and your classmates discussing all the elements that could be associated with *darkness*. All the choices given in this question would qualify except for *exploration*.

12. **C.** Line 1 gives you the answer. The Thames is the river that runs through the heart of London.

13. **D.** A careful reading of the passage will introduce you to a speaker who is *thinking* about the past, *thinking* about exploration and conquest, and *thinking* about the conqueror and the conquered.

14. **A.** Here, the speaker is asking his listeners to picture the past. Therefore, it is *not* pointing to the future. The feelings of a commander have nothing to do with a future event; whereas each of the other choices hints at a future concept.

15. **B.** The second paragraph is about ancient Rome and its conquests. The third paragraph has the speaker considering "us" and what saves "us." This is past and present.

16. **B.** The first ten lines support inclusion of A. Choice B is NOT part of the speaker's conversation. Choice C is supported in the second paragraph. Choice D may be found in lines 5–8. Lines 36–47 support Choice E.

17. **D.** Lines 26–30 and 39–45 indicate the speaker's attitude toward the human condition. There is no evidence in the passage to support any of the other choices.

18. **A.** The question assumes you know the definition of *paradox*. Therefore, you should

be able to see that to be fascinated by that which is repulsive, awful, and horrible is a paradox.

19. **D.** "A sea," "a sky," "a kind," "or orders," "or what" are examples of parallel structure. The simile is "ship about as rigid as a concertina."

20. **E.** This is a straightforward, factual question. The answer is found in line 37.

21. **D.** In lines 45–47 the speaker is philosophizing about what it is that "redeems" the "conquest of the earth." It is the *idea*.

22. **B.** This question asks you to locate the antecedent of "this." You could use the substitution method here. Just replace "this" with the word or phrase. Or, you could look carefully at the text itself. The omniscient narrator is describing the speaker as a Buddha. Lines 45–46 come after "this." D and E are not real possibilities. Also, they are too far away from the pronoun.

23. **E.** A careful reading of the passage allows you to find references to A and D and to locate the quoted phrases in B and C. What you will *not* find are any references to "punishment for a crime."

Sonnet 73
by William Shakespeare

24. **B.** The difficulty with this question lies in the similarity between B and E. However, it should be apparent from the numerous references to death and the contrast to youth that the poet is speaking of a literal time period in life and not of a state of emotional development.

25. **E.** Use the process of substitution and work backward in the poem to find the antecedent. Recognize the appositive phrase, which is set off by commas, to spot the previous image—"black night." Another trick is to recast the line into a directly stated sentence instead of the poetic inversion. Asking "who or what is Death's second self" will help you locate the subject of the line.

26. **A.** Once again you are being tested on terminology and your ability to recognize an example. Deconstruct the line and find its

essence; here it is obvious that "consumed" and "nourished" are contradictory.

27. **B.** Even without returning to the poem, you should notice that A, C, D, and E suggest death or diminishment. The only image of intensity and life appears in choice B.

28. **D.** The keys to this question can be found in lines 10–12 and line 14, which restate the irony of the beloved's devotion and the speaker's mortality. A good technique is to always check the previous and subsequent lines in order to clarify your answer. Also, careful reading would eliminate A and B. Passion is not mentioned in the poem.

29. **D.** For the prepared student, this question is a giveaway. Definitions of these terms in Chapter 9 clarify the differences among the types of sonnets. The rhyme scheme should lead you to choose D.

30. **A.** The sonnet depends on several extended comparisons with nature—the seasons, day and night, and fire. Although there may be a contradiction in the final three lines, the primary means of development is metaphor. (See Chapter 8 for examples of synecdoche.)

31. **E.** Since contradiction and paradox are techniques that create irony, you should be able to see that choice E restates the essential opposing forces in the sonnet.

32. **C.** You must reread and interpret the entire third quatrain to clearly figure out this question. You need to decode the metaphor and realize that fires must be fed and that they expire when they exhaust the source of fuel.

33. **D.** Even though E is a lovely thought, the speaker never expresses the desire to have the beloved age along with him. This answer depends on the pun in the title of choice D—fall. Here it may refer to the season of age as well as to the decline of the speaker and the relationship. No other choice is supported in the sonnet.

34. **A.** At first glance, one might think the speaker is submissive to the greater force of death; however, at no time does he acquiesce to the demands of mortality. The speaker thinks about and reflects on his circumstances.

35. **E.** You should notice that three of the five choices are negative. If you have read carefully,

you will be aware that the poem is laudatory and positive with regard to the depth of the beloved's love. And, at no time is the speaker looking forward to his lover's departure.

White Teeth
by Zadie Smith

36. **D.** A diatribe is a bitter, verbal attack. Even though the first paragraph is negative, it does not meet the criteria for a diatribe. Without specific details of time or place, this paragraph could be anywhere. There is no real indication of a conflict brewing between characters that will be developed, and Ophelia is introduced in the second paragraph. The best answer is D, supported with details like "don't fit," "put up with this," "for the sake of appearance."

37. **B.** The second paragraph presents Archie as a character who goes along to get along without too much introspection. This, together with the chaotic attic and the Hoover that Archie had promised to fix and never did, lead to the inference stated in choice B.

38. **E.** A halo is a universal symbol of saintliness, holiness. Wanting his women and the resulting love to wear halos is indicative of his desire for perfection in his women.

39. **C.** Without the first paragraph as a lead-in, choice E could be viable. However, given the entire first paragraph and the first part of the second, marriage is the best choice.

40. **A.** What the home-helper says, how she says it, and what she does ("cut her eyes at him," "spat on the doormat next his shoes,") support the choice of hostility and belittling. The other choices do not have any support in this passage.

41. **D.** Third-person subjective has a narrator speaking through the viewpoint of a specific character at a specific time and place so that the reader can experience the thoughts of that character. In paragraph seven, the narrator moves from a reportorial overview of the general ambiance of the house to what are obviously Archie's personal thoughts.

42. **B.** Choice B is almost a paraphrasing of the last sentence. Choices A, C, and E are all the cause of his desire to fix the Hoover. Choice D is not supported in the text.

43. **D.** It is the world inside this house that is pushing Archie to try to prove his worth, to prove he can do things. At this point in the narrative, Ophelia is not an active player.

44. **E.** Archie is carrying a heavy load of life's baggage. This is emphasized in line 59 with the metaphor "…Life was an enormous rucksack."

45. **A.** Since the attitude of the home-helper would be the same with or without her dialect, it can best be seen as a way to inject a bit of realism into both the characterization and the situation.

46. **C.** "Losing everything," "walk into blackness," "I felt like the end of the world," "This stuff's all dead weight," "feel nothing in particular": These phrases and sentences, plus others, build a picture of a character who is less and less able to deal with his life. The last two paragraphs are about ONLY Archie and his personal situation. None of the other choices are supported in this set of paragraphs.

47. **C.** The flipping of the coin with one side being life and the other death is not hopeful, nor does it indicate loss of control, anger, or redemption. What it does signify is Archie's willingness to leave his living or dying up to a flip of a coin and his nonchalant acceptance of its outcome.

Litany
by Billy Collins

48. **D.** Rhymed iambic pentameter, a pattern of specific rhyme, and specific meter are NOT part of the construction of this poem. Because of this, the poem is classified as free verse.

49. **E.** The ordinary language, the contrasts, the everyday details, and the personal comments best leads the reader to conclude that the tone is casual and playful. Remember that BOTH descriptors have to be applicable to the text.

50. **A.** "Suddenly" indicates surprise among the marsh in early morning. This surprise forces the birds to flee. This suggests a sense of uncertainty. None of the other choices will allow for this sudden flight to the birds.

51. **E.** As the title of the poem suggests, this is a listing of the qualities the speaker primarily attributes to the beloved. It is not a poem

mourning a death, nor a description of the beloved's appearance, nor a song or apology to the beloved.

52. C. In the first line of the fifth stanza, the speaker switches from addressing *you* to speaking about *I*. Here the focus switches from the beloved to the speaker.

53. D. Metaphors based on "You are . . ." and "I am . . ." are found throughout the poem. "You are" is repeated frequently. Alliteration is found in lines 24 and 25. Rhyme is used with "show" and "know." Simile is the only listed literary device not found in this poem.

54. B. The speaker introduces counterbalance in the second stanza when he stops repeating "you are" with "However," together with "It might interest you to know" in the fifth stanza. This, combined with switching between addressing both the negative and the positive aspects of the beloved and the speaker as well as the creation of several rather absurd comparisons, provide the components of the poem's humor.

55. B. The first three lines of the last stanza imply that the speaker accepts the beloved, "But" he will still have his own take on life. The last two lines with "You will always" implies the speaker and the beloved will be forever connected. This negates choices A, C, D, and E.

CHAPTER 5

The Prose Passage Essay

IN THIS CHAPTER

Summary: Complete explanation of the prose passage essay and its purpose as it is presented on the AP English Literature exam

Key Ideas

○ Learn the types of prose passage prompts you might encounter on the AP English Literature exam

○ Learn about the rubrics and rating of the AP English Literature prose passage essay

○ Learn the basics of reading and notating a given passage

○ Learn the basics of constructing your response to the prompt

○ Examine the student models that respond to the diagnostic exam's prose passage essay prompt

○ Learn how the rubrics were used to rate the student sample essays

Introduction to the Prose Passage Essay

This section of the exam gives you an opportunity to read and analyze a prose piece of literature. This is your chance to become personally involved in the text and to demonstrate your literary skills.

The free-response prose fiction essay will present a prose fiction passage of approximately 500 to 700 words. You will be expected to:

• Respond to the prompt with a thesis that presents an assertion that requires defense and support

• Select and use evidence to support your line of reasoning

- Explain how the evidence supports your line of reasoning
- Use appropriate grammar and punctuation in communicating your argument

The wording of the prose fiction prompt will be consistent. Only the title of the text and information about it will differ. For example: "The following excerpt is from [text and author, date of publication]. In this passage, [comment on what is being addressed in the passage]. Read the passage carefully. Then, in a well-written essay, analyze how [author] uses literary elements and techniques to [convey/portray/develop a thematic, topical, or structural aspect of the passage that is complex and specific to the passage provided]." (*AP English Literature and Composition Course and Exam Description*, The College Board, 2020, p. 139.)

What Is an AP Literature Prose Passage?

Generally, it is a one-page excerpt from a work of fiction. More often than not, the selection will be from a novel or short story. Be aware that the exam may also present an excerpt from a drama.

What Is the Purpose in Writing an Essay About a Prose Piece?

First, the people at the College Board want to determine your facility in reading and interpreting a sustained piece of literature. It requires you to understand the text and to analyze those techniques and devices the author uses to achieve his or her purpose.

Second, the AP exam is designed to allow you to demonstrate your ease and fluency with terminology, interpretation, and criticism. Also, the level of your writing should be a direct reflection of your critical thinking.

Third, the AP exam determines your ability to make connections between analysis and interpretation. For example, when you find a metaphor, you should identify and connect it to the author's intended purpose or meaning. You should not just list items as you locate them. You must connect them to your interpretation.

> Before beginning to work with an actual prose passage, read the review of processes and terms in the Comprehensive Review section of this book. You should also have completed some of the activities in that section.

Types of Prose Passage Essay Questions

Let's look at a few prose passage questions that have been asked on the AP Literature exam in the past:

- Analyze narrative and literary techniques and other resources of language used for characterization.
- How does a narrator reveal character? (i.e., tone, diction, syntax, point of view)
- How does the author reveal a character's predicament? (i.e., diction, imagery, point of view)
- Explain the effect of the passage on the reader.
- Compare/contrast two passages concerning diction and details for the effect on the reader.
- How does the passage provide characterization and evaluation of one character over another? (i.e., diction, syntax, imagery, tone)
- What is the attitude of the speaker toward a particular subject?

- Analyze the effect of revision when given both the original and the revised version of a text.
- Analyze style and tone and how they are used to explore the author's attitudes toward his or her subject.
- How is the reader prepared for the conclusion of the piece?

You should be prepared to write an essay based on any of these prompts. Practice. Practice. Practice anticipating questions. Keep a running list of the kinds of questions your teacher asks.

Don't be thrown by the complexity of a passage. Remember, *you* choose the references you wish to incorporate into your essay. So, even if you haven't understood everything, you are still able to write an intelligent essay—*as long as you address the prompt* and refer to the parts of the passage you do understand.

Watch out for overconfidence when you see what you believe to be an easy question with an easy passage. You are going to have to work extra hard to find the nuances in the text that will allow you to write a mature essay.

Rating the Prose Passage Essay

You will be relieved to know that the rating of your essay is *not* based on whether or not the reader likes you or agrees with your point of view.

How Do the Test Readers Evaluate My Essay?

It's important to understand just what it is that goes into rating your essay. This is called a *rubric*, but don't let that word frighten you. A rubric is a word that simply refers to the <u>rating standards that are set and used by the people who read the essays</u>. These standards are fairly consistent, no matter what the prompt might be. The primary change is in the citing of the specifics in a particular prompt.

Let us assure you that, as experienced readers of the AP English exams, we know that the readers are trained to reward those things you do well in addressing the question. They are *not* looking to punish you. They are aware of the time constraints, and they read your essay just as your own instructor would read the first draft of an essay you wrote on a 40-minute exam. <u>These readers look forward to an interesting, insightful, and well-constructed essay</u>.

So, let's take a look at the following rubrics:

Prose Passage Essay Rubric

- 1 point for thesis/claim/introduction that is appropriate to the prompt
- 4 points for evidence/support of the thesis/claim
  - Clear and appropriate references to the text
  - Clear presentation of how the references relate to the thesis
- 1 point for complexity of the commentary and syntax

Remember, the essay is really a first draft. The test readers know this and approach each essay with this in mind.

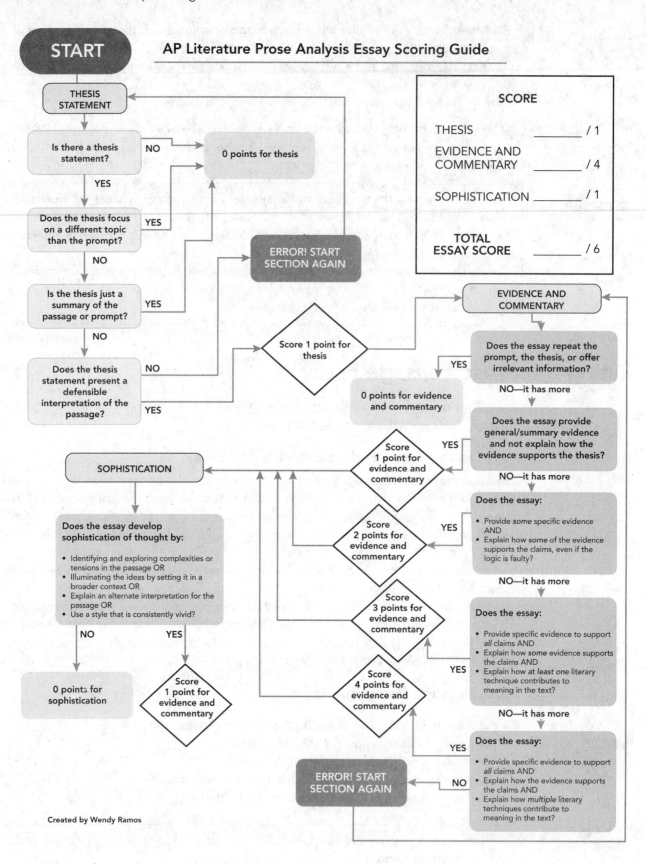

AP Literature Prose Analysis Essay Scoring Guide

START

THESIS STATEMENT

Is there a thesis statement? **NO** → 0 points for thesis

YES

Does the thesis focus on a different topic than the prompt? **YES** → ERROR! START SECTION AGAIN

NO

Is the thesis just a summary of the passage or prompt? **YES**

NO

Does the thesis statement present a defensible interpretation of the passage? **NO** / **YES**

Score 1 point for thesis

SCORE

THESIS _____ / 1

EVIDENCE AND COMMENTARY _____ / 4

SOPHISTICATION _____ / 1

TOTAL ESSAY SCORE _____ / 6

EVIDENCE AND COMMENTARY

Does the essay repeat the prompt, the thesis, or offer irrelevant information? **YES** → 0 points for evidence and commentary

NO—it has more

Does the essay provide general/summary evidence and not explain how the evidence supports the thesis? **YES** → Score 1 point for evidence and commentary

NO—it has more

Does the essay:
- Provide *some* specific evidence AND
- Explain how *some* of the evidence supports the claims, even if the logic is faulty?

YES → Score 2 points for evidence and commentary

NO—it has more

Does the essay:
- Provide specific evidence to support *all* claims AND
- Explain how *some* evidence supports the claims AND
- Explain how *at least one* literary technique contributes to meaning in the text?

YES → Score 3 points for evidence and commentary

NO—it has more

Does the essay:
- Provide specific evidence to support *all* claims AND
- Explain how the evidence supports the claims AND
- Explain how *multiple* literary techniques contribute to meaning in the text?

YES → Score 4 points for evidence and commentary

NO → ERROR! START SECTION AGAIN

SOPHISTICATION

Does the essay develop sophistication of thought by:
- Identifying and exploring complexities or tensions in the passage OR
- Illuminating the ideas by setting it in a broader context OR
- Explain an alternate interpretation for the passage OR
- Use a style that is consistently vivid?

NO → 0 points for sophistication

YES → Score 1 point for evidence and commentary

Created by Wendy Ramos

Timing the Essay

Timing is crucial. With that in mind, here's a workable strategy:

- 1–3 minutes reading and "working the prompt."
- 5 minutes reading and making marginal notes about the passage. Try to isolate 2 quotations that strike you. This may give you your opening and closing.
- 5–10 minutes preparing to write. (Choose one or two of the following methods that you feel comfortable with.)
  - Underlining, bracketing, circling
  - Marginal notations
  - Charts or key word/one word/line number outlining
- 20–25 minutes to write your essay, based on your preparation.
- 3 minutes for proofreading.

Using a highlighter is not allowed during the exam. However, it is a strong tool for practice in critical reading.

Note: Throughout this book, the term **highlight** will also refer to underlining, circling, or bracketing.

> In the margin, note what time you should be finished with each essay. For example, the test starts at 1 P.M. You write 1:40 in the margin. Time to move on.

Working the Prompt

You can't write clearly unless you know *Why* you are writing and *What's Expected* of you. When you "Work the Prompt," you are maximizing both of these areas.

How Should I Go About Reading the Prose Prompt?

To bring the answer home to you, we will deconstruct a prompt for you now. (This is the same question that is in the Diagnostic/Master exam.) Plan to spend 1–3 minutes carefully reading the question. This will give you time to really digest what the question is asking you to do.

Here's the prompt:

In the following passage from his 1914 short story "The Dead," James Joyce presents an insight into the character of Gabriel. Read the passage carefully. Then, in a well-written essay analyze how Joyce uses literary strategies and techniques to reveal various aspects of Gabriel's complex character to the reader and to Gabriel himself.

Here are three reasons why you should do a 1–3-minute careful analysis of the prompt.

1. Once you know what is expected, you will read in a more directed manner.

2. Once you internalize the question, you will be sensitive to those details that will apply.

3. Once you know all the facets that need to be addressed, you will be able to write a complete essay demonstrating adherence to the topic.

> Topic adherence, which means sticking to the question, is key to achieving a high score.

Do this now. Underline, circle, or bracket the essential terms and elements in the prompt. Time yourself. How long did it take you? _____ Don't worry if it took you longer than 1–3 minutes in this first attempt. You will be practicing this technique throughout this review, and it will become almost second nature to you.

Compare our working of the prompt with yours.

In the following passage from his 1914 <u>short story</u> "<u>The Dead</u>," <u>James Joyce</u> presents an <u>insight</u> into the <u>character of Gabriel</u>. Read the passage carefully. Then, in a well-written essay <u>analyze</u> how Joyce uses <u>literary strategies and techniques</u> to reveal various aspects of Gabriel's complex character to the reader and to Gabriel himself.

In this prompt, anything else you may have highlighted is extraneous.

When the question uses the expression "such as," you are *not* required to use only those ideas presented; you are free to use your own selection of techniques and devices. Notice that the prompt requires more than one technique. One will not be enough. You *must* use more than one. If you fail to use more than one technique, no matter how well you present your answer, your essay will be incomplete.

Reading and Notating the Prose Passage

Depending on your style and comfort level, choose one of these approaches to your reading:

1. A. Read quickly to get the gist of the passage.
    B. Reread, using the visual and marginal notes approach.
2. A. Read slowly, using highlighting and making marginal notes.
    B. Reread to confirm that you understand the full impact of the passage.

Note: In both approaches, you *must* highlight and make marginal notes. There is no way to avoid this. Ignore what you don't immediately understand. It may become clear to you after you finish reading the passage. Practice. Practice. Concentrate on those parts of the passage that apply to what you highlighted in the prompt.

There are many ways to read and interpret any given passage. You have to choose which one to use and which specifics to include for support. Don't be rattled if there is leftover material.

We've reproduced the passage for you below so that you can practice both the reading and the process of deconstructing the text. Use highlighting, arrows, circles, underlining, notes, numbers, and whatever you need to make the connections clear to you.

Do this now. Spend 8–10 minutes working the material. *Do not skip this step.* It is time well spent and is a key to the high-score essay.

The Dead

She was fast asleep.

Gabriel, leaning on his elbow, looked for a few moments unresentfully on her tangled hair and half-open mouth, listening to her deep-drawn breath. So she had had that romance in her life: a man had died for her sake. It hardly pained him now to think how poor a part   5 he, her husband, had played in her life. He watched her while she slept as though he and she had never lived together as man and wife. His curious eyes rested long upon her face and on her hair and, as he thought of what she must have been then, in that time of her first girlish beauty, a strange friendly pity for her entered his soul. He did not like to say   10 even to himself that her face was no longer beautiful but he knew that it was no longer the face for which Michael Furey had braved death.

Perhaps she had not told him all the story. His eyes moved to the chair over which she had thrown some of her clothes. A petticoat string dangled to the floor. One boot stood upright, its limp upper fallen down: 15 the fellow of it lay upon its side. He wondered at his riot of emotions of an hour before. From what had it proceeded? From his aunt's supper, from his own foolish speech, from the wine and dancing, the merry-making when saying good-night in the hall, the pleasure of the walk along the river in the snow. Poor Aunt Julia! She, too, would soon be a shade with the   20 shade of Patrick Morkan and his horse. He had caught that haggard look upon her face for a moment when she was singing *Arrayed for the Bridal*. Soon, perhaps, he would be sitting in the same drawing-room dressed in black, his silk hat on his knees. The blinds would be drawn down and Aunt Kate would be sitting beside him, crying and blowing her nose and   25 telling him how Julia had died. He would cast about in his mind for some words that might console her, and would find only lame and useless ones. Yes, yes: that would happen very soon.

KEY IDEA Now, compare your reading notes with what we've done below. Yours may vary from ours, but the results of your note-taking should be similar in scope.

The Dead

who?

alike?

Bible?   *angel?*   *death?*   She was fast asleep. ———— *short sentence*

time

Gabriel, leaning on his elbow, looked for a few moments

he hears

unresentfully on her tangled hair and half-open mouth, listening to her

time deep-drawn breath. So she had had that romance in her life: a man had

not him

last? died for her sake. It hardly pained him now to think how poor a part

he thinks

detached? he, her husband, had played in her life. He watched her while she slept

he sees

death as though he and she had never lived together as man and wife. His

death-like?

time curious eyes rested long upon her face and on her hair and, as he thought

of what she must have been then, in that time of her first girlish beauty,

time—again

he's kind? a <u>strange friendly pity</u> for her entered his <u>soul</u>. <u>He did not like to say</u> *back to death*

weak <u>even to himself</u> that <u>her face was no longer beautiful</u> but he knew that it *time*
coward? *fury?*
self-image *time* was <u>no longer</u> the face for which Michael <u>Furey</u> had <u>braved death</u>. *not a coward*

Perhaps she had not told him all the story. His eyes moved to the chair over which she had thrown some of her clothes. A petticoat string

dangled to the floor. One boot stood upright, its <u>limp</u> upper <u>fallen down</u>: *weak? lack of*

the fellow of it lay upon its side. He wondered at his <u>riot</u> of emotions of *control? afraid to*

time an <u>hour before</u>. From what had it proceeded? From his aunt's supper, *let go?*
self-image

death? from his own <u>foolish speech</u>, from the wine and dancing, the merry-making

cold death? when saying <u>good-night</u> in the hall, the pleasure of the walk along the river

ghost? in the <u>snow</u>. Poor Aunt Julia! She, too, would <u>soon</u> be a <u>shade</u> with the *time*
cold *cold*

time <u>shade</u> of Patrick Morkan and his horse. He had caught that haggard look

upon her face for a <u>moment</u> when she was singing *Arrayed for the Bridal.*

time <u>Soon</u>, perhaps, he would be sitting in the same drawing-room <u>dressed in</u> *mourning*
closed off
death <u>black, his silk hat on his knees</u>. The <u>blinds would be drawn down</u> and *mourning*

Aunt Kate would be sitting beside him, <u>crying and blowing</u> her nose and *self-image*

death <u>telling him how Julia had died</u>. <u>He would cast about in his mind for some</u> *detached*

weak? words that might console her, and would find only <u>lame and useless</u> ones.
uncertain?
Yes, yes: that would happen very <u>soon</u>. —— *time* *weakness*

After you have marked the passage, review the prompt. You are asked to look for ways Joyce reveals Gabriel's character. When you consult your notes, certain categories will begin to pop out at you. These can be the basis for the development of the body of your essay. For example, we saw details and images that support the concepts of:

- Death
- Passivity
- Time
- Detachment
- Insecurity

In addition, stylistically, we noticed the use of short sentences.

Here's how one category developed using the notations made on the passage. Notice that we have ignored notes that did not apply to the prompt.

Concept: Time

Words/Phrases from the Text:

"a few moments"	"no longer the face"
"had had that romance"	"an hour before"
"he thought of what she must have been then"	"soon be a shade"
	"for a moment"
"girlish beauty"	"soon"
"no longer beautiful"	"that would happen very soon"

Conclusion: Gabriel moves from the distant past to the near future. He becomes aware of the change in the marital relationship with his wife and with his own passage.

Your Turn

Now you choose a concept you are able to explore and defend that reveals Gabriel's character.

Concept:

Words/Phrases from the Text:

Conclusion:

In response to the prompt, we have decided that the techniques/devices we will analyze are:

- Imagery
- Diction
- Style
- Motif

Here's one technique/device and how it is developed in the passage. Again, notice that we use our margin notes to trace this development.

Technique/Device: Imagery

Words/Phrases from the Text:

the title "The Dead"	Gabriel's very name
"entered his soul"	"braved death"
"fallen down"	"good-night"
"in the snow"	"would soon be a shade"
"dressed in black"	"the blinds would be drawn"
"crying and blowing her nose"	

Conclusion: These images foreshadow and emphasize that there is a coldness and a loss in relationships and self-image.

Your Turn

Now you choose the technique/device you are able to explore and defend that reveals Gabriel's character.

Technique/Device:

Words/Phrases from the Text:

Conclusion:

If you expand the above techniques/devices and categories into interpretive statements and support those statements with appropriate details that you've already isolated, you will be writing a detailed essay.

Writing the Opening Paragraph

Your opening statement is the one that sets the tone of your essay and possibly raises the expectations of the reader. Spend time on your first paragraph to maximize your score.

Make certain that your topic is very clear. This reinforces the idea that you fully understand what is expected of you and what you will communicate to the reader. Generally, identify both the text and its author in this first paragraph.

A suggested approach is to relate a direct quotation from the passage to the topic.

Consider the "philosophy of firsts." It is a crucial strategy to spend focused time on the first part of the question and on the first paragraph of the essay because:

1. It establishes the direction and tone of your essay.

2. It gives you the guidelines for what to develop in your essay.

3. It connects you to the reader.

Remember our philosophy: **In the Beginning:** if you focus on the beginning, the rest will fall into place. A wonderful thing happens after much practice, highlighting, and note-taking. Your mind starts to focus automatically. Trust us on this. It is the winning edge that can take an average essay and raise it to a higher level.

Do this now. Take 5 minutes to write your opening paragraph for "The Dead" prompt. Write quickly, referring to your notes.

Let's check what you've written:

Highlight these points to see if you've done them. You may be surprised at what is actually there.

• Have you included author and title? _____ Yes _____ No

• Have you addressed the character of Gabriel? _____ Yes _____ No

• Have you specifically mentioned the techniques you will refer to in your essay?

_____ Yes _____ No

Here are four sample opening paragraphs that address all of the criteria:

A

In "The Dead" by James Joyce, the character Gabriel is revealed through diction, point of view, and imagery as he watches his wife sleep.

B

Poor Gabriel! Who would have thought he knew so little about himself and his life. And yet, in "The Dead," James Joyce, through diction, point of view, and imagery, makes it clear to the reader and to Gabriel that there is much to reveal about his character.

C

"Yes, yes: that would happen very soon." And, yes, very soon the reader of the excerpt from Joyce's "The Dead" gets to know the character of Gabriel. Through diction, point of view, and imagery, we are introduced to Gabriel and what he thinks of himself.

D

"The Dead." How apt a title. James Joyce turns his reader into a fly on the wall as Gabriel is about to realize the many losses in his life. Death pervades the passage, from his sleeping wife to his dying aunt.

Each of these opening paragraphs is an acceptable beginning to an AP Literature exam essay. Note what each of these paragraphs accomplishes:

• Each has identified the title and author.
• Each has stated which techniques/devices will be used.
• Each has stated the purpose of analyzing these techniques/devices.

Now, note what is different about each opening paragraph:

• Sample **A** restates the question without anything extra. It is to the point, so much so that it does nothing more than repeat the question. It's correct, but it does not really pique the reader's interest. (Use this type of opening if you feel unsure of or uncomfortable with the prompt.)
• Sample **B** reveals the writer's attitude toward the subject. The writer has already determined that Gabriel is flawed and indicates an understanding of how Gabriel's character is revealed in the passage.
• Sample **C**, with its direct quotation, places the reader immediately into the passage. The reader quickly begins to hear the writer's voice through his or her choice of words (diction).
• Sample **D**, at first glance, reveals a mature, confident writer who is not afraid to *imply* the prompt's criteria.

Note: There are many other types of opening paragraphs that could do the job as well. The paragraphs above are just a few samples.

Into which of the above samples would you classify your opening paragraph?

Writing the Body

When you write the body of your essay, take only 20–25 minutes. Time yourself and try your best to finish within that time frame.

Since this is practice, don't panic if you can't complete the essay within the allotted time. You will become more and more comfortable with the tasks presented to you as you gain experience with this type of question.

What Should I Include in the Body of the Prose Passage Essay?

1. Obviously, this is where you present your interpretation and the points you wish to make that are related to the prompt.

2. Use specific references and details from the passage.
- Don't always paraphrase the original; refer directly to it.
- Place quotation marks around those words and phrases that you extract from the passage.

3. Use "connective tissue" in your essay to establish adherence to the question.
- Use the repetition of key ideas from your opening paragraph.
- Try using "echo words" (i.e., synonyms, such as death/loss/passing or character/persona/personality).
- Create transitions from one paragraph to the next.

To understand the process, carefully read the following sample paragraphs. Each develops one of the categories and techniques/devices asked for in the prompt. Notice the specific references and the "connective tissue." Also, notice that details that do not apply to the prompt have been ignored.

A

This paragraph develops **imagery**.

Joyce creates imagery to lead his reader to sense the cloud of death that pervades Gabriel's world. From its very title "The Dead," the reader is prepared for loss. Just what has Gabriel lost: his wife, his confidence, his job, a friend, a relative, what? As his "wife slept," Gabriel sees her "half-open mouth" and "listens" to her "deep-drawn breath." The reader almost senses this to be a death watch. The images about the room reinforce this sense of doom. One boot is "limp" and the other is "upon its side." Picturing the future, Gabriel sees a "drawing-room dressed in black" with blinds "drawn down" and his Aunt Kate "crying" and "telling him how Julia had died." And to underscore his own feelings of internal lifelessness, he can only find "lame and useless" words of comfort.

B

This paragraph develops the **motif of time**.

Time is a constant from the beginning to the end of the passage. In the first paragraph, Gabriel is in the present while thinking of the past. He is an observer, watching his wife as he, himself, is observed by the narrator, and as we, as readers, observe the entire scene. Time moves the reader and Gabriel through the experience. Immediately, we spend a "few moments" with Gabriel as he goes back and forth in time assessing his relationship with his wife. He recognizes she "had had romance in her life." But, "it hardly pains him now." He thinks of what she had been "then" in her "girlish" beauty, which may indicate his own aging. His "strange friendly pity," because she is "no longer beautiful," may be self-pity, as well. In the next paragraph, we are with Gabriel as he reflects on his emotional "riot" only an hour before. However, he jumps to the future because he can't sustain self-examination. He chooses to allow himself to jump to this future and a new subject—Aunt Julia's death. In this future, he continues to see only his inability and incompetence. For Gabriel, all this will happen "very soon."

C
This passage develops **diction**.

Gabriel appears to be a man who is on the outside of his life. Joyce's diction reveals his passive nature. Gabriel "looked on" and "watched" his wife sleeping. He spent time "listening to her breath" and was "hardly pained by his role in her life." His eyes "rest" on her, and he "thinks of the past." All of Gabriel's actions are as weak as a "limp" and "fallen down" boot, "inert in the face of life." He is in direct contrast to Michael Furey, who has "braved death." And he knows this about himself. The narrator's diction reveals that Gabriel "did not like to say even to himself," implying that he is too weak to face the truth.

Later in the text, Gabriel's word choice further indicates his insecurity. He is troubled by his "riot of emotions," his "foolish speech." It is obvious that Gabriel will not take such risks again.

D
This passage develops **style**.

Joyce's very straightforward writing style supports the conclusions he wishes the reader to draw about the character of Gabriel. Most sentences are in the subject/verb, simple sentence form, reflecting the plain, uncomplicated character of Gabriel.

Joyce employs a third person narrator to further reinforce Gabriel's detachment from his own circumstances. We watch him observing his own life with little or no connection on his part. He wonders at his "riot of emotions." All this is presented without Joyce using obvious poetic devices. This punctuates the lack of "romance" in Gabriel's life when compared with that of Michael Furey.

Start a study group. Approach an essay as a team. After you've deconstructed the prompt, have each person write a paragraph on a separate area of the question. Then come together and discuss what was written. You'll be amazed at how much fun this is because the work will carry you away. This is a chance to explore exciting ideas.

Again, sharing your writing with members of your class or study group will allow you to gain experience and find a comfort zone with requirements and possibilities.

We urge you to spend more time developing the body paragraphs than worrying about a concluding paragraph, especially one that begins with "In conclusion," or "In summary." In such a brief essay, the reader will have no problem remembering what you have already stated. It is not necessary to repeat yourself in a summary-type final paragraph.

If you want to make a final statement, try to link your ideas to a particularly effective line or image from the passage.

Note: Look at the last line of Sample **B** on motif. For Gabriel, all this will happen "very soon." This final sentence would be fine as the conclusion to the essay. A conclusion does not have to be a paragraph. It can be the writer's final remark or observation presented in a sentence or two.

Do this now. Write the body of your essay. Time yourself. Allow 15–20 minutes to complete this task.

Sample Student Essays

Following are two actual student essays followed by a rubric and comments on each. Read both of the samples in sequence to clarify the differences between "high" and "mid-range" essays.

Student Essay A

A picture is worth a thousand words, but James Joyce manages to paint a pretty vivid one in only two short paragraphs. Joyce offers tremendous insight into the character of Gabriel in the short story "The Dead." He captures the essence of a scene laden with death and laced with tones of despair and hopelessness. By employing third person narration alternating with a stream of consciousness, Joyce demonstrates his abilities to delve deep into Gabriel's mind, illustrating this somewhat detached disposition and low self-image.

The passage takes us through Gabriel's reflections upon past, present, and future events while his inner character unfolds. Joyce's careful use of diction suggests that Gabriel has emotionally closed himself off to the world as he tries to cope with some aforementioned incident. He was "hardly pained" to think about a situation which caused a "riot of emotions" just a little earlier on that evening. Here, Joyce is emphasizing Gabriel's way of coping with an unfavorable event by blocking it out. He continues to "unresentfully" reflect upon what had occurred, closing himself off from any pain he obviously experienced a short while ago.

With the powerful omniscience of a third-person narrator, Joyce is able to describe the workings of Gabriel's inner consciousness without writing from the first-person point of view. Gabriel further detaches himself as he thinks about his wife. He watches her from the point of view of an outsider, as if they were never married. The mere fact that Gabriel is able to do this suggests that he and his wife do not have a truly loving relationship. This assertion is underscored by the "friendly" pity Gabriel feels for his wife, emphasizing the lack of true love in their relationship. Gabriel later questions his wife's honesty, further emphasizing a troubled relationship. The reader may be inclined to infer that Gabriel is completely devoid of compassion; however, this idea is refuted. Gabriel proceeds to express an element of sorrow when he thinks back to his wife's youth and beauty.

The evening's events had evidently triggered some type of emotional outburst which Gabriel cannot stop thinking about. His mental state is paralleled by the chaotic state of disorder in the room he is in. With a masterful control of language and syntax, Joyce describes in short, choppy sentences the array of clothing strewn around the room. This is followed by one of the longest sentences in the passage. Joyce reveals this series of events all at once, paralleling Gabriel's release of a multitude of emotions at once.

Joyce weaves a motif of darkness and death into the story. His aunt's "haggard" appearance ironically catches Gabriel's attention during the recitation of <u>Arrayed for the Bridal</u>, a seemingly happy song. This image of happiness and marriage is further contrasted with images of the woman's funeral and a detailed description of how Gabriel will mourn for her. Joyce also takes time to underscore Gabriel's low self-esteem, in that he will only think of "lame and useless" words at a time when comforting tones are necessary. He is essentially describing himself, since it has been established that he failed as a husband and that he is emotionally distraught even though he blocks out the pain he feels. "The blinds would be drawn down," Gabriel says, as he describes both the room at his aunt's funeral and his mental state of affairs.

The true originator of "stream-of-consciousness" techniques, Joyce delves deep into Gabriel's mind, describing his wide range of emotions and state of mind. His powerful diction reveals a great deal about Gabriel's character while his implied insights penetrate into the reader's mind, reinforcing the abstract meanings behind the actions and events that transpire throughout the course of his story.

Student Essay B

In the excerpt from the short story "The Dead" from Dubliners by James Joyce, the author describes some personality traits of the character Gabriel as he sits watching a sleeping woman. The point of view from which this excerpt is expressed helps the reader to get to know Gabriel because the narrator is omniscient and knows how Gabriel perceives things and what he is thinking. With the use of many literary devices such as imagery, diction, and syntax, the reader is able to see that Gabriel is an observant and a reflective person, but he is also detached.

Gabriel comes across as observant, because throughout the entire passage he is observing a woman, his wife, sleeping. He scans the room looking over everything and taking note of everything. An example of this is looking at "her tangled hair and half-open mouth, listening to her deep-drawn breath." The author uses the technique of syntax ("deep-drawn breath" and "half-open mouth") in the above quotation to show us exactly what Gabriel is seeing. Gabriel notices many details, and they are described so that the reader can clearly formulate a picture of what he is gazing at. This imagery can be seen in lines such as the one where the woman's boots are being described. "One boot stood upright, its limp upper fallen down: the fellow of it lay upon the side." The diction used such as "limp" and "upright," are concrete words that create clear pictures. Another reason that Gabriel comes across as observant is because he catches and notices little things. For example, he "caught" the "haggard look" on his Aunt Julia's face.

Resulting from the fact that Gabriel is observant, he is also reflective. He thinks over past events that had happened and wonders what caused them and why he did what he did. In the first paragraph he reflects on his wife's "fading beauty," what she used to look like, and the story of the death of Michael Furey. He realizes that it is a possibility that she had not told him the entire story concerning the boy's death. He further reflects when he is thinking about his emotional outburst. He asks himself many questions including "From what had it proceeded?"

A feeling of detachment is also present. The way he looks at his wife "as though he and she had never lived together as man and wife" shows that he is viewing his own life from an objective standpoint. He is able to look at his own life as though it wasn't his. The sentence that reads "it hardly pained him now to think how poor a part he, her husband, had played in her life," further exemplifies this feeling of detachment. Feelings that he used to feel no longer even touched him. He was able to recognize them, yet remain separate. In the second paragraph Gabriel continues

to come across as remote. He is able to picture and describe in great detail the 35
death and funeral of his Aunt Julia. He narrates the future drastic event in a
matter-of-fact way. Gabriel goes so far as to describe what he will be thinking at
the time of his Aunt Julia's death which is "he would cast about in his mind for some
words that might console her (his Aunt Kate), and would find only lame and useless 40
ones." This statement finalizes the idea that Gabriel is a person who is, at least to
some degree, detached from his own life.

Even though the passage is fairly short, the author is able to impart a fair
amount of information concerning the character Gabriel. It becomes apparent that
he possesses the qualities of observance, reflection, and detachment. These 45
qualities are all interconnected because of the fact that he is observant leading to
his ability to reflect on his actions and actions of others. This in turn leads to his
detachment, because when he reflects on his life he does it from the standpoint of a
third-person narrator. The author's use of literary techniques helps to convey these
personality traits of Gabriel to a reader.

Let's take a look at a set of rubrics for this prose passage essay. (If you want to see
actual AP rubrics used in a recent AP Lit. exam, log on to the College Board website:
<www.collegeboard.org/ap>). As you probably know, essays are rated on a 6–1 scale, with
6 the highest and 1 the lowest. Since we are not there with you to personally rate your
essay and to respond to your style and approach, we are going to list the criteria for high-,
middle-, and low-range papers. These criteria are based on our experience with rubrics and
reading AP Literature essays.

A HIGH-range essay can be a 6 or a 5. MIDDLE refers to essays in the 4–3 range. And
the LOW-scoring essays are rated 2–1.

After reading the following rubrics, evaluate the two essays that you have just read.

Rating the Student Essays

High-Range Essay (5, 6)
- The thesis statement presents a defensible assertion related to the prompt.
- The thesis clearly presents a possible interpretation and indicates how the support will be developed (line of reasoning).
- Distinguishes between what Gabriel acknowledges about himself and what the reader comes to know about him.
- Explores the complexity of Gabriel's character.
- Identifies and analyzes Joyce's literary techniques, such as imagery, diction, point of view, motif, and style.
- Cites specific references to the passage.
- Illustrates and supports the points being made.
- The line of reasoning is clear, well-organized, and coherent.
- Relates points made to a broader context.
- Reflects the ability to manipulate language at an advanced level.
- Contains only minor errors or flaws, if any.

Middle-Range Essay (3, 4)

- Refers accurately to the prompt.
- Refers accurately to the literary devices used by Joyce.
- Provides a less thorough analysis of Gabriel's character than the higher-rated paper.
- Is less adept at linking techniques to the purpose of the passage and a broader context.
- Demonstrates writing that is adequate to convey the writer's intent.
- May not be sensitive to the implications about Gabriel's character.

Low-Range Essay (1, 2)

- Does not respond adequately to the prompt.
- Demonstrates insufficient and/or inaccurate understanding of the passage.
- Does not link literary devices to Gabriel's character.
- Underdevelops and/or inaccurately analyzes literary techniques.
- Fails to demonstrate an understanding of Gabriel's character.
- Demonstrates weak control of the elements of diction, syntax, and organization.

How would you rate these student essays?

Now, compare your evaluation of the two student essays with ours.

Note: With specific reference to the 6-point rubric, we will use the following abbreviations to indicate into which column the comment would fall: **T** = **thesis, E** = **evidence, C** = **complexity, S** = **sophistication**.

Student Essay A

This is a high-range paper for the following reasons:

- Thesis presents a defensible assertion that is clearly related to the prompt and indicates a probable line of reasoning. T
- Indicates perceptive, subtle analysis (line 8). E/C
- Maintains excellent topic adherence (lines 9, 17, 28, 39). E
- Uses good "connective tissue" (repetition of key words). S
- Chooses good specific references (lines 11, 12, 21, 35). E
- Knows how to distinguish between the author and the narrator. C
- Understands point of view well. E
- Makes suggestions and inferences (lines 7, 20). C/S
- Demonstrates good critical thinking. S
- Is perceptive about syntax and the style of the author (lines 27–33). S
- Links techniques with character (line 34). C
- Demonstrates mature language manipulation (line 34). S
- Understands function of diction and motif (lines 40–44). S

It's best to omit extraneous judgmental words from your essay (line 45).

This is obviously a mature, critical reader and writer. Using subtle inferences and implications, the writer demonstrates an understanding of the character of Gabriel both as Joyce presents him and as Gabriel views himself. There is nothing extraneous or repetitious in this essay. Each point leads directly and compellingly to the next aspect of Gabriel's character.

Student Essay B

This is a middle-range essay for the following reasons:

- Sets up an introduction that indicates the line of reasoning, but it neglects to clearly set up the required discussion of how Gabriel views himself. T
- Immediately establishes that the essay will address Gabriel's character as drawn by the narrator and seen by the reader. T
- Addresses three aspects of Gabriel's character without fully developing the analysis of literary techniques. E
- Adheres to the essay's topic. E
- Uses "connective tissue" (lines 21, 28). E
- Uses "echo words" (lines 8, 9, 10). E
- Uses citations from the passages. E
- Isolates some details to illustrate Gabriel's character (lines 31–32, 39). C
- Lacks development of literary technique in paragraph 4. E/C
- Displays faulty diction and syntax. S
- Does not develop an important part of the prompt—how Gabriel views himself. E/C
- Incorporates faulty logic at times (lines 44–49). C

This essay is a solid, middle-range paper. The writer has a facility with literary analysis. Even though there are flashes of real insight, they are not sustained throughout the essay. There is a strong opening paragraph that makes it clear to the reader what the topic of the paper is. The writer obviously grasps Gabriel's character and the needed details to support the character analysis. But the weakness in this paper is the writer's incomplete development of the relationship of literary techniques to character analysis.

Note: Both essays have concluding paragraphs that are repetitive and largely unnecessary. It is best to avoid this type of ending.

Your Turn

How about sharing these samples with members of your class or study group and discussing possible responses?

Try a little reverse psychology. Now that you are thoroughly familiar with this passage, construct two or three alternative prompts. (Walk a little in the examiner's shoes.) This will help you gain insight into the process of test-making. Create two questions of your own. (See the Types of Prose Passage Essay Questions section of this chapter for ideas.)

1ˢᵗ alternative prompt for "The Dead"

_____

_____

_____

_____

_____

2ⁿᵈ alternative prompt for "The Dead"

_____

_____

_____

_____

_____

Rapid Review

After you've absorbed the ideas in this chapter, the following points will provide you with a quick refresher when needed:

- Familiarize yourself with the types of prose questions (prompts).
- Highlight the prompt and understand all the required tasks.
- Time your essay carefully.
- Spend sufficient time "working the passage" before you begin writing.
- Mark up the passage.
- Create a strong opening paragraph.
- Refer often to the passage.
- Use concrete details and quotes to support your ideas.
- Always stay on topic.
- Avoid plot summary.
- Include transitions and echo words.
- Check the models and rubrics for guidance for self-evaluation.
- Practice—vary the question and your approach.
- Share ideas with others.

CHAPTER 6

The Poetry Essay

IN THIS CHAPTER

Summary: Examination of the poetry essay and its purpose as it is presented in the AP English Literature exam

Key Ideas

✪ Learn the types of poetry prompts you might encounter in the AP English Literature exam
✪ Learn the basics of reading and notating a given poem
✪ Learn the basics of constructing your response to the poetry prompt
✪ Learn about the rubrics and rating of the AP poetry essays
✪ Examine model student essays
✪ Learn how rubrics were used to rate student essays

Introduction to the Poetry Essay

It's obvious to any reader that poetry is different from prose. And, writing about each is different also. This chapter will guide you through the expectations and processes associated with the AP Poetry section.

The free-response poetry essay will present a complete poem or a passage from a poem of approximately 100 to 300 words. According to The College Board, you will be expected to:

• respond to the prompt with a thesis that presents a defensible interpretation
• select and use evidence to support your line of reasoning
• explain how the evidence supports your line of reasoning
• use appropriate syntax and diction in communicating your argument

The following is the format for the poetry prompt:

"In the following poem [or excerpt from poem] by [author, date of publication], the speaker [comment on what is being addressed in the poem]. Read the poem carefully. Then, in a well-written essay, analyze how [author] uses [poetic or literary] elements and techniques to [convey/portray/develop a thematic, topical, or structural aspect of the poem that is complex and specific to the passage of the poem provided]." (*AP English Literature and Composition Course and Exam Description*, The College Board, 2020, p. 138.)

What Is the Purpose of the Poetry Essay?

The College Board wants to determine your facility in reading and interpreting a sustained piece of literature. You are required to understand the text and to analyze those techniques and devices the poet uses to achieve his or her purpose.

The AP Lit exam is designed to allow you to demonstrate your ease and fluency with terminology, interpretation, and analysis. The level of your writing should be a direct reflection of your critical thinking.

The AP Lit exam is looking for connections between analysis and interpretation. For example, when you find a metaphor, you should identify it and connect it to the poet's intended purpose or meaning. You shouldn't just list items as you locate them. You must connect them to your interpretation.

Before beginning to work with an actual poem, read the review of processes and terms in the Comprehensive Review section of this book. Make certain to complete some of the activities in that section.

Types of Prompts Used for the Poetry Essay

Not every poetry essay prompt is the same. Familiarizing yourself with the various types is critical. This familiarity will both increase your confidence and provide you with a format for poetry analysis.

What Will the Poetry Prompt Ask Me to Do?

Let's look at several typical tasks that have been used for the poetry essay in the AP Literature exam in the past:

- How does the language of the poem reflect the speaker's perceptions, and how does that language determine the reader's perception?
- How does the poet reveal character? (i.e., diction, sound devices, imagery, allusion)
- Discuss how poetic elements, such as language, structure, imagery, and point of view, convey meaning in a poem.
- Relate the imagery, form, or theme of a particular section of a poem to another part of that same poem. Discuss changing attitude or perception of speaker or reader.
- Analyze a poem's extended metaphor and how it reveals the poet's or speaker's attitude.
- Discuss the way of life revealed in a poem. Refer to such poetic elements as tone, imagery, symbol, and verse form.
- Discuss the poet's changing reaction to the subject developed in the poem.
- Discuss how the form of the poem affects its meaning.
- NOTE: There will be NO "paired poem prompts" on the exam.

You should be prepared to write an essay based on any of these prompts. Apply these questions to poems you read throughout the year. Practice anticipating questions. Keep a running list of the kinds of questions your teacher asks. Practice. Practice.

Timing and Planning the Poetry Essay

Successful writing is directly related to both thought and structure, and you will need to consider the following concepts related to pre-writing.

How Should I Plan to Spend My Time Writing the Poetry Essay?

Remember, timing is crucial. With this in mind, here's a workable strategy:

- 1–3 minutes reading and "working the prompt."
- 5 minutes reading and making marginal notes about the poem. Try to isolate two references that strike you. This may give you your opening and closing.
- 5–10 minutes preparing to write. (Choose one or two of the following methods that you feel comfortable with.)
  - Highlighting, underlining, circling, bracketing
  - Marginal mapping (see Chapter 5 for samples)
  - Key word/one word/line number outlining
  - Numerical clustering
- 20–25 minutes to write your essay, based on your preparation.
- 3 minutes for proofreading.

Working the Prompt

It is important to understand that the quality of your essay greatly depends upon your correctly addressing the prompt.

How Should I Go About Reading the Poetry Prompt?

As we did in the prose section, we will deconstruct a poetry essay prompt for you now. (This is the same question that is in the Diagnostic/Master exam earlier in this book.)

You should plan to spend 1–3 minutes carefully reading the question. This will give you time to really digest what the question is asking you to do.

Here's the prompt:

In her 1987 poem "On the Subway," Sharon Olds brings two worlds into close proximity. Read the poem carefully. Then, in a well-written essay analyze how Olds uses poetic elements and techniques to develop the complex contrasts and insights the speaker comes to as a result of the experience.

In the margin, note what time you should be finished with this essay. For example, the test starts at 1 P.M. You write 1:40 in the margin. Time to move on.

Here are three reasons why you should do a 1–3-minute careful analysis of the prompt:

1. Once you know what is expected, you will read in a more directed manner.

2. Once you internalize the question, you will be sensitive to the details that will apply as you read the poem.

3. Once you know all the facets that need to be addressed, you will be able to write a complete essay that demonstrates adherence to the topic.

Do this now. Highlight, circle, or underline the essential terms and elements in the prompt. Time yourself. How long did it take you?

Compare our highlighting of the prompt with yours.

In her 1987 poem "<u>On the Subway</u>," <u>Sharon Olds</u> brings <u>two worlds into close proximity</u>. Read the poem carefully. Then, in a well-written essay analyze how Olds uses <u>poetic elements and techniques</u> to develop the <u>complex contrasts and insights</u> the speaker comes to as a result of the experience.

In this prompt, anything else you may have highlighted is extraneous.

You are free to use your own selection of techniques and devices. Notice that the prompt requires more than one technique. One will not be enough. You must use more than one. If you fail to use more than one technique, no matter how well you present your answer, your essay will be incomplete.

Reading and Notating the Poetry Selection

Finally, read the poem. Depending on your style and comfort level, choose one of these approaches to your reading:

1. A. Read quickly to get the gist of the poem.
   B. Reread, using the highlighting and marginal notes approach.

2. A. Read slowly, as if speaking aloud. Let the structure of the poem help you with meaning. (See the terms *enjambment* and *caesura* in the Glossary at the back of this book.)
   B. Reread to confirm that you understand the full impact of the poem. Do your highlighting and make marginal notes.

Note: In both approaches, you *must* highlight and make marginal notes. There is no way to avoid this. Ignore what you don't immediately understand. It may become clear to you after reading the poem. Practice. Practice. Concentrate on those parts of the poem that apply to what you highlighted in the prompt.

There are many ways to read and interpret any poetry. You have to choose your own approach and which specifics to include for support. *Don't be rattled if there is leftover material.*

We've reproduced the poem for you below so that you can practice both the reading and the process of deconstructing the text. Use highlighting, arrows, circles, underlining, notes, numbers, and whatever you need to make the connections clear to you.

Do this now. Spend 8–10 minutes working the material. *Do not skip this step.* It is time well spent and is a key to the high-score essay.

On the Subway
by Sharon Olds

The boy and I face each other
His feet are huge, in black sneakers
laced with white in a complex pattern like a
set of intentional scars. We are stuck on

opposite sides of the car, a couple of   5
molecules stuck in a rod of light
rapidly moving through darkness.
He has the casual cold look of a mugger,
alert under hooded lids. He is wearing
red, like the inside of the body   10
exposed. I am wearing dark fur, the
whole skin of an animal taken and
used. I look at his raw face,
he looks at my fur coat, and I don't
know if I am in his power—   15
he could take my coat so easily, my
briefcase, my life—
or if he is in my power, the way I am
living off his life, eating the steak
he does not eat, as if I am taking   20
the food from his mouth. And he is black
and I am white, and without meaning or
trying to I must profit from his darkness,
the way he absorbs the murderous beams of the
nation's heart, as black cotton   25
absorbs the heat of the sun and holds it. There is
no way to know how easy this
white skin makes my life, this
life he could take so easily and
break across his knee like a stick the way his   30
own back is being broken, the
rod of his soul that at birth was dark and
fluid and rich as the heart of a seedling
ready to thrust up into any available light

KEY IDEA

Now compare your reading notes with what we've done below. Yours may vary from ours, but the results of your note-taking should be similar in scope.

On the Subway
by Sharon Olds

*first part = narrator as
observer*
                                   first person   *oppositions*
The boy and I face each other
His feet are huge, in black sneakers
laced with white in a complex pattern like a ——— *dark*
light ——— set of intentional scars. We are stuck on
violence? ——— opposite sides of the car, a couple of ——— *no control*   5
opposite sides of molecules stuck in a rod of light
the "tracks" rapidly moving through darkness. ——— *light and dark
metaphor*

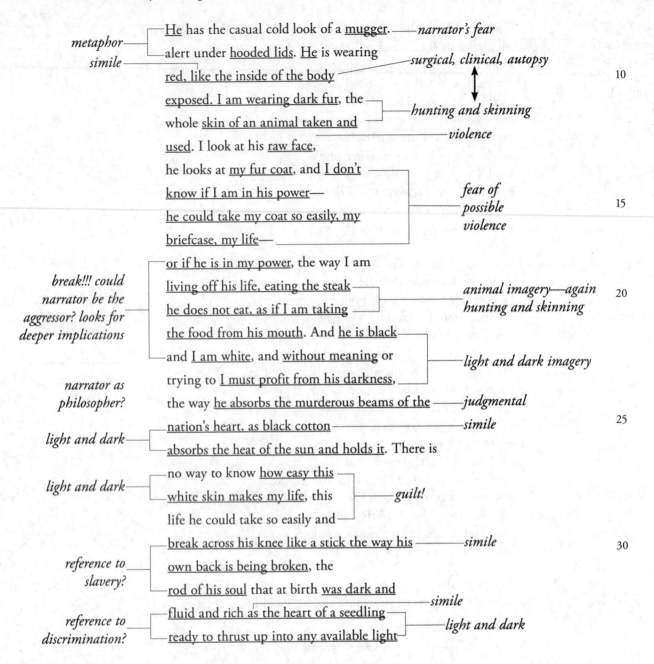

metaphor ——┐
simile ——┘
He has the casual cold look of a <u>mugger</u>. —— *narrator's fear*
alert under <u>hooded lids</u>. <u>He</u> is wearing
<u>red, like the inside of the body</u> —— *surgical, clinical, autopsy*   10
<u>exposed</u>. <u>I am wearing dark fur</u>, the —— *hunting and skinning*
whole <u>skin of an animal taken and</u>
<u>used</u>. I look at his <u>raw face</u>, —— *violence*
he looks at <u>my fur coat</u>, and <u>I don't</u>
<u>know if I am in his power</u>——
<u>he could take my coat so easily</u>, <u>my</u>
<u>briefcase, my life</u>—— *fear of possible violence*   15

break!!! could narrator be the aggressor? looks for deeper implications ——
<u>or if he is in my power</u>, the way <u>I am</u>
<u>living off his life, eating the steak</u> —— *animal imagery—again hunting and skinning*   20
<u>he does not eat, as if I am taking</u>
<u>the food from his mouth</u>. And <u>he is black</u>
and <u>I am white</u>, and <u>without meaning</u> or —— *light and dark imagery*

narrator as philosopher?
trying to <u>I must profit from his darkness</u>,
the way <u>he absorbs the murderous beams of the</u> —— *judgmental*
light and dark —— <u>nation's heart, as black cotton</u> —— *simile*   25
<u>absorbs the heat of the sun and holds it</u>. There is
light and dark —— no way to know <u>how easy this</u>
<u>white skin makes my life</u>, this —— *guilt!*
life <u>he could take so easily</u> and

reference to slavery? ——
<u>break across his knee like a stick</u> the way his —— *simile*   30
<u>own back is being broken</u>, the
<u>rod of his soul</u> that at birth <u>was dark and</u>
reference to discrimination? ——
<u>fluid and rich as the heart of a seedling</u> —— *simile*
<u>ready to thrust up into any available light</u> —— *light and dark*

STRATEGY

After you have marked the poem, review the prompt. When you look at your notes, certain categories will begin to pop out at you. These can be the basis for the development of the body of your essay. For example:

- Light and dark imagery
- Speaker's insights
- Contrast in status
- Metaphors

- Animal imagery
- Implied violence
- Shift in middle of poem
- Similes

Here's how we saw one category develop in the poem. Notice that we have ignored notes that did not apply to the prompt.

Category: Light and dark imagery

Examples:

"black sneakers"   "laced with white"   "rod of light"

"moving through darkness"   "profit from his darkness"   "he is black"

"and I am white"   "heat of the sun"   "murderous beams"

"black cotton"   "thrust up into any   "dark and fluid"

"how easy this white skin   available light"

makes my life"

Comment: The use of black and white imagery emphasizes the opposite ends of the spectrum represented by the speaker and the boy.

Your Turn

Now you choose a category that seems to pop out at you and trace its use through the poem.

Category:

Examples:

Comment:

We chose to examine poetic devices used in "On the Subway."

Category: Poetic devices

Examples:

Simile	lines 3–4	"complex … scars"
Metaphor	lines 4–6	"We are … molecules"
Simile	lines 9–11	"He is wearing … exposed"
Simile	lines 24–26	"he absorbs … holds it"
Simile	lines 29–30	"he could … stick"
Simile	line 32	"rod of his soul"
Simile	lines 32–34	"rod of his soul … light"

Comment: By definition, similes and metaphors are comparisons. The poet uses these comparisons to develop and flesh out the juxtaposition of the life and situation of the speaker and the boy.

Your Turn

Refer to this chapter's earlier section about the types of poetry prompts to expect on the exam. Construct two alternative prompts for Sharon Olds's "On the Subway."

1st Alternative prompt:

2nd Alternative prompt:

Notice that we have ignored notes that did not apply to the prompt.

Now choose the techniques that develop the contrasting portraits and reveal the narrator's perceptions.

In response to the prompt, we have decided that the techniques/devices we will analyze are:

- Imagery
- Poetic devices
- Organization

If you expand the above techniques/devices and the above categories into interpretive statements and support those statements with appropriate details that you've already isolated, you will be writing a defended essay.

Writing the Opening Paragraph

Your opening statement is the one that sets the tone of your essay and possibly raises the expectations of the reader. Spend time on your first paragraph to maximize your score.

Make certain that your topic is very clear. This reinforces the idea that you fully understand what is expected of you and what you will communicate to the reader. Generally, identify both the text and the poet in this first paragraph.

Do this now. Take 5 minutes to write your opening paragraph for the prompt. Write quickly, referring to your notes.

Let's check what you've written.

Highlight these points to see if you've done them. You may be surprised at what is actually there.

- Have you included the poet and the title?
- Have you addressed the portraits, contrasts, and insights?
- Have you specifically mentioned the techniques you will refer to in your essay?

Here are three sample opening paragraphs that address each of the above criteria.

A

Sharon Olds in the poem, "On the Subway," presents a brief encounter between two people of different races which leads to several insights of one participant. This is accomplished through Olds's use of poetic devices, imagery, and imagination.

B

The observer and the observed. One has control over the other. In her poem, "On the Subway," Sharon Olds asks her readers to enter the mind of a white woman who observes a young, black man as they travel together, neither knowing the other. Using poetic devices, imagery, and organization, Olds takes the reader on a ride through the contrasts and images that spark the imagination of the white onlooker.

C

"And he is black and I am white" establishes the basic contrast and conflict in Sharon Olds's poem, "On the Subway." Through imagery, organization, and poetic devices, Olds creates two contrasting portraits. The narrator's confrontation becomes the reader's also as she reveals her troubling fears and insights through her images and comments concerning her encounter with the black youth.

These three introductory paragraphs identify the poet and the title and clearly indicate an understanding of the prompt. Now, let's note what is different about each.

Sample **A** is a straightforward, unadorned restatement of the prompt. It is correct, yet lacks a writer's voice. (If you are unsure of how to proceed, this is the type of opening you may want to consider.) This type of opening paragraph will at least allow you to get into the essay with as little complexity as possible.

Sample **B** immediately reveals the writer's confidence and mature writing style. The prompt is addressed in a provocative and interesting manner, letting the reader know the tone of the essay.

Sample **C** incorporates a direct quotation from the poem which indicates the writer is comfortable with citation. The writer also links the reader with the poem and feels confident that his or her judgments about the encounter are supportable.

Note: There are many other types of opening paragraphs that could do the job as well. The paragraphs above are just a few samples.

Does your opening paragraph resemble any of these samples?

_____Yes_____No

Writing the Body of the Poetry Essay

When you write the body of your essay, take only 15–20 minutes. Time yourself and try your best to finish within that time frame.

Since this is practice, don't panic if you can't complete the essay within the allotted time. You will become more and more comfortable with the tasks presented to you as you gain experience with this type of question.

What Should I Include in the Body of the Poetry Essay?

STRATEGY

1. Obviously, this is where you present your interpretation and the points you wish to make that are related to the prompt.

2. Use specific references and details from the poem.
   - Refer directly to the original. Don't always paraphrase.
   - Place quotation marks around those words and phrases that you extract from the poem.

3. Use "connective tissue" in your essay to establish adherence to the question.
   - Use the repetition of key ideas from your opening paragraph.
   - Try using "echo words" (i.e., synonyms such as *insight* can be inference/observation/perception; *fear* can be apprehension/insecurity).
   - Create transitions from one paragraph to the next.

To understand the process, carefully read the following sample paragraphs. Each develops one of the categories and techniques/devices asked for in the prompt. Notice the specific references and the "connective tissue." Also, notice that details that do not apply to the prompt have been ignored.

A
This paragraph develops **poetic devices**.

"Black sneakers laced with white in a complex pattern like a set of intentional scars" is the jarring simile Olds uses to establish the relationship between the woman and the "boy" on the subway. Immediately, the poetic device implies the bondage and pain of the oppressed minority and the deliberate complexity of race relations. This idea of interwoven lives is further developed by the metaphor that links both as "molecules stuck in a rod of light." The youth, however, is compared to a reptile with "hooded lids," and all the fear and repulsion associated with this creature is transferred to the boy who is hiding his true intentions with such a look. The woman follows her fearful insights with still another extreme simile—worrying about "this life he could take so easily and break across his knee like a stick." Still, she proves the complexity of her thoughts by creating a sympathetic metaphor to ponder "the rod of his soul—the heart of a seedling" yearning to grow into the light.

B
This paragraph develops **imagery**.

The images in the poem are predominantly drawn from the contrast between light and dark. "Black sneakers," "white laces," "rod of light rapidly moving through darkness" are all images that immediately establish the contrast that is at the heart of the meaning of the poem. This juxtaposition becomes reality in lines 21–22 when we learn that "he is black and I am white." The problem is how the "white" profits from his "darkness." [line 23] What should be light, "the beams of the nation's heart," is murderous, and he "as black cotton," absorbs this heat. This angry contrast leads the speaker to her insight about her life in lines 26–28. Empathizing with the black youth, the narrator moves beyond her prejudices and finds promise in the last three lines which see the dark being born into the light.

C
This paragraph develops **organization**.

The organization of "On the Subway" is rather linear. Olds's narrator proceeds from a frightened observer to a philosophical questioner to finally a mature, sympathetic forecaster of the promise of the young, black man. The first thirteen lines provide the interior monologue of a woman who sits across from a young, black male and looks him over from head to toe. In line 10 she begins to move deeply into the hidden person across from her, with this "introspection" ending in lines 14–16 with her questioning who actually has power over whom. Line 18 presents a true shift from personal observation to an almost societal conscience which is sympathetic to the plight of all blacks in America as seen in lines 21–26. Bringing the reader back to the opening section of the poem, the speaker intimates at the promise of the young man with "the rod of his soul . . . rich as the heart of a seedling/ready to thrust up into any available light." [lines 32–34]

Refer to our list of recommended poets at the back of this book. Look for poems similar in length and complexity to those we've provided and apply a variety of prompts. You can try these alone, with a study group, or with your class.

Note: Look at the last sentence of Sample B on imagery: "Empathizing with the black youth, the narrator moves beyond her prejudices and finds promise in the last three lines which see the dark being born into the light."

This final sentence would be fine as the conclusion to the essay. A conclusion does not have to be a paragraph. It can be the writer's final remark, observation, or reference and may be only a sentence or two.

Do this now. Write the body of your essay. Time yourself. Allow 15–20 minutes to complete this task.

Sample Student Essays

Following are two actual student essays followed by a rubric and comments on each.

Student Essay A

The three sections of "On the Subway" by Sharon Olds express the complicated relationship between Caucasians and African-Americans. In the first section the author presents an exposition that contrasts a white person with a black (lines 1–13). In the second, the speaker begins to develop the apparent disparities so that inter-relationships emerge (lines 13–20). In the third, the narrator gains insight into how this scene is representative of American culture at large (lines 20–34).

The imagery Olds uses in the first section emphasizes the difference between the white woman who is the narrator and the observer and the black boy, who is the observed, as they ride the subway. The shoes he is wearing are black "laced with white" (line 3). The speaker describes the white zigzags as "intentional scars" (line 4). The scars allude to the discrimination against the black man by white society. The adjective "intentional" denotes that whites purposely harm blacks. The image contrasts whites with blacks: whites are powerful; blacks are subservient. Similarly, the two characters are described as being "stuck on opposite sides" of the subway car; they are separated permanently from each other (lines 4–5). The description of the clothing is a third contrasting element. Here, the black man is "exposed," while the speaker is covered in fur (line 11). This image reinforces the opposition between the white woman and the black boy.

The second section sees a shift in tone. Where the first section is composed of finite physical descriptions, the second is more philosophical and indicates the speaker's apprehension. She is uncertain and writes that "I don't/know if I am in his power . . . or if he is in my power" (lines 14–15, 18). Such a statement is important because it illustrates that the boundaries between whites and blacks are not as clearcut as they may seem. Perhaps the speaker begins to realize that the image of the subservient black and the powerful white presented in the first section of the poem is incorrect. The repetition of the word "Life" is another way the interconnection between the two characters is developed. The narrator cannot decide whether her wealth usurps the power of the black man or whether his potential aggression usurps her power (lines 17, 19).

5

10

15

20

25

The tone, again, shifts in the third segment. Here, it is clear that the speaker is trying to gain an understanding of the relationship between the white world and that of the black boy. At first, she realizes that they are different because "he is black and I am white" (lines 21–22). The image of the "black cotton" alludes to slavery, once again referring to the scars, or distinctions, imposed by the white society. Yet, at the end of this section, the differences between the two people are strangely reconciled. This is accomplished using the technique of repetition. Instead of repeating a word as in the second section, an image is repeated. Lines 29–31 state that the black man could hurt the white woman; he could "break [her] across his knee . . . the way his own back is being broken." In other words, both whites and blacks can hurt; both races can be injured by either repression or aggression, and so they are connected through their pain and unrealized dreams.

Student Essay B

In the poem "On the Subway" by Sharon Olds, she contrasts the worlds of an affluent white person and a poor black person. The two people have many opposing characteristics, and the author uses literary techniques such as tone, poetic devices, and imagery to portray these differences. The narrator is the white woman, and she realizes how people get "stuck" in places of society based on their skin color. The word "stuck" is repeated twice to stress this idea.

The major difference between the two people is obviously their skin color. This one difference causes many aspects of each person's life to be unlike the other's. The white woman is above the black man in the eyes of much of society. The narrator states that "without meaning or trying to I must profit from his darkness." This is basically saying that the black man is living in a white man's world, where his skin color alone has given him a predisposition in the eyes of many. This idea is further supported when the speaker thinks "There is no way to know how easy this white skin makes my life." Olds uses the following simile to show the black man's situation: ". . . he absorbs the murderous beams of the nation's heart, as black cotton absorbs the heat of the sun and holds it."

Another contrast that is in the poem is the rawness of the black man versus the sheltered and refined look of the white woman. Olds uses a simile to describe the red that the black youth is wearing: "Like the inside of the body exposed." The white woman is the outside of the animal wearing a fur coat. The black man is the inside of the body, the true animal, while the white woman is not; she is simply wearing the outer covering of an animal.

As a result of this experience, the narrator realizes that there is a balance of power and control between her and the young man. She realizes that at times, and in certain situations, she rules, while in others the black man does. Her life, her "easier" life, can be taken away by the black youth. Who has the power on the train? The big, strong, raw black man or the weaker, but richer, white woman? Society has given the white woman a false sense of superiority and security. She is protected by wealth, her job, and her possessions, but when alone on the subway with this black man, she feels fear. She is confronted by her own vulnerability. The black youth who is being broken by society can break the white woman who is society.

Overall, this poem effectively contrasts the two people and exposes a fallacy of society. The black man must live in eternal darkness because he is never allowed to "thrust up into any available light."

Rating the Student Essays

Let's take a look at a set of rubrics for the poetry essay.

- 1 point for thesis/claim/introduction that is appropriate to the prompt
  - The thesis clearly presents a possible interpretation and indicates how the support will be developed.
- 4 points for evidence/support of the thesis/claim
  - Clear and appropriate references to the text
  - Clear presentation of how the references relate to the thesis
- 1 point for complexity of the commentary and syntax

> *Note:* The essay is really a first draft. The readers know this and approach each essay with this in mind.

Note: With specific reference to the 6-point rubric, we will use the following abbreviations to indicate into which column the comment would fall: **T** = **thesis, E** = **evidence, C** = **complexity, S** = **sophistication**.

Student Essay A

This is a high-range essay (5, 6) for the following reasons:

"Even though I hate doing it, my writing really improves when I spend the time revising what I've written."
—Mike T.
  AP student

- A sophisticated, indirect indication of the task of the prompt and line of reasoning. T
- Tightly constructed and thorough discussion of the contrasts and opposition in the poem. E/C
- Effective analysis of imagery (lines 1–13, 15–17). E/C
- Effective and coherent analysis of tone. E
- Understanding of the subtleties of tone (lines 19–21). C
- Strong support for assertions and interpretations (lines 22–29). C
- Effective analysis of literary techniques (lines 11, 33–34, 36–38). E
- Mature syntax, diction, and organization. S

   This high-ranking essay is subtle, concise, and on target. There is nothing that takes away from the writer's focus. Each paragraph grows out of the previous one, and the reader always knows where the author is taking him or her.

Student Essay B

This is a middle-range essay (3, 4) for the following reasons:

- Clearly identifies the task, the poem, and the poet. T
- States the techniques that will be discussed in the essay and indicates a line of reasoning. T
- Lacks a transition to the body of the essay (lines 6–7). S
- Provides an adequate discussion of the insights of the speaker (lines 23–25). C
- Cites appropriate specifics to support the thesis of the essay (lines 14–16). E
- Uses standard style, diction, and structure, but does not reflect a sophisticated or mature writer. S
- Attempts a universal statement within a rather repetitive and summary-like conclusion (lines 32–34). S

How about sharing these samples with members of your class or study group and discussing possible responses?

While adhering to the prompt, this mid-range essay is an adequate first draft. It shows promise but comes dangerously close to paraphrasing lines. The analysis is basic and obvious, depending on only one device, that of simile. The writer hints at the subtleties but misses the opportunity to respond to further complexities inherent in the poem.

Note: Both essays have concluding paragraphs that are repetitive and mostly unnecessary. It is best to avoid this type of ending.

Rapid Review

Need a Quick Review? Spend a minute or two reading through…that'll do.

- Review terms and techniques.
- Become familiar with types of poetry questions (prompts).
- Highlight the prompt to make certain you are aware of required tasks.
- Time your essay carefully.
- Read the poem a couple of times.
- Spend sufficient time "working the poem" before writing.
- Mark up the poem.
- Create a strong opening paragraph, including prompt information.
- Refer often to the poem for concrete details and quotes to support your ideas.
- Always stay on topic.
- Avoid simply paraphrasing.
- Include transitions and echo words.
- Practice—vary the prompt and your response.
- Consult the models and rubrics for self-evaluation.
- Share ideas with others.

CHAPTER 7

The Free-Response Essay/Literary Argument

IN THIS CHAPTER

Summary: Examination of the free-response essay and its purpose as it is presented in the AP English Literature exam

Key Ideas

✪ Learn the types of free-response prompts you might encounter in the AP English Literature exam
✪ Practice various ways of organizing the information based on your chosen literary work
✪ Learn the basics of constructing your response to the free-response prompt
✪ Learn about the rubrics and rating of the AP free-response essays
✪ Examine model student essays
✪ Learn how rubrics were used to rate student essays
✪ Learn how the synthesis essay differs from the argumentative and analysis essays
✪ Learn the process of dealing with many texts

Introduction to the Free-Response Essay/Literary Argument

Nothing in life is free, but this essay does indicate that the end is near. So, hang in there. This chapter will provide the information and the practice you need to "knock their socks off."

You will be given a literary idea or comment. This idea will be followed by a list of 30 to 40 texts deemed to have literary merit. You will then:

- Select one of these works or a work of literary merit from your own reading
- Analyze how your literary work relates to the prompt and to the work as a whole
- Select and discuss appropriate evidence to support your thesis
- Employ appropriate diction and syntax

The wording of the free-response prompt will be consistent. Only the statement of the idea/concept and the list of literary works will differ.

For example: "Either from your own reading or from the list below, choose a work of fiction in which [some aspect of the lead is addressed]. Then, in a well-written essay, analyze how [that same aspect of the lead] contributes to an interpretation of the work as a whole. Do not merely summarize the plot." (*AP English Literature and Composition Course and Exam Description*, The College Board, 2020, p. 139.)

What Is a Free-Response Essay?

The free-response essay is based on a provocative question that highlights specific insights applicable to a broad range of literary texts. The question provides for varied personal interpretations and multiple approaches. It allows students to truly create the specific substance of their own essay.

What Is the Purpose of the Free-Response Essay?

The College Board wants to assess your ability to discuss a work of literature in a particular context. The illustrations you include in your essay will demonstrate your insights and critical thinking as well as your writing ability.

What Makes This Essay "Free"?

Although the question is the same for all students, you have total freedom to choose the piece of literature to which you will refer. Once chosen, you have total freedom to select the specifics that will support your thesis. Unlike the other two essays, which have rubrics based on certain concrete interpretations and directions of the text, your free-response essay will be uniquely your own.

If This Is Total Freedom of Expression, How Can I Ever Get Less Than a 6?

The test reader is expecting an essay that demonstrates a mature understanding and defense of the prompt. Your paper must be specific and well organized. It must also adhere to the topic. You will lose major credit for providing only plot summary. Your illustrations should be cogent and insightful rather than obvious or superficial. For a high score, you must bring something specific and relevant to the conversation that is logically related to the thesis.

What Are the Pitfalls of the Free-Response Essay?

It is our experience that the free-response question is a double-edged sword. Students can suffer from overconfidence because of the open nature of this essay. They depend on memory rather than on preparation and often go for the most obvious illustrations. They tend to ramble on in vague and unsupported generalities, and they frequently provide incorrect information. *The failure to plan and limit can undermine this essay.*

Students often have trouble choosing the appropriate work and lose valuable time pondering a variety of choices. It is important to be decisive and confident in your presentation.

What Kinds of Works May I Refer to in This Essay?

Generally, you are asked to choose a full-length work, almost always a novel or play. However, if the prompt says "choose a work," you may use a poem, short story, novella, or work of nonfiction. *Note*: You may *never* use a film.

Note: The list of suggested texts for FRQ3 will have 36–42 works on it, NONE of which will be works in translation or ancient texts (e.g., *The Odyssey*, *The Iliad*). Students will be allowed to write about works in translation (e.g., *Crime and Punishment*, *Madame Bovary*), but translated works will not be listed in the prompt.

- What constitutes "literary merit" will no longer be an issue. Works of literature characterized by "complexity" will be acceptable choices.
- Literary nonfiction (e.g., *The Bell Jar*, *In Cold Blood*, *Night*) will be acceptable choices.

Must I Use the List of Works Provided at the Bottom of the Prompt?

<u>Absolutely not!</u> Since this is a free-response essay, the choice of a literary work is up to you. You should choose a work that is appropriate to the prompt, one that is appropriate to AP students, and one that is comfortable for you.

Must I Use Works Read This Year?

No, but why would you choose any work that could be a faded memory or unsuitable for AP-level analysis? We always recommend using works that you studied in class and have read and discussed throughout the year. One exception occurs when you have written a lengthy literary research paper or a sustained critical analysis. In this situation, you may have real in-depth familiarity with a work that you could adapt to a free-response question. By all means, go for it!

How Do I Prepare for the Free-Response Essay?

You need to tell yourself in September or October that you will be taking the exam next May. This will emphasize the point that throughout the year you will have to keep some type of record of the works you have read and some specific points you want to make about each of them. (In Chapter 8, we introduce several techniques and processes that will enable you to keep these records.)

By the time of the exam in May, you need to be thoroughly conversant with at least three to five full-length works from different genres, eras, and literary movements.

You also need to practice. Practice writing questions, practice choosing appropriate works, and practice writing responses to questions. Practice!

What Criteria Do the AP Readers Use to Rate a Free-Response Essay?

The readers are looking for literary insights and awareness of character, comprehension of theme, and the ability to transfer specific ideas and details to a universal concept. In addition, the readers are hoping to see a writer who reveals and understands the relationships among form, content, style, and structure and their effects on the meaning of the work. The essay should indicate the writer's ability to choose appropriate illustrations from a full-length work and to connect them in a thoughtful way. The sophisticated writer will refer to plot but will not summarize. As always, the reader is looking for a well-organized essay written in a mature voice.

According to The College Board, the scoring of a student's free-response will be based on how well the student:

- Responds to the prompt with a thesis that presents a defensible interpretation
- Provides evidence to support your line of reasoning
- Explains how the evidence supports your line of reasoning
- Uses appropriate grammar and punctuation in communicating your argument

What Happens If I Use a Work That the Reader Doesn't Know?

This should not be a major concern to you. Throughout the year, your AP instructor has provided you with appropriate literary experiences suitable for addressing this prompt. In addition, be assured that any work we mention in this book will be appropriate. Be sure to consult our suggested reading list to increase your range of choices. Any other works by the same author would probably be on an appropriate AP level. For the most part, the AP prefers works from the literary canon because they exhibit breadth and complexity for literary scholarship. Don't fight these requirements. <u>You do yourself a disservice when you insist on trying to outwit or beat the system.</u>

Having said all this, if by chance you do choose an obscure work and present it well, the reader will respond accordingly.

Types of Free-Response Prompts

Here are some topics that could be the basis for a free-response prompt. We also include some suggested works for these.

- The journey as a major force in a work. (*Gulliver's Travels*, *As I Lay Dying*, *The Stranger*, *The Kite Runner*, etc.)
- What happens to a dream deferred? (*Hedda Gabler*, *Desire Under the Elms*, *Their Eyes Were Watching God*, etc.)
- Transformation (literal and/or figurative). (*Dr. Jekyll and Mr. Hyde*, *Black Like Me*, *Metamorphosis*, etc.)
- Descent into madness/hell. (*Medea*, *Heart of Darkness*, *Secret Sharer*, etc.)
- An ironic reversal in a character's beliefs or actions. (*Heart of Darkness*, *The Stranger*, *Oedipus*, etc.)
- Perception and reality—"What is, is not." (*Twelfth Night*, *Hamlet*, *Who's Afraid of Virginia Woolf?*, etc.)
- A child becomes a force to reveal _____ . (*Jane Eyre*, *Huckleberry Finn*, *Lord of the Flies*, etc.)
- Ceremony or ritual plays an important role. (*The Stranger*, *Lord of the Flies*, *The Sun Also Rises*, *Suddenly Last Summer*, etc.)
- The role of the fool, comic character, or wise servant who reveals _____ . (*King Lear*, *The Importance of Being Earnest*, *Tartuffe*, etc.)

Note: Fill in works you would use to respond to the above prompts.

_____

_____

_____

_____

"I really like hearing and reading how the other students do the same questions. It helps me evaluate my own ideas and essays."
—Adam S.
 AP student

Here's another set of possible free-response prompts for development:

- How an opening scene or chapter establishes the character, conflict, or theme of a major literary work.
- How a minor character is used to develop a major character.
- How violence relates to character or theme.
- How time is a major factor.
- The ways in which an author changes the reader's attitude(s) toward a subject.
- The use of contrasting settings.
- Parent/child or sibling relationships and their significance.
- The analysis of a villain with regard to the meaning of the work.
- The use of an unrealistic character or element and its effect on the work.
- The relevance of a nonmodern work to the present day.
- The conflict between passion and responsibility.
- The conflict between character and society.

Note: To our knowledge, a free-response question has never been repeated. Therefore, we suggest:

1. Use the prompts cited earlier when you discuss works you read or when you write about those works throughout the year.

2. Generate a list of topics that would also be suitable for free-response prompts. Discuss, outline, or prepare sample essays utilizing these questions.

Anticipating prompts and responses is a productive way to prepare for this exam.

General Rubrics for the Free-Response Essay

Let's take a look at a set of rubrics for the free-response essay.

- 1 point for thesis/claim/introduction that is appropriate to the prompt
  - The thesis clearly cites a major work related to the prompt and indicates how the support will be developed.
- 4 points for evidence/support of the thesis/claim
  - Clear and appropriate references to the text
  - Clear presentation of how the references relate to the thesis
- 1 point for complexity of the commentary and syntax

Timing and Planning the Free-Response Essay

This essay is the real challenge of the exam. Keep in mind that with the other two essay questions, half the job was done for you; the material was limited and provided for you. But now you are faced with the blank page that you must fill. Therefore, you must plan this essay carefully and completely. With this in mind, here's a workable strategy:

- 1–3 minutes working the prompt. (At this point, you might even chart the prompt.)
- 3–5 minutes choosing your work. (You should mentally run through two or three works that might be appropriate.) This is a crucial step for laying the foundation for your essay.

- 5–10 minutes for brainstorming, charting, mapping, outlining, and so on the specifics you plan to use in your essay. (Remember, a vague, general, unsupported essay will cost you points.)
- 20–25 minutes to write your essay based on your preparation.
- 3 minutes for proofreading.

Working the Prompt from the Diagnostic/Master Exam

Before you read the prompt, immediately cover the list of suggested works. There are several good reasons for this:

- It requires time to read the list.
- Chances are you will have read very few works on the list. If you are like many students, this could make you feel insecure and rattle your confidence.
- If you are familiar with a work or two, you may be predisposed to use the work to answer the question even if it is not necessarily your best choice. You may find yourself considering a work that you would not have considered if it were not listed, and you may find yourself taking precious time to fit that choice unsuccessfully to the prompt.

Here is the PROMPT:

Often in literature, a literal or figurative journey is a significant factor in the development of a character or the meaning of the work.

Either from your own reading or from the list below, choose a work of fiction that presents the effect(s) of a literal or figurative journey on a character or on the meaning of the entire work. Then, in a well-written essay analyze how the journey affects the character or the meaning of the work as a whole.

As I Lay Dying	*Beloved*
The Handmaid's Tale	*Heart of Darkness*
The Odyssey	*Moby Dick*
Brave New World	*The Sun Also Rises*
To the Lighthouse	*The Grapes of Wrath*
A Streetcar Named Desire	*The Poisonwood Bible*
A Passage to India	*Their Eyes Were Watching God*
Gulliver's Travels	*The Bonesetter's Daughter*
Jasmine	*Twelfth Night*
The Kite Runner	*The Brief Wondrous Life of Oscar Wao*

Notating the Prompt

We recommend that you chart or map the prompt. This is a simple visualization of your task. Before you look at our samples, you might want to try charting or mapping the prompt on your own.

Following is a sample chart:

Jane Eyre

	JOURNEY	EFFECT ON CHARACTER	EFFECT ON THEME
LITERAL			
FIGURATIVE			

Here is a sample map:

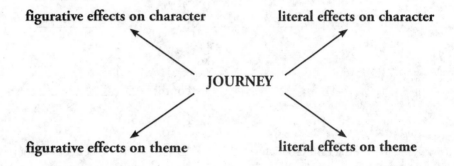

Following is a sample topic outline:

Journey

- Literal effect
  - character
  - theme
- Figurative effect
  - character
  - theme

Your Turn

Carefully read and highlight the following prompt.

Frequently, the tension in a literary work is created by the conflict between a character and society. Choose a full-length literary work and discuss the nature of the conflict, its effect on the character, on society, and on the resulting thematic implications.

A. **Construct a chart** that addresses the requirements of the prompt.

Title of literary work:

	NATURE OF CONFLICT	EFFECT OF CONFLICT
ON CHARACTER		
ON SOCIETY		
ON THEMATIC IMPLICATIONS		

B. Using the same literary work you chose for the chart, **create a map**.

(character) _____   (society) _____   (thematic) _____

_____   _____   _____

_____   _____   _____

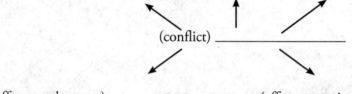

(conflict) _____

(effect on character) _____   (effect on society) _____

_____   _____

_____   _____

C. With the same literary work and prompt in mind, **construct an outline**.

Conflict

Nature of conflict
– On character:
– On society:

Effect of conflict
– On character:
– On society:

Thematic implications
– On character:
– On society:

When you provide the specifics, either mentally or by writing them down, you will ensure that you have addressed all parts of the prompt. This also will provide the basic structure of your essay.

Note: Although it may feel awkward and contrived at first, if you actually practice this technique, it will become automatic and help you to immediately get into the writing of your essay.

Now that you are familiar with the prompt, take a few moments to think about works that might be appropriate for this question. One or two will immediately pop into your mind. Mentally examine them for scenes or details that you might be able to use. *If you can't think of specifics, abandon this choice.*

If you wish, now take a look at the list of suggested works, because:

- You may find your choice there, and you will feel very validated.
- You may see a different work by the same author, which may also boost your confidence.
- You might see another work or author you recognize you had not considered that could possibly spark a better response to the prompt.

This process should only take a minute or so.

Do this now. Spend 8–10 minutes working your choice to fit the requirements of the prompt. For example, prior to the exam, you will have prepared a cross section of works from various genres, time periods, and literary movements. Since these are works with depth, you will be able to take your basic scene or references and modify them to suit the task of the given prompt.

Using *Hamlet* as an example, let's assume you reviewed the graveyard scene prior to the exam. This scene would be appropriate to illustrate your thoughts on such varied prompts as:

- The use of humor—the gravedigger.
- The role of a minor character—Horatio.
- The concept of death as the great leveler—motif.
- Use of ritual—funeral.
- The impact of a character *not* seen in the work—Yorick.
- The use of coincidence or irony in the work—Ophelia's grave.
- The use of setting to develop theme or character—"To be or not to be."

You get the point. Obviously, you could not answer a question about the effectiveness of a work's conclusion by using this scene, which is exactly why you prepare *several* different literary examples.

We know that Shakespeare is so universal that any work could be used to answer almost any free-response question. Therefore, we urge you to prepare at least one Shakespearean play as a "safe" work.

There is another reason to spend several minutes planning your essay. Frequently, your first responses and examples are the obvious and common ones. This is not to say that you could not write an adequate essay using these. But, if they came to you this quickly, they probably also came to many thousands of other students taking the exam. It is usually more challenging and rewarding to find a unique focus for your essay. For example: choosing the gravedigger's scene in *Hamlet* rather than the "To be or not to be" scene may reveal a more creative thinker.

Sometimes, as you are planning, you realize that your work will answer only part of the prompt and that it would be better to switch to another work. If you have prepared well prior to the test, you will be able to do this without taking up much time. Sometimes it's better to abandon your initial choice in favor of the second and more productive one. This is why you have not yet begun to write.

Developing the Opening Paragraph

Now you are ready to write. Remember, your opening paragraph is the one that raises the expectations of the reader and sets the tone of your essay. Spend time on your first paragraph to maximize your score.

Make certain that your topic is very clear to the reader. This reinforces the idea that you fully understand what is expected of you and what you will communicate to the reader. Generally, identify both the text and the author in this first paragraph.

Do this now. Take 5 minutes and write your opening paragraph for this prompt. Write quickly, referring to your notes.

Let's check what you've written:

Actually highlight these to see if you've done it. You may be surprised at what is actually there.

- Have you included the author and title?
- Have you addressed the literal and figurative journeys?
- Have you addressed characterization and theme?

Here are three sample opening paragraphs that address each of the above criteria.

A

"There was no possibility of taking a walk that day" says young Jane in Chapter One of Charlotte Brontë's novel, *Jane Eyre*. Little did she know that her very existence would evolve from her personal odyssey as she journeyed from Gateshead to Lowood to Thornfield and beyond; from child to adolescent to woman. This literal and figurative journey enables Brontë to develop both the character and the theme of her work.

B

Up the hill, down the street, across the road from cafe to cafe, the characters in Ernest Hemingway's novel, *The Sun Also Rises*, wander interminably. Hemingway employs this aimless journey to reveal the lost nature of his characters and his theme of the search for meaning and direction in their post–World War I existence.

C

In *Heart of Darkness* by Joseph Conrad, a literal journey from England to Africa becomes a nightmare of realization and epiphany for the main character, Marlowe. Conrad develops his themes through Marlowe's observations and experiences on his figurative journey from innocence to corruption, idealism to cynicism, and optimism to despair.

Note: These three introductory paragraphs identify the author and the title and clearly indicate an understanding of the prompt. Let's note what is different about each.

Sample **A** begins with an appropriate, direct quotation. It clearly delineates the two types of journeys and their relationship to the character. The writer indicates an understanding of the difference between literal and figurative interpretation.

Sample **B** has a clear writer's voice. The writer is not afraid to be judgmental. The tone of the essay is apparent and sustained.

Sample **C** alludes to the content of the body of the essay and touches on vague generalities. However, the maturity of the vocabulary and thought indicate the writer's understanding of Conrad's complex themes and their relationship to the prompt.

Note: There are many other types of opening paragraphs that could also do the job. The paragraphs above are just a few samples. Does your opening paragraph resemble any of these samples? When you write the body of your essay, take only 15–20 minutes. Time yourself and try your best to finish within that time frame.

Developing the Body of the Essay

Time to pump some mental iron and to firm up and tone those flabby ideas and turn them into examples of intellectual fitness.

What Should I Include in the Body of the Free-Response Essay?

1. Obviously, this is where you present your interpretation and the points you wish to make that are related to the prompt.

2. Use specific references and details from the chosen work.
   • Incorporate direct quotations when possible.
   • Place quotation marks around those words or phrases taken directly from the work.

3. Use connective tissue in your essay to establish adherence to the question.
   • Use the repetition of key ideas in the prompt and in your opening paragraph.
   • Try using "echo words" (i.e., synonyms such as journey/wanderings/travels or figurative/symbolic/metaphoric).
   • Use transitions from one paragraph to the next.

To understand the process, carefully read the following sample paragraphs. Each illustrates an aspect of the prompt. Notice the specific references and the connective tissue.

A

At Gateshead, despite its material comforts, Jane was an orphaned outcast who felt "like a discord." She was, like Cinderella, abused by her cousins and aunt and nurtured only by Bessie, a servant. Jane's immaturity and rebellious nature cause her to be jealous and vengeful which culminates in a violent confrontation with her repulsive cousin, John. Her subsequent eviction from Gateshead forces her to embark on a journey that will affect her forever. The stark privations of Lowood humble Jane and open her to the true riches of friendship with Helen Burns. It is here she learns the academic, religious, and social skills that will enable her to move on to her destiny at Thornfield.

B

Throughout the novel Jake escorts the reader on the journeys that become the only purpose the group exhibits. The trip to San Fermin for the fiesta is also a journey to hell, away from civilization and morality. The fiesta "explodes" and for seven days any behavior is acceptable, for there is no accountability during this time. No one "pays the bill," yet. Brett is worshiped as a pagan idol; garlic is strung around her neck, and men drink to her powers. She is compared to Circe, and, indeed, she turns her companions into swine as they fight over her. This trip to the fiesta reinforces the lack of spirituality and direction that is a theme of the novel.

C

Referring to the map of the Congo, Marlowe states that "the snake had charmed me." This primal description prepares us for the inevitable journey up the river that will change the very core of his character. The snake implies temptation, and Marlowe is seduced by the mysteries of Africa and his desire to meet Kurtz in the interior. He is too naive and pure to anticipate the abominations that await him at the inner station. Like a descent into hell, the journey progresses. The encounters with Fresleven, the workers without rivets, the pilgrims shooting into the jungle, all foreshadow Marlowe's changing understanding of the absurdity of life and the flawed nature of man. Only when he is totally aware of "the horror, the horror" can he journey back to "another dark place of the universe," London, to see the Intended and to corrupt his own values for her sake.

Let's examine these three body paragraphs.

Sample **A** is about *Jane Eyre*. It addresses one aspect of the prompt—Jane's character at the beginning of the journey—and continues with the first major change in her life. The writer demonstrates familiarity with the novel through concrete details and quotations. Theme is implied and leads the reader to anticipate further development in the rest of the body of the essay.

Sample **B** refers to *The Sun Also Rises*. This paragraph uses a single incident to develop the discussion of the journey as it affects character and theme. The writer includes very specific details of the San Fermin fiesta to support comments about Brett and Jake. The integration of these details is presented in a cohesive, mature style.

Sample **C** delves into *Heart of Darkness*. This paragraph is a philosophical approach, which assumes the reader is familiar with the novel. It focuses on theme and how the development of the character is used to illustrate that theme. The ending of the paragraph presents an insight that invites the reader to "stay tuned."

Do this now. Write the body of your essay. Time yourself. Allow 15–20 minutes to complete this task.

Sample Student Essays

Here are two actual student essays that are followed by a rubric and comments on each essay.

Student Essay A

The journey taken by Edna in Kate Chopin's <u>The Awakening</u> exemplifies the journey that is a very common feature in many works of literature. This journey is not a commonplace journey; it is one that brings about development and change in the story's main character. In <u>The Awakening</u>, the spiritual journey that Edna takes changes the way she thinks, acts, and lives. The ramifications of her journey change her life.   5

The story takes place in New Orleans around the turn of the century. The women of society were treated as possessions, either of their fathers or their husbands, or even of their religion. The story's protagonist, Edna, is introduced as the respectable wife. She is a good mother and is faithful to her husband. The   10
family vacations for the summer in Grand Isle. While there, Edna befriends Robert who every summer devotes himself to being an attendant to one of the married women, Edna being his current choice. While there, she undergoes a series of "awakenings" which begin her journey. One such push was Edna's learning to swim. Although she was previously afraid of the water and of swimming, one day   15
she tried, and is successful. Her newfound ability signifies the steps she is taking towards no longer being a possession. It is one of the first signs that Edna is ready

to break free and to be her own person. The water gives her a sense of freedom, and she relishes this sensation.

Edna's growing love for Robert alerts her of the journey upon which she has unknowingly embarked. After Robert leaves, giving very short notice, she misses him tremendously. She realizes that she is in love with him but has no such love for her husband, Leonce. While Robert gives into her every whim, Leonce only cares about Edna as if she were his possession. He does not consider her feelings and emotions, only his own. He leaves the family often to go into the city for work, sending candy and chocolates to Edna and her children in order to compensate for his absence. He constantly neglects Edna's emotional needs, and as a result, intensifies the strength of her journey. However, Leonce is not the only person who sees Edna merely as a possession. Even Robert, who is in love with her, feels that Edna belongs to Leonce. Because he knows that she cannot be his, Robert refuses to let their relationship progress any further than it has, and the only way for him to achieve this is to go away and cut off contact with Edna.

When the family returns to their home in New Orleans, Edna is not content with her life and begins to neglect performing some of her expected activities and duties, such as entertaining the wives of her husband's clients. Edna's refusal to accompany her husband on a business trip is the pinnacle of her journey. Leonce is shocked and appalled by her noncompliance, but he feels that she is going through a phase and will soon come to her senses.

While her husband is gone, Edna's children are sent to live with their grandmother. During this time, Edna is free and independent. She meets a variety of new people who she begins to spend time with. One of these people is Alcee Arobin, who becomes her lover. This relationship is important in Edna's journey because it represents a further rift from her previous life as a possession. More and more, Edna becomes her own person. Moreover, although he tries to make her his own possession as well, Edna refuses to let Alcee have the upper hand in their relationship. She refuses to let anyone control her life ever again. She even goes so far as to close up her house and rent a much smaller place to dwell in. Edna's actions come as a shock to many people, especially her husband, but she is really just trying to assert her individuality. However, no one understands what she is going through. In fact, many people, including her husband, blame her behavior on mental illness. Edna realizes that she cannot continue to live in this manner.

At the novel's conclusion, Edna decides to commit suicide. She swims into the ocean and drowns herself. It is fitting that she chooses the ocean, the place where she feels she has the most freedom, to end the journey. Edna decides that she would rather not live at all than to live a life where she cannot be her own person.

Student Essay B

It is easy to interpret the novel, Things Fall Apart, as a denouncement of white colonization, or simply as a detailed portrayal of African culture. But that would be all too banal; it has already been said and done by many authors. What makes this novel distinctive is the development and depiction of Okonkwo's journey through life and how his journey effects the novel's themes.

Given Okonkwo's rugged personality, he encounters many conflicts on his journey to self-awareness. Okonkwo clashes with his father, his wives, his children, his village, and perhaps every other character, but his greatest struggle is with himself. It seems as if Okonkwo's enemy is his father's flaws, but in reality, Okonkwo's hidden enemy is his fear of his father's reflection upon himself. Okonkwo spends his whole life on a journey away from the values of his father, so much up to the point where he ruins his life as well as the lives of those around him. His tragic flaw is his obsessive aversion to his father's laid back character. Okonkwo is so engulfed by his life's mission to become a rejection of his father's character, that he fails to see Unoka's positive traits such as tenderness, wisdom, and a passion for life, which Okonkwo lacks.

Even though Okonkwo is the protagonist in this book, he is also the antagonist; clearly, he is on a trip to disaster. He has not journeyed inside himself to understand what makes him act the way he does. He is extremely rash and explosive and does not think twice about throwing a fatal punch. He foolishly thinks that his aggressiveness is the only way for a man to act; it is this misconception that ultimately ruins him. Unfortunately for Okonkwo, he never realizes his flaw, and in the end, it is as if he cannot flee his father's reflection, for just like his father, he dies with shame and disgrace.

He had the ambition; he had the intelligence; he had the passion; but he had all of these for the wrong reasons. Perhaps <u>Things Fall Apart</u> portrays Okonkwo's lack of development rather than his development through time. From his early youth he forms this strong aversion to weakness and ineptitude, and this controls all his actions throughout his life. In actuality, the fact that he is totally ruled by this fear of ineptitude underscores how internally weak Okonkwo is. In the end, when he realizes that there is no possible way to triumph, that he cannot control people with his violent actions, and that he cannot control his fate, what does he do? He gives up and commits the most cowardly act of suicide.

10

15

20

25

30

Note: With specific reference to the 6-point rubric, we will use the following abbreviations to indicate into which column the comment would fall: **T = thesis, E = evidence, C = complexity, S = sophistication**.

Rating the Student Essays

Student Essay A

This is essay is rated within the high-range for several reasons:

- It presents a defensible thesis that addresses all aspects of the prompt with a clear indication of a line of reasoning. T
- It is highly detailed (lines 13–14, 25–26, 34–35). E
- It demonstrates strong topic adherence (lines 5–6, 14–15, 20, 36–37, 50–51). E/C
- There is strong integration of specifics to support the thesis (lines 16–17, 29–32, 42–43). E/C
- There is perceptive character analysis (lines 33–36, 49–51). C
- There is clear linear development of the essay (lines 9, 13–14, 33, 39, 48). C/S
- The essay is frequently repetitive and needs echo words. S
- There are some syntax and diction errors. S

This is an example of an essay that makes the jump into the high-range area because of its organization, its use of detail, and its insights. It's obvious that the writer thoroughly understands the work and presents various specifics to support the thesis. The diction and syntax are, at times, not as mature as would be found in more sophisticated essays.

Student Essay B

Student Essay B is a mid-range essay for the following reasons:

- It addresses the prompt with a defensible thesis and indicates a line of reasoning. T
- It identifies character and theme. T
- It refers to the character's journeys but does not really develop any of them (paragraphs 2–3). E/C
- There are many generalizations that need more specific support (lines 10–16, 25–27). E/C
- It does contain several perceptive insights that are unevenly developed. C/S
- The essay loses its clear connection to the prompt at times (paragraph 4). T/S
- The diction and syntax, although adequate, lack a maturity seen in higher-level papers. S

This mid-range essay demonstrates that the writer understands the prompt. This is obviously a first draft in need of further revision. As it stands, it relies too heavily on generalizations.

Final Comments

Warning! Although the free-response essay may appear to be the easiest and most accessible on the exam, it is fraught with danger. The worst danger is relying on vague references and general statements that are not supported by specific details or lines. In addition, you have to develop the organizational pattern of the essay and control its progression. All too often the essays read like capsule summaries of the plots.

Your lifesaver in this essay situation is preparation. We say this again because it bears repeating:

- Review full-length works you've read during the year.
- Choose a minimum of five works you've connected with.
- Classify the five works to ensure a broad spectrum of types, literary movements, and themes.
- Isolate several *pivotal* scenes, moments, or episodes from each of the five works and examine the suitability of those scenes for a variety of questions.
- Select quotations and details from these pivotal scenes.
- If necessary, reread only the pivotal scenes before you take the exam.

Rapid Review

- Remember the pitfalls of the free-response essay: vagueness and plot summary.
- Choose AP-level full-length novels or plays that you thoroughly recall and understand.
- Generally, use this year's material.
- Familiarize yourself with sample free-response prompts.
- Anticipate free-response prompts.

- Develop specific review materials for several full-length works.
- Practice applying your knowledge to a variety of prompts.
- Highlight the prompt to make certain you are addressing the requirements of the question.
- Do not waste time looking at the suggested works. Choose from your own memory bank.
- Plan the essay thoroughly before you begin writing.
- Briefly chart your response. Fill in with concrete details and quotes, if possible.
- Write an engaging opening paragraph that reflects the question's requirements.
- Stay on topic.
- *Avoid plot summary.*
- Include transitions and echo words.
- Review our models and rubrics for self-evaluation.
- Share your ideas with others.

Steps to Achieving Six Points for the AP English Literature Exam Essays

I. (Row A, 1 pt.) The thesis

    A. Clearly address the elements of the essay prompt.

    B. Structure your argument by drawing from the text.

    Note: An essential requirement of this section is a "defensible interpretation." This is a phrase used for the 1-point Thesis component for all three essays.

    C. Make sure your argument is clear and logical.

II. (Row B, 4 pts.) Using evidence and providing commentary

    A. Provide specific evidence to support ALL claims in your line of reasoning.

        1. For prose and poetry arguments, you will supply specific, direct evidence from the text.

        2. For the literary argument, you will draw from specific scenes, characterizations, and settings.

        3. Supporting ALL claims puts you in the best position to be receive either 3 or 4 points for this section. While incorporation of developed commentary and literary elements will also be essential to scoring 4 points, the support of ALL claims establishes a strong foundation to achieve a 4.

    B. Consistently explain HOW the evidence supports your line of reasoning (Commentary).

        1. Demonstrate control of your argument by not merely presenting evidence but by also integrating clear connections between that material and the underlying reasoning.

        2. Establish a line of reasoning and be consistent. This is essential in putting you in the best possible position to gain all 4 points in this section. Point deductions result from the absence of a line of reasoning and inconsistent explanations of evidence.

    C. Explain how multiple literary elements of techniques contribute to a work's meaning.

        1. This rubric element applies directly to the poetry and prose essays. However, your integration of literary elements into the literary argument could very well help you achieve the demonstration of sophistication (Row C) by presenting a complex literary argument.

        2. Using multiple literary elements of techniques puts you in the best position to achieve 4 points in this section. Using one literary element or technique puts you in the 3-point range while using no elements or techniques drops you to 2 points or fewer.

III. (Row C, 1 pt.) Sophistication of thought and/or development of a complex literary argument

    A. To earn this point, you must demonstrate sophistication of thought by doing any of the following:

        1. Identifying and exploring complexities or tensions within the poem, passage, or selected work.

        2. Illuminating [your] interpretation by situating it within a broader context.

        3. Accounting for alternative interpretations of the poem, passage, or selected work.

        4. Employing a style that is consistently vivid and persuasive.

    B. The preceding criteria are consistent for all three essays.

Note: The requirement of "doing any one of the following" allows you to approach sophistication based on the specific text you are considering. In other words, the ambiguity in a poem might lead you to examine alternative interpretations, while an historically situated prose passage might call for placing the interpretation into a broader context.

    C. Demonstrate consistent development when you are incorporating any one of the preceding four opportunities.

Note: The final note of this "sophistication" (Row C) stipulates: This point should be awarded only if the sophistication of thought or complex understanding is part of the student's argument, not merely a phrase or reference. Therefore, you need to integrate this sophistication fully into your essay.

STEP 4

Review the Knowledge You Need to Score High

Introduction to Review Section

Why a Review Section? Why Not Just Provide a Series of Practice Exams?

Since the AP Lit exam is the culminating, evaluative tool for your high school English career, it would be wonderful if it could be truly representative of all that you have learned. But, it is only a 3-hour test. Therefore, it must of necessity be general, and it must be wide ranging enough to provide equity and opportunity for every student who takes the exam. What the test makers assume about the students who take the AP Lit exam is a common background of terminology and skills.

The following two chapters are not a replacement for your serious in-class study and practice. Instead, they provide a resource for terminology and skills when you need clarification or explanation. We want the information to enhance your analytical skills and to present you with direction you might not have considered.

CHAPTER 8

Comprehensive Review—Prose

IN THIS CHAPTER

Summary: A brief review of terms and processes associated with prose analysis

Key Ideas
- ✪ Understand the components of a narrative
- ✪ Explore various types of novels
- ✪ Learn literary terminology related to analysis
- ✪ Understand various levels of interpretation

Introduction to Prose

Our desire to know ourselves and others, to explore the unknown mysteries of existence, to make sense out of chaos, and to connect with our own kind are all primary reasons for engaging in the process of literary analysis.

The benefits to self and society that result from this interaction include a sense of wonder at the glory of humanity's imagination, a sense of excitement at the prospect of intellectual challenge, and a sense of connection with the universe.

You have already engaged in these lofty experiences. This section will provide a brief review of terms and processes associated with the study of literature. Included are some suggested activities for you to try which will help you prepare for the exam.

What Is Prose?

As you know, prose is the written equivalent of the spoken language. It is written in words, phrases, sentences, paragraphs, and chapters. It utilizes punctuation, grammar, and vocabulary to develop its message. Prose is made up of fiction and nonfiction. For the AP Lit exam, you are required to be well read in the areas of:

- Fiction, which includes:
  - Novels
  - Short stories
- Nonfiction, which includes:
  - Essays
  - Autobiographies and biographies
  - Speeches
  - Journals
  - Articles

Note: A brief word about drama. Since this section is a review of prose designed to prepare you for the AP Lit exam, it is not feasible to address every literary distinction and definition. Therefore, we wish to stress the following:

- Specific terminology can be found in the Glossary at the back of this book.
- All the techniques examined for prose can be used to analyze drama as well.
- The overlapping nature of the analytical skills makes them suitable for prose, poetry, and drama.

Five Aspects of Every Narrative

There is a certain degree of universality regarding definitions of terms when analyzing literature. For clarity and understanding, you should be aware of the following terms.

Plot

The plot is a series of episodes in a *narrative* carried out by the *characters*. Here are the primary terms related to plot. You should be familiar with all of them. Obviously each work manipulates these concepts in its own unique way.

- *Initial incident:* the event that puts the story in gear.
- *Rising action:* the series of complications in the narrative.
- *The climax:* the highest point of interest, action, or tension. More subtly, it is a turning point in the protagonist's behavior or thoughts.
- *Falling action:* the series of events occurring after the climax.
- *Denouement:* the resolution that ties up the loose ends of the plot.

These form the skeleton of a discussion about plot. But there are also other elements that add to your comprehension.

- *Foreshadowing:* hints at future events.
- *Flashbacks:* cut or piece a prior scene into the present situation.
- *In medias res:* literally, to be in the middle. This is a device that places the reader immediately into the action.

- *Subplot:* secondary plot that explores ideas that are different from the main story line.
- *Parallel plot:* a secondary story line that mimics the main plot.

Setting

Traditionally, setting is the time and place of a work, but it is also so much more. Setting is not accidental. It is a vital part of the narrative, and it can serve many functions. You should consider setting in light of the following:

- *General:* to underscore the universality of the work ("The Open Boat").
- *Specific:* to create a definitive ambiance that impacts on the work's possibilities (*The Kite Runner*).
- *Character or foil:* in relation to the protagonist (*Brave New World*).
- *Limiting factor:* to allow the plot, character, and theme to develop (*Lord of the Flies*).
- To *reveal style* (*To the Lighthouse*).
- To *reveal character* (*Hedda Gabler*).
- To *reveal theme* (*Heart of Darkness*).

Your Turn

Choose a literary text you've read during the past two years and examine a particularly effective setting.

1. Jot down the major specifics of the setting.

2. Identify the function(s) of that setting.

Title: _____

Setting: _____

_____

Details/Specifics	**Function(s)**
_____	_____
_____	_____
_____	_____
_____	_____
_____	_____
_____	_____

Character

Character development can be both simple and complex. The author has a variety of methods from which to choose. Here's a mnemonic device that may help you analyze character: Use the word **STAR**.

- **S**—what the character *says*;
- **T**—what the character *thinks*;
- **A**—how the character *acts* and interacts; and
- **R**—how the character *reacts*.

Traditionally, characters carry out the plot, and it is around the characters that the plot revolves and the theme is developed. There can be many types of characters in a given work:

- *Protagonist:* the main character who is the central focus of the story. For example, Hamlet is the eponymous protagonist.
- *Antagonist:* the opposing force. It does not always have to be a person. For example, the sea or the fish in *The Old Man and the Sea.*
- *Major:* the character or characters who play a significant role in the work.
- *Minor:* the characters who are utilized for a specific purpose, such as moving the plot along or contrasting with a major character.
- *Dynamic:* refers to characters who undergo major changes, such as Jane Eyre.
- *Static:* generally refers to characters who remain the same throughout the story. For instance, Brutus in *Julius Caesar* always considers himself to be an "honorable man."
- *Stereotype:* a character who is used to represent a class or a group.
- *Foil:* a character who provides the opportunity for comparison and contrast. For example, in Shakespeare's *Julius Caesar*, Brutus and Cassius are foils for each other.

Character as Hero

Once again, you may encounter many variations on the concept of hero:

- Aristotelian tragic hero:
  - Of noble birth; larger than life
  - Basically good
  - Exhibits a fatal flaw
  - Makes error in judgment
  - Possesses hubris (excessive arrogance or pride) which causes the error in judgment
  - Brings about his own downfall
  - Has a moment of realization, an epiphany
  - Lives and suffers
  - Examples: Creon in *Antigone*, Oedipus in *Oedipus*, Jason in *Medea*

- Classical hero: a variation on the tragic hero:
  - Examples: Macbeth in *Macbeth*, Lear in *King Lear*, Hamlet in *Hamlet*

- Romantic hero:
  - Larger than life
  - Charismatic
  - Possesses an air of mystery
  - "Saves the day" or the heroine

"Be consistent and persistent in maintaining a literary journal. Students who do this have greater recall of information that they can incorporate into their literary essays."
—Charles V.
    AP teacher

- Embodies freedom, adventure, and idealism
- Often outside the law
- Examples: Robin Hood, James Bond

- Modern hero:
  - May be everyman
  - Has human weaknesses
  - Caught in the ironies of the human condition
  - Struggles for insight
  - Examples: Willy Loman in *Death of a Salesman*, Tom Joad in *Grapes of Wrath*

- Hemingway hero:
  - Brave
  - Endures
  - Maintains a sense of humor
  - Exhibits grace under pressure
  - Examples: Santiago in *The Old Man and the Sea*, Jake Barnes in *The Sun Also Rises*

- Antihero: Protagonist is notably lacking in heroic qualities:
  - Examples: Meursault in *The Stranger*, Randall McMurphy in *One Flew Over the Cuckoo's Nest*, Homer Simpson of cartoon fame

Theme

Theme is the main idea, the moving force, what it's all about, the "why" behind the "what," the universal concept or comment, the big picture, the major insight, the *raison d'être*. But theme is much more than a simple checklist. And, we cringe each time we hear, "What is the theme?" Remember, the enlightened, complex mind questions, ponders, responds. A literary work evolves and can be validly interpreted in so many ways that it would be a disservice to limit it to any single, exclusive theme.

Keeping an open mind, understand that the following is an overview of ways of assessing themes. All elements of a literary work point toward the development of the theme. Therefore, you will apply all that you have been learning and practicing in your search for a discernible, supportable theme.

Motif   In its most general sense, motif is the repetition of an image. It may be closely connected to symbol, or it may be a thematic restatement.

The following is a preparation process for discovering and analyzing the function of motif. You can try this with any work.

- Isolate some general motifs you've noticed in a work.
- Provide specific examples to illustrate the motif.
- Draw inferences from your observations.

These rough inferences may lead you to a better understanding of character and theme. The following is a sample worksheet that uses the above process to analyze motif in Tennessee Williams's *A Streetcar Named Desire*.

Motif in *A Streetcar Named Desire*

MOTIF	EXAMPLE	THEMATIC IMPLICATIONS
Color	White woods (Blanche DuBois) Blue piano Red pajamas—Stanley Allan Grey	Red/white/blue = American theme Blue/gray—Civil War? Rape of Old South? Destruction of a way of life
Music	The blues "Only a Paper Moon" (if you believed in me) Captive maiden	Loss/sorrow, betrayal Lack of reality—insanity Control/slavery

Animals	<u>Blanche</u>:
	   fine feathered/wildcat
	   trapped bird/tiger
	   moth to light
	<u>Stanley</u>:
	   rooster/pig
	   ape
	   goat/Capricorn
		
		ego/id
		duality
		self-destruction
		
		survival of the fittest
		Darwinism/primitivism
		Dionysian—rape

Here's another way to work through an idea about theme. Sometimes it's easier to input a theme and then prove it with support from a work. If you can defend an idea with several specifics, you probably have identified a theme. Let's look at Shakespeare's *Hamlet*:

Hamlet

POSSIBLE THEME	EVIDENCE
What is, is not	1. Hamlet is not mad, only north-northwest. 2. Polonius is not Claudius in Gertrude's chamber. 3. Ophelia is not disinterested in Hamlet's overtures. 4. Rosencrantz and Guildenstern are not Hamlet's "friends."
Vengeance	1. Old Hamlet's charge to Hamlet to redress his murder. 2. Laertes's vow to avenge his father's death. 3. Fortinbras's victory to avenge his father.

Obviously, we have provided the organization in our samples, but these two techniques are solid, reliable processes. They will work on the exam, too, especially as you interrelate ideas for your essays or identify points that may be the topic of multiple-choice questions.

Keep a section in your notes where you enter important motifs, images, and so on and their implications from works you study. These concrete details will be invaluable when you write the free-response essay. Keep in mind that motif, imagery, symbol, and theme build on one another and are interrelated.

Point of View

Point of view is the method the author utilizes to tell the story. It is the vantage point from which the narrative is told. You've had practice with this in both reading and writing.

- *First person*: The narrator is the story's protagonist. (I went to the store.)
- *Third-person objective*: The narrator is an onlooker reporting the story. (She went to the store.)
- *Third-person omniscient*: The narrator reports the story and provides information unknown to the character(s). (She went to the store unaware that in three minutes she would meet her long-lost mother selling apples on the corner.)
- *Stream of consciousness*: This is a narrative technique that places the reader in the mind and thought processes of the narrator, no matter how random and spontaneous that may be (e.g., James Joyce's *Ulysses*).
- *Chorus*: Ancient Greek plays employed a chorus as a narrative device. The chorus, as needed, could be a character, an assembly, the playwright's voice, the audience, an omniscient forecaster. This function can be seen in modern works as well.
- *Stage manager*: This technique utilizes a character who comments omnisciently (e.g., *Our Town*, *The Glass Menagerie*).
- *Interior monologue*: This technique reflects the inner thoughts of the character.

    Note: In modern literature, authors often use multiple forms of narration. For example, in *As I Lay Dying* by William Faulkner, every chapter has a different narrator.

Types of Novels

There are many types of novels you will encounter during your study of English literature. Some novels exhibit several qualities. A few of the most common genres are:

- *Epistolary*: These novels utilize the convention of letter writing and are among the earliest novel forms (e.g., *Pamela*, *Dracula*, *The Color Purple*).
- *Picaresque*: This early, episodic novel form concentrates on the misadventures of a young rogue (e.g., *Huckleberry Finn*, *Don Quixote*, *Tom Jones*, *Candide*).
- *Autobiographical*: This readily identifiable type is always told in the first person and allows the reader to directly interact with the protagonist (e.g., *David Copperfield*, *Catcher in the Rye*).
- *Gothic*: This type of novel is concerned with the macabre, supernatural, and exotic (e.g., *Frankenstein*, *Beloved*, *Dr. Jekyll and Mr. Hyde*).
- *Historical*: This form is grounded in a real context and relies heavily on setting and factual detail (e.g., *A Tale of Two Cities*, *War and Peace*).
- *Romantic*: This novel form is idealistic, imaginative, and adventuresome. The romantic hero is the cornerstone of the novel, which often includes exotic locales (e.g., *Wuthering Heights*, *Madame Bovary*).
- *Allegorical*: This type of novel is representative and symbolic. It operates on at least two levels. Its specifics correspond to another concept (e.g., *Animal Farm*, *Handmaid's Tale*, *Lord of the Flies*).

Consider this. *Jane Eyre* has elements of all these types, as do many other novels. List and loosely categorize some of the major novels you've read.

_____

_____

_____

_____

_____

Literary Terminology

Literary analysis assumes the working knowledge of a common vocabulary.

The Kaleidoscope of Literary Meaning

Literary meaning is developed and revealed through various devices and techniques. What follows is a brief listing of those terms and devices most often used in prose, poetry, and drama.

- *Allusion*: An allusion is a reference to another work, concept, or situation which generally enhances the meaning of the work that is citing it. There are many types of allusions, and they may be implicit or explicit, highly limited or broadly developed. Often, modern readers may miss the context of a particular reference because they have a limited frame of reference. A few common categories of allusion follow:

  - *Mythological allusions*: These often cite specific characters. Common allusions might refer to the beauty of Aphrodite or the power of Zeus. "She followed like Niobe, all tears" (*Hamlet*). Sometimes the entire work may refer to a mythological event. The play *Desire Under the Elms* is a sustained allusion to the Phaedra legend, as well as the Oedipal myth.

  - *Biblical allusions*: These references may deal with circumstances as familiar as "the mark of Cain," "the fall from paradise," "the tribulations of Job," or "destruction by flood or fire." A character may have the "strength of Samson" or the "loyalty of Ruth."

  - *Historical allusions*: These kinds of allusions might refer to major historical events, such as Napoleon meeting his Waterloo or Nixon dealing with Watergate.

  - *Literary allusions*: Often works will refer to other well-known pieces. For example, *West Side Story* expects you to think of *Romeo and Juliet*. To describe a character as "quixotic" refers to Cervantes's great novel *Don Quixote*.

  - *Political allusions*: These references would be sustained in works like *Gulliver's Travels* or *Alice in Wonderland*. They might also be used briefly. If a character were called the next Julius Caesar, we might sense that he would be betrayed in some manner. *The Crucible* is a historical allusion to the Salem witch trials and is also a statement about McCarthyism in the 1950s.

  - *Contemporary allusions*: These are often lost when the current context is no longer in the public eye. For example, "valley girls" or "Beavis and Butthead" may not remain in vogue, and, therefore, references to them would lose their effectiveness.

- *Ambiguity*: This is the seemingly incongruous and contradictory interpretations of meaning in a work. James Joyce and William Faulkner utilize ambiguity often in their writing.

- *Allegory*: A work that operates on another level. The characters and events may be interpreted for both literal and symbolic meaning. For example, *Of Mice and Men* by Steinbeck is an indictment of the exploitation of the masses and a call to unionism as well as a story of doomed friendship. Other allegorical works include *The Old Man and the Sea* by Hemingway, *Animal Farm* by Orwell, *Candide* by Voltaire, and *Pilgrim's Progress* by John Bunyan.
- *Parable*: A parable is an allegorical story that is intended to teach. It generally provides a moral lesson or illustrates a guiding principle. "The Nun's Priest's Tale" in *The Canterbury Tales* by Chaucer is a parable about vanity and pride.
- *Symbol*: This is an image that also represents something else. Some symbols appear to be extremely specific. In Hawthorne's *The Scarlet Letter* the scarlet letter is a symbol of Hester's impropriety. It can also represent Hester's pride, talent, responsibility, and shame. The reader should always be open to the broadest interpretation of the concept of symbol, whether about character, setting, situation, detail, or whatever. Another example of symbol is the splitting of the chestnut tree in *Jane Eyre*. Here Brontë symbolizes the breach in the relationship between Jane and Rochester. The white hat in *The Secret Sharer* by Conrad is a symbol of man's compassion and pity for his own kind.
- *Connotation*: This is the implication that is suggested by a word or phrase rather than the word or phrase's actual, literal meaning. For example, the use of "antique land" instead of "ancient land" brings a richer connotation to Shelley's "Ozymandias." The reader must be especially open to the varied levels of meaning in poetry.
- *Denotation*: The literal meaning of a word or phrase. If a reader is attempting to present a valid interpretation of a literary work, he or she must pay attention to both the denotation and the connotation of the language.
- *Tone*: Tone is difficult to define but is relatively easy to assess. It is a subtle feeling that the author creates through diction. The following is a short list of words often used to describe tone. Notice that they are adjectives.

bitter	objective	idyllic
sardonic	naive	compassionate
sarcastic	joyous	reverent
ironic	spiritual	lugubrious
mocking	wistful	elegiac
scornful	nostalgic	gothic
satiric	humorous	macabre
vituperative	mock-serious	reflective
scathing	pedantic	maudlin
confidential	didactic	sentimental
factual	inspiring	patriotic
informal	remorseful	jingoistic
facetious	disdainful	detached
critical	laudatory	

- *Transition*: Do not be fooled into thinking that "transition" is an unimportant term. An author will give you a road map through his or her story's journey, and one of the best indicators of direction is the transition word or phrase. Transitions help to move the reader smoothly from one part of the text to another. Below is a list of the most effective commonly used transitions:

and	also	as a result	after
but	besides	for example	although
for	consequently	in addition	because
nor	furthermore	in the same way	once
or	however	on the contrary	since
so	likewise	on the other hand	unless
yet	moreover	otherwise	until
	nonetheless	unlike the former	while
	similarly		
	still		
	therefore		

Prose Analysis

A word about this section: There are many processes that will help you to understand prose, poetry, and drama.

These approaches may not all be suitable for every work, but they certainly are worth considering as methods for responding to subtleties that are in the work.

Name Analysis

Consider your name. Did your folks have a specific reason for choosing it? Does it have a family significance or a special cultural meaning? What would you choose for your name and why? Remember, names and identity are closely linked.

Authors often choose names that bring another dimension to a character or place. A good reader is sensitive to the implications of names. Here are a few interesting names and observations about each:

- Oedipus—swollen foot, seeker of truth
- Billy Budd—simple, melodic, young growth, ready to bloom
- Jane Eyre—Janus/beginning, air, err, heir, ere, eerie, ire
- Helen Burns—fever, fervor, mythological inspiration
- Mr. Mason—the Masons are a secret fraternity; he holds the secret
- Stella—star, light
- Kurtz—short, curt
- Willy Loman—low man

Your Turn

Create your own listing of literary names and their interpretations and implications. (This could also include place names, etc.)

Literary Work	Name	Interpretations

It's an Open-and-Closed Case

The first thing that catches your attention should be the title. By all means, consider it carefully. *David Copperfield* lets you know it will be a novel about character. *As I Lay Dying* involves plot and theme. *One Flew Over the Cuckoo's Nest* involves you immediately in symbol, character, and theme.

Authors place special emphasis on the first and last impressions they make on a reader. The opening and closing lines of chapters or scenes are, therefore, usually very significant and should be closely examined. (This is much like an establishing shot in a movie that sets up the audience for future developments.)

Here's the opening line from Chapter 1 of *Jane Eyre*:

> *There was no possibility of taking a walk that day.*

Here are some implications of this one line: no independence, locked in, no sense of curiosity, outside force preventing a journey, not ready to leave. Obviously, the character is not ready to experience the outside world or to embark on her journey.

Contrast that with the last line of Chapter 1:

> *Four hands were laid upon me and I was borne upstairs.*

This line introduces a spiritual level to the novel. It also implies that a new Jane will emerge, and indeed she does.

Take a look at one of the last lines of the novel:

> *We wended our way into the wood.*

This lovely, alliterative line completes the journey. Jane and Edward have come full circle as they stroll their way together.

In a Shakespearean play, often a couplet at the end of a scene or act will neatly summarize or foreshadow events. In *Julius Caesar*, for example:

> *And after this, let Caesar seat him sure*
> *For we will shake him, or worse days endure (Julius Caesar)*

Keep a written record of opening and closing lines of complete literary works, chapters, scenes, acts. Not only will this develop your interpretative skills, but it will also provide you with a list of quotations for later use in essays.

Levels of Interpretation

Complex works of literature afford many avenues of interpretation. After you read a work, consider the following areas of exploration. We use Ibsen's *Hedda Gabler* as a model.

- *Literal level*: A young woman is frustrated in her life and eventually commits suicide.
- *Social level*: Ibsen explores the role of women in society and presents the despair connected with a male-dominated existence.
- *Psychological level*: The play traces a descent into madness and the motivations for aberrant human behavior.
- *Religious level*: The loss of a soul to temptation, the encounter with the devil, and the inspiration of godliness are all in the play.
- *Sexual level*: Gender issues, the Electra complex, phallic symbols, abortion, and homosexuality are all developed and explored through numerous love triangles.
- *Political level*: The play could be read as a treatise on socialism. It denigrates capitalism and pays homage to the ideas of Marx's *Communist Manifesto*.

Obviously, you need to supply the evidence from the works to develop your interpretations in a concrete manner.

Note: A word about **subtext**:

Subtext refers to the implied meaning of a work or section of a work. It involves reading between the lines to discover subtle attitudes, comments, and observations within the piece. The exploration of subtext utilizes all of the interpretative skills you've been developing in your AP course.

Practice looking beyond the literal presentation of the plays, novels, and short stories you read. The following are richly suitable for such study:

Heart of Darkness	Joseph Conrad
Dubliners	James Joyce
The Grapes of Wrath	John Steinbeck
Les Miserables	Victor Hugo
The Kite Runner	Khaled Hosseini
Beloved	Toni Morrison

Final Comments

One of the most rewarding forms of preparation you can do involves developing a sensitivity to the words of a piece of literature.

Get a journal or set aside a section of your notebook for recording lines you respond to for their beauty, appeal, meaning, or relevance. For each work you read:

- Enter the lines.
- Identify the speaker and situation.

- Interpret, connect, comment, or reflect on your choice.
- Free-associate as well as relate the quotation to the original text.
- Make connections to other works you read.
- Project and expand on the lines.

For each full-length work, record at least ten references. Write these quotations out and include the page numbers so you can easily find them if you need to. Try to take them from throughout the work. Here is what is going to happen. Soon, you will automatically identify and respond to significant lines and passages. It will become second nature for you to identify lines of import and meaning in a work as you read. You will also begin to remember lines from a work and to connect them to important details, episodes, and themes. You will be able to understand and analyze a character in light of his or her own language. In other words, you will be interpreting literature based on text.

Rapid Review

- Every narrative is composed of plot, setting, character, theme, and point of view.
- Motifs develop characters and themes.
- Themes require specific illustrations to support them.
- There are many types of characters and heroes.
- There are many forms of narration.
- Novels may exhibit many characteristics.
- Meaning may be revealed via multiple approaches.
- Parables and allegories operate on symbolic levels. Connotations of words reveal the subtext of a work.
- Tone is a description of the attitude found in a piece of literature.
- Transitions aid movement and unity in a written work.
- Titles and names are important areas for analysis.
- First and last lines often carry great meaning in a work and demand careful attention.
- Works may be interpreted literally, socially, psychologically, sexually, politically, and so on.
- Quotations from works are an accurate way of understanding meaning and characterization. They also provide support for your interpretations.

Comprehensive Review—Poetry

IN THIS CHAPTER

Summary: Overview, including definitions, examples, and practice with poetic forms

Key Ideas

✪ Learn the differences between poetry and prose
✪ Understand the structure of poetry
✪ Explore various types of poetry
✪ Practice interpreting selected poems
✪ Compare and contrast given poems

Introduction to Poetry

Poetry—the very word inspires fear and trembling, and well it should because it deals with the intensity of human emotion and the experiences of life itself. But there is no reason to fear that which elevates, elucidates, edifies, and inspires. Poetry is a gift of language, like speech and song, and with familiarity comes pleasure and knowledge and comfort.

However, it may still be intimidating to read poetry. After all, we've been speaking and reading prose our entire lives. This review assumes that by the time you reach an AP-level literature course, you have some experience and facility with poetry. We provide you with definitions, examples, and practice with interpretation. Hopefully, you will provide the interest, diligence, and critical thinking necessary for a joyful and meaningful experience.

Remember our philosophy of firsts? First, we believe that you should read as much poetry as possible. Early in the year, pick up an anthology of poetry and read, read, read. Open to any page and read for pleasure and interest. Don't try to "study" the poems; just respond to them on an emotional level. Consider the following:

- Identify subjects that move you or engage you.
- Are there certain themes you respond to? Are there certain poets you like? List them and read more poetry by them.
- Are there certain types or styles of poems you enjoy? What do they seem to have in common?
- Are there images or lines you love? Keep a record of some of your favorites.

Make this a time to develop a personal taste for poetry. Use this random approach to experience a broad range of form and content. You should find that you are more comfortable with poetry simply because you have been discovering it at your own pace.

When you are comfortable and have honestly tried reading it for pleasure, it is time to approach it on a more analytical level.

The Structure of Poetry

What Makes Poetry Different from Prose?

How do you know when you're working with poetry and not prose? Simple. Just look at it. It's shorter; it's condensed; it's written in a different physical form. The following might help you to visualize the basic differences:

Prose	Poetry
Words	Syllables
Phrases	Feet
Sentences	Lines
Paragraphs	Stanzas
Chapters	Cantos

It should not be news to you when we say that poetry sounds different from prose. It is more musical, and it often relies on sound to convey meaning. In addition, it can employ meter, which provides rhythm. Did you know that poetry is from the ancient oral tradition of storytelling and song? Rhyme and meter made it easier for the bards to remember the story line. Try to imagine Homer in a dimly lit hall chanting the story of Odysseus.

As with prose, poetry also has its own jargon. Some of this lingo is specifically related to form and meter. The analysis of a poem's form and meter is termed **scansion**.

The Foot

The **foot** is the basic building block of poetry. It is composed of a pattern of syllables. These patterns create the meter of a poem. **Meter** is a pattern of beats or accents. We figure out this pattern by counting the stressed and unstressed syllables in a line. Unstressed syllables are indicated with a ˘, and stressed syllables are indicated with a ´.

There are five common patterns that are used repeatedly in English poetry. They are:

- The *iamb* ˘ ´ (tŏ dáy) (bĕ cáuse)
- The *trochee* ´ ˘ (háp p̆y) (líght l̆y)
- The *anapest* ˘ ˘ ´ (ŏb vĭ oús) (rĕ gŭ lár)
- The *dactyl* ´ ˘ ˘ (cĭg ă reʹte) (íń tĕr rŭpt)
- The *spondee* ´ ´ (dówn tówn) (slíp shód)

The Line

Unlike the prose sentence, which is determined by subject, verb, and punctuation, the poetic line is measured by the number of feet it contains.

- 1 foot   monometer
- 2 feet   dimeter
- 3 feet   trimeter
- 4 feet   tetrameter
- 5 feet   pentameter
- 6 feet   hexameter
- 7 feet   heptameter
- 8 feet   octameter
- 9 feet   nonometer

Your Turn

Now answer the following. How many stressed syllables are in a line of:

Iambic pentameter   _____
Dactylic trimeter   _____
Anapestic dimeter   _____
Spondaic monometer   _____
Trochaic tetrameter   _____

Note: Answers can be found at the end of the definition of "meter" in the Glossary of terms.

The Stanza

You should now understand that syllables form feet, feet form lines, and lines form stanzas. Stanzas also have names:

- 1 line   a line
- 2 lines   couplet
- 3 lines   tercet
- 4 lines   quatrain
- 5 lines   cinquain
- 6 lines   sestet
- 7 lines   septet
- 8 lines   octave

Your Turn

What is the total number that results from adding up all of the metric references in the following, make-believe poem?

- The poem is composed of 3 quatrains, 2 couplets, and 1 sestet.
- Each quatrain is written in iambic tetrameter.
- The couplets are dactylic dimeter.
- The sestet is trochaic trimeter.

The total number is _____.

Note: You can find the answer at the end of the definition of "rhythm" in the Glossary of terms.

You will never have to be this technical on the AP exam. However, you will probably find a question on meter, and technical terms may be included in the answer choices to the multiple-choice questions. In addition, sometimes in the poetry essay you may find an opportunity to use your knowledge of scansion, or your analysis of the rhyme and meter of the poem, to develop your essay. This can be very effective if it is linked to interpretation.

Rhyme

One of the first processes you should become familiar with concerns the identification of a poem's rhyme scheme. This is easily accomplished by assigning consecutive letters of the alphabet to each new sound at the end of a line of poetry. Traditionally, rhyme scheme is indicated with italicized, lowercase letters placed to the right of each line of the poem.

- *a* for the first
- *b* for the second
- *c* for the third
- *d, e*, and so forth

Try this with the opening stanza from "Peace" by George Herbert.

> *Sweet Peace, where dost thou dwell? I humbly crave,*
>   *Let me once know.*
> *I sought thee in a secret cave,*
>   *And asked if Peace were there.*
> *A hollow wind did seem to answer, "No,*
>   *Go seek elsewhere."*

You may restart the scheme with each new stanza or continue throughout the poem. Remember, the purpose is to identify and establish a pattern and to consider if the pattern helps to develop sound and/or meaning. Here's what the rhyme scheme looks like for the above selection: *a b a c b c*.

When you analyze the pattern of the complete poem, you can conclude that there is a very regular structure to this poem which is consistent throughout. Perhaps the content will also reflect a regular development. Certainly the rhyme enhances the sound of the poem and helps it flow. From now on we will refer to rhyme scheme when we encounter a new poem.

The rhymes we have illustrated are called **end rhymes** and are the most common. **Masculine rhyme** is the most frequently used end rhyme. It occurs when the last stressed syllable of the rhyming words matches exactly. ("The play's the thing/Wherein I'll catch the conscience of the king.") However, there are **internal rhymes** as well. These rhymes occur within the line and add to the music of the poem. An example of this is *dreary*, in Poe's "The Raven" ("Once upon a midnight dreary, while I pondered, weak and weary"). **Feminine rhyme** involves two consecutive syllables of the rhyming words, with the first syllable stressed. ("The horses were prancing / as the clowns were dancing.")

Types of Poetry

Because of its personal nature, poetry has evolved into many different forms, each with its own unique purpose and components. What follows is an examination of the most often encountered forms.

Most poetry falls into one of two major categories. ***Narrative poetry*** tells a story. ***Lyric poetry*** presents a personal impression.

The Ballad

The ***ballad*** is one of the earliest poetic forms. It is a narrative that was originally spoken or sung and has often changed over time. It usually:

- Is simple.
- Employs dialogue, repetition, minor characterization.
- Is written in quatrains.
- Has a basic rhyme scheme, primarily *a b c b*.
- Has a refrain which adds to its songlike quality.
- Is composed of two lines of iambic tetrameter which alternate with two lines of iambic trimeter.

The subject matter of ballads varies considerably. Frequently, ballads deal with the events in the life of a folk hero, like Robin Hood. Sometimes they retell historical events. The supernatural, disasters, good and evil, love and loss are all topics found in traditional ballads.

The following is a typical folk ballad. Read this poem out loud. Listen to the music as you read. Get involved in the story. Imagine the scene. Try to capture the dialect or sound of the Scottish burr.

Bonny Barbara Allan
by Anonymous

It was in and about the Martinmas* time,
When the green leaves were falling,
That Sir John Graeme, in the West Country,
Fell in love with Barbara Allan.

He sent his man down through the town,   5
To the place where she was dwelling:
"O haste and come to my master dear,
Gin ye be Barbara Allan."

Slowly, slowly rose she up,
To the place where he was lying,   10
And when she drew the curtain by:
"Young man I think you're dying."

"O it's I'm sick, and very, very sick,
And 'tis a' for Barbara Allan."
O the better for me ye's never be,   15
Though your heart's blood were a-spilling.

"O dinna ye mind, young man," said she,
"When ye was in the tavern a drinking,

---

* St. Martin's Day, commemorates the funeral of St. Martin, also known as old Halloween Eve, the end of harvest.

That ye made the healths gae round and round,
And slighted Barbara Allan?"   20

He turned his face unto the wall,
And death was with him dealing:
"Adieu, adieu, my dear friends all,
And be kind to Barbara Allan."

And slowly, slowly raise she up,   25
And slowly, slowly left him,
And sighing said, she could not stay,
Since death of life had reft him.

She had not gane a mile or twa,
When she heard the dead-bell ringing,   30
And every jow* that the dead bell geid,
It cried, "Woe to Barbara Allan."

"O mother, mother, make my bed!
O make it saft and narrow!
Since my love died for me to-day,   35
I'll die for him to-morrow."

_____
* Tolling of a bell.

After you've read the ballad, consider the following:

1. Check the rhyme scheme and stanza form. You should notice it is written in quatrains. The rhyme scheme is a little tricky here; it depends on pronunciation and is what is called a **_forced rhyme_**. If you soften the "g" sound in the word "falling," it more closely rhymes with "Allan." Try this throughout the ballad, recognizing that the spoken word can be altered and stretched to fit the intention of rhyme. This falls under the category of "poetic license."

2. Follow the plot of the narrative. Poor Barbara Allan, poor Sir John. They are a classic example of thwarted young lovers, a literary pattern as old as Antigone and Haemon or Romeo and Juliet. Love, unrequited love, and dying for love are all universal themes in literature.

3. Observe the use of repetition and how it unifies the poem by sound and structure. "Barbara Allan/Hooly, hooly/Adieu, adieu/Slowly, slowly/Mother, mother."

4. Notice that dialogue is incorporated into the poem for characterization and plot development.

Don't be too inflexible when checking rhyme or meter. Remember, never sacrifice meaning for form. You're smart; you can make intellectual leaps.

Here are some wonderfully wicked and enjoyable ballads to read:

"Sir Patrick Spens"—the tragic end of a loyal sailor
"The Twa Corbies"—the irony of life and nature
"Edward"—a wicked, wicked, bloody tale

"Robin Hood"—still a great, grand adventure
"Lord Randall"—sex, lies, and death in ancient England
"Get Up and Bar the Door"—a humorous battle of the sexes
"La Belle Dame Sans Merci"—John Keats's fabulous tale of a demon lover
"Ballad of Birmingham"—Dudley Randall's recounting of the bombing of a church in Birmingham, Alabama, in 1963

Have you read ballads? Traditional or modern? List them here. Jot down a few details or lines to remind you of important points. If you're musical, try singing one out loud.

_____

_____

_____

_____

_____

The Lyric

Lyric poetry is highly personal and emotional. It can be as simple as a sensory impression or as elevated as an ode or elegy. Subjective and melodious, it is often reflective in tone.

The following is an example of a lyric:

A Red, Red Rose
by Robert Burns

O my luve's like a red, red rose,
That's newly sprung in June;
O my luve's like the melodie
That's sweetly played in tune.

As fair art thou, my bonnie lass,   5
So deep in luve am I;
And I will luve thee still, my dear,
Till a' the seas gang dry.

Till a' the seas gang dry, my dear,
And the rocks melt wi' the sun: 10
O I will luve thee still, my dear,
While the sands o' life shall run.

And fare the weel, my only luve,
And fare the weel awhile!
And I will come again, my luve,   15
Though it were ten thousand mile.

Now answer the following questions:

1. The stanza form is _____

2. The rhyme scheme is _____

3. The meter of line 6 is _____

4. The first stanza depends on similes. Underline them. _____

5. Cite assonance in stanza one. _____

6. Line 8 is an example of _____

7. Highlight alliteration in the poem. _____

8. Did you recognize iambic trimeter? How about hyperbole? _____

The following are wonderful lyric poems. Read a few.

> Edna St. Vincent Millay—"Childhood Is the Kingdom Where Nobody Dies"
> Emily Dickinson—"Wild Nights, Wild Nights"
> Dylan Thomas—"Fern Hill"
> Matthew Arnold—"Dover Beach"
> Andrew Marvell—"To His Coy Mistress"
> Carol Ann Duffy—"Syntax"
> Elizabeth Alexander—"Praise for the Day"
> Louise Glück—"Vita Nova"

The Ode

The *ode* is a formal lyric poem that addresses subjects of elevated stature. One of the most beautiful odes in English literature is by Percy Bysshe Shelley.

Ode to the West Wind

O wild West Wind, thou breath of Autumn's being,
Thou, from whose unseen presence the leaves dead
Are driven, like ghosts from an enchanter fleeing,

Yellow, and black, and pale, and hectic red,   5
Pestilence-stricken multitudes: O thou,
Who chariotest to their dark wintry bed

The wingéd seeds, where they lie cold and low,
Each like a corpse within the grave, until
Thine azure sister of the Spring shall blow

Her clarion* o'er the dreaming earth, and fill   10
(Driving sweet buds like flocks to feed in air)
With living hues and odors plain and hill:

Wild Spirit, which art moving everywhere;
Destroyer and preserver; hear, oh, hear!

2

Thou on whose stream, mid the steep sky's commotion,   15
Loose clouds like earth's decaying leaves are shed,
Shook from the tangled boughs of Heaven and Ocean,

Angels of rain and lightning: there are spread
On the blue surface of thine aery surge,
Like the bright hair uplifted from the head   20

*Melodious trumpet call

Of some fierce Maenad,* even from the dim verge
Of the horizon to the zenith's height,
The locks of the approaching storm. Thou dirge

Of the dying year, to which this closing night
Will be the dome of a vast sepulcher,   25
Vaulted with all thy congregated might

Of vapors, from whose solid atmosphere
Black rain, and fire, and hail will burst: oh, hear!

3

Thou who didst waken from his summer dreams
The blue Mediterranean, where he lay,   30
Lulled by the coil of his crystalline streams

Beside a pumice isle in Baiae's† bay,
And saw in sleep old palaces and towers
Quivering within the wave's intenser day,

All overgrown with azure moss and flowers   35
So sweet, the sense faints picturing them! Thou
For whose path the Atlantic's level powers

Cleave themselves into chasms, while far below
The sea-blooms and the oozy woods which wear
The sapless foliage of the ocean, know   40

Thy voice, and suddenly grow gray with fear,
And tremble and despoil themselves: oh, hear!

4

If I were a dead leaf thou mightest bear;
If I were a swift cloud to fly with thee;
A wave to pant beneath thy power, and share   45

The impulse of thy strength, only less free
Than thou, O uncontrollable! If even
I were as in my boyhood, and could be

The comrade of thy wanderings over Heaven,
As then, when to outstrip thy skiey speed   50
Scarce seem a vision; I would ne'er have striven

As thus with thee in prayer in my sore need.
Oh, lift me as a wave, a leave, a cloud!
I fall upon the thorns of life! I bleed!

———————

*Frenzied dancer
†A village near Naples, Italy

A heavy weight of hours has chained and bowed   55
One too like thee: tameless, and swift, and proud.

5

Make me thy lyre,* even as the forest is:
What if my leaves are falling like its own!
The tumult of thy mighty harmonies

Will take from both a deep, autumnal tone,   60
Sweet though in sadness. Be thou, Spirit fierce,
My spirit! Be thou me, impetuous one!

Drive my dead thoughts over the universe
Like withered leaves to quicken a new birth!
And, by the incantation of this verse,   65

Scatter, as from an unextinguished hearth
Ashes and sparks, my words among mankind!
Be through my lips to unawakened earth

The trumpet of a prophecy! O Wind,   70
If Winter comes, can Spring be far behind?

---

*Small, harplike instrument

    As always, read the poem carefully. (Find a private place and read it aloud. You'll be carried away by the beauty of the sounds and imagery.) Now answer the following questions.

1. Look at the configuration of the poem. It is divided into five sections. What function might each section serve? _____

2. Count the lines in each section. How many? _____ Name the two stanza forms you encountered. _____

3. Check the rhyme scheme. Did you come up with *a b a b c b c d c d e d e e*? The first four tercets are written in a form called *terza rima*. Notice how this rhyme scheme interweaves the stanzas and creates unity throughout the poem. Did it cross your mind that each section might be a variation on the sonnet form? _____

4. Check the meter. You should notice that it is very irregular. (Freedom of form was a tenet of the Romantic Movement.)

5. Stanza one: Did you catch the *apostrophe*? The direct address to the wind places us in the poem's situation and provides the subject of the ode. Highlight the *alliteration* and trace the similes in line 3. _____

6. Stanza two: What are the "pestilence-stricken multitudes"? In addition to leaves, could they be the races of man? _____

7. Stanza three: See how the enjambment pulls you into this line. Find the simile. _____ Alliteration can be seen in "azure," "sister," "Spring," "shall."

8. Stanza four: What images are presented? _____ Locate the simile. _____ Find the contrast between life and death. _____ Highlight the personification.

9. Identify the essential paradox of the poem and life itself in the couplet.

We are not going to take you through the poem line by line. You may isolate those lines that speak to you. Here are a few of our favorites that are worth a second look:

- Lines 29–31
- Lines 35–42 for assonance
- Lines 53–54
- Lines 55–56
- Lines 57–70

You should be able to follow the development of ideas through the five sections. Were you aware of:

- The land imagery in section 1?
- The air imagery in section 2?
- The water imagery in section 3?
- The comparison of the poet to the wind in section 4?
- The appeal for the spirit of the wind to be the poet's spirit in section 5?

After you have read the poem, followed the organization, recognized the devices and images, you still have to interpret what you've read.

This ode has many possibilities. One interpretation linked it with the French Revolution and Shelley's understanding of the destructive regeneration associated with it. Another valid reading focuses on Shelley's loss of faith in the Romantic Movement. He asks for inspiration to breathe life into his work again. Try to propose other interpretations for this "Ode to the West Wind."

Here is a brief list of some odes you may want to consider:

"Ode on Intimations of Immortality"—William Wordsworth
"Ode to My Socks"—Pablo Neruda
"Homage to My Hips"—Lucille Clifton
"Ode on a Grecian Urn"—John Keats
"Ode to Silence"—Edna St. Vincent Millay
"Ode to Dirt"—Sharon Olds

The Elegy

The *elegy* is a formal lyric poem written in honor of one who has died. *Elegiac* is the adjective that describes a work lamenting any serious loss.

One of the most famous elegies is by Percy Bysshe Shelley. It was written to mourn the loss of John Keats. Here is the first stanza of "Adonais." It contains all the elements of an elegy.

Adonais*

I weep for Adonais—he is dead!
O, weep for Adonais! Though our tears
Thaw not the frost which binds so dear a head!
And thou, sad Hour, selected from all years
To mourn our loss, rouse thy obscure compeers,   5
And teach them thine own sorrow, say: "With me
Died Adonais; till the Future dares
Forget the Past, his fate and fame shall be
An echo and a light unto eternity!"

---

* An elegy on the death of John Keats, author of "Endymion," "Hyperion," etc.

Read this stanza several times. Try it aloud. Get carried away by the emotion. Respond to the imagery. Listen to the sounds; let the meter and rhyme guide you through. Consider the following:

1. Adonais, Shelley's name for Keats, is derived from Adonis. This is a mythological allusion to associate Keats with love and beauty. (The meter will tell you how to pronounce Adonais.)

2. Check the rhyme scheme. Did you come up with *a b a b b c b c c*? See how the last two lines are rhymed to set this idea apart.

3. Line 1 contains a major *caesura* in the form of a dash. This forces the reader to pause and consider the depth of emotion and the finality of the event. The words that follow are also set off by the caesura and emphasized by the exclamation point. Notice that the meter is not interrupted by the caesura. (˘ ´ ˘ ´ ˘ ´ ˘ ´ ˘ ´ is perfect iambic pentameter.) This line is a complete thought which is concluded by punctuation and is an example of an *end-stopped line*.

4. Line 2 utilizes repetition to intensify the sense of loss. Here the caesura is an exclamation point. Notice that the last three words of the line fulfill the meter of iambic pentameter but do not express a complete thought as did line 1. The thought continues into line 3. This is an example of *enjambment*.

5. Lines 2 and 3 contain *alliteration* ("Though," "tears," "Thaw," "the") and *consonance* ("not," "frost," continuing into line 4 with "thou").

6. Line 3 contains *imagery* and *metaphor*. What does the frost represent? _____
   _____

7. Line 4 contains an *apostrophe*, which is a direct address to the sad Hour, which is personified. To what event does the "sad Hour" refer? _____
   _____

8. Lines 4, 5, and 6 incorporate *assonance*. The vowel sounds provide a painful tone through "ow" sounds ("thou," "Hour," "our," "rouse," "sorrow").

9. Notice how the enjambment in lines 7–9 speeds the stanza to the final thought. This helps the pacing of the poem.

10. Reread the poem. Choose images and lines you respond to.

Have you read any elegies? List them here. Jot down the poet, title, and any images and lines you like. Add your own thoughts about the poem.

_____

_____

_____

Following is a list of some of the most beautiful elegies in the English language. Make it a point to read several. You won't be sorry.

"Elegy for Jane" by Theodore Roethke—a teacher's lament for his student.
"Elegy in a Country Church Yard" by Thomas Gray—a reflective look at what might have been.
"When Lilacs Last in the Dooryard Bloomed" and "O Captain, My Captain" by Walt Whitman—tributes to Abraham Lincoln.
"In Memory of W. B. Yeats" by W. H. Auden—a poet's homage to a great writer.
"Lycidas" by John Milton on the death of a college friend.
"Timer" by Tony Harrison reflects on the death of his mother.
"Song for the Last Act" by Louise Bogen on the death of someone she cares for deeply.
"Minstrel Man" by Langston Hughes laments the stereotype of the minstrel slave.
"Candle in the Wind" by Elton John mourns the death of Princess Diana.

The Dramatic Monologue

The *dramatic monologue* relates an episode in a speaker's life through a conversational format that reveals the character of the speaker.

Robert Browning is the acknowledged master of the dramatic monologue. The following is an example of both the dramatic monologue and Browning's skill as a poet.

Porphyria's Lover

The rain set early in tonight,
    The sullen wind was soon awake,
It tore the elm-tops down for spite,
    And did its worst to vex the lake:
    I listened with heart fit to break.   5
When glided in Porphyria; straight
    She shut the cold out and the storm,
And kneeled and made the cheerless grate
    Blaze up, and all the cottage warm;
    Which done, she rose, and from her form   10
Withdrew the dripping cloak and shawl,
    And laid her soiled gloves by, untied
Her hat and let the damp hair fall,
    And, last, she sat down by my side
    And called me. When no voice replied,   15
She put my arm about her waist,
    And made her smooth white shoulder bare,
And all her yellow hair displaced,
    And, stooping, made my cheek lie there,
    And spread, o'er all, her yellow hair,   20

Murmuring how she loved me—she
  Too weak, for all her heart's endeavor,
To set its struggling passion free
  From pride, and vainer ties desever,
    And give herself to me forever.   25
But passion sometimes would prevail,
  Nor could tonight's gay feast restrain
A sudden thought of one so pale
  For love of her, and all in vain:
    So, she was come through wind and rain.   30
Be sure I looked up at her eyes
  Happy and proud; at last I knew
Porphyria worshipped me: surprise
  Made my heart swell, and still it grew
    While I debated what to do.   35
That moment she was mine, mine, fair,
  Perfectly pure and good: I found
A thing to do, and all her hair
  In one long yellow string I wound
    Three times her little throat around,   40
And strangled her. No pain felt she;
  I am quite sure she felt no pain.
As a shut bud that holds a bee,
  I warily oped her lids: again
    Laughed the blue eyes without a stain.   45
And I untightened next the tress
  About her neck; her cheek once more
Blushed bright beneath my burning kiss:
  I propped her head up as before,
    Only, this time my shoulder bore   50
Her head, which droops upon it still:
  The smiling rosy little head,
So glad it has its utmost will,
  That all it scorned at once is fled,
    And I, its love, am gained instead!   55
Porphyria's love: she guessed not how
  Her darling one wish would be heard.
And thus we sit together now,
  And all night long we have not stirred,
    And yet God has not said a word!   60

Read the poem aloud, or have someone read it to you. Try for a conversational tone.

1. Concentrate on following the storyline. (Were you surprised by the concluding events?)

---

2. Once you know the "story," look closely at the poem for all the clues concerning character and episode.

3. Automatically check for the relationship between form and content. Quickly scan for rhyme scheme and meter. You should notice a definite presence of rhyme in an unusual form *a b a b b c d c d d e f e f f*, etc. You should be able to recognize that the meter is iambic tetrameter. Rather than scan the entire poem, try lines throughout to see if a pattern exists.

4. *Lines 1–5:* What does the setting indicate or foreshadow? _____

_____

Lines 6–9: What diction and imagery is associated with Porphyria?

_____

Lines 10–12: Why are we told her gloves were soiled?

_____

Lines 20–25: Try to understand what the narrator is telling you here.

This reveals what is important to him. _____

Lines 30–37: Have you found the turning point? _____

Remember, literary analysis is like unraveling a mystery. Find motivational and psychological reasons for the narrator's behavior. _____

_____

Line 41: Notice how the caesura emphasizes the finality of the event. You are forced to confront the murder directly because of the starkness of the syntax. This is followed by the narrator's justification.

Line 43: Did you catch the simile? It's a little tricky to spot when "as" is the first word.

_____

Line 55: What character trait is revealed by the narrator? _____

_____

Lines 59–60: Notice how the rhyming couplet accentuates the final thought and sets it off from the previous lines. Interpret the last line. Did you see that the last two lines are end-stopped, whereas the majority of the poem utilizes enjambment to create a conversational tone? _____

_____

5. Did you enjoy this poem? Did you feel as if you were being spoken to directly? _____

_____

The AP often uses dramatic monologues because they can be very rich in narrative detail and characterization. This is a form you should become familiar with by reading several from different times and authors. Try one of these: Robert Browning —"My Last Duchess," "The Soliloquy of the Spanish Cloister," "Andrea Del Sarto"; Alfred Lord Tennyson —"Ulysses," T. S. Eliot—"The Love Song of J. Alfred Prufrock," Ai—"Killing Floor," Federico Garcia Lorca—"The Unfaithful Housewife," Joshua McCarter Simpson—"No, Master, Never!," Alice Moore Dunbar-Nelson—"I Sit and Sew."

How many dramatic monologues have you read? List them here and add details and lines that were of interest and /or importance to you.

_____

_____

_____

_____

The Sonnet

The **sonnet** is the most popular fixed form in poetry. It is usually written in iambic pentameter and is always made up of 14 lines. There are two basic sonnet forms: the *Italian* or *Petrarchan* sonnet, named after Petrarch, the poet who created it, and the *English* or *Shakespearean* sonnet, named after the poet who perfected it. Each adheres to a strict rhyme scheme and stanza form.

The subject matter of sonnets varies greatly, from expressions of love to philosophical considerations, religious declarations, or political criticisms. The sonnet is highly polished, and the strictness of its form complements the complexity of its subject matter. As you know by now, we like to explore the relationship between form and function. The sonnet effectively integrates these two concepts.

Let's compare the two forms more closely. The **Italian sonnet** is divided into an octave and a sestet. The rhyme scheme is:

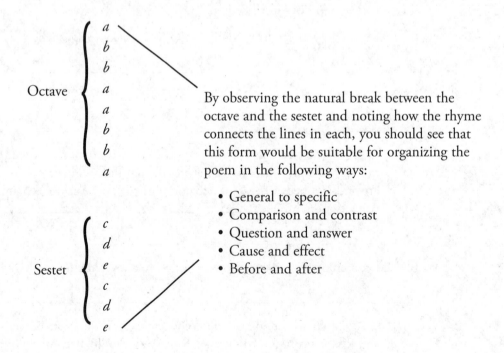

Octave
- a
- b
- b
- a
- a
- b
- b
- a

Sestet
- c
- d
- e
- c
- d
- e

By observing the natural break between the octave and the sestet and noting how the rhyme connects the lines in each, you should see that this form would be suitable for organizing the poem in the following ways:

- General to specific
- Comparison and contrast
- Question and answer
- Cause and effect
- Before and after

The **Shakespearean sonnet** has a different rhyme scheme and stanza form:

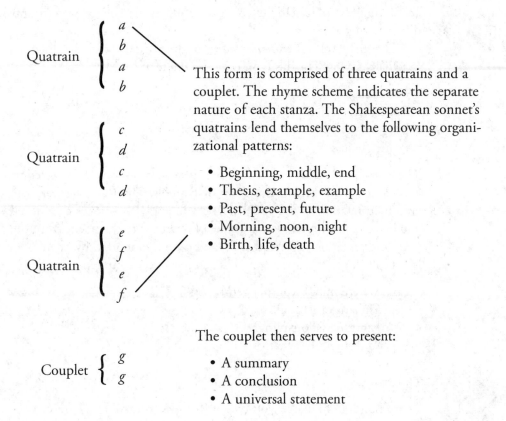

Quatrain
{
a
b
a
b
}

This form is comprised of three quatrains and a couplet. The rhyme scheme indicates the separate nature of each stanza. The Shakespearean sonnet's quatrains lend themselves to the following organizational patterns:

Quatrain
{
c
d
c
d
}

- Beginning, middle, end
- Thesis, example, example
- Past, present, future
- Morning, noon, night
- Birth, life, death

Quatrain
{
e
f
e
f
}

The couplet then serves to present:

Couplet
{
g
g
}

- A summary
- A conclusion
- A universal statement

Modern sonnets often vary rhyme and stanza form, but they will always have 14 lines.

For more practice with the sonnet, see Poems for Comparison and Contrast in this chapter. We recommend you read sonnets written by Shakespeare, Milton, Wordsworth, e e cummings, Edna St. Vincent Millay, and Keats. You might also want to examine some late twentieth and early twenty-first century sonnets, such as "Tapestry" by Amy Foreman, "America" by Clause McKay, "Potpourri" by Joseph Salem, and "Petrarch on West 115th Street" by Marion Shore.

The Villanelle

The **villanelle** is a fixed form in poetry. It has six stanzas: five tercets, and a final quatrain. It utilizes two refrains: The first and last lines of the first stanza alternate as the last line of the next four stanzas and then form a final couplet in the quatrain.

As an example, read: "Do Not Go Gentle Into That Good Night" by Dylan Thomas. Other villanelles that are worth a close reading include "The Art of Losing" by Elizabeth Bishop and "The Waking" by Theodore Roethke.

Interpretation of Poetry

Interpretation is not license for you to say just anything. Your comments/analysis/interpretation must be based on the given text.

How Do I Begin to Interpret Poetry?

To thoroughly understand a poem, you should be able to view it and read it from three different angles or viewpoints.

The first level is the *literal reading* of the poem. This is the discovery of what the poem is actually saying. For this, you only use the text:

- Vocabulary
- Structure
- Imagery
- Poetic devices

The *second level* builds on the first and draws conclusions from the connotation of the form and content and the interpretation of symbols. The *third level* refers to your own reading and interpretation of the poem. Here, you apply the processes of levels one and two, and you bring your own context or frame of reference to the poem. Your only restriction is that your interpretation is grounded in, and can be supported by, the text of the poem itself.

To illustrate this approach, let's analyze a very simple poem.

> Where ships of purple gently toss
> On seas of daffodil,
> Fantastic sailors mingle
> And then, the wharf is still.

1. Read it.

2. Respond. (You like it; you hate it. It leaves you cold. Whatever.)

3. Check rhyme and meter. We can see there is some rhyme, and the meter is iambic and predominantly trimeter. The first and third lines are irregular. (If this does not prove to be critical to your interpretation of the poem, move on.)

4. Check the vocabulary and syntax. Are there any words you are not familiar with?

5. Look for poetic devices and imagery.

6. Highlight, circle, connect key images and words.

7. Begin to draw inferences from the adjectives, phrases, verbs.

As an example, we have provided the following notes:

Movement

- Toss
- Mingle   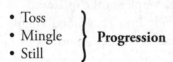 **Progression**
- Still

Images

- Ships
- Seas   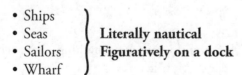 **Literally nautical**
- Sailors   **Figuratively on a dock**
- Wharf

Syntax

- Ships of purple = purple ships (Where or when do you see purple ships?)
- Seas of daffodil = daffodil seas (When would seas be yellow?)
- Fantastic sailors = sailors of fantasy = clouds moving, birds flying (What might they be?)
- Wharf is still = place is quiet = ?

   Put your observations together and formulate your interpretation. Write it below.

_____

_____

_____

   Some students have said that they saw a field of flowers, bees and butterflies, a coronation, a celebration, and/or a royal event. These are all valid interpretations. Remember, this is only a simple exercise to acquaint you with the approaches you can use to analyze complex poetry. By the way, Emily Dickinson was writing about a sunset over Boston harbor.

Poetry for Analysis

This section will walk you through the analysis of several poems, presenting the poetry and a series of directed questions for you to consider. For maximum benefit, work with a highlighter and refer often to the poem. *Always* read the entire poem before you begin the analysis.

The Snake
by D. H. Lawrence

A snake came to my water-trough
On a hot, hot day, and I in pyjamas for the heat
To drink there.

In the deep, strange-scented shade of the great dark carobtree
I came down the steps with my pitcher   5
And must wait, must stand and wait, for there he was at the trough
      before me.

He reached down from a fissure in the earth-wall in the gloom
And trailed his yellow-brown slackness soft-bellied down, over the
      edge of the stone trough,   10
And rested his throat upon the stone bottom,
And where the water had dripped from the tap, in a small clearness,
He sipped with his straight mouth,
Softly drank through his straight gums, into his slack long body,
Silently.   15

Someone was before me at my water trough,
And I, like a second comer, waiting.
He lifted his head from his drinking, as cattle do,
And looked at me vaguely, as drinking cattle do,

And flickered his two-forked tongue from his lips, and mused a   20
    moment,
And stooped and drank a little more,
Being earth-brown, earth-golden from the burning bowels of the earth
On the day of Sicilian July, with Etna smoking.

The voice of my education said to me   25
He must be killed,
For in Sicily the black, black snakes are innocent, the gold are
    venomous.

The voice in me said, If you were a man
You would take a stick and break him now, and finish him off.   30

But must I confess how I liked him,
How glad I was he had come like a guest in quiet, to drink at my
    water-trough
And depart peaceful, pacified, and thankless,
Into the burning bowels of this earth?   35

Was it cowardice, that I dared not kill him?
Was it perversity, that I longed to talk to him?
Was it humility, to feel so honoured?
I felt so honoured.

And yet those voices: 40
If you were not afraid, you would kill him!
And truly I was afraid, I was most afraid,
But even so, honoured still more
That he should seek my hospitality
From out the dark door of the secret earth.   45

He drank enough
And lifted his head, dreamily, as one who has drunken,
And flickered his tongue like a forked night on the air, so black,
Seeming to lick his lips,
And looked around like a god, unseeing, into the air,   50
And slowly turned his head,
And slowly, very slowly, as if thrice a dream,
Proceeded to draw his slow length curving round
And climb again the broken bank of my wall-face.

And as he put his head into that dreadful hole,   55
And as he slowly drew up, snake-easing his shoulders, and entered
    farther,
A sort of horror, a sort of protest against his withdrawing into that
    horrid black hole,
Deliberately going into blackness, and slowly drawing himself   60
    after,
Overcame me now his back was turned.

I looked round, I put down my pitcher,
I picked up a clumsy log
And threw it at the water-trough with a clatter.   65

I think it did not hit him,
But suddenly that part of him that was left behind convulsed in
     undignified haste,
Writhed like lightning, and was gone
Into the black hole, the earth-lipped fissure in the wall-front,   70
At which, in the intense still noon, I stared with fascination.

And immediately I regretted it.
I thought how paltry, how vulgar, what a mean act!
I despised myself and the voices of my accursed human education.
And I thought of the albatross,   75
And I wished he would come back, my snake.

For he seemed to me again like a king,
Like a king in exile, uncrowned in the underworld,
Now due to be crowned again.
And so, I missed my chance with one of the lords   80
Of life.
And I have something to expiate:
A pettiness.

1. Since there is no regular rhyme scheme or length of lines or stanza form, we may conclude that this is *free verse*. _____ Yes _____ No

2. After reading the poem, you should be able to determine the situation, which is _____, and the speaker, who is _____.

3. The first stanza establishes the conflict, which is _____ _____.

4. Find evidence of the developing conflict in lines 4–6. _____

5. Find examples of alliteration and assonance in lines 7–13. Notice how the sounds are appropriate for a snake rather than just random sounds.

6. Read line 12 aloud. Hear how slowly and "long" the sounds are, like the body of the snake itself.

7. Circle or highlight the imagery in lines 16–24. _____ Notice how the scene is intensifying.

8. Restate the speaker's position in lines 25–28. _____

9. In lines 31–38, identify the conflict and the thematic ideas of the poem. Highlight them.

10. Identify the opposition facing the speaker in lines 36–39. State it. _____

_____

11. In lines 46–54, highlight the similes presented. Explore the nature of a snake and the connotation associated with one. _____

12. Interpret the setting as presented in lines 55–62. _____

13. The poem breaks at line 63. Highlight the change in the speaker at this point. Who is to blame for this action? _____

14. In line 75 there is a reference or allusion to the "Rime of the Ancient Mariner" by Coleridge, which is a poem in which a man learns remorse and the meaning of life as the result of a cruel, spontaneous act. Is this a suitable comparison for this poem's circumstances? Why? _____

15. Identify the similes and metaphor in lines 66–71. _____

16. Elaborate on the final confession of the speaker. May we conclude that the poem is a modern dramatic monologue? _____

After you have considered these ideas, expand your own observations. Might the entire poem be a metaphor? Can it be symbolic of other pettinesses? Can you interpret this poem socially, religiously, politically, psychologically, sexually?

The following poem is particularly suitable for the interpretation of symbolism. Apply what you have learned and reviewed and respond to this sample.

The Sick Rose
by William Blake

O Rose, Thou Art Sick!
The Invisible Worm
That flies in the night
In the howling Storm,

Has found out thy bed
Of Crimson joy,
And his dark secret love
Does thy life destroy.

Try your hand at interpreting this poem:

1. Literally

2. Sexually

3. Philosophically

4. Religiously

5. Politically

Apply the following thematic concepts to the poem:

1. Passion

2. Deceit

3. Betrayal

4. Corruption

5. Disease

6. Madness

Interesting, isn't it, how much can be found or felt in a few lines. Read other poems by Blake, such as "Songs of Innocence" and "Songs of Experience."

Poems for Comparison and Contrast

Sometimes the AP exam requires you to compare and contrast two poems or prose selections in the essay section. Do not panic. The selections will usually be short and the points of comparison or contrast plentiful and accessible. This type of question can be interesting and provide you with a chance to really explore ideas.

Following are two poems suitable for this kind of analysis. Read each poem carefully. Take a minute to look at them and allow a few ideas to take shape in your mind. Then plan your approach logically. Remember, form and content are your guidelines.

She Walks in Beauty
by Lord Byron

She walks in Beauty, like the night
    Of cloudless climes and starry skies;
And all that's best of dark and bright
    Meet in her aspect and her eyes:
Thus mellowed to that tender light   5
    Which heaven to gaudy day denies.

One shade the more, one ray the less,
    Had half impaired the nameless grace
Which waves in every raven tress,
    Or softly lightens o'er her face;   10
Where thoughts serenely sweet express,
    How pure, how dear their dwelling-place.

And on that cheek, and o'er that brow,
    So soft, so calm, yet eloquent,
The smiles that win, the tints that glow,   15
    But tell of days in goodness spent,
A mind at peace with all below,
    A heart whose love is innocent!

Sonnet 130
by William Shakespeare

My mistress' eyes are nothing like the sun;
Coral is far more red than her lips' red;
If snow be white, why then her breasts are dun;
If hairs be wires, black wires grow on her head.
I have seen roses damasked red and white,   5
But no such roses see I in her cheeks;
And in some perfumes is there more delight
Than in the breath that from my mistress reeks.
I love to hear her speak, yet well I know
That music hath a far more pleasing sound;   10
I grant I never saw a goddess go:
My mistress, when she walks, treads on the ground.
And yet, by heaven, I think my love as rare
As any she belied with false compare.

It is essential that you read each poem again, marking, highlighting, connecting, etc. those points you will develop. List or chart your findings before you begin to write your essay.

Common Elements

- Both have the same topic—to a lover
- Both use similes: "She Walks"—"like the night"; "Sonnet 130"—"nothing like the sun"
- Both rely on nature imagery: "She Walks"—"starry skies"; "Sonnet 130"—"Coral, roses"
- Both deal with light or dark
- Both include references to lover's hair: "She Walks"—"raven tress"; "Sonnet 130"—"black wires"
- Both appeal to the senses: "She Walks"—"raven tress"; "Sonnet 130"—perfume, roses, music, garlic stink
- Both use alliteration: "She Walks"—"cloudless climes"; "Sonnet 130"—"goddess go"

Differences

"Practice. Practice. Practice."
—Martha W.
  AP teacher

- Form: "She Walks" lyric, has sestets; "Sonnet 130," 12 + 2 (3 quatrains and couplet)
- Kind of love: "She Walks" serious and adoring; "Sonnet 130"—critical and humorous
- Diction: "She Walks"—positive; "Sonnet 130"—negative
- Ending: "She Walks"—adoring; "Sonnet 130"—realistic
- Tone: "She Walks"—idyllic; "Sonnet 130"—realistic

To recap: If you are given two selections, consider the following:

- What is the form or structure of the poems?
- What is the situation or subject of each?
- How are the poetic devices used?
- What imagery is developed?
- What thematic statements are made?
- What is the tone of each poem?
- What is the organization or progression of each poem?
- What attitudes are revealed?
- What symbols are developed?

Rapid Review

- Poetry has its own form.
- The foot, line, and stanza are the building blocks of poetry.
- Meter and rhyme are part of the sound of poetry.
- There are many types of rhyme forms.
- There are many types of poetic feet. They may be iambic, trochaic, anapestic, dactylic, or spondaic.
- There are several stanza forms.
- Narrative poetry tells stories.
- Ballads are simple narratives.
- Lyric poetry is subjective and emotional.
- Odes are formal lyrics that honor something or someone.
- Elegies are lyrics that mourn a loss.
- Dramatic monologues converse with the reader as they reveal events.
- The sonnet is a 14-line form of poetry.
- The villanelle is a fixed form that depends on refrains.
- Levels of interpretation depend on the literal and figurative meaning of poems.
- Symbols provide for many levels of interpretation.
- When comparing and contrasting poems, remember to consider speaker, subject, situation, devices, tone, and theme.

STEP 5

Build Your Test-Taking Confidence

Practice Exam 1
Practice Exam 2

PRACTICE EXAM 1
ANSWER SHEET FOR MULTIPLE-CHOICE QUESTIONS

1. _____   20. _____   39. _____

2. _____   21. _____   40. _____

3. _____   22. _____   41. _____

4. _____   23. _____   42. _____

5. _____   24. _____   43. _____

6. _____   25. _____   44. _____

7. _____   26. _____   45. _____

8. _____   27. _____   46. _____

9. _____   28. _____   47. _____

10. _____   29. _____   48. _____

11. _____   30. _____   49. _____

12. _____   31. _____   50. _____

13. _____   32. _____   51. _____

14. _____   33. _____   52. _____

15. _____   34. _____   53. _____

16. _____   35. _____   54. _____

17. _____   36. _____   55. _____

18. _____   37. _____

19. _____   38. _____

"I need to honestly time myself on the practice exams, or else I don't really concentrate the way I should."
—Carol K.
  AP student

I _____ did _____ did not complete this part of the test in the allotted 1 hour.

I had _____ correct answers. I had _____ incorrect answers. I left _____ blank.

I have carefully reviewed the explanations of the answers, and I think I need to work on the following types of questions:

PRACTICE EXAM 1
ADVANCED PLACEMENT ENGLISH LITERATURE

Section I

Total time—1 hour

Questions 1–12 are based on a careful reading of the following 2015 poem by Juan Felipe Herrera.

Almost Livin' Almost Dyin'
by Juan Felipe Herrera

for all the dead
& hear my streets
with ragged beats & the beats
are too beat to live so the graves push out with
hands that cannot touch the makers of light & the   5
sun flames down through the roofs & the roots that slide
to one side & the whistlin' fires of the cops & the cops
in the shops do what they gotta do & your body's
on the fence & your ID's in the air & the shots
get fired & the gas in the face & the tanks   10
on your blood & the innocence all around & the
spillin' & the grillin' & the grinnin' & the game of Race
no one wanted & the same every day so U fire &
eat the smoke thru your long bones & the short mace
& the day? This last sweet Swisher[1] day that turns to love   15
& no one knows how it came or what it is or what it says
or what it was or what for or from what gate
is it open is it locked can U pull it back to your life
filled with bitter juice & demon angel eyes even though
you pray & pray mama says you gotta sing she says   20
you got wings but from what skies from where could
they rise what are the things the no-things called love
how can its power be fixed or grasped so the beats
keep on blowin' keep on flyin' & the moon tracks your bed
where you are alone or maybe dead & the truth   25
carves you carves you & calls you back still alive
cry cry the candles by the last four trees still soaked
in Michael Brown[2] red and Officer Liu[3] red and
Officer Ramos[4] red and Eric Garner[5] whose
last words were not words they were just breath   30
askin' for breath they were just burnin' like me like
we are all still burnin' can you hear me
can you can you feel me swaggin' tall & driving low &
talkin' fine & hollerin' from my corner crime & fryin'
against the wall   35

almost livin' almost dyin'
almost livin' almost dyin'

---

[1]**Swisher day:** local day set aside for fun, games, and celebration
[2]**Michael Brown:** an unarmed black teenager shot and killed in 2014 by a white police officer
[3]**Officer Liu:** slain NYC police officer
[4]**Officer Ramos:** slain NYC police officer
[5]**Eric Garner:** killed by NYC police officers while being arrested for selling single cigarettes; remembered for crying out, "I can't breathe."

1. The pace of this poem can best be described as
   A. processional
   B. breathless
   C. contemplative
   D. ambling
   E. steady

2. The effect of using the ampersand throughout the poem is to
   A. set up a hyperbole
   B. direct the reader's attention to the next item in a list
   C. gives the impression of person who doesn't care about language
   D. act like a quickening heartbeat
   E. act as a symbol of the neighborhood's character

3. Lines 1 to the beginning of line 15 is a recounting of
   A. a street fair
   B. a robbery of a local grocery store
   C. a confrontation between neighborhood young men and police
   D. the life around a low-income, urban neighborhood
   E. a conflict between rival gangs

4. The speaker is most probably
   A. an onlooker from outside the community
   B. a reporter for a national newspaper
   C. the mother of one of the young men
   D. a politician
   E. a young person who lives in the neighborhood

5. The poem contains examples of all of the following literary devices *except*
   A. internal rhyme
   B. alliteration
   C. metaphor
   D. repetition
   E. synecdoche

6. Lines 15–18 indicate the speaker's
   A. longing for a life that is filled with love
   B. hoping for his mother to rescue him
   C. giving up any hope for the future
   D. blaming life's uncertainty on "the system"
   E. believing he will have a better life in the future

7. The pace and rhythm of the poem is created primarily with a combination of
   A. playful imagery, repetition, ampersands
   B. similes and repetition
   C. appeals to emotions, metaphors
   D. single syllable words, no punctuation, repetition
   E. ampersands, extended analogy

8. Lines 18–26 can best be summarized as:
   A. Love can conquer violence.
   B. There is no real escape from this life of violence and fear.
   C. Hope lies in prayer.
   D. There is no truth.
   E. Enjoy life as it comes.

9. "Its" in line 23 refers to
   A. angel eyes (19)
   B. wings (21)
   C. skies (21)
   D. love (22)
   E. no-things (22)

10. In the context of the poem, "you" in line 33 can best be understood to be
    A. the speaker
    B. the friends of the speaker
    C. those in power
    D. the speaker's mother
    E. neighborhood rivals

11. "we all are still burnin'" in line 32 can best be interpreted to mean
  A. Nothing is able to end the fear and violence.
  B. There eventually will be a rebellion.
  C. The deaths of those mentioned in lines 28 and 29 should be avenged.
  D. Only love can save the speaker.
  E. Hope lies in remembering those who have lost their lives to violence.

12. The last six lines of the poem are a(n)
  A. accusation
  B. litany
  C. eulogy
  D. promise
  E. plea

Carefully read the following passages and answer the questions that follow. Questions 13–25 are based on the following passage.

Bleak House
by Charles Dickens (1853)

Excerpt from Chapter 1—"In Chancery"

LONDON. Michaelmas Term lately over, and the Lord Chancellor sitting in Lincoln's Inn Hall. Implacable November weather. As much mud in the streets as if the waters had but newly retired from the face of the earth, and it would not be wonderful to meet a Megalosaurus, forty feet long or so, waddling like an elephantine lizard up Holborn Hill. Smoke lowering down from chimney-pots, making a soft black drizzle, with flakes of soot in it as big as full-grown 5
snowflakes—gone into mourning, one might imagine, for the death of the sun. Dogs, undistinguishable in mire. Horses, scarcely better; splashed to their very blinkers. Foot passengers, jostling one another's umbrellas in a general infection of ill-temper, and losing their foot-hold at street-corners, where tens of thousands of other foot passengers have been slipping and sliding since the day broke (if the day ever broke), adding new deposits to the crust upon 10
crust of mud, sticking at those points tenaciously to the pavement, and accumulating at compound interest.

Fog everywhere. Fog up the river, where it flows among green aits and meadows; fog down the river, where it rolls defiled among the tiers of shipping and the waterside pollutions of a great (and dirty) city. Fog on the Essex marshes, fog on the Kentish heights. Fog creeping into the 15
cabooses of collier-brigs; fog lying out on the yards, and hovering in the rigging of great ships; fog drooping on the gunwales of barges and small boats. Fog in the eyes and throats of ancient Greenwich pensioners, wheezing by the firesides of their wards; fog in the stem and bowl of the afternoon pipe of the wrathful skipper, down in his close cabin; fog cruelly pinching the toes and fingers of his shivering little 'prentice boy on deck. Chance people on the bridges peeping over 20
the parapets into a nether sky of fog, with fog all round them, as if they were up in a balloon, and hanging in the misty clouds.

Gas* looming through the fog in divers places in the streets, much as the sun may, from the spongey fields, be seen to loom by husbandman and ploughboy. Most of the shops lighted two hours before their time—as the gas seems to know, for it has a haggard and unwilling look. 25

The raw afternoon is rawest, and the dense fog is densest, and the muddy streets are muddiest near that leaden-headed old obstruction, appropriate ornament for the threshold of a leaden-headed old corporation, Temple Bar. And hard by Temple Bar, in Lincoln's Inn Hall, at the very heart of the fog, sits the Lord High Chancellor in his High Court of Chancery.

---

* (23) *gas*: gas lights

Never can there come fog too thick, never can there come mud and mire too deep, to assort   30
with the groping and floundering condition which this High Court of Chancery, most pestilent of
hoary sinners, holds this day in the sight of heaven and earth.

On such an afternoon, if ever, the Lord High Chancellor ought to be sitting here—as here he
is—with a foggy glory round his head, softly fenced in with crimson cloth and curtains,
addressed by a large advocate with great whiskers, a little voice, and an interminable brief, and   35
outwardly directing his contemplation to the lantern in the roof, where he can see nothing but
fog. On such an afternoon some score of members of the High Court of Chancery bar ought to be
—as here they are—mistily engaged in one of the ten thousand stages of an endless cause,
tripping one another up on slippery precedents, groping knee-deep in technicalities, running their
goat-hair and horse-hair* warded heads against walls of words and making a pretence of equity   40
with serious faces, as players might. On such an afternoon the various solicitors in the cause,
some two or three of whom have inherited it from their fathers, who made a fortune by it, ought
to be—as are they not?—ranged in a line, in a long matted well (but you might look in vain for
truth at the bottom of it) between the registrar's red table and the silk gowns, with bills, cross-bills,
answers, rejoinders, injunctions, affidavits, issues, references to masters, masters' reports,   45
mountains of costly nonsense, piled before them. Well may the court be dim, with wasting
candles here and there; well may the fog hang heavy in it, as if it would never get out; well may
the stained-glass windows lose their colour and admit no light of day into the place; well may the
uninitiated from the streets, who peep in through the glass panes in the door, be deterred from
entrance by its owlish aspect and by the drawl, languidly echoing to the roof from the padded   50
dais where the Lord High Chancellor looks into the lantern that has no light in it and where the
attendant wigs are all stuck in a fog-bank! This is the Court of Chancery, which has its decaying
houses and its blighted lands in every shire, which has its worn-out lunatic in every madhouse
and its dead in every churchyard, which has its ruined suitor with his slipshod heels and
threadbare dress borrowing and begging through the round of every man's acquaintance, which   55
gives to monied might the means abundantly of wearying out the right, which so exhausts
finances, patience, courage, hope, so overthrows the brain and breaks the heart, that there is not
an honourable man among its practitioners who would not give—who does not often give—the
warning, "Suffer any wrong that can be done you rather than come here!"

———————

*(40) *goat-hair and horse-hair warded heads*: wigs worn by members of the court

13. In context, "Implacable November weather"
[line 2] serves as
A. the major theme of the passage
B. the introduction to the extinction imagery
C. a contrast to the tone of the passage
D. the introduction to the controlling
   metaphor of the passage
E. personification of "Michaelmas Term"

14. The juxtaposition of "Megalosaurus" [line 3]
with London town has as its purpose
A. indicating a natural disaster
B. foreshadowing an outdated legal system
C. reinforcing the animalistic nature of man
D. indicating the magnitude of London's
   poverty
E. revealing the onslaught of civil unrest

15. "Gone into mourning" in line 6 refers to
A. snow-flakes
B. smoke
C. death of the sun
D. flakes of soot
E. drizzle

16. In the context of the passage, "death of the
sun" [line 6] can be seen as parallel to the
A. philandering of the Lord High Chancellor
B. degradation of London
C. indifference of the wealthy class
D. blighted lands
E. corruption of justice

17. "For it has a haggard and unwilling look" [line 25] refers to
    A. the fog
    B. the gas
    C. the shops
    D. the husbandman and ploughboy
    E. the sun

18. The purpose of lines 26–29 is to
    A. provide the major shift in the subject
    B. solidify the implacable nature of November weather
    C. reemphasize the nature of the fog
    D. proceed from setting to theme
    E. foreshadow a religious conversion

19. The attitude of the speaker in lines 26–29 can best be described as
    A. self-serving platitude
    B. vitriolic indictment
    C. disconsolate resignation
    D. unfounded aspiration
    E. pathetic desperation

20. Lines 37–41, beginning with "On such an afternoon" and ending with "as players might," reinforce which of the following lines?
    A. 4–6
    B. 13–15
    C. 17–20
    D. 23–25
    E. 30–32

21. The imagery created in lines 46–52 serves to
    A. emphasize the poverty of London
    B. reinforce the crowded court condition
    C. characterize the role of lawyers in the court
    D. reveal the author's attitude toward his subject
    E. separate the exterior from the interior

22. One could best summarize lines 52–59 with which of the following statements?
    A. The court system is not just
    B. The court system needs to be revised
    C. The lawyers are corrupt
    D. The court system has the support of the attorneys
    E. The courts exist only to help the poor

23. The second and last paragraphs are primarily developed through the use of
    A. comparison and contrast
    B. simple sentences
    C. parallel structure
    D. rhetorical questions
    E. animal imagery

24. The organization of the passage moves from
    A. past to present
    B. positive to negative
    C. cause to effect
    D. general to specific
    E. literal to figurative

25. The overall tone of the passage can best be described as
    A. remorseful and resigned
    B. outraged and exhortative
    C. scathing and bitter
    D. victimized and vengeful
    E. dispassionate and objective

Questions 26–36 are based on the following poem.

The Writer
by Richard Wilbur (1969)

In her room at the prow of the house
Where light breaks, and the windows are tossed with linden,
My daughter is writing a story.

I pause in the stairwell, hearing
From her shut door a commotion of typewriter-keys   5
Like a chain hauled over a gunwale.

Young as she is, the stuff
Of her life is a great cargo, and some of it heavy:
I wish her a lucky passage.

But now it is she who pauses,   10
As if to reject my thought and its easy figure.
A stillness greatens, in which

The whole house seems to be thinking,
And then she is at it again with a bunched clamor
Of strokes, and again is silent.   15

I remember the dazed starling
Which was trapped in that very room, two years ago;
How we stole in, lifted a sash

And retreated, not to affright it;
And how for a helpless hour, through the crack in the door,   20
We watched this sleek, wild, dark

And iridescent creature
Batter against the brilliance, drop like a glove
To the hard floor, or the desk-top,

And wait then, humped and bloody,   25
For the wits to try it again; and how our spirits
Rose when, suddenly sure,

It lifted off from a chair-back,
Beating a smooth course for the right window
And clearing the sill of the world.   30

It is always a matter, my darling,
Of life or death, as I had forgotten. I wish
What I wished you before, but harder.

26. The last line of the poem "What I wished you before, but harder" implies that
   A. the speaker loves his daughter more than at the beginning of the poem
   B. the speaker realizes the intensity of life's challenges
   C. the speaker cannot be as creative as she
   D. the speaker feels he has failed her
   E. the daughter will never be a successful writer

27. Which of the following is used to develop the poem?
   A. cause and effect
   B. argument
   C. general to specific examples
   D. definition
   E. parallel analogy

28. Line 13 is an example of
   A. allusion
   B. alliteration
   C. personification
   D. simile
   E. apostrophe

29. "A smooth course for the right window" in line 29 parallels line(s)
   A. 1
   B. 5–6
   C. 8
   D. 9
   E. 11

30. The poem breaks after line
   A. 3
   B. 6
   C. 8
   D. 15
   E. 27

31. The final stanza serves all the following purposes *except*
   A. to restate the theme
   B. to reemphasize the father's love for his daughter
   C. to solidify the daughter's character
   D. to connect the two major sections of the poem
   E. to allow the father to be more sympathetic

32. Stanzas 1–3 include all the following analogies *except*
   A. the house as a ship
   B. the daughter's room as a ship's cabin
   C. life's problems as a ship's cargo
   D. writing as a safe harbor
   E. life as a sea journey

33. The father's sensitivity is supported by line(s)
   A. 3
   B. 4
   C. 11
   D. 19
   E. 21–22

34. Contrasts developed in the poem include all the following *except*
   A. stillness and clamor
   B. house and cargo
   C. bird and daughter
   D. life and/or death
   E. light and dark

35. According to the poem, the daughter, as young as she is, has
   A. endured hardships
   B. published her writing
   C. fought for her independence
   D. saved a starling
   E. left home and returned

36. The poet alludes to all the following as part of the process of a creative life *except*
   A. "Batter against the brilliance"
   B. "drop like a glove to the hard floor"
   C. "clearing the sill of the world"
   D. "the wits to try it again"
   E. "Beating a smooth course for the right window"

Questions 37–47 are based on the following passage.

Jane Eyre
by Charlotte Brontë (1847)

Miss Temple got up, took her hand and . . . returned to her own seat: as she resumed
it, I heard her sigh low. She was pensive a few minutes, then rousing herself, she
said cheerfully:—

"But you two are my visitors to-night; I must treat you as such." She rang her bell.

"Barbara," she said to the servant who answered it, "I have not yet had tea; bring   5
the tray, and place cups for these two young ladies."

And a tray was soon brought. How pretty, to my eyes, did the china and bright
teapot look, placed on the little round table near the fire! How fragrant was the steam of the
beverage, and the scent of the toast! of which, however, I, to my dismay (for I was
beginning to be hungry), discerned only a very small portion: Miss Temple discerned it   10
too:—

"Barbara," said she, "can you not bring a little more bread and butter? There is not
enough for three."

Barbara went out: she returned soon:—

"Madam, Mrs. Harden says she has sent up the usual quantity."   15

Mrs. Harden, be it observed, was the housekeeper: a woman after Mr.
Brocklehurst's own heart, made up of equal parts of whalebone and iron.

"Oh, very well!" returned Miss Temple; "we must make it do, Barbara, I
suppose." And as the girl withdrew, she added, smiling, "Fortunately, I have it in my
power to supply deficiencies for this once."   20

Having invited Helen and me to approach the table, and placed before each of us a
cup of tea with one delicious but thin morsel of toast; she got up, unlocked a drawer, and
taking from it a parcel wrapped in paper, disclosed presently to our eyes a good-sized
seed-cake.

"I meant to give each of you some of this to take with you," said she; "but as there   25
is so little toast, you must have it now," and she proceeded to cut slices with a generous
hand.

We feasted that evening as on nectar and ambrosia; and not the least delight of the
entertainment was the smile of gratification with which our hostess regarded us, as we
satisfied our famished appetites on the delicate fare she liberally supplied. Tea over and the 30
tray removed, she again summoned us to the fire; we sat one on each side of her, and now a
conversation followed between her and Helen, which it was indeed a privilege to be
admitted to hear.

Miss Temple had always something of serenity in her air, of state in her mien, of
refined propriety in her language, which precluded deviation into the ardent, the excited, the 35
eager: something which chastened the pleasure of those who looked on her and listened to
her, by a controlling sense of awe; and such was my feeling now: but as to Helen Burns, I
was struck with wonder.

The refreshing meal, the brilliant fire, the presence and kindness of her beloved
instructress, or, perhaps, more than all these, something in her own unique mind, had   40
roused her powers within her. They woke, they kindled: first, they glowed in the bright tint
of her cheek, which till this hour I had never seen but pale and bloodless; then they shone in

the liquid lustre of her eyes, which had suddenly acquired a beauty more singular than that
of Miss Temple's—a beauty neither of fine colour nor long eyelash, nor pencilled brow,
but of meaning, of movement, of radiance. Then her soul sat on her lips, and language 45
flowed, from what source I cannot tell: has a girl of fourteen a heart large enough, vigorous
enough to hold the swelling spring of pure, full, fervid eloquence? Such was the
characteristic of Helen's discourse on that, to me, memorable evening; her spirit seemed
hastening to live within a very brief span as much as many live during a protracted
existence. 50

They conversed of things I had never heard of ! Of nations and times past; of
countries far away: of secrets of nature discovered or guessed at: they spoke of books: how
many they had read! What stores of knowledge they possessed! They seemed so
familiar with French names and French authors: but my amazement reached its climax
when Miss Temple asked Helen if she sometimes snatched a moment to recall the Latin her 55
father had taught her, and taking a book from a shelf, bade her read and construe a page of
"Virgil"; and Helen obeyed, my organ of Veneration expanding at every sounding line.
She had scarcely finished ere the bell announced bedtime: no delay could be admitted;
Miss Temple embraced us both, saying, as she drew us to her heart:—

"God bless you, my children!" 60

Well has Solomon said—"Better is a dinner of herbs where love is, than a stalled ox
and hatred therewith."

37. From the passage, it can be concluded that Mrs. Harden is
A. in love with Mr. Brocklehurst
B. generous with the girls
C. a confidante of Miss Temple's
D. strong-willed and inflexible
E. Miss Temple's superior

38. Religious imagery in this passage is developed by all the following *except*
A. Miss Temple's name
B. feasting on nectar and ambrosia
C. the taking of tea and toast
D. Miss Temple's benediction
E. being summoned to sit by the fire

39. The "smile of gratification with which our hostess regarded us" (line 29) indicates that Miss Temple derives pleasure from
A. having power over the girls
B. being a role model for the girls
C. keeping secrets
D. outsmarting the girls
E. providing for the girls

40. For the speaker, the most nourishing part of the evening was
A. the seed cake
B. the tea and toast
C. the company of an adult
D. the conversation
E. the brilliant fire

41. ". . . her spirit seemed hastening to live within a very brief span as much as many live during a protracted existence" (lines 48–49) is an example of
A. circular reasoning
B. satire
C. foreshadowing
D. denouement
E. digression

42. The reader can infer from lines 45– 47 ("Then her soul sat on her lips . . . eloquence") that
A. Helen has traveled the world
B. Helen likes to show off intellectually
C. Miss Temple has been tutoring Helen
D. the speaker is afraid of Helen
E. Helen is an instrument of divine inspiration

43. The last sentence of the passage may be best interpreted to mean
   A. It is better to be rich than poor
   B. Everything in moderation
   C. The greatest of all riches is love
   D. Denial of riches leads to love
   F. Riches lead to hatred

44. The tone developed in the passage is best described as
   A. amused indifference
   B. subdued admiration
   C. pedantic
   D. reverent wonder
   E. remorseful

45. The reader may infer all the following *except* that
   A. the evening has transformed Helen
   B. the speaker is observant of and sensitive to human nature
   C. the evening is in contrast to their daily lives
   D. Miss Temple will save the two children
   E. love of learning is important to the speaker

46. The description of Miss Temple in lines 34–38 reveals her to be a woman of
   A. religious fervor
   B. restraint and reservation
   C. passionate beliefs
   D. submissive inclinations
   E. dominating sensibilities

47. Based on the passage, all the following can be inferred about Jane's character *except that* she is
   A. cognizant of her limitations
   B. a great observer
   C. of an inquisitive nature
   D. highly impressionable
   E. religious

Questions 48–55 are based on a careful reading of the following 2011 poem by Tracy K. Smith.

The Good Life
by Tracy K. Smith

When some people talk about money
They speak as if it were a mysterious lover
Who went out to buy milk and never
Came back, and it makes me nostalgic
For the years I lived on coffee and bread,   5
Hungry all the time, walking to work on payday
Like a woman journeying for water
From a village without a well, then living
One or two nights like everyone else
On roast chicken and red wine.   10

48. This poem is an example of
   A. a ballad
   B. free verse
   C. a sonnet
   D. blank verse
   E. rhymed verse

49. In line 2, "it" refers to
   A. "The Good Life"
   B. milk
   C. mysterious lover
   D. coffee and bread
   E. money

50. The tone of the poem can best be described as
   A. formal and didactic
   B. uncaring and suspicious
   C. informal and satirical
   D. brusque and patronizing
   E. casual and conversational

51. Lines 2–4 are developed using
   A. personification
   B. hyperbole
   C. allusion
   D. alliteration
   E. onomatopoeia

52. Line 5 is an indication that the speaker is speaking about her
   A. future
   B. present condition
   C. past
   D. nightmares
   E. fears

53. Examples of similes are found in all of the following lines *except*
   A. 2
   B. 5
   C. 6
   D. 7
   E. 9

54. Based on the poem as a whole, the title "The Good Life" can best be described as
   A. accusatory
   B. sentimental
   C. mournful
   D. sarcastic
   E. hopeful

55. In context, the reader can infer that the speaker is
   A. bitter
   B. indigent
   C. successful
   D. envious
   E. indifferent

END OF SECTION I

Section II

Total time—2 hours

Question 1

(Suggested time 40 minutes. This question counts as one-third of the total score for Section II.)

The following is the 1973 short story "The Flowers" by Alice Walker. Carefully read the passage. Then, in a well-written essay analyze how Walker uses literary elements and techniques to convey the complex meaning of "The Flowers" and how she prepares the reader for the ending of this short story.

In your response you should do the following:

- Respond to the prompt with a thesis that presents an assertion that requires defense and support.
- Select and use evidence to support your line of reasoning.
- Explain how the evidence supports your line of reasoning.
- Use appropriate grammar and punctuation in communicating your argument.

The Flowers
by Alice Walker

It seemed to Myop as she skipped lightly from her house to pigpen to smokehouse
that the days had never been as beautiful as these. The air held a keenness that made her
nose twitch. The harvesting of the corn and cotton, peanuts and squash, made each day a
golden surprise that caused excited little tremors to run up her jaws.

Myop carried a short, knobby stick. She struck out at random at chickens she liked,   5
and worked out the beat of a song on the fence around the pigpen. She felt light and good
in the warm sun. She was ten, and nothing existed for her but her song, the stick clutched
in her dark brown hand, and the tat-de-ta-ta-ta of accompaniment.

Turning her back on the rusty boards of her family's sharecropper cabin, Myop
walked along the fence till it ran into the stream made by the spring. Around the spring,   10
where the family got drinking water, silver ferns and wildflowers grew. Along the shallow
banks pigs rooted. Myop watched the tiny white bubbles disrupt the thin black scale of soil
and the water that silently rose and slid away down the stream.

She had explored the woods behind the house many times. Often, in late autumn, her
mother took her to gather nuts among the fallen leaves. Today she made her own path,   15
bouncing this way and that way, vaguely keeping an eye out for snakes. She found, in
addition to various common but pretty ferns and leaves, an armful of strange blue flowers with
velvety ridges and a sweetsuds bush full of the brown, fragrant buds.

By twelve o'clock, her arms laden with sprigs of her findings, she was a mile or more
from home. She had often been as far before, but the strangeness of the land made it not as   20
pleasant as her usual haunts. It seemed gloomy in the little cove in which she found herself.
The air was damp, the silence close and deep.

Myop began to circle back to the house, back to the peacefulness of the morning.

It was then she stepped smack into his eyes. Her heel became lodged in the broken
ridge between brow and nose, and she reached down quickly, unafraid, to free herself. It was   25
only when she saw his naked grin that she gave a little yelp of surprise. He had been a tall
man. From feet to neck covered a long space. His head lay beside him. When she pushed
back the leaves and layers of earth and debris Myop saw that he'd had large white teeth, all
of them cracked or broken, long fingers, and very big bones. All his clothes had rotted away

except some threads of blue denim from his overalls. The buckles of the overalls had turned green.   30

    Myop gazed around the spot with interest. Very near where she'd stepped into the head was a wild pink rose. As she picked it to add to her bundle she noticed a raised mound, a ring, around the rose's root. It was the rotted remains of a noose, a bit of shredding plow-line, now blending benignly into the soil. Around the overhanging limb of a great spreading   35
oak clung another piece, frayed, rotted, bleached, and frazzled—barely there—but spinning restlessly in the breeze. Myop laid down her flowers.

    And the summer was over.

Question 2

(Suggested time 40 minutes. This question counts as one-third of the total score for Section II.)

In his 1957 poem "The Naked and the Nude," Robert Graves contemplates the distinguishing differences between the complex connotations of the two main words in the title. Read the poem carefully. Then, in a well-written essay, analyze how Graves uses poetic elements and techniques to portray these differences.

    In your response you should do the following:

- Respond to the prompt with a thesis that presents an assertion that requires defense and support.
- Select and use evidence to support your line of reasoning.
- Explain how the evidence supports your line of reasoning.
- Use appropriate grammar and punctuation in communicating your argument.

The Naked and the Nude
by Robert Graves

For me, the naked and the nude
(By lexicographers construed
As synonyms that should express
The same deficiency of dress
Or shelter) stand as wide apart   5
As love from lies, or truth from art.

Lovers without reproach will gaze
On bodies naked and ablaze;
The Hippocratic eye will see
In nakedness, anatomy;   10
And naked shines the Goddess when
She mounts her lion among men.

The nude are bold; the nude are sly
To hold each treasonable eye.
While draping by a showman's trick   15
Their dishabille in rhetoric,
They grin a mock-religious grin
Of scorn at those of naked skin.

The naked, therefore, who compete
Against the nude may know defeat;
Yet when they both together tread   20
The briary pastures of the dead,
By Gorgons with long whips pursued,
How naked go the sometime nude!

Question 3

(Suggested time 40 minutes. This question counts as one-third of the total score for Section II.)

Often in your study of literature you encounter a character or group that intentionally dissembles in order to advance a specific agenda. Either from your own reading or from the list below, choose a work of fiction in which intentional dissembling occurs. Then, in a well-written essay analyze how the complex nature of the deceit or misrepresentation contributes to the development of the character or to the interpretation of the work as a whole. Do not merely summarize.

In your response you should do the following:

- Respond to the prompt with a thesis that presents an assertion that requires defense and support.
- Select and use evidence to support your line of reasoning.
- Explain how the evidence supports your line of reasoning.
- Use appropriate grammar and punctuation in communicating your argument.

The Adventures of Huckleberry Finn	*A Streetcar Named Desire*
Oedipus	*Major Barbara*
Jane Eyre	*Hamlet*
The Scarlet Letter	*The Brief Wondrous World of Oscar Wao*
Heart of Darkness	*King Lear*
Brave New World	*The Great Gatsby*
Beloved	

END OF SECTION II

ANSWERS TO MULTIPLE-CHOICE QUESTIONS

Answer Key

1. B	20. E	39. E
2. D	21. D	40. D
3. C	22. A	41. C
4. E	23. C	42. E
5. E	24. E	43. C
6. A	25. C	44. D
7. D	26. B	45. D
8. B	27. E	46. B
9. D	28. C	47. E
10. C	29. D	48. B
11. A	30. D	49. E
12. E	31. C	50. E
13. D	32. D	51. A
14. B	33. D	52. C
15. A	34. B	53. B
16. E	35. A	54. D
17. B	36. B	55. C
18. A	37. D	
19. B	38. E	

Answers and Explanations

Almost Livin Almost Dyin
by Jose Felipe Herrera

1. **B.** The lack of internal and end punctuation, single syllable words, and the use of ampersands create a quick, relentless movement from one word to another and one line to another.
2. **D.** The ampersand acts like the sound of a heart monitor. The quickening pace is pushed forward with this sign. It is the heartbeat of the world that is portrayed in the poem.
3. **C.** The event described is like a filmed police chase in the movies. It's quite visual: from the rooftops to the fence climbing, to the chase through the neighborhood.
4. **E.** The poem is not objective and reportorial. It is told from the vantage point of experience, not from the perspective of a caring parent or a politician seeking office. It is the story of a passionate insider.
5. **E.** Internal rhyme (6, 20, 21), alliteration (6, 7, 27), metaphor (4, 5, 19), and repetition (7, 26, 30) are all included in the construction of the poem. Synecdoche is not.
6. **A.** "This last sweet Swisher day that turns to love" is a nostalgic plea for hope. It is not asking for help or to lay blame.
7. **D.** There is nothing playful about or in this poem. Its pace, rhythm, beat are hard, fast, and furious. This is constructed with diction and syntax that forces the momentum.
8. **A.** A close look at the diction and imagery ("bitter, demon, alone, death, the truth carves you") negates any feeling of hope, love, truth, or joy.
9. **D.** This is a predictable question related to antecedents. In this case, "its" refers to "love" in line 22.
10. **C.** This is a plea for those who have power to do the right thing so that love and hope may survive. None of the other choices has this ability.
11. **A.** The key to the meaning lies in consideration of ALL and EACH of the words in this line. For the speaker, burning was, is, and will always be without end. For the speaker, this applies to himself and everyone he knows. Love and hope are not a possibility as things now stand.
12. **E.** When the speaker says "can you hear me/ can you feel me," he is pleading for a way to regain hope and love, some way to delete almost.

Bleak House
by Charles Dickens

13. **D.** All of the weather images illustrate and reinforce the conditions that exist within the legal system.
14. **B.** The image of an extinct, gigantic, lumbering creature in the midst of London is as out of place as the efficacy of the court system that Dickens describes in the passage.
15. **A.** This is another basic reference question. The image is one of smoke-flakes wearing black for mourning.
16. **E.** The key here is "In the context of the passage." The death of the sun symbolizes the end of enlightenment, warmth, hope, and nurturing—all of which are characteristic of the High Court of Chancery.
17. **B.** This is a basic antecedent question. You need to trace "it" back to "gas."
18. **A.** The author takes the two major images and combines them (fog:court).
19. **B.** The deliberate repetition and diction (for example: "leaden-headed," "obstruction") is evidence of the bitter accusation.
20. **E.** "Mud," "mire," "groping," and "floundering" are echoed by "endless cause," "tripping," "slippery," and "knee-deep."
21. **D.** Phrases such as "court be dim," "wasting candles," "admit no light of day," "lantern that has no light" all reveal the author's attitude toward the court.
22. **A.** The listing of the effects of the court on the people specifically indicate how justice is not being served. There is no direct call for revision of the court in this passage.
23. **C.** In paragraph 2 the repetition of "fog," and the repetition of "On such," "Well may," and "which has" in the last paragraph, all serve to

tightly structure both the description and the indictment presented in the excerpt.

24. **E.** The excerpt begins with a specific description of London in November and progresses to a symbolic depiction of the Court of Chancery.

25. **C.** The previous questions should have pointed you toward this answer. There is no resignation in the author. He rails against the system (A). While it is obvious the writer is outraged, he does not call for action on the part of the reader (B). We may infer that he has been victimized, but there is no evidence of that in this excerpt (D). His sarcasm, diction, and imagery reveal a subjective point of view (E).

The Writer
by Richard Wilbur

26. **B.** The entire poem hinges on the speaker's epiphany about life and creativity, which occurs in the last stanza. It is this realization that points to choice B. Choice A is silly and should be eliminated immediately. There is no discussion of the daughter's talent, which eliminates choice E. Although C and D sound plausible and may even be insights raised by the reader, once again there is no concrete evidence in the poem to support these choices.

27. **E.** The careful reader should recognize that the poem introduces a new idea in lines 16–30, and he or she should question the reason for this. It is obvious that the episode of the starling is meant to parallel the intensity of the creative process the daughter is experiencing.

28. **C.** The house is personified as "thinking." This is a question that is really a freebie if you've done your preparation. The answer depends on your knowledge of simple terms and your ability to identify examples of them in a work.

29. **D.** A question of this type demands that you actually refer to the passage. (You might try highlighting or underlining to emphasize line 29 and the various choices. This will prevent you from losing your place or focus.) Use the process of elimination until you find an "echo" word or phrase. In line 9, "passage" parallels "course" and points to choice D. It is a good

idea to follow the choices in order for clarity and continuity because each rereading may give you help with another question.

30. **D.** Question 2 may help you with this answer. Skim the poem from line 1 until you strike a new idea—the dazed bird. The answer has to be D. A, B, and C all describe the daughter and are on topic, while line 27 refers to the previous idea, in this case, the starling introduced earlier.

31. **C.** The perceptive reader will understand that the stanza is not about the daughter at all, whereas each of the other ideas is valid and can be supported in the context of the stanza.

32. **D.** The use of nautical terms dominates the first section of the poem, establishing the concept of life as a sea journey or passage. The words, "prow" (line 1), "gunwale" (line 6), and "great cargo" (line 8) all support choices A, B, C, and E. The only image not stated concerns writing as a safe harbor.

33. **D.** This is essentially a reading question and one you should find easy to answer. Start with the first choice and work your way through each of the others. Highlight or underline lines, look for concrete evidence, and eliminate unsupported choices. Line 19 indicates the sensitivity shown by the father's consideration for the trapped bird.

34. **B.** This type of question is more complicated than the others because there are many steps involved in finding the answer. Don't just rely on memory. Actually circle or highlight the contrasts as you skim the poem. You may have a quick flash. If so, look immediately to prove it. If you can't, you have your answer. In this case, B. To illustrate the process, here are the images that prove that the other choices are contained in the poem.
A. Line 5: commotion; line 12: stillness
C. Lines 22–23: the implied analogy of child and bird
D. Line 32: life and death
E. Line 2: light breaks; line 21: dark

35. **A.** This simple reading question is a giveaway. Stanza three tells the reader that "the stuff of her life is a great cargo, and some of it heavy." You should be able to interpret the metaphor as life's difficulties.

36. **B.** All the choices, with the exception of B, reflect the need to persist in order to achieve

a goal—freedom and creation. Only B is grounded to the hard floor.

Jane Eyre
by Charlotte Brontë

37. D. The answer is obvious if you carefully read lines 15–17. A heart made up of whalebones and iron is synonymous with strong-willed and inflexible.

38. E. Temple, feasting, food of the gods, and benediction can all imply religious connotations. Tea and toast can be a direct allusion to taking communion. Being asked to "come sit by the fire" is simply a request, nothing more.

39. E. "Gratification" involves thankfulness. And, in this case, Miss Temple is pleased that she is able to give the girls some special foods during their visit.

40. D. This is a metaphorical construction. With it, Jane lets the reader know that having the opportunity to be part of engaging and exciting conversation was like food for her mind and soul.

41. C. This is one of those questions that assumes the student is familiar with the definitions of specific terms. "Seemed hastening" is almost a literal flag waving in front of the reader's eyes signaling that something will happen in the future.

42. E. Helen's "soul sitting on her lips," her "secret sources of language," and her "purity and radiance" all relate to the realm of the divine.

43. C. Herbs are simple and of small quantity. An ox, on the other hand, is overwhelmingly large and overabundant. Love is better than hate. This analogy is straightforward and obvious.

44. D. If you read the passage carefully, Jane's wonder and deference are apparent. Look at lines 39–50 to see her sense of awe. Look at line 38. It clearly states Jane's wonder at Helen.

45. D. There is nothing in this passage that indicates either of the two girls needs to be saved.

46. B. "Serenity," "state in her mien," "refined propriety" in lines 34–35 are synonymous

with one who is restrained. The remainder of the lines illustrates and supports this characterization.

47. E. Although there is considerable religious diction and imagery in the passage, none of it directly relates to Jane's character and her being a religious person.

The Good Life
by Tracy K. Smith

48. B. This short poem does not have a rhyme scheme nor a regular meter. This is generally termed free verse. If you have any doubt about the definitions of the other choices, you should review them in Chapter 9 of this book.

49. E. You can count on questions asking you to locate a pronoun's antecedent. In this case, it is "money" in line 1. If you have any doubts, just exchange "it" with any of the other choices.

50. E. The details and diction are common, ordinary, and simple. Informal is a possibility, but the word "it's" paired with is not. None of the other choices is supported in the text.

51. A. The speaker gives "money" the qualities of a living being. This question assumes you have a working knowledge of literary devices. Take a few minutes to review them in the glossary of this book.

52. C. "For the years I lived . . ." is written in the past tense. Make certain you are familiar with verbs and their tenses. Choices D and E are not supported in this line.

53. B. Line 5 simply states a factual situation. The other lines cited contain or further develop a comparison using "like" or "as."

54. D. Remember what sarcasm means: an ironic indication of bitterness or contempt. The diction, subject matter, and literary devices are used to convey a tough life lived by the speaker. To title the poem "The Good Life" is sarcastic and quite the opposite of what is portrayed in the poem.

55. C. The key to this answer is in line 4. It is the word "nostalgic." This relates to remembering the past, and it is further developed in line 5.

Rating the Essay Section

Rubrics for "The Flowers" by Alice Walker

A high-range score (5, 6):

- Thesis indicates complete understanding and support of the prompt with an indication of the line of reasoning.
- Analyzes appropriate literary techniques that illustrate how Walker prepares the reader for the ending of the story.
- Thoroughly explores the contrasts/complexities inherent in the story.
- Fully presents Myop's character.
- Recognizes the underlying theme related to prejudice and innocence. (Very much related to sophistication.)
- Responds insightfully to image, diction, and setting.
- Presents suitable and unique interpretations of the text.
- Demonstrates a mature, sophisticated writing style.

A mid-range score (3, 4):

- The thesis refers accurately to the prompt and indicates the probable line of reasoning.
- Utilizes appropriate devices in the analysis of Walker's preparation for the surprise ending.
- Adequately supports the thesis with appropriate evidence.
- Uses obvious references and details.
- May miss the subtleties of the story.
- Inferences are based on an acceptable reading of the text.
- Demonstrates writing that is adequate to convey the writer's intent.
- May exhibit a few errors in syntax and/or diction.

Sample Student Essays

Student Essay A

". . . the days had never been as beautiful as these . . . each day a golden surprise." Surprise is the element Alice Walker presents in her story "The Flowers." It is at the heart of the meaning of this story which is driven forward by imagery, setting, and diction.

In the beginning of the story, Walker utilizes diction that creates an atmosphere of euphoric childhood innocence. Myop, the main character, "skipped lightly." Walker describes the harvests, which evince "excited little tremors" in Myop as she anticipates the new day.   5

This jocund diction continues into the second paragraph. Specifically, Myop feels "light and good" in the heat of the warm sun. In addition, ten year old Myop creates her own world in which nothing exists "but her song." In line 8, the use of onomatopaeia, "tat-de-ta-ta-ta" reinforces the idea of a happy, carefree youth.   10

Paragraph three, however, marks a small yet significant shift in the passage. Walker begins the paragraph with "Turning her back on the rusty boards of her family's sharecropper cabin, Myop . . . " Myop's world is not behind her, but moves forward to the familiar woods.   15

As the story progresses, there is a significant shift in paragraphs four and five. Walker begins to prepare the reader for her profound conclusion. While Myop has often explored the woods behind the house with her mother, today she sets out alone and "made her own path." As she walks through the woods, she cautiously keeps an eye out for snakes. The solitude of her journey, and the possibility of danger, builds suspense and prepares the reader for the dark surprise of the ending. 20

The diction of paragraphs four and five also contributes to the sudden 25 shift in the passage. While the diction in the beginning was blithe, describing "beautiful," the language in paragraph five is negative, foreshadowing the conclusion. Specifically, Myop is disoriented by the, "strangeness of the land." It was "not as pleasant" as her usual expeditions. Furthermore, words such as "gloomy" and "damp" reiterate the dark setting and prepare the reader for the 30 grotesque conclusion of the story.

Paragraph six, which is only one sentence long, marks a brief transition into the ending of the passage. Myop wants to return to her house, to the "peacefulness of the morning." But, while she was able to turn her back on the reality of her poverty, she will not be able to ignore the next truth that hits her. 35

"Stepping smack into his eyes," Myop encounters death, but is unafraid as she "frees herself." She is filled with innocent curiosity and gazes "around the spot with interest." Ironically, as she picks her "wild pink rose," a symbol of beauty, she spots the noose and has her epiphany.

The transition in image, setting, and diction all propel Walker's theme— 40 the coming of age. In the last paragraph Myop picks up the flowers and places her bouquet in front of the lynched man. It is as if she is at a funeral, as if she has sobered from her carefree state to one of realization. For, in the last line, the images of the beginning are finally crushed. Myop can no longer return to the world of flower-gathering or sun-lit skipping. For Myop, the "summer is over." 45

Note: With specific reference to the 6-point rubric, we will use the following abbreviations to indicate into which column the comment would fall: **T = thesis, E = evidence, C = complexity, S = sophistication**.

This is a high-ranking essay for the following reasons:

KEY IDEA

- Thesis presents a defensible assertion with a clear relationship to the prompt and an indication of the line of reasoning. T
- Cites appropriate details to support the thesis: E
  - Imagery (lines 15, 25–30, 36) E
  - Diction (lines 5–6, 10, 30) E
  - Setting (lines 1, 15–16) E
- Thoroughly explores contrasts (lines 12, 16–17, 45). E/C
- Presents unique insights into the underlying theme (lines 16–17, 22–23, 41–43). C/S
- Adheres well to topic; exhibits transitions and connective tissue. S
- Has a definite, clear progression of thought and a strong writer's voice. S

This high-ranking essay presents a solid, mature, and insightful discussion and analysis of Myop's "epiphany" and how Walker prepares the reader for it.

Student Essay B

In the short story "The Flowers" by Alice Walker, the author conveys the meaning of the story and prepares the reader for the ending by using various literary techniques. Some of these are symbol, narrative pace, and style.

The narrative pace starts out as slow and relaxed as Myop explores the land around her family's sharecropper cabin. Every little detail is described creating an image of the blissful summer day. Myop's exuberance is portrayed through diction such as "skipped lightly," "she felt light and good," "bouncing," and "she was singing." Her innocence is shown by the way she is able to block out everything but her happiness and her song. The colors used in the beginning of the story further form the image that is being set up because they are earthy yet shiny colors such as "golden," "silver," and "dark brown."

The fifth paragraph is a transition of narrative pace. The diction and tone change from peaceful and relaxed to tense and dark. Diction such as "strangeness" and "gloomy" take over. When describing the new atmosphere, Walker uses syntax like "the air was damp, the silence close and deep."

From here, the story continues to darken and reaches a climax when Myop steps on a dead man's face. She then discovers his body—in parts and decaying. Walker's use of colors suddenly changes too. Now, "blue," "green," and "wild pink" are used. Although these colors can be seen as positive, in this story, they represent "rotting." Myop finds the noose as she picks up a flower. Such irony.

The last paragraph/sentence is brief and compact. It simply reads, "And the summer was over." The summer can be seen as a symbol of Myop's innocence. With the end of her summer, when she lays down her flowers, her innocence is gone forever. She can no longer exist "for nothing but her song." She had seen death in the midst of her paradise.

5

10

15

20

25

This is a mid-range essay (3, 4) for the following reasons:

- Presents a defensible thesis based on the prompt and indicates a probable line pf reasoning. T
- Makes an adequate, expedient presentation of the details in developing the thesis. E
- Illustrates an understanding of the selected literary devices used in the story, but does not fully link or expand them with regard to the thesis (lines 9–10, 14–15). E
- Has unsupported interpretation in lines 18–19. C
- In many places, the syntax resembles a list because ideas are not fully developed (lines 16–20). S

This mid-range essay addresses the prompt and provides details to support the thesis. While the writer obviously understood both the story and the author's process, the subtleties are not fully explored and the syntax lacks fluidity.

Rubrics for "The Naked and the Nude" by Robert Graves

A high-range score (5, 6):

- Thesis presents a defensible assertion related to the prompt and indicates the line of reasoning.
- Analysis demonstrates a complete understanding of the requirements for discussing the differences in connotation between "naked" and "nude."
- Recognizes and identifies the many differences between the two words.
- Analyzes how Graves uses appropriate literary techniques to present a coherent distinction between the two words.
- Responds to the irony in the final stanza.
- Perceives Graves's tone and preference for one of the words.
- Interprets allusions, images, symbols, etc.
- Uses smooth transitions and clear connective tissue.
- Demonstrates a mature writing style.

A mid-range score (3, 4):

- Presents a thesis with a defensible assertion related to the prompt and a probable line of reasoning.
- Adequately supports the thesis with appropriate evidence.
- Is less adept at interpreting the poem.
- May not be sensitive to the complex allusions and images or vocabulary.
- Demonstrates writing that is adequate to convey the writer's intent, may have minor errors in syntax and diction.

Sample Student Essays

Student Essay A

Many people tend to use the words "naked" and "nude" interchangeably. Yet Robert Graves objects to this misconception in his poem "The Naked and the Nude." Although both words mean "without clothes," Graves interprets them differently with regard to their connotations. He points out that "naked" refers to the body itself, whereas, "nude" refers to a personality or state of mind. Through his use of various allusions and imagery, Graves contrasts the two synonyms.

Graves dedicates one stanza apiece to explain his perception of each word. When describing the "naked," Graves uses several classical allusions. He points out that "the Hippocratic eye will see in nakedness, anatomy." Likewise, "naked shines the Goddess when she mounts her lion among men." It's clear that nakedness only refers to the naked body. However, Graves uses allusions to deception and trickery to explain his concept of the nude. He says, "the nude are bold, the nude are sly . . . they grin a mock-religious grin of scorn at those of naked skin." The concept of nude seems to be more of a cunning state of mind—"being naked with attitude."

The poet uses these details to create a certain imagery that clearly explains this discrepancy. His use of classical allusions creates images of peace, beauty, and spirituality which imply the inherent beauty of the human body on a physical level.

5

10

15

Yet, the imagery created by the second set of details does not deal with the physical body. Graves explains that the nude have a cunning state of mind, "while draping by a showman's trick their dishabille in rhetoric." 20

The contrast described in the poem, body versus mind, is reinforced when Graves tells us that the naked are physical bodies that are admired by "Lovers without reproach" and men of medicine. The nude, however, are more than that; they "are sly" and "hold each treasonable eye." The writer concludes that the naked, therefore, who 25 compete against the nude may know defeat because the nude are more complex and cynical.

Graves's final stanza transfers the vulnerability of the naked to the nude. When treading "the briary patches of the dead," the nude will not have artifice to protect them from the Gorgons' whips—they will be the naked as well as the nude. 30

Note: With specific reference to the 6-point rubric, we will use the following abbreviations to indicate into which column the comment would fall: **T = thesis, E = evidence, C = complexity, S = sophistication**.

This is a high-ranking essay for the following reasons:

KEY IDEA

- Thesis states a defensible assertion clearly related to the prompt and indicates a line of reasoning. T
- Immediately presents an accurate distinction between "naked" and "nude" (lines 4–5). E/C
- Utilizes allusion and imagery correctly and links examples to meaning (lines 8–11, 12–15, 17–18). E/C
- Reinforces the contrast throughout the essay (lines 16, 22, 29–30). E
- Indicates perceptive, subtle analysis (lines 20–21, 29). E/C
- Is well organized. S
- Demonstrates a mature writing style. S

This essay is indicative of a confident writer and thinker. The paper is well focused, and it exhibits the writer's facility with literary terminology and analysis.

Student Essay B

The poem "The Naked and the Nude" written by Robert Graves explicitly shows how connotations can change the meaning of a thought or statement through images and other poetic devices. Those who are "naked" and those who are "nude" are not, according to the poem, in the same state of undress.

The speaker of the poem describes the differences between the naked and the 5 nude using a variety of images and descriptions. He feels that one who is naked is hiding nothing while one who is nude is a picture of deception and art. The images of "Lovers without reproach will gaze on bodies naked and ablaze" depicts the honesty and truth that is given with love. Also the "Hippocratic eye will see in nakedness, anatomy." When this "eye" sees a naked person it is seeing what is really there and 10 not what could be held in the deception of a person who is nude.

Although the naked are personified as "love" and "truth," when they "compete against the nude they may know defeat." This statement shows how those who are naked can sometimes be deceived and beaten by those who are artful liars. However, when it comes to the life after death, those who have been nude will also be naked, meaning that no matter what they were in life, when they die there will be no hiding behind the art of the body. Also, the facade that was built in life to hide from the truth will not work when it comes to the end.   15

Tone is another device that is used to convey the different connotations of naked and nude. When those who are naked are being discussed, the tone is not only positive, it presents an image of those who are happy with their position in life. For example, nakedness is linked with words such as "love," "truth," "shines," and "Goddess." However, when the speaker directs his attention on the nude, the tone is just the opposite. Nude is associated with "scorn," "showman," and "mock-religious." The speaker's tone in the descriptions of the two states of undress presents a clear difference in the connotations of the two words in the title of the poem.   20   25

The style and structure of the poem also contribute to conveying the two different connotations of naked and nude. The simple rhyme scheme shows how simplistic those who are naked can be as opposed to the deception and intricacies of those who are nude. The four stanza's each have a theme that it conveys. The first stanza exhibits the differences between the naked and the nude. The second stanza has the theme of the freedom of the naked, while the third shows the deception of the nude. The fourth and final stanza reinforces the theme that everyone will be naked after death.   30

This is a mid-range essay for the following reasons:

- Accurately addresses the prompt with a defensible assertion and an indication of a probable prompt. T
- Understands deception and artifice (lines 6–7). E
- Refers to suitable textual material to support the thesis (lines 8–9, 22–24). E
- Demonstrates an ability to handle literary analysis (19–25, 27–29). E
- Adheres to the implied line of reasoning. T/E/C
- Has several awkward sentences and punctuation and agreement errors (lines 10–11, 13–29, and 30). S
- Uses transitions and connective tissue. S

It's obvious that the writer of this mid-range essay understands both the prompt and process of literary analysis. The second half of the paper is not as strong as the first. Perhaps, this writer was feeling the time pressure.

Rubrics for the Free-Response Essay

A high-range score (5, 6):

- Clearly incorporates a chosen work of fiction into the thesis that addresses the prompt and provides an indication of the line of reasoning.
- Chooses an appropriate novel or play.
- Effectively and coherently addresses the intentional dissembling of a character or group.
- Effectively and coherently analyzes how the dissembling contributes to character development.

- Effectively and coherently analyzes how the dissembling contributes to the meaning of the work.
- Uses references insightfully to support and illustrate the dissembling.
- Thoroughly discusses the character's nature and its relation to the theme.
- Strongly adheres to the topic using transitions and a clear line of reasoning.
- Substantiates development of the thesis.
- Exhibits mature writing style.

A mid-range score (3, 4):

- Addresses the prompt with a defensible thesis and indicates a probable line of reasoning.
- Identifies the intentional dissembling of a character or group.
- Chooses an acceptable novel or play.
- Adequately addresses the prompt with respect to intentional dissembling and how it contributes to both character development and meaning.
- Uses obvious references to support the prompt.
- Discussion of the character's nature and its relation to the theme is less developed.
- Adheres to topic, but may have lapses in coherence.
- Discussion of the theme is less developed.
- Writing style is acceptable but may show lapses in syntax and/or diction.

Sample Student Essays

Student Essay A

"To thine own self be true," advises Polonius in Shakespeare's *Hamlet*. Too bad he doesn't follow his own counsel when he continually dissembles to advance his own position in Claudius's court. This deceitfulness is the cause of the destruction of the lives of his children, himself, and ultimately the kingdom. His seemingly minor deceits reinforce the theme of betrayal and deception in the play. 5

Our first impression of Polonius is a positive one when we see him supporting Laertes's desire to return to his studies in Paris. However, his fatherly advice, "to not be false to any man" is ironic because he has already hired Reynaldo to spy on his son. He tells Reynaldo to use a "bait of falsehood" to see if Laertes's friends will be faithful 10 and true. Polonius plans for this to include starting rumors and even malicious lies. Later in the play, Shakespeare has Rosencrantz and Guildenstern play out a parallel scene with Hamlet.

As with his son, Polonius seems to be genuinely concerned with the well-being of his daughter Ophelia. He tells her to reject the "love" letters and tokens from Hamlet 15 because he fears Hamlet only wants to take advantage of her and will not and cannot marry her. But soon we see the other side of this paternal scheme when Polonius willingly uses his daughter's emotional connections to Hamlet for his own purpose of furthering his service to Claudius. Hoping to prove that Hamlet's madness is caused by love sickness, he permits himself to advance his own agenda even though he has to 20 know that it will cause pain and distress for both Ophelia and Hamlet.

Inevitably, Polonius's dissembling leads to his own destruction. Ever the deceitful sycophant, he suggests to Claudius that he hide behind the arras in Gertrude's chamber in order to spy on both her and Hamlet. While eavesdropping, he cries out when he believes that Hamlet is attacking the Queen. Believing the voice to be that of   25
Claudius, Hamlet thrusts his sword through the curtain, fatally wounding Polonius. Here, the irony lies in his death resulting from an attempt to protect Gertrude.

It is this act that is the catalyst for the subsequent tragic events: Ophelia's madness and death, Laertes's desire for revenge, and Hamlet's fleeing Denmark. The final tragedies of the play—the deaths of Ophelia, Laertes, Gertrude, Claudius, and   30
Hamlet—are all the results of further dissembling which is foreshadowed by Polonius's deceit.

Although Polonius dies in Act III, he sets the foundation for the theme of deceit and murder throughout the remainder of the drama. Truly, something was rotten in the state of Denmark, and it was Polonius.   35

Note: With specific reference to the 6-point rubric, we will use the following abbreviations to indicate into which column the comment would fall: **T = thesis, E = evidence, C = complexity, S = sophistication**.

This is a high-range essay for the following reasons:

- Presents a clear thesis with a defensible assertion and an indication of a line of reasoning. T
- Exhibits solid evidence of knowledge of the chosen work. E
- Demonstrates the ability to garner insights from the work. C
- Uses appropriate illustrations and details (lines 8–9, paragraphs 3 and 4). E/C
- Uses strong connective tissue. S
- Demonstrates thorough development of ideas that are linked to the meaning of the work (lines 3–6, 11–13, 19–21). E/C/S
- Strongly adheres to topic and organization. S
- Uses mature vocabulary and syntax (lines 22–23, 28). S

This essay is in the high-range because of its clear voice and strong organization. (S) The introductory paragraph establishes the premise, which is fully supported in the body paragraphs. (E/C) Rather than a summary, the concluding paragraph makes an insightful final comment.

Student Essay B

Often, in literature, there is a gap between the appearance of a situation and the meaning of the truth behind it. In Shakespeare's *Hamlet*, the protagonist assumes the antic disposition as a means of investigating the veracity of the ghost's admonition, "The serpent that did sting thy father's life, now wears his crown." In addition to contributing to the psychological development of Hamlet's character, this deceit augments many of the important themes in the play. In a work whose main topic is the search for truth, Hamlet's misrepresentation acts as a warning to sift through the surface appearance of things to discover purpose in this world.

Throughout the play, nothing is really as it seems. Hamlet's feigned madness is perhaps the most egregious example of this pattern. The melancholy Dane becomes a different man behind the mask of insanity. He is free to taunt Polonius regarding his lack of intelligence, or to scold his mother for her sexual improprieties, or to chastise Ophelia for her attempt to trick him. He is free to express himself without the fear of being held responsible for his insolence. This is a psychological coping method for Hamlet to deal with the trauma of a father's death and a mother's betrayal. Hamlet represses his anger and is paralyzed by it. The course of the play is a struggle for Hamlet to overcome his repression and to deal with the problems before him. Pretending to be mad is symbolic of this inner struggle and Hamlet's shield from the world.

Many of the major themes in *Hamlet* are also embodied in Hamlet's misrepresentation. The pervading irony in the play is that the "madman" is really thinking rationally. He sees what others do not and recognizes that his father was killed at Claudius's hands. Hamlet is a man who can and does make plans to seek the truth, and he carries these plans out. Another major theme is that of appearance versus reality. Connected to and with Hamlet's situation is a king who is a murderer, a mystery involving a ghost, a play within a play, a royal request which will turn into an invasion of Denmark, spying for proof of madness, fatherly advice to his children, and friends who are enemies. Each of these separately and all of them together enhance this theme of the play.

Hamlet is a search for truth. Through the protagonist's discovery of self and the revelation of Claudius's guilt, he embodies everyman's striving for understanding. Dissembling as a madman, Hamlet is able to work toward his goal of gaining authentic knowledge of past events and future battles.

This is a solid mid-range essay for the following reasons:

- Provides a clear thesis statement with a defensible assertion and an indicated line of reasoning. T
- Decisively identifies theme and character. C
- References are appropriate. E
- Indicates cause and effect with supporting details. E/C
- Uses inferences rather than plot. E/C

- Good use of connective tissue. S
- Uses strong vocabulary. S
- Uses parallel structure well. S

Here is a paper that shows great promise and strength in the first half, but it loses continuity and lacks development in the second half. It seems that the writer has run out of time and is anxious to complete the essay. This student is a real thinker, but appears to be trapped by time constraints.

this object to describing the people who inhabit that house. It transitions from reportorial to personal.

21. D. The use of "I" does not allow for a strictly objective or reportorial perspective. There is no mention of a death, nor are there any techniques or devices used to suggest bitterness. Relating the dining event and the family interactions with each other supports the idea of an involved memoirist.

22. A. The final paragraph is all about the grandmother: her actions and the actions of those around her as they respond to her demands. This is on whom the narrator centers her attention.

23. C. The pair of words that correctly apply to the entire passage is frank and thoughtful. Nostalgia could be applied, but it is paired with a word that cannot be correctly used to describe the tone of the passage.

24. B. The detailed description of a typical dinner with Mammy and the interactions of all of those gathered around the table provide the opportunity for the narrator to imply and the reader to conclude that this is a family with a multitude of stories.

25. E. Lines 44–45 and 50–51 are the telling signs that the narrator was not happy with her mother's passivity.

Love Poem
by John Frederick Nims

26. C. You should use the context of lines 7–8 to help you. "Steady" implies a lack of movement and leads you to the best choice, "wavy," which implies motions.

27. D. The entire poem lists the beloved's faults, yet the speaker adores her for them. This contradiction is the essence of the ironic title. Choice A is close, but it refers to the situation of the entire poem, not just the title.

It is easy to jump to the conclusion that the [speak]er has broken yet another object. However, [B,] C, D, and E all support that idea; therefore, [they] cancel one another out.

[You] are required to reread the lines prior [to the] word "only" in order to realize that [it prov]ides a contrast. B and C are readily [elimina]ted with a glance, and D and E are not [support]ed by the poem.

30. D. Pay careful attention to the word "except." Then use substitution to find the one quality she does not exhibit. The answer is supported in line 15 with "wit," line 1 with "clumsiest," line 14 with "at ease," and line 19 with "gayly."

31. E. By definition, an apostrophe is an example of direct address.

32. D. Even though there is some exaggeration and humor, they are used to develop the character of the beloved, and a narrative requires elements of a story.

33. A. As you can see, it is imperative that you know terminology. To make sense, lines 5 and 6 must be read smoothly to the punctuation rather than to the end of the line.

34. E. The tone is revealed clearly in lines 16, 19, 23, and 24. The speaker adores his beloved.

35. C. This is a question that is almost too easy. Use your information from questions 30, 31, and 34 to help you recognize that all the other choices are negative.

36. A. As toys bring joy and delight, so, too, does the lover bring pleasure to the speaker's life. She holds toys and the speaker in her hands.

37. E. The clocks and solar system represent time and space. (See metonymy in Chapter 8.) "Wrench" indicates a breakdown of a system (e.g., "throwing a wrench into the system").

38. C. A straightforward, factual question. Again, you need to know your terms.

39. A. This is a poetic term and example question. The two metaphors are that palms are "bulls" and "burs in linen."

40. E. This is a subtle question which asks you to hear the sound of the line. All the open "O" sounds reinforce the idea of floating. None of the other given devices is present in this line.

As I Lay Dying
by William Faulkner

41. C. One of the universal symbols of freedom is flight. To refer to "wild geese going north" is to reinforce Addie's desire to be free.

42. E. "I" indicates a first person narrator point of view. The phrases "little dirty snuffling nose," "damp and rotting leaves," and "it was worst then" are indicative of conflict, setting, and tone. What is *not* mentioned in this first paragraph is a central event.

43. A. These lines are primarily composed of dialogue, so it is here that you should look for your answer. Vocabulary, similes, and syntax all point to colloquial (informal, conversational) diction.

44. D. The similes found in these two sets of lines are examples of figurative language. The other lines are factual and reportorial.

45. C. The concepts and images associated with alienation are found in phrases containing "secret," "blood strange," "cemetery," and "got no people." C, on the other hand, is cause and effect.

46. D. There is no evidence of any of the other choices in the passage. The very last line begins with the word "so." It is indicative of a matter-of-fact result of Anse being in the right place at the right time.

47. B. In this passage, Addie's conversation and interaction with Anse always place him in a subservient, uncomfortable position. See lines 27–28 and 31–33 to support the idea of her dominance.

48. E. Lines 17 and 46 indicate a straightforward cause and effect that just so happens to lead to Addie marrying Anse. Ambivalence, irony, setting, and highlighting an event are *not* references of the given phrase.

49. A. The "it" in this question is used the second time in the same way. See lines 4–6: The early spring, longing, potential, and desire to be free as wild geese lead to the conclusion that Addie has a restless nature.

50. D. Lines 1–15 give you the direct answer. ". . . and I would think with each blow of the switch: Now you are aware of me!"

51. E. A careful reading of the passage will lead you through Addie's experiences and thoughts about living and dying, about being alone, about being in a relationship, and about being free. Therefore, you need to recognize that, for Addie, hope and liberation is not in her future.

52. B. The second paragraph gives you the correct answer. It directly refers to the father.

53. C. Contrast demands difference. The only appropriate choice, therefore, is "rotting leaves . . . new earth." Rotting and new are the contrast here.

54. A. Paragraphs 1, 2, and 4 allow the reader into Addie's psyche. The one characteristic *not* associated with her seeking quiet is hatred.

55. D. This is another universal symbol. The associations with spring, especially early spring, center around renewal, regeneration, hope, fertility, and the continuance of life.

Rating the Essay Section

Rubrics for "Reginald's Choir Treat" by Saki

A high-range score (5, 6):

- Presents a prompt with a defensible assertion and indicates a line of reasoning.
- Identifies the two views of life presented in the story.
- Recognizes which view is preferred by the author.
- Effectively and coherently analyzes Saki's craft.
- Is cognizant of satire.
- Recognizes the humor in the allusions.
- Understands the irony and tone of the essay.
- Delineates Reginald's character.
- Cites appropriate textual references.
- Presents advanced insight and complexity.
- Strongly adheres to topic and uses connective tissue.
- Demonstrates an ability to manipulate language in a mature style.

A mid-range score (3, 4):

- Refers accurately to the prompt with a defensible assertion and probable line of reasoning.

- Presents the two philosophies.
- Refers accurately to Saki's craft.
- Infers the narrator's preference of lifestyle.
- Presents less-developed discussion of the two views of life.
- Adequately links elements of the discussion.
- May miss the satire of the story.
- Concentrates on the obvious rather than on the inferences and implications.
- Organization is adequate.
- May exhibit a few errors in syntax and/or diction.

Sample Student Essays

Student Essay A

In the short story "Reginald's Choir Treat" Saki contrasts two philosophies of life. One is a daring, cynical, and whimsical approach to life, like Reginald's. The other is a conservative, intellectual, religious, reforming approach to life like Anabel's. The author's sarcastic tone with a hint of diffidence indicates that he agrees with Reginald's cause, but he pities the fact that few people can relate to or understand "pioneers." Saki contrasts and shows the irony of both Anabel and Reginald's actions and perspectives about life to help the reader understand the two philosophies. However, even Anabel's philosophy shares some similarities to Reginald's and is more appealing to Saki's story than that of Reginald's family, which lives a modest, pedestrian, and uncompromising life, with no tolerance for the whims of Reginald.

Reginald does not fit in with his family's lifestyle. He questioned the universe and pleased himself with unconventional fantasies. Anabel is a gifted vicar's daughter who leads a charitable life and tries to be worldly at the same time. She attempts to make Reginald more religious and to coax him with her womanly charms but is unsuccessful. Saki ironically has her traveling to a French resort to pick up a good French accent from the Americans living there. She also persuades Reginald to lead a more virtuous life like herself and then ironically leaves Reginald to complete one of her charitable obligations without her. In a dialogue between the two main characters, Saki uses conversation to contrast Reginald with Anabel's perspectives. She speaks against the "sin of an empty life," and Reginald recalls the artistic "simplicity of the lilies" that simply sit and look beautiful. The greatest humorous irony of the story is Reginald turning religious charity work in the form of a choir outing into a whimsical pagan festival which is an allusion to the mythological Bacchus, the god of wine and pleasure. He shows his carefree and sarcastic approach to life by giving choirboys "tin whistles" and parading them through the streets with symbols of Bacchus. Another irony is that he has children honor Bacchus (god of wine) with a temperance hymn familiar to them, and that the parade which was intended to be gay turns out to be a lugubrious procession with the "miserable wailing of pipes."

A sign that Saki sides with Reginald's unappreciated actions over those of Anabel, or especially those of his family, is in the story's conclusion. Reginald's family never forgives him, and Saki adds that they felt this way because "they had no sense of humour."

This makes it clear that the unfortunate and almost bitter ending is their flaw and not Reginald's because they should have appreciated the humor of the situation.

Saki shows that he shares some of Reginald's philosophy with his frequent use of irony and sarcasm. He shows that people who share Anabel's philosophy will not be able to reform those whimsical pioneers like Reginald. But, they should be amiable and attempt to appreciate the sense of humor in the actions of those like Reginald. If not, they will be doomed to live an ill-humored, mundane life like that of Reginald's family.

Note: With specific reference to the 6-point rubric, we will use the following abbreviations to indicate into which column the comment would fall: **T = thesis, E = evidence, C = complexity, S = sophistication**.

This is a high-ranking essay for the following reasons:

- Introduction contains a clear thesis with a defensible assertion that sets up the organization of the essay. T
- Contains a clear opening, which sets up the organization of the essay. T
- Clarifies distinction between the two views and the characters (lines 5–10, 11–14). E/C
- Establishes Saki's attitude. C
- Introduces sarcasm and defends it (lines 3–5). E
- Contains strong textual references. E/C
- Draws appropriate conclusions based on the evidence presented (lines 34–37). C
- Addresses the writer's craft. E/C
- Juxtaposes the two characters and their opposing views (lines 18–20). E/C
- Provides a perceptive interpretation of a grammatical detail (lines 29–31). S
- Strongly adheres to topic using transitions and echo words. S
- Is direct and accurate. S
- Organization, syntax, and diction are adequate. S

This is an essay that can be categorized as high. Its strong textual references and understanding of the subtleties allow it to be in the high range even though there are some lapses in syntax.

Student Essay B

Saki's short story "Reginald's Choir Treat" contrasts two different philosophies of life. Each philosophy is represented by different characters. Conformity is represented by Anabel and nonconformity is represented by Reginald. In this story, Anabel and Reginald's parents try to make Reginald conform to the rest of society. Yet, his choir treat demonstrates that their goal failed. Through his use of tone, dialogue, and contrast, Saki indirectly shows his support of Reginald's nonconformity.

Saki uses a sarcastic tone, particularly towards Anabel and the other conformists. The first line of the story has an adage from Reginald: "never be a pioneer. It's the Early Christian that gets the fattest lion." This saying sets the sarcastic tone for the rest of the story. Later on, in his description of Anabel, Saki notes that, "if you abstain from tennis and read Maeterlinck in a small country village, you are of necessity intellectual." Likewise, in his description of Reginald's family, Saki points out that the rest of his family used "primroses as a table decoration." Saki is mocking all the

conformists because of their desire to conform to society. He uses this sarcastic tone to
demonstrate his partiality towards Reginald's free nature.   15

Saki also uses a contrast between Reginald and Anabel. The only direct
description of Reginald is that "[He], in his way, is a pioneer." On the other hand, the
author describes many details about Anabel. He calls Anabel, "the vicar's one extravagance."
Yet, in this case, Saki uses the pronoun "it" to refer to Anabel's fanciful name,
demonstrating his distaste for her. He sarcastically relates that "Anabel was accounted   20
a beauty and intellectually gifted" because "she had been twice to Fecamp to pick up a good
French accent from the Americans staying there." Saki presents the notion that many
believe the conformists are better than the nonconformists and uses Anabel to refute that
notion. Despite these accolades Saki has attributed to her, he mocks her and her philosophy.

Similarly, Saki uses dialogue to demonstrate his favoring nonconformity. The   25
conversation between Reginald and Anabel revolves around trying to convince Reginald to
abandon his nonconformity. She tries to do so by insulting him. Anabel tells him that
"[He is] really indecently vain in [his] appearance." For a woman who is supposed to be
smart and sweet, she does not display any of those qualities here. Her nasty nature
towards Reginald in this dialogue further emphasizes Saki's distaste for her and   30
her philosophy.

Obviously, Saki views individual expression as important and nonthreatening.
He recognizes that the best weapon to fight conformity is humor.

This is a mid-range essay for the following reasons:

- Clearly presents a thesis related to the prompt and the organization of the essay (lines 1–6). T
- Establishes the characters of Reginald and Anabel. E/C
- Recognizes and discusses sarcasm (lines 10–11). E
- Presents dialogue as indicative of character (lines 25–30). E
- Makes inferences and understands satire. E/C
- Presents author's preference and defends it (lines 7, 13–15). E/C
- Draws threads of the essay together and synthesizes technique with interpretation (lines 32–33). C/S

The syntax and diction shortcomings do not allow this essay to be rated in the high range.

Rubrics for the Poetry Essay

A high-range score (5, 6):

- Effectively and coherently analyzes the poet's attitude toward education.
- Effectively and coherently analyzes the similarities and differences between Nemerov and Wordsworth.
- Indicates a fluency with poetic analysis.
- Identifies and analyzes appropriate references to support an interpretation.
- Exhibits strong line of reasoning.
- Draws mature inferences.
- Responds to subtleties in the poem.
- Writer's syntax and diction demonstrate a mature style.

A mid-range score (3, 4):

- Adequately addresses the prompt.
- Identifies and discusses the writers' techniques.
- Adequately discusses the similarities and differences between Nemerov and Wordsworth.
- Presents an adequate discussion of the poet's attitude.
- Displays acceptable writing skills.
- May not be sensitive to inference and tone.
- Focuses on the obvious and may not recognize the subtleties in both poems.
- Writing may have a few errors in syntax and/or diction.

Student Essay A

If weirdly possible, Wordsworth and Nemerov would probably have a heated conversation about education. While they would both agree that being taught and learning are important and necessary, they would probably disagree about where the lessons should come from, they may agree about the purpose and direction of education, and the value of education. Nemerov's "To David, About His Education" poetically promulgates his views about education which are facilitated through the poem's structure, tone, and imagery.

"To David, About His Education" suggests that what the world sees as important parts of life are learned through books rather than Wordsworth's experience and nature. In the opening lines of the poem, Nemerov makes the case that the world's "invisible things" can only be learned in books. Lines 2–3 call for "putting the mind's eye/or its nose, in a book" to receive a proper education for learning these "invisible things." Continuing, the speaker states that studying from books is a more effective way to learn but cannot procure a benefit to the method. He questioningly states, "You will have to learn them/ in order to become one of the grown-ups" (14–15), not to any kind of an enlightened, educated person. This begins to place a doubt in the reader's mind about the real value of book learning.

Perhaps in line with with Wordsworth's belief in an education based soley on experience and living in nature, "To David, About His Education" presents examples of the intellectual pursuit of an education in which the images are of ridiculous facts and esoteric information, such as "the square root of Everest" (4) or the humorous "calorie content of the Diet of Worms" (13). The images are hyperbolic examples of the studies in an education through books. According to the speaker, only this kind of an education will produce the answers to such questions presented by "mostly invisible things." And, the reader may be led to ask whether or not this kind of information is of any value.

An answer to this type question is created by the tone established in the poem which is tongue-in-cheek or a bit sarcastic. Using parallel examples (4–13) that enumerate almost useless facts and information, the speaker describes the results of book learning to his son, but he does not praise these results. Rather, he seems to put it down in lines 15–19, "In order to become one of these grown-ups/ Who keeps invisible things neither steadily nor whole,/ But keeps gravely the grand confusion of the world." Nemerov is sarcastically saying that education has value, but for what and for whom?

So, it would seem Wordsworth and Nemerov have more in common than one would originally conclude. Both see the value of education, as most of the modern world does. Their differences most likely lie in the how, not the why.

Note: With specific reference to the 6-point rubric, we will use the following abbreviations to indicate into which column the comment would fall: **T** = **thesis**, **E** = **evidence**, **C** = **complexity**, **S** = **sophistication**.

This is a high-ranking essay for the following reasons:

- Contains a sophisticated and complex thesis and introduction to the task at hand (lines 1–7). T
- Clearly and concisely identifies the attitude of the poet toward education and supports it with references to the text (lines 10–11, 23–25). E/C
- Perceives implications arising from the poem (lines 12–16, 22–24, 32–34). C
- Uses connective tissue well (paragraphs 2, 3, 4, 5). S
- Analyzes the purpose of the imagery and tone (paragraphs 2, 3, 4). C

This spare essay falls into the high range because it is packed with appropriate detail and effective and coherent analyses and interpretation that is clearly related to the thesis and indicates a wider application.

Student Essay B

As shown in his poem "To David, About His Education" Howard Nemerov would disagree with William Wordsworth about how one should be educated. Wordsworth believes that true education is only gotten through experience and living in nature. But, from the very opening line of his poem, Nemerov makes it clear that a proper education is achieved through school which is something almost everyone would agree with. This is made obvious by Nemerov's tone and imagery.

Throughout the poem Nemerov illustrates that he is very educated. At times, it seems as if Nemerov has a sarcastic, almost cynical approach toward school, with his mocking of things taught in school, such as "the square root of Everest" and "how many times Byron goes into Texas." He also uses humor in the line "calorie content/Of the diet of Worms." Seeming to realize the underlying benefits of a proper education, Nemerov points out that "such things are said to be good for you." However, he also states in lines 10–13 that "I don't know/What you will do with the mean annual rainfall/of Plato's Republic."

Nemerov uses a very unusual sarcasm in this poem, as he applies two or more academic subjects which may have nothing in common except that they are both taught in school, and he is able to tie them together to make sense, almost in joking manner. Statements such as "the law of the excluded middle applies west of the Rockies" illustrate this method, as does the "calorie content of the Diet of Worms." Although Diet of Worms has nothing to do with eating, Nemerov connects the two almost as if his brain has been overloaded with useless information, similar to the way a student might accidentally confuse the material of multiple subjects he is studying. Nemerov fully understands the value of an education "in order to become one of the grown-ups."

Nemerov and Wordsworth have blatantly opposing opinions about the best method of education. While Wordsworth believes that an education through Nature is more valuable than spending hours reading books, Nemerov understands that in order to be accepted by society, a knowledge of academic subjects is vital.

5

10

15

20

25

This is a mid-range essay for the following reasons:

- Presents a clear thesis that addresses the prompt and indicates a line of reasoning (paragraph 1). T
- Adequately illustrates a facility with analysis with respect to imagery (paragraph 2) and tone (paragraph 3). E/C
- Provides adequate evidence to defend interpretations (paragraphs 2, 3). E/C
- Transitions logically lead from one claim to another. S
- Support is adequate but needs more analysis of purpose. E/C
- Lacks implications for a wider view and applicaton. S

This is a mid-range essay with clear analysis, topic adherence, and support. Details chosen are obvious and limited in scope with a few lapses in syntax and diction.

Rubrics for the Free-Response Essay

A high-range score (5, 6):

KEY IDEA

- Clearly states the thesis with a defensible assertion and presents a line of reasoning.
- Effectively and coherently addresses the nature of the transformation.
- Effectively and coherently discusses the effects of the transformation on character and meaning.
- Insightful choice of details from an appropriate novel or play.
- Differentiates between actual and symbolic transformations.
- Focuses on the results of the transformation with regard to character and theme.
- Thoroughly discusses a specific character in context.
- Strongly adheres to topic.
- Demonstrates mature writing style.

A mid-range score (3, 4):

- States a clear thesis with a defensible assertion and probable line of reasoning.
- Adequately identifies and discusses the transformation.
- Adequately addresses the transformation's effect on the character and theme.
- Results of transformation are presented with less-developed discussion and/or analysis.
- Relies on obvious details to support the prompt or discussion.
- Adequately adheres to topic and uses connective tissue.
- Demonstrates some errors in syntax and diction.

Sample Student Essays

Student Essay A

In the novel <u>The Color Purple</u> by Alice Walker, the heroine, Celie, grows and develops tremendously as an individual. Throughout the course of the story, Celie undergoes major spiritual and psychological transformations. In essence, Celie is reborn. The novel's themes of the power of faith, a united sisterhood, and rebirth are all emphasized by Celie's dramatic character evolution.

The novel begins with Celie writing a letter to God, telling him how her father has been raping her. Only fourteen years old, Celie is naive and still somewhat immature. She doesn't understand what her father is doing to her, and even more

5

unfortunately, she doesn't have anyone to confide in. Thus, the reader senses Celie's immense isolation as she shares her confusion with, and only with, God.

Celie's life takes on a turn for the worse when she is sent to live with her arranged husband, Mr.—, who beats her and doesn't appreciate her. She does all of his work for him and his children, and again she has not a friend to turn to. However, when Mr.—'s son, Harpo, marries Sophia, Celie comes into contact with another woman. Celie doesn't really understand Sophia because she is a strong-willed, independent person who actually stands up to men. Thus, the reader senses the weakness in Celie's character when she advised Harpo to beat Sophia. Celie has been abused her whole life, and to her, being beaten is part of being a woman. She is totally numb to abuse; she even imagines herself to be a tree when being abused. This is her way to escape and void all feelings, to be indifferent to the pain.

Naturally, she is envious of Sophia's strength and character, and so she feels a beating would do Sophia good. When Sophia discovers that it was Celie who told Harpo to beat her, she is both furious and hurt. Sophia confronts Celie, and this a pivotal point in the novel. Celie realizes that she meant enough to Sophia for her to be upset, which means that Celie has actually affected another person. The two women quickly mend their relationship and begin a quilt to symbolize their friendship. This ties into the theme of sisterhood because now Celie has a friend, and the unity that the two share becomes an amazing force throughout the novel.

Celie's character undergoes the strongest transformation after meeting another "sister," Shug Avery. The circumstances under which Shug and Celie become friends are incredible, for Shug is Mr.—'s mistress. However, their unlikely bond is the main cause of Celie's rebirth. It was Shug who first expressed appreciation to Celie for helping her get better after a serious illness. No one had ever thanked Celie before, but Shug was so gratified for her care that she wrote a song for Celie. This small act of appreciation becomes the turning point in Celie's life. She now feels she is no longer as numb as a lifeless tree.

Shug's influence leads Celie to go from being a passive victim to becoming an assertive, vibrant, independent woman. Shug was the one who makes Mr.— stop beating Celie, as well as the one who found Celie's lost sister Nettie's letters which Mr.— had been hiding. Shug even inspires Celie to begin her own pants-making business, giving Celie total economic independence and creative freedom. Thus, the theme of rebirth is emphasized. Walker stresses how the human soul is an unbelievably powerful force, and how it contains the strength to emerge victorious despite adversity.

Shug Avery is also responsible for giving Celie a new spiritual outlook on life. She explains to Celie that God isn't necessarily an old, white-bearded man. Shug's view is that God is everything and is everywhere. The title becomes significant when Shug tells Celie that God becomes angry if you walk past the color purple in a field and don't notice it. This is a significant step in Celie's spiritual life because she now doesn't feel that God is a man who is indifferent and deaf to her prayers. She has renewed her belief, and the theme of the power of faith is reinforced, for Celie's faith has remained strong.

The Color Purple is a perfect example of a work of literature where the character undergoes a dramatic transformation. Celie changes from a numb, unassertive victim to being an aggressive, creative, vibrant, and independent woman. The unity of her female confidants and her unending faith allowed her to undergo such a deep transformation. 55

Note: With specific reference to the 6-point rubric, we will use the following abbreviations to indicate into which column the comment would fall: **T = thesis, E = evidence, C = complexity, S = sophistication.**

This essay is within the high-range parameters for the following reasons:

- Presents a clear, strong thesis with a a defensible assertion and indication of the line of reasoning. T
- Presents clear, appropriate evidence/support for thesis. E
- Incorporates connected meaning with every point made. E/C
- Thoroughly presents Celie's character. E/C
- Provides pivotal moments and details to illustrate the prompt. C
- Organization allows presentation to build chronologically and from the merely physical to the metaphysical. S
- Indicates both a perceptive reading of the novel and an understanding of some of its complexities. S
- Strongly adheres to topic. E/C/S
- Uses good connective tissue. S
- Demonstrates mature manipulation of language. S

This is a solid high-range essay that clearly indicates a reader who not only "got" the novel but also "got" the tasks demanded of the prompt.

Student Essay B

Set in the malevolent, shadowy era of the Cold War, Ian McEwan's The Innocent centers on a fervent young Brit working for a covert anti-Soviet intelligence agency. His youthful good nature, manners, and naiveté are what make Leonard Marnham "the innocent." The new threat constantly slithering around the corner is 5 the dreaded red snake of Communism, ensnaring and asphyxiating the world with its wicked omnipotence. Leonard travails scrupulously and surreptitiously for its willful opposition and relies on his innocence throughout his occupation and life. When suddenly thrust into a spiral of new and exciting, but vaguely frightening experiences exploring 10 the life he never lived, something immense in Leonard changes. This flagrant transformation is momentous and permanent.

The most vital characterization of the protagonist is his underlying innocence, which is repeatedly and implicitly emphasized throughout the novel. The reader and revolving characters are drawn into Leonard's 15 ingenuousness until he chooses to walk a path unknown to him which results in his surrendering his innocence. This transformation begins when Leonard becomes enraptured by the discovery of his own sexuality. He is an innocent in the purest sense of the word. Maria, his young, German lover, uncorks a surge of forceful new sensations and emotions in Leonard. This unleashing of unbridled passion allows him to give in to urges that ultimately push him over the edge. His exploration of sexuality brings new found masculinity and confidence. Leonard officially enters manhood and undergoes a tremendous transformation of temperament. His behavior is increasingly unrestrained. At a crucial turning point, Leonard willfully imposes himself on Maria, ignoring all cries of distress of his lover. It is then that the reader becomes fully aware of Leonard's grave potential to give rein to his basest nature.

Following this traumatic incident with Maria, Leonard distinctly apologizes and makes a conscious effort to reform himself. The two scarred companions reconcile only superficially and suffer perceptible losses of intimacy. The plot is complicated by the appearance of Maria's inebriated and disgruntled husband who attacks Leonard. After a crushing blow to his genitals, Leonard unleashes a shocking display of malice and murders and mutilates his assailant.

When Leonard callously forces himself onto Maria, we see his capability for harsh insensitivity, resulting in severe damage. But when Leonard slaughters Otto, and severs all his limbs, in order to fit the body into a suitcase, with the intent of eschewing penalty, it is all but too clear that Leonard Marnham is no longer the shy, unripe innocent the author introduced us to.

In reference to Leonard's inhumanity the author uses irony to convey the idea that human actions during this time period were largely inhumane. McEwan's assessment of humanity and essentially his thesis by writing The Innocent is that man is inherently evil, requiring only the slightest corruption (such as Leonard's entrance into manhood and the decadence exemplified by society) to unveil his intrinsic iniquity.

This essay is within the mid-range parameters for the following reasons:

- Presents a clear thesis with a defensible assertion and probable line of reasoning. T
- Uses specifics from the text to illustrate points (paragraphs 2 and 3). E
- Organization builds to a strong conclusion. S
- Adheres to topic well. S
- Does not provide a balanced characterization of Leonard. E/C
- Does not provide proof of Leonard's innocence other than his sexuality. E/C
- Demonstrates a willingness to stretch with regard to syntax and diction. S
- Demonstrates a clear voice. S
- Exhibits instances of awkward word choice (lines 7, 12, 37). S

- Exhibits instances of awkward sentences (lines 9–11, 25–27). S
- Veers dangerously close to plot summary. E/C

It is obvious that this is an eager, intelligent, and thoughtful reader and writer. However, the results of the transformation on Leonard are not as fully developed as the prompt demands. It is only at the end of the essay that the transformation is connected to theme.

5 Minutes to a 5

180 Activities and Questions in

5 Minutes a Day

This section is written by Barbara L. Murphy and Michael Hartnett.

Check off each activity as it is completed.

1. ❏	46. ❏	91. ❏	136. ❏
2. ❏	47. ❏	92. ❏	137. ❏
3. ❏	48. ❏	93. ❏	138. ❏
4. ❏	49. ❏	94. ❏	139. ❏
5. ❏	50. ❏	95. ❏	140. ❏
6. ❏	51. ❏	96. ❏	141. ❏
7. ❏	52. ❏	97. ❏	142. ❏
8. ❏	53. ❏	98. ❏	143. ❏
9. ❏	54. ❏	99. ❏	144. ❏
10. ❏	55. ❏	100. ❏	145. ❏
11. ❏	56. ❏	101. ❏	146. ❏
12. ❏	57. ❏	102. ❏	147. ❏
13. ❏	58. ❏	103. ❏	148. ❏
14. ❏	59. ❏	104. ❏	149. ❏
15. ❏	60. ❏	105. ❏	150. ❏
16. ❏	61. ❏	106. ❏	151. ❏
17. ❏	62. ❏	107. ❏	152. ❏
18. ❏	63. ❏	108. ❏	153. ❏
19. ❏	64. ❏	109. ❏	154. ❏
20. ❏	65. ❏	110. ❏	155. ❏
21. ❏	66. ❏	111. ❏	156. ❏
22. ❏	67. ❏	112. ❏	157. ❏
23. ❏	68. ❏	113. ❏	158. ❏
24. ❏	69. ❏	114. ❏	159. ❏
25. ❏	70. ❏	115. ❏	160. ❏
26. ❏	71. ❏	116. ❏	161. ❏
27. ❏	72. ❏	117. ❏	162. ❏
28. ❏	73. ❏	118. ❏	163. ❏
29. ❏	74. ❏	119. ❏	164. ❏
30. ❏	75. ❏	120. ❏	165. ❏
31. ❏	76. ❏	121. ❏	166. ❏
32. ❏	77. ❏	122. ❏	167. ❏
33. ❏	78. ❏	123. ❏	168. ❏
34. ❏	79. ❏	124. ❏	169. ❏
35. ❏	80. ❏	125. ❏	170. ❏
36. ❏	81. ❏	126. ❏	171. ❏
37. ❏	82. ❏	127. ❏	172. ❏
38. ❏	83. ❏	128. ❏	173. ❏
39. ❏	84. ❏	129. ❏	174. ❏
40. ❏	85. ❏	130. ❏	175. ❏
41. ❏	86. ❏	131. ❏	176. ❏
42. ❏	87. ❏	132. ❏	177. ❏
43. ❏	88. ❏	133. ❏	178. ❏
44. ❏	89. ❏	134. ❏	179. ❏
45. ❏	90. ❏	135. ❏	180. ❏

Day 1

AN INTRODUCTION

Before You Begin…

The following 180 questions and activities are based on the material presented in the formal text of *5 Steps to a 5: AP English Literature and Composition.* These questions and activities are created as supplementary material to both the text AND your own AP English Literature course. There are FOUR major sections presented in the order of the original contents: Multiple Choice, Poetry, Prose, and Free Response. The material progresses from basic to complex in each section. Some activities stand alone, while others have two or more connected activities. We recommend that you work your way through each section in the given order. However, you can certainly peruse the activities and pick and choose as you desire. Whatever works best for you.

You will find answers with explanations at the end of the activities. If you need further clarification of a question or explanation, you should review the related material in the *5 Steps* text.

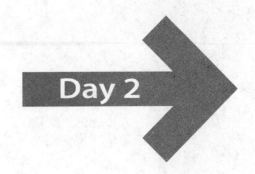

Day 2

Introduction to *5 Steps to a 5: AP English Literature*

Before doing anything else, acquaint yourself with *5 Steps to a 5: AP English Literature*. Then, complete this first 5-minute activity to quickly review what you found after scanning the text.

	YES	NO
1. I've looked over the table of contents.	——	——
2. I've found out the date of the AP English Literature exam.	——	——
3. I've carefully reviewed the three approaches to preparing for the exam located on pages 11–14.	——	——
4. I've made a decision about which approach would be best for me, or I've decided to develop my own study plan.	——	——
5. I've completed the walk-through of the Diagnostic/Master Exam in Chapter 3.	——	——

GENERAL

Definition/Examples of Literary Terms

Define or provide an example of the following literary terms regarding sound.

1. Alliteration:

2. Assonance:

3. Onomatopoeia:

4. Euphony:

5. Cacophony:

Terminology

It is assumed that an AP English Literature student has a working knowledge of terminology related to the reading, understanding, and analysis of literary texts. With this assumption in mind, the test makers create their multiple-choice questions and essay prompts. Two of the most frequently used terms are *literary devices* (tools) and *rhetorical strategies* (plan). Although the difference between the two can be viewed as minimal, it's a good idea to practice determining when one or the other term is the better choice in a given situation where these terms are being used.

Identify each of the following statements, items, events as either a Literary Device (LD) or Rhetorical Strategy (RS).

_____ **1.** Onomatopoeia

_____ **2.** Eulogy

_____ **3.** A particular word pattern or combination of words used in a literary work to evoke a desired effect or arouse a desired reaction in the audience

_____ **4.** Narrative

_____ **5.** Metaphor

_____ **6.** Satire

_____ **7.** A technique a writer uses to produce a special effect in her writing

_____ **8.** An epic poem

_____ **9.** Motif

_____ **10.** Synecdoche

Day 5

Levels of Interpretation

List four levels or approaches to consider when analyzing literature.

For example, a work may be read on a simple literal level. Other levels include:

1.

2.

3.

4.

Name Analysis

Often, a character's name adds to our understanding of meaning in a work.

The following names should provide an opportunity for you to make predictions, jot down possibilities, examine character, or explore insights for interpretation.

Do not be concerned about prior knowledge; just write your thoughts based on the names. Have fun exploring ideas.

1. Abbie and Eben

2. Seymour Glass

3. Ruth Hartwell

4. Holly Golightly

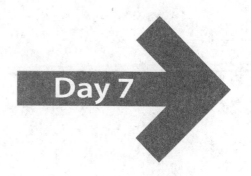

Structure of Prose vs. Poetry

Arrange the following words into two columns, one indicating the form found in prose, and the other the form found in poetry. Arrange the columns in order of complexity. Some words will *not* be used.

foot   stanza   phrase   chapter   syllable   rhyme   paragraph

word   transition   sentence   line   canto   antecedent

Prose

1.

2.

3.

4.

5.

Poetry

1.

2.

3.

4.

5.

Tone-Descriptive Assessment

There are hundreds of words that can describe the tone that an author develops through diction. List 10 adjectives that could be used to assess a specific tone in a work. Rely on the works you have read.

1.

2.

3.

4.

5.

6.

7.

8.

9.

10.

Types of Irony

Carefully read each of the following statements or situations. Then, identify the type of irony each illustrates.

Three Types of Irony

A. Verbal Irony: What is said and what the speaker actually means are two different things. (Sarcasm is a form of verbal irony.)

B. Dramatic Irony: The audience knows something the character or characters are not aware of.

C. Situational Irony: The exact opposite of what was expected occurs.

_____ **1.** In the novel *Animal Farm* by George Orwell, the readers are aware of many more facts than the animals.

_____ **2.** Antony calls Brutus "honorable" but all the while means to imply he is not honorable.

_____ **3.** *Fahrenheit 451* is one of the top banned books in the United States.

_____ **4.** Iago, whom Othello considers a friend, plots Othello's demise throughout the entire play. Othello does not know that Iago is the one pulling the strings, but the audience does.

_____ **5.** "Wow! This 750-page report on shades of orange really looks exciting."

_____ **6.** Toward the end of the short story "The Story of an Hour," by Kate Chopin, the wife of a controlling Mr. Brently is told that he has died in a train accident. She comes to feel content to living a long life with freedom and no restrictions imposed by her husband. However, at the end of the story, her husband comes back unexpectedly. When she sees him, she instantly dies from this shock.

Tone, Film Opening Sequence—*Henry V*

- We first meet Henry V when he enters his courtroom where the members of his court are awaiting his arrival.

- Watch the first 45 seconds of Henry's entrance.
  https://www.youtube.com/watch?v=EhGiSfv5FJk

- After your initial viewing, look over the questions asked of you.

- Watch the scene one more time

- Then respond to the questions.

1. The tone of this scene can best be described as

    A. angry and satirical
    B. condescending and reverent
    C. imperial and provocative
    D. magisterial and cunning
    E. prosecutorial and mysterious

2. Cite THREE details from the scene that led to your conclusion about the tone.

    Detail 1:

    Detail 2:

    Detail 3:

Introductory Paragraphs, 1

Assume you are given this prompt:

> Carefully read "We Grow Accustomed to the Dark" by Emily Dickinson and Robert Frost's "Acquainted with the Night." Then write a well-developed essay that addresses the attitude of each poet toward the subject.

Consider the following first draft of an introduction to an essay in response to the prompt:

> Though these two poems by Dickinson and Frost share the element of dark or night, the poets speak from very different perspectives. The speaker of Frost's poem gives night a far more negative and desolate meaning than Dickinson's "darkness," which connotes uncertainty and change.

Each of the following is specifically related to the first draft of the introduction. When revising, consider:

1. Keeping the prompt in mind, the organization of the essay should be _____ first and _____ second.

2. Changing "Though" to _____

3. _____ Including _____ not including the titles of the poems

4. Changing "gives" to _____

5. Defining "perspectives" (Hint: perspectives on what?)

Day 12

Introductory Paragraphs, 2

Using the prompt and the questions related to the first draft of the introduction provided in the previous activity, write the revised introduction below.

Style, 1

You've learned in English classes, especially AP English, that style is the way an author writes that differentiates his or her writing from that of others. It's the way an author addresses a subject given the subject, purpose, or audience: diction, syntax, voice.

Here are examples of writing by Ernest Hemingway and William Faulkner. Carefully read each example. Then complete the activity that follows.

Manuel drank his brandy. He felt sleepy himself. It was too hot to go out into the town. Besides there was nothing to do. He wanted to see Zurito. He would go to sleep while he waited.

—Men Without Women, Ernest Hemingway (1927)

He did not feel weak, he was merely luxuriating in that supremely gutful lassitude of convalescence in which time, hurry, doing, did not exist, the accumulating seconds and minutes and hours to which in its well state the body is slave both waking and sleeping, now reversed and time now the lip-server and mendicant to the body's pleasure instead of the body thrall to time's headlong course.

—The Hamlet, William Faulkner (1931)

Based on these two examples and with the elements of style in mind, identify which author is associated with each of the following characteristics.

A. HEMINGWAY   B. FAULKNER

_____ **1.** Thoughtful

_____ **2.** Direct

_____ **3.** Solitary

_____ **4.** Tense

_____ **5.** Reportorial

_____ **6.** Complex

_____ **7.** Tense

_____ **8.** Simple

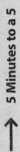

Style, 2

Carefully read these three poems by Emily Dickinson. Then respond to the questions that follow.

A Day

I'll tell you how the sun rose,
A ribbon at a time.
The steeples swam in amethyst,
The news like squirrels ran.
The hills untied their bonnets,
The bobolinks begun.
Then I said softly to myself,
"That must have been the sun!"

But how he set, I know not.
There seemed a purple stile
Which little yellow boys and girls
Were climbing all the while

Till when they reached the other side,
A dominie in gray
Put gently up the evening bars,
And led the flock away.

Pain

Pain has an element of blank;
It cannot recollect

A time when it was not.
has no future but itself,
Its infinite realms contain
    The distant strains of triumph
New periods of pain.
Pain has an element of blank,
It cannot recollect
When it began, or if there was
A time when it was not.

It has no future but itself,
Its infinite realms contain
Its past, enlightened to perceive
New periods of pain.

Success is counted sweetest . . .

Success is counted sweetest
By those who ne'er succeed
    To comprehend a nectar
    Requires sorest need.

Not one of all the purple host
Who took the flag to-day
    When it began, or if there was
    So clear, of victory

As he, defeated, dying,
Its past, enlightened to perceive
    Can tell the definition,
    Burst agonized and clear!

———————————————

Based on these poems, one could conclude that Dickinson's poetry exhibits all of the following characteristics except

    A. lyric
    B. no exact rhyme pattern
    C. blank verse
    D. common meter
    E. simple but complex

MULTIPLE CHOICE
Identifying Types of Questions

Each of the following is an example of which of the following types of multiple-choice stems?

FACTUAL   **TECHNICAL**   **ANALYTICAL**   **INFERENTIAL**

If you are not certain about the description of these categories, check Chapter 3 of the main text.

_____ 1. The passage uses all of the following literary devices except . . .

_____ 2. The phrase in lines 4–7 refers to . . .

_____ 3. According to the author, a poet is a combination of . . .

_____ 4. The passage is an example of . . .

_____ 5. The text is primarily developed by . . .

_____ 6. The setting of the sun is a symbol for . . .

_____ 7. One may conclude from the passage that the speaker . . .

_____ 8. The tone of the passage is . . .

_____ 9. "She" in line 7 refers to . . .

_____ 10. An apt title for the text is . . .

Factual

Read the passage carefully and answer the following questions.

From *Julius Caesar*

There is a tide in the affairs of men,
Which taken at the flood, leads on to fortune.
Omitted, all the voyage of their life is bound in shallows and in miseries.
On such a full sea are we now afloat.
And we must take the current when it serves, or lose our ventures.

1. The antecedent of "Which" in line 2 is

 A. men
 B. affairs
 C. flood
 D. tide
 E. fortune

2. Lines 3-4 refer to

 A. men
 B. fortune
 C. flood
 D. affairs
 E. ventures

Technical

Carefully read the following passage from The Scarlet Letter by Nathaniel Hawthorne.

Chapter 1 The Prison-Door

A throng of bearded men, in sad-colored garments and gray, steeple-crowned hats, intermixed with women, some wearing hoods, and others bareheaded, was assembled in front of a wooden edifice, the door of which was heavily timbered with oak, and studded with iron spikes.

The founders of a new colony, whatever Utopia of human virtue and happiness they might originally project, have invariably recognized it among their earliest practical necessities to allot a portion of the virgin soil as a cemetery, and another portion as the site of a prison. In accordance with this rule, it may safely be assumed that the forefathers of Boston had built the first prison-house, somewhere in the vicinity of Cornhill, almost as seasonably as they marked out the first burial-ground, on Isaac Johnson's lot, and round about his grave, which subsequently became the nucleus of all the congregated sepulchres in the old church-yard of King's Chapel. Certain it is, that, some fifteen or twenty years after the settlement of the town, the wooden jail was already marked with weather-stains and other indications of age, which gave a yet darker aspect to its beetle-browed and gloomy front. The rust on the ponderous iron-work of its oaken door looked more antique than anything else in the new world. Like all that pertains to crime, it seemed never to have known a youthful era. Before this ugly edifice, and between it and the wheel-track of the street, was a grass-plot, much overgrown with burdock, pig-weed, apple-peru, and such unsightly vegetation, which evidently found something congenial in the soil that had so early borne the black flower of civilized society, a prison. But, on one side of the portal, and rooted almost at the threshold, was a wild rose-bush, covered, in this month of June, with its delicate gems, which might be imagined to offer their fragrance and fragile beauty to the prisoner as he went in, and to

5

10

15

20

25

the condemned criminal as he came forth to his doom, in token that the deep heart of Nature could pity and be kind to him.

This rose-bush, by a strange chance, has been kept alive in history; 30 but whether it had merely survived out of the stern old wilderness, so long after the fall of the gigantic pines and oaks that originally overshadowed it,—or whether, as there is fair authority for believing, it had sprung up under the footsteps of the sainted Ann Hutchinson, as she entered the prison-door, —we shall not take upon us to determine. 35 Finding it so directly on the threshold of our narrative, which is now about to issue from that inauspicious portal, we could hardly do otherwise than pluck one of its flowers and present it to the reader. It may serve, let us hope, to symbolize some sweet moral blossom, that may be found along the track, or relieve the darkening close of a tale of 40 human frailty and sorrow.

Line 34, beginning with "it had sprung up under the footsteps of the sainted Ann Hutchinson," contain an example of

A. analogy
B. anticlimax
C. alliteration
D. allusion
E. apostrophe

Analytical

Read the following passage carefully and answer the following questions.

From *Julius Caesar*

> There is a tide in the affairs of men,
> Which taken at the flood, leads on to fortune.
> Omitted, all the voyage of their life is bound in shallows and in miseries.
> On such a full sea are we now afloat.
> And we must take the current when it serves, or lose our ventures.

1. The primary poetic device employed to develop this passage is

   A. Alliteration
   B. Assonance
   C. Personification
   D. Metaphor
   E. Simile

2. The passage is primarily concerned with

   A. The beauty of Nature
   B. Business images
   C. Cause and effect
   D. Planning an assassination
   E. Rhyme and meter

Inferential

Read carefully the following poem by Stephen Crane.

"A Man Said to the Universe"

> A man said to the universe:
> "Sir, I exist!"
> "However," replied the universe,
> "The fact has not created in me
> A sense of obligation."

1. The tone of this poem may best be described as

A. Whimsical and nonrealistic
B. Regretful and bitter
C. Indifferent and detached
D. Irreligious and critical
E. Brief and concise

2. The attitude of the man is most likely

A. Accepting and passive
B. Insistent and assertive
C. Fearful and cowering
D. Questioning and belligerent
E. Prayerful and pleading

Day 20

Context

> Read carefully the following poem by William Ernest Henley (1849–1903).
>
> **"Invictus"**
>
> Out of the night that covers me,
> Black as the Pit from pole to pole,
> I thank whatever gods may be
> For my unconquerable soul.
>
> In the fell clutch of circumstance   5
> I have not winced nor cried aloud.
> Under the bludgeonings of chance
> My head is bloody, but unbowed.
>
> Beyond this place of wrath and tears
> Looms but the Horror of the shade,   10
> And yet the menace of the years
> Finds, and shall find, me unafraid.
>
> It matters not how strait the gate,
> How charged with punishments the scroll.
> I am the master of my fate: 15
> I am the captain of my soul.

1. In the context of line 5 and the poem, the word *fell* most likely means

A. Lower
B. Terrible
C. Full
D. Conquered
E. Remembered

2. In context "the Horror of the shade" probably refers to

A. Night
B. Isolation
C. Regret
D. Afterlife
E. The Pit

Content and Inferences

> ### from "*Outcasts of Poker Flat*"
> ### by Hart Crane (1869)
>
> As Mr. John Oakhurst, gambler, stepped into the main street of Poker Flat on the morning of the twenty-third of November, 1850, he was conscious of a change in its moral atmosphere since the preceding night. Two of three men, conversing earnestly together, ceased as he approached, and exchanged significant glances. There was a Sabbath[1] lull in the air, which, in a settlement unused to Sabbath influences, looked ominous.
>
> Mr. Oakhurst's calm, handsome face betrayed small concern in these indications. Whether he was conscious of any predisposing cause was another question. "I reckon they're after somebody," he reflected; "likely it's me." He returned to his pocket the handkerchief with which he had been whipping away the red dust of Poker Flat from his neat boots, and quietly discharged his mind of any further conjecture.
>
> ---
>
> [1]Sabbath: a religious day of observance

1. This opening passage of a short story accomplishes which of the following?
   A. Presents an original and probing argument about the nature of small Western towns
   B. Establishes a humorous, playful tone about the charming local color of regional provincialism
   C. Offers a first-person account of everyday life in the mid-nineteenth century
   D. Introduces the possibility the central character might be confronting troubling circumstances
   E. Negates any opportunity for the reader to be unclear about what is about to transpire

2. This passage reveals Mr. Oakhurst to be

    A. rash and impetuous
    B. composed and observant
    C. nervous and cowardly
    D. bold and heroic
    E. kind and generous

3. The two of three men conversing appear to be

    A. predatory
    B. oblivious
    C. fearful
    D. insecure
    E. unrefined

4. The mood established in this opening scene is one of

    A. sentimental
    B. nightmarish
    C. passionate
    D. hopeful
    E. apprehensive

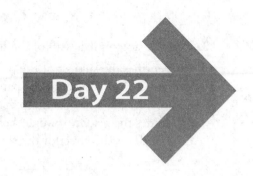

All-Except

Carefully read the following poem aloud. Seriously, hear the poem as you read it at least twice.

"The Dance"
> **by William Carlos Williams**

> In Brueghel's great picture, The Kermess,
> the dancers go round, they go round and
> around, the squeal and the blare and the
> tweedle of bagpipes, a bugle and fiddles
> tipping their bellies (round as the thick   5
> sided glasses whose wash they impound)
> their hips and their bellies off balance
> to turn them. Kicking and rolling
> about the Fair Grounds, swinging their butts, those
> shanks must be sound to bear up under such   10
> rollicking measures, prance as they dance
> in Brueghel's great picture, The Kermess.

1. All of the following are present in the poem except
   A. Simile
   B. Onomatopoeia
   C. Repetition
   D. Foreshadowing
   E. Meter

2. The title accomplishes all of the following except

    A. Identifies the subject of the poem
    B. Explains the subject of the painting
    C. Provides the author's interpretation of the painting
    D. Guides the reader through the imagery of the poem
    E. Introduces the effect of the rhyme and meter in the poem

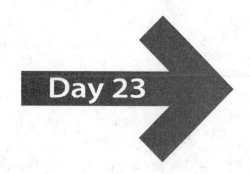

Characterization

from *The Awakening*
by Kate Chopin (1899)

Mrs. Pontellier's eyes were quick and bright; they were a yellowish brown, about the color of her hair. She had a way of turning them swiftly upon an object and holding them there as if lost in some inward maze of contemplation or thought.

Her eyebrows were a shade darker than her hair. They were thick and almost horizontal, emphasizing the depth of her eyes. She was rather handsome than beautiful. Her face was captivating by reason of a certain frankness of expression and a contradictory subtle play of features. Her manner was engaging.

1. Mrs. Pontellier is a woman distinguished by her

A. insecurity and awkwardness
B. pulchritude and loveliness
C. recklessness and lack of restraint
D. alertness and awareness
E. blandness and lack of imagination

2. The description of Mrs. Pontellier is presented in

A. a murky, ambiguous setting
B. a series of direct, relatively simple sentences
C. an ironic and humorous manner
D. a serpentine series of conflicting characterizations
E. a first-person account from an acquaintance

3. Mrs. Pontellier exudes all of the following qualities except

    A. watchfulness
    B. pensiveness
    C. openness
    D. attractiveness
    E. superciliousness

4. The primary literary technique in this passage is

    A. personification
    B. theme
    C. imagery
    D. setting
    E. characterization

Structure and Meaning

> **"To Memory"**
> **by Mary Elizabeth Coleridge**
>
> Strange Power, I know not what thou art,
> Murderer or mistress of my heart.
> I know I'd rather meet the blow
> Of my most unrelenting foe
> Than live—as now I live—to be   5
> Slain twenty times a day by thee.
>
> Yet, when I would command thee hence,
> Thou mockest at the vain pretence,
> Murmuring in mine ear a song
> Once loved, alas! forgotten long;   10
> And on my brow I feel a kiss
> That I would rather die than miss

1. The entire poem employs which literary technique?

   A. Understatement
   B. Simile
   C. Allusion
   D. Apostrophe
   E. Iambic pentameter

2. In the context of the poem, which of the following can be considered valid definitions for the word *vain* (line 8)?

I. conceited   II. futile   III. cruel

A. I only
B. II only
C. III only
D. I and II
E. I, II, and III

3. How does the structure of the two stanzas function?

A. The second stanza serves as a reinforcement of the view expressed in the first stanza.
B. The first stanza presents a concept while the second stanza presents a logical explanation.
C. The first stanza serves as an attack on a force while the second stands as a qualified defense.
D. The first stanza is an emotional plea while the second stanza is a calm, measured response.
E. The first stanza introduces a personal philosophy while the second provides a moral allegory.

4. What is the narrator's ultimate point about memory?

A. It offers great visceral pleasure, despite the pain.
B. It serves as a soothing solace for a turbulent past.
C. It is too painful and not worth having, given how meager its offerings.
D. It provides unadulterated bliss.
E. It fades as time passes and experiences march forward.

Context and Meaning

from "*The Cask of Amontillado*"
by Edgar Allan Poe (1846)

The thousand injuries of Fortunato I had borne as I best could, but when he ventured upon insult, I vowed revenge. You, who so well know the nature of my soul, will not suppose, however, that I gave utterance to a threat. At length I would be avenged; this was a point definitely settled—but the very definitiveness with which it was resolved precluded the idea of risk. I must not only punish, but punish with impunity. A wrong is unredressed when retribution overtakes its redresser. It is equally unredressed when the avenger fails to make himself felt as such to him who has done the wrong.

It must be understood that neither by word nor deed had I given Fortunato cause to doubt my good will. I continued, as was my wont, to smile in his face, and he did not perceive that my smile now was at the thought of his immolation.

He had a weak point—this Fortunato—although in other regards he was a man to be respected and even feared. He prided himself on his connoisseurship in wine. Few Italians have the true virtuoso spirit. For the most part their enthusiasm is adopted to suit the time and opportunity—to practice imposture upon the British and Austrian millionaires. In painting and gemmary,[1] Fortunato, like his countrymen, was a quack, but in the matter of old wines he was sincere. In this respect I did not differ from him materially: I was skillful in the Italian vintages myself, and bought largely whenever I could.

----

[1]Gemmary: the scientific knowledge of gems

1. As a necessary requirement for his revenge, the narrator must make certain that

A. Fortunato knows who his assailant is
B. Fortunato departs with his dignity in tact
C. Fortunato discovers the inner nature of his soul
D. Fortunato rejects every opportunity for escape
E. Fortunato never knows who has dragged him to his doom

2. The narrator explains that his smile to Fortunato

A. betrays a surprising level of kindness
B. appears to be benevolent but is actually malignant
C. exposes the narrator's hazy ambivalence
D. appears to be more malevolent than his intentions
E. serves as sincere testimony to his good will

3. The narrator wants to avoid

A. acting nice to Fortunato
B. concealing his true intentions from Fortunato
C. engaging Fortunato in cultured conversations
D. putting himself in a situation where he can get caught
E. having to indulge in consuming fine vintages

4. The narrator of the passage can be best characterized as

A. logical and charitable
B. nervous and insecure
C. charming and lighthearted
D. impersonal and distant
E. calculating and menacing

Structure and Content

"The Man He Killed"
          by Thomas Hardy (1902)

Had he and I but met
By some old ancient inn,
We should have set us down to wet
Right many a nipperkin!

But ranged as infantry,   5
And staring face to face,
I shot at him as he at me,
And killed him in his place.

I shot him dead because—
Because he was my foe,   10
Just so: my foe of course he was;
That's clear enough; although

He thought he'd 'list, perhaps, Off-
hand like—just as I—
Was out of work—had sold his traps—   15
No other reason why.

Yes; quaint and curious war is!
You shoot a fellow down
You'd treat, if met where any bar is,
Or help to half a crown.   20

1. In "The Man He Killed" the redundancy of "old ancient" (2) indicates

    I. The meeting's irrelevance   II. The location's inappropriateness

        III. The theme's timelessness

A. I only
B. II only
C. III only
D. I and II
E. E I, II, and III

2. The author repeats the word *because* to convey

    I. A hesitation   II. A groping for a reason

        III. The narrator's speech impediment

A. I only
B. II only
C. III only
D. I and II
E. I, II, and III

3. The narrator reiterates his points in line 11 to

A. justify his action
B. stall for time
C. plan to shoot others
D. play around with the wording
E. regulate his hatred for his enemy

4. The line "quaint and curious" can best be defined as

A. homey
B. antique
C. distant
D. vivid
E. absurd

5. What technique is represented in the final stanza of "The Man He Killed"?

A. Metaphor
B. Irony
C. Apostrophe
D. Allusion
E. Hyperbole

6. The reader can infer the narrator of this poem is
   A. an innkeeper
   B. an assassin
   C. a general
   D. a foot soldier
   E. an aristocrat

POETRY

Poetic Devices, Terminology

Briefly define or provide an example of the following poetic terms.

1. Metaphor

2. Simile

3. Personification

4. Hyperbole

Day 28

Identifying Poetic Devices

Identify the poetic device illustrated by the example.

1. The moon doth with delight look round her.

2. The furrow followed free.

3. Thy soul was like a star.

4. England has become a fen of stagnant waters.

5. Tyger, Tyger burning bright in the forest of the night

6. From the jingling and the tinkling of the bells

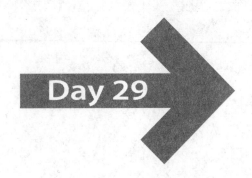

Poetic Sound Devices in Poetry and Prose

Define or provide an example of the following literary terms:

1. Alliteration:

2. Assonance:

3. Onomatopoeia:

4. Euphony:

5. Cacophony:

Day 30

Analyzing Poetic Devices

"A Patch of Old Snow"
        by Robert Frost (1920)

There's a patch of snow in the corner
That I should have guessed
Was a blow-away paper the rain
Had brought to rest.

It is speckled with grime as if   5
Small print overspread it,
The news of a day I've forgotten—
If I ever read it.

1. The phrase "should have guessed" indicates that a piece of paper on the ground

   A. seems more plausible than snow
   B. blocks the author's view of the snow
   C. blends with the snow
   D. becomes moist from the wet snow
   E. captures words fraught with meaning

2. The author uses vowel sounds to

   A. quicken the pace of the poem
   B. make the poem more frightening
   C. brighten the mood of the poem
   D. slow the pace of the poem
   E. generate a passionate sensibility

3. The comparison to small print leads the reader to interpret **all of the following** about the snow except

A. it has been around a while
B. it is innocent
C. it has been penetrated by substances
D. it has lost its purity
E. its markings are hard to read

4. What is the author saying happens to most patches of snow?

A. They pass away from our thoughts.
B. They are always remembered.
C. They become connected to great events.
D. They end up covered with newspaper print.
E. They represent mankind's colder inclinations.

Day 31

Deconstructing the Poetry Prompt

Read the Prompt!

Carefully read the following post–World War I poem by Archibald MacLeish. Then in a well-developed essay analyze the different techniques the poet uses to convey his attitude toward his subject. You may want to consider form, literary devices, and tone.

"The End of the World"
by Archibald MacLeish

> Quite unexpectedly, as Vasserot[1]
> The armless ambidextrian[2] was lighting
> A match between his great and second toe,
> And Ralph the lion was engaged in biting
> The neck of Madame Sossman while the drum   5
> Pointed, and Teeny was about to cough
> In waltz-time swinging Jocko by the thumb
> Quite unexpectedly to top blew off:
> And there, there overhead, there, there hung over
> Those thousands of white faces, those dazed eyes,   10
> There in the starless dark, the poise, the hover,
> There with vast wings across the cancelled skies,
> There in the sudden blackness the black pall
> Of nothing, nothing, nothing—nothing at all.

---

[1]French, 1900 Olympic cyclist
[2]a person who can use both arms equally well

Deconstruct the above prompt by underlining, highlighting, and/or notating the requirements of the task.

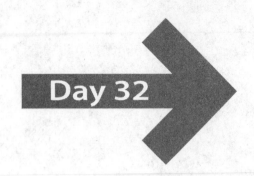
Metaphor and Meaning

***As You Like It*, Act II, Scene 7,**
by William Shakespeare

Jaques to Duke Senior

All the world's a stage,
And all the men and women merely players;
They have their exits and their entrances,
And one man in his time plays many parts,
His acts being seven ages. At first, the infant,   **5**
Mewling and puking in the nurse's arms.
Then the whining schoolboy, with his satchel
And shining morning face, creeping like snail
Unwillingly to school. And then the lover,
Sighing like furnace, with a woeful ballad   **10**
Made to his mistress' eyebrow. Then a soldier,
Full of strange oaths and bearded like the pard,
Jealous in honor, sudden and quick in quarrel,
Seeking the bubble reputation
Even in the cannon's mouth. And then the justice,   **15**
In fair round belly with good capon lined,
With eyes severe and beard of formal cut,
Full of wise saws and modern instances;
And so he plays his part. The sixth age shifts
Into the lean and slippered pantaloon,   **20**
With spectacles on nose and pouch on side;
His youthful hose, well saved, a world too wide

For his shrunk shank, and his big manly voice,
Turning again toward childish treble, pipes
And whistles in his sound. Last scene of all,   25
That ends this strange eventful history,
Is second childishness and mere oblivion,
Sans teeth, sans eyes, sans taste, sans everything.

1. The central metaphor of this passage is _____.

2. All of the following are included in the seven ages of man except
   A. infant
   B. schoolboy
   C. lover
   D. soldier
   E. scholar

3. If the reader follows the extended metaphor in the passage, the seven ages of man are similar to _____.

4. The tone of this passage can best be described as
   A. disillusioned
   B. sad
   C. anxious
   D. indifferent
   E. hostile

Metaphor, Political Imagery

***The Building of the Ship*, "The Republic" (1849)
by Henry Wadsworth Longfellow**

Thou, too, sail on, O Ship of State!
Sail on, O Union, strong and great!
Humanity with all its fears,
With all the hopes of future years,
Is hanging breathless on thy fate!   5
We know what Master laid thy keel,
What Workmen wrought thy ribs of steel,
Who made each mast, and sail, and rope,
What anvils rang, what hammers beat,
In what a forge and what a heat   10
Were shaped the anchors of thy hope!
Fear not each sudden sound and shock,
'T is of the wave and not the rock;
'T is but the flapping of the sail,
And not a rent made by the gale!   15
In spite of rock and tempest's roar,
In spite of false lights on the shore,
Sail on, nor fear to breast the sea!
Our hearts, our hopes, are all with thee,
Our hearts, our hopes, our prayers, our tears,   20
Our faith triumphant o'er our fears,
Are all with thee,—are all with thee!

1. The controlling metaphor in this poem is _____.

2. This poem is constructed of five major points.
   A. The first, in lines 1–2, addresses _____.
   B. The second, in lines 3–5, says humanity is _____.
   C. Lines 6–11 describe _____.
   D. The subject of the fourth point (lines 12–18) is _____.
   E. The last lines (19–22) address _____ and the promise to _____.

Close Reading and Antecedents

> **from *Merchant of Venice***
> **by William Shakespeare, 1564–1616**
>
> The quality of mercy is not strained;
> It droppeth as the gentle rain from heaven
> Upon the place beneath. It is twice blest;
> It blesseth him that gives and him that takes:
> 'T is mightiest in the mightiest; it becomes.   **5**
> The thronèd monarch better than his crown:
> His sceptre shows the force of temporal power,
> The attribute to awe and majesty,
> Wherein doth sit the dread and fear of kings;
> But mercy is above this sceptred sway;   **10**
> It is enthronèd in the hearts of kings,
> It is an attribute to God himself;

1. What is the antecedent of lines 5 and 6?

2. What is the symbol of "dread and fear," line 9?

3. What poetic device is present in lines 1 and 2?

4. What is "the attribute to awe and majesty" in line 8?

5. What is "the attribute to God himself" in line 12?

Antecedents/Metaphor

> **from *Julius Caesar***
> **by William Shakespeare**
>
> FLAVIUS. It is no matter; let no images
>   Be hung with Caesar's trophies. I'll about
>   And drive away the vulgar from the streets;
>   So do you too, where you perceive them thick.
>   These growing feathers pluck'd from Caesar's wing   5
>   Will make him fly an ordinary pitch,
>   Who else would soar above the view of men,
>   And keep us all in servile fearfulness.
>
> **1.** "These growing feathers pluck'd from Caesar's wing" (line 5) refers to
> _____ .
>
> **2.** To what is Caesar compared?
>
> **3.** List the images that further develop the metaphor.

Poetic Terminology and Antecedents

"London, 1802"
            by William Wordsworth

Milton! thou shouldst be living at this hour:
England hath need of thee: she is a fen
Of stagnant waters: altar, sword, and pen,
Fireside, the heroic wealth of hall and bower,
Have forfeited their ancient English dower   5
Of inward happiness. We are selfish men;
Oh! raise us up, return to us again;
And give us manners, virtue, freedom, power.
Thy soul was like a Star, and dwelt apart:
Thou hadst a voice whose sound was like the sea: 10
Pure as the naked heavens, majestic, free,
So didst thou travel on life's common way,
In cheerful godliness; and yet thy heart
The lowliest duties on herself did lay.

1. An example of an apostrophe can be found in which line?

2. List the lines that refer back to the apostrophe.

Extended Metaphor

"I Like to See It Lap the Miles"
by Emily Dickinson

I like to see it lap the Miles,
And lick the valleys up,
And stop to feed itself at tanks;
And then, prodigious, step

Around a pile of mountains,   5
And, supercilious, peer
In shanties by the sides of roads;
And then a quarry pare

To fit its sides, and crawl between,
Complaining all the while   10
In horrid, hooting stanza;
Then chase itself down hill

And neigh like Boanerges[1];
Then, punctual as a star,
Stop—docile and omnipotent—   15
At its own stable door.

---

[1]sons of thunder

1. The subject of this poem is _____.

2. Having carefully read each of the four stanzas, the reader can easily conclude that this poem is constructed entirely using a(n) _____.

3. In the poem a _____ is compared to a _____.

Allusion

> **from *Paradise Lost***
> **by John Milton (1667)**
>
> OF MAN'S first disobedience, and the fruit
> Of that forbidden tree whose mortal taste
> Brought death into the World, and all our woe,
> With loss of Eden, till one greater Man
> Restore us, and regain the blissful Seat. . . .
>
> These five lines from Milton's *Paradise Lost* are an example of a(n) _____.

Tone and Detail

---

from "Ulysses"
      by Alfred Lord Tennyson (1842)

Come, my friends,
'T is not too late to seek a newer world.
Push off, and sitting well in order smite
The sounding furrows; for my purpose holds
To sail beyond the sunset, and the baths   **5**
Of all the western stars, until I die.
It may be that the gulfs will wash us down.
It may be we shall touch the Happy Isles,
And see the great Achilles, whom we knew.
Tho' much is taken, much abides; and tho'   **10**
We are not now that strength which in old days
Moved earth and heaven, that which we are, we are;
One equal temper of heroic hearts,
Made weak by time and fate, but strong in will
To strive, to seek, to find, and not to yield.   **15**

1. The tone of the poem can best be described as

  A. inquisitive and irritated
  B. proud and optimistic
  C. ashamed and alienated
  D. hopeful and sarcastic
  E. insecure and aggressive

2. Examples of enjambment can be found in which lines?

Day 40

Literary Devices

> **"Sympathy"**
>> **by Paul Laurence Dunbar**
>
> I know what the caged bird feels, alas!
>> When the sun is bright on the upland slopes;
> When the wind stirs soft through the springing grass,
> And the river flows like a stream of glass;
>> When the first bird sings and the first bud opes,
> And the faint perfume from its chalice steals—
> I know what the caged bird feels!
>
> I know why the caged bird beats his wing
>> Till its blood is red on the cruel bars;
> For he must fly back to his perch and cling
> When he fain would be on the bough a-swing;
>> And a pain still throbs in the old, old scars
> And they pulse again with a keener sting—
> I know why he beats his wing!
>
> I know why the caged bird sings, ah me,
>> When his wing is bruised and his bosom sore,—
> When he beats his bars and he would be free;
> It is not a carol of joy or glee,
>> But a prayer that he sends from his heart's deep core,
> But a plea, that upward to Heaven he flings—
> know why the caged bird sings!

5

10

15

20

1. The poet employs all of the following literary devices except

   A. alliteration
   B. imagery
   C. litotes
   D. simile
   E. anaphora

2. In the second stanza, the bird struggles so much in the cage that it

   A. faints
   B. cries
   C. falls
   D. dies
   E. bleeds

3. This description in the second stanza suggests that the bird

   A. has recently been caged after a long period of freedom
   B. has beaten his wings many times before
   C. no longer has any desire to return to the upland slopes
   D. refuses to ask for help, spiritual or otherwise
   E. has completely forgotten how to fly

4. According to the third stanza, the bird sings as a means of

   A. expressing exultation
   B. revealing its lethargy
   C. releasing its anger
   D. offering an invocation
   E. invoking laughter

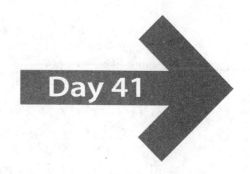

Dashes

Dashes can offer dramatic pauses preceding any activity from an external revelation or internal epiphany. They can also set off a particular idea, reinforce a previous thought, and shift the direction of a piece. In "The Man He Killed" the dash is used on a singular, but crucial, occasion in stanza three and numerous times in stanza four.

In the space below, describe the role these dashes play in these stanzas and how they help the author convey meaning

"The Man He Killed"
      by Thomas Hardy (1902)

Had he and I but met
By some old ancient inn,
We should have set us down to wet
Right many a nipperkin!

But ranged as infantry,   5
And staring face to face,
I shot at him as he at me,
And killed him in his place.

I shot him dead because—
Because he was my foe,   10
Just so: my foe of course he was;
That's clear enough; although

He thought he'd 'list, perhaps,
Off-hand like—just as I—
Was out of work—had sold his traps—   15
No other reason why.

Yes; quaint and curious war is!
You shoot a fellow down
You'd treat, if met where any bar is,
Or help to half a crown.   20

Day 42

Consonance

Consonance is the repetition of consonant sounds. A key distinction from alliteration is that consonance can appear at any point in a word. The first stanza of "Pied Beauty" is riddled with consonance.

"Pied Beauty"
by Gerard Manley Hopkins (1877)

Glory be to God for dappled things—
    For skies of couple-colour as a brinded cow;
        For rose-moles all in stipple upon trout that swim; Fresh-
firecoal chestnut-falls; finches' wings;
    Landscape plotted and pieced—fold, fallow, and plough;   5
      And áll trádes, their gear and tackle and trim.

All things counter, original, spare, strange;
    Whatever is fickle, freckled (who knows how?)
      With swift, slow; sweet, sour; adazzle, dim;
He fathers-forth whose beauty is past change: 10
    Praise him.

Go through the first stanza and mark off all the repeated consonants. Come up with a system for marking each letter (say a circle for *l*s, a square for *p*s, an underline for *d*s, a triangle for *t*s, etc.). In the space below, describe how consonance influences the sound of the stanza and how it contributes to the author's conveyance of meaning.

from "The Weary Blues"
          by Langston Hughes

Droning a drowsy syncopated tune,
Rocking back and forth to a mellow croon,
I heard a Negro play.
Down on Lenox Avenue the other night
By the pale dull pallor of an old gas light   5
He did a lazy sway. . . .
He did a lazy sway. . . .
To the tune o' those Weary Blues.
With his ebony hands on each ivory key
He made that poor piano moan with melody.   10
O Blues!
Swaying to and fro on his rickety stool
He played that sad raggy tune like a musical fool.
Sweet Blues!
Coming from a black man's soul.   15
O Blues!
In a deep song voice with a melancholy tone
I heard that Negro sing, that old piano moan—
"Ain't got nobody in all this world,
Ain't got nobody but ma self.   20
I's gwine to quit ma frownin'
And put ma troubles on the shelf."

1. Line 5 ("By the pale dull pallor of an old gas light") features which literary device?

   A. Personification
   B. Metaphor
   C. Consonance
   D. Paradox
   E. Hyperbole

2. The mood of this excerpt can best be characterized as

   A. world weary
   B. exuberant
   C. hostile
   D. apathetic
   E. spooky

3. The poet employs all of the following literary devices except

   A. imagery
   B. repetition
   C. onomatopoeia
   D. assonance
   E. allusion

4. At the end of the excerpt, the song intimates that the "Negro" pianist uses his music

   A. to cope with his suffering
   B. to elevate the audience
   C. to thrust his suffering onto the audience
   D. to reveal his anger about racial injustice
   E. to offer a joyous cry of hope

Pacing Via Assonance

Just as the "Negro" in "The Weary Blues" does a "lazy sway," Langston Hughes's poem has slow, deliberate pacing. Analyze how Hughes achieves this effect through the use of assonance (the repetition of a vowel sound).

To foster this analysis, read the poem out loud steadily and carefully, listening for how the vowel sounds affect the pace of the lines.

from "The Weary Blues"
       by Langston Hughes

    Droning a drowsy syncopated tune,
    Rocking back and forth to a mellow croon,
    I heard a Negro play.
    Down on Lenox Avenue the other night
    By the pale dull pallor of an old gas light   5
    He did a lazy sway. . . .
    He did a lazy sway. . . .
    To the tune o' those Weary Blues.
    With his ebony hands on each ivory key
    He made that poor piano moan with melody.   10
    O Blues!
    Swaying to and fro on his rickety stool
    He played that sad raggy tune like a musical fool.

Sweet Blues!
Coming from a black man's soul.   **15**
O Blues!
In a deep song voice with a melancholy tone
I heard that Negro sing, that old piano moan—
"Ain't got nobody in all this world,
Ain't got nobody but ma self.   **20**
I's gwine to quit ma frownin'
And put ma troubles on the shelf."

Allegory

An allegory can be defined as a work which offers another layer of meaning. Write a paragraph about the allegorical nature of "A Patch of Old Snow." In your commentary, be sure to incorporate specific language from the poem.

"A Patch of Old Snow"
by Robert Frost

There's a patch of snow in the corner
That I should have guessed
Was a blow-away paper the rain
Had brought to rest.

It is speckled with grime as if   5
Small print overspread it,
The news of a day I've forgotten—
If I ever read it.

Hyperbole in Narrative Voice

Hyperbole is the exaggeration of concepts or ideas to drive home a point. While hyperbole courses through the entire first stanza of "To Memory," it is employed most dramatically in the final lines of that stanza.

"To Memory"
          by Mary Elizabeth Coleridge

> Strange Power, I know not what thou art,
> Murderer or mistress of my heart.
> I know I'd rather meet the blow
> Of my most unrelenting foe
> Than live—as now I live—to be   5
> Slain twenty times a day by thee.
>
> Yet, when I would command thee hence,
> Thou mockest at the vain pretence,
> Murmuring in mine ear a song
> Once loved, alas! forgotten long;   10
> And on my brow I feel a kiss
> That I would rather die than miss

Particularly in the final two lines of the first stanza, what is the role of hyperbole in this poem? How does it address the narrator's tone, mental state, and outlook?

Language, Structure, and Meaning

"I Saw in Louisiana a Live-Oak Growing"
        by Walt Whitman

I saw in Louisiana a live-oak growing,
All alone stood it and the moss hung down from the branches,
Without any companion it grew there uttering joyous leaves of dark
        green,
And its look, rude, unbending, lusty, made me think of myself,
But I wonder'd how it could utter joyous leaves standing alone there   5
        without its friend near, for I knew I could not,
And I broke off a twig with a certain number of leaves upon it, and
        twined around it a little moss,
And brought it away, and I have placed it in sight in my room,
It is not needed to remind me as of my own dear friends,
(For I believe lately I think of little else than of them,)
Yet it remains to me a curious token, it makes me think of manly love;   10
For all that, and though the live-oak glistens there in Louisiana solitary in
        a wide flat space,
Uttering joyous leaves all its life without a friend a lover near,
I know very well I could not.

1. The structure of the poem is

A. blank verse
B. terza rima
C. consonance
D. free verse
E. ballad meter

---

2. The narrator connects himself to the oak in all of these ways except

    A. desire

    B. coarseness

    C. companionship

    D. stubbornness

    E. aspect

3. All of the following verbs relate to the oak's independent nature except

    A. stood (line 2)

    B. hung (line 2)

    C. grew (line 3)

    D. utter (line 5)

    E. glistens (line 11)

4. The narrator's "curious token" provides

    A. a dark and disturbing recollection that he'd much rather do without

    B. a note of irony, since the memory of the tree being all alone makes him think of male companionship

    C. a curious dismissal, since the narrator seems to forget the tree about which he'd previously written

    D. a reluctant confession of his mistreatment of his own dear friends who occupy his thoughts

    E. an epiphany about the nature of suffering, loss, and death

Finding Meaning Through Repetition

Repetition in literature can serve to express any of the following:

obsession	preoccupation	unbridled joy	a pause in thought
a mockery	a rallying cry	a sob	an affirmation
	a moment of realization		

The possibilities are large, but if the purpose of repetition is not readily apparent, start with this list.

Consider the meaning of Paul Laurence Dunbar's "Sympathy." List the examples of repetition and how this develops the rhythm, meaning, and structure of the poem.

"Sympathy"
         by Paul Laurence Dunbar

I know what the caged bird feels, alas!
        When the sun is bright on the upland slopes;
When the wind stirs soft through the springing grass,
And the river flows like a stream of glass;
        When the first bird sings and the first bud opens,   5
And the faint perfume from its chalice steals—
I know what the caged bird feels!

I know why the caged bird beats his wing
        Till its blood is red on the cruel bars;
For he must fly back to his perch and cling   10

5 Minutes to a 5

When he fain would be on the bough a-swing;
    And a pain still throbs in the old, old scars
And they pulse again with a keener sting—
I know why he beats his wing!

I know why the caged bird sings, ah me,   15
    When his wing is bruised and his bosom sore,—
When he beats his bars and he would be free;
It is not a carol of joy or glee,
    But a prayer that he sends from his heart's deep core,
But a plea, that upward to Heaven he flings—   20
I know why the caged bird sings!

List the repetition + line(s) + effect/purpose

Example of Repetition	Line(s)	Effect/Purpose

Organization and Imagery

from "Thunderstorms"
by W.H. Davies

My mind has thunderstorms,
That brood for heavy hours:
Until they rain me words;
My thoughts are drooping flowers
And sulking, silent birds.   5

Yet come, dark thunderstorms,
And brood your heavy hours;
For when you rain me words,
My thoughts are dancing flowers
And joyful singing birds.   10

1. The organization of this poem is based on

   A. exemplification
   B. choice
   C. cause/effect
   D. narration
   E. allusions

2. The imagery in the poem is created primarily by the use of

   A. simile
   B. metaphor
   C. hyperbole
   D. onomatopoeia
   E. oxymoron

Structure

from "Thunderstorms" (continued)

> My mind has thunderstorms,
> That brood for heavy hours:
> Until they rain me words;
> My thoughts are drooping flowers
> And sulking, silent birds.   5
>
> Yet come, dark thunderstorms,
> And brood your heavy hours;
> For when you rain me words,
> My thoughts are dancing flowers
> And joyful singing birds.   10

1. The shift in the development of the poem occurs in line _____.

2. Rewrite this poem as a compound sentence using the shift cited in question 1 as the connecting feature.

Lyric Poetry

"Pied Beauty"
      by Gerard Manley Hopkins (1877)

   Glory be to God for dappled things –
      For skies of couple-colour as a brinded cow;
         For rose-moles all in stipple upon trout that swim; Fresh-
   firecoal chestnut-falls; finches' wings;
      Landscape plotted and pieced – fold, fallow, and plough;   5
         And áll trádes, their gear and tackle and trim.

   All things counter, original, spare, strange;
      Whatever is fickle, freckled (who knows how?)
         With swift, slow; sweet, sour; adazzle, dim;
   He fathers-forth whose beauty is past change: 10
         Praise him.

1. The variety and sophistication of the language used in the first stanza of "Pied Beauty"

I. Represents the multiplicity of nature   II. Celebrates things with mottled markings

III. Speaks to the frightening confusion of hybrids

A. I only
B. II only
C. III only
D. I and II
E. I, II, and III

2. All of the following techniques are employed in the first stanza except

    A. cataloging
    B. personification
    C. assonance
    D. simile
    E. consonance

3. In what sense is Hopkins imitating in language the "Pied Beauty" depicted in nature?

    I. The staccato one-syllable words   II. The mixture of disparate images

                  III. The varied and layered consonance

    A. I only
    B. II only
    C. III only
    D. I and II
    E. I, II, and III

4. The dappled things are all of the following except

    A. God
    B. trout
    C. finches' wings
    D. brinded cows
    E. landscape

5. What best describes the narrator's response to God's creations?

    A. contrariness
    B. wonder
    C. certainty
    D. silent prayer
    E. confusion

Theme and Poetic Devices

"My Parents"
> **by Stephen Spender**

My parents kept me from children who were rough
Who threw words like stones and wore torn clothes
Their thighs shown through rags. They ran in the street
And climbed cliffs and stripped by the country streams.

I feared more than tigers their muscles like iron   5
Their jerking hands and their knees tight on my arms
I feared the salt coarse pointing of those boys
Who copied my lisp behind me on the road.

They were lithe, they sprang out behind hedges
Like dogs to bark at my world. They threw mud   10
While I looked the other way, pretending to smile
I longed to forgive them but they never smiled.

1. Cite the line(s) that contain examples of each of the following poetic devices.

  A. Enjambment:
  B. Simile:
  C. Caesura:
  D. Alliteration:
  E. Internal rhyme:

2. The narrator of the poem can best be described as

    A. hostile and aggrieved
    B. despairing and frightened
    C. somber and forgiving
    D. confused and overwhelmed
    E. reflective and ambivalent

3. In one sentence state the theme of the poem.

Extended Metaphor

> **from** *Julius Caesar*
> **by William Shakespeare**
>
> However he puts on this tardy form.
> This rudeness is a sauce to his good wit,
> Which gives men stomach to digest his words
> With better appetite.
>
> **1.** An extended metaphor is termed a _____.
>
> **2.** List the words that extend the metaphor.
>
> **3.** What do these lines reveal about the speaker?
>
> **4.** What do we learn about the subject of the passage?

Symbol and Theme

"Fire and Ice"

      by Robert Frost (1920)

Some say the world will end in fire,
Some say in ice.
From what I've tasted of desire
I hold with those who favor fire.
But if it had to perish twice,   5
I think I know enough of hate
To know that for destruction ice
Is also great
And would suffice.

1. What is the poem's rhyme scheme?

2. In which line and with which word does the shift in the poem occur?

3. Frost associates fire with ＿＿＿＿＿＿ in lines ＿＿＿＿＿＿.

4. Frost associates ice with ＿＿＿＿＿＿ in lines ＿＿＿＿＿＿.

5. What is the poet's position on how the world will be destroyed?

5 Minutes to a 5

The Sonnet, Content/Detail

"Sonnet 30"
  by William Shakespeare

When to the sessions of sweet silent thought
I summon up remembrance of things past,
I sigh the lack of many a thing I sought,
And with old woes new wail my dear time's waste:
Then can I drown an eye, unus'd to flow,   5
For precious friends hid in death's dateless night,
And weep afresh love's long since cancell'd woe,
And moan th' expense of many a vanish'd sight;
Then can I grieve at grievances foregone,
And heavily from woe to woe tell o'er.   10
The sad account of fore-bemoaned moan,
Which I new pay as if not paid before.
But if the while I think on thee, dear friend,
All losses are restor'd, and sorrows end.

1. In one sentence state the subject of the sonnet.

2. The major points are constructed using cause and effect.

The first cause is indicated in lines _____.

Line(s) _____ contain(s) the second cause.

The first effect is described in lines _____.

The second effect is given in lines _____.

Line(s) _____ present(s) the third cause.

The final effect is found in line(s) _____.

3. The shift in the poem occurs in line _____ with the word _____.

4. The narrator is _____ (**accusatory** or **complimentary**) toward _____.

"Sonnet 37"
by William Shakespeare

As a decrepit father takes delight
To see his active child do deeds of youth,
So I, made lame by Fortune's dearest spite,
Take all my comfort of thy worth and truth;
For whether beauty, birth, or wealth, or wit,   5
Or any of these all, or all, or more,
Entitled in thy parts, do crowned sit,
I make my love engrafted to this store:
So then I am not lame, poor, nor despised,
Whilst that this shadow doth such substance give   10
That I in thy abundance am sufficed,
And by a part of all thy glory live.
      Look what is best, that best I wish in thee:
      This wish I have; then ten times happy me!

1. In context, "decrepit" (line 1) is best interpreted as

  A. cruel
  B. creepy
  C. happy
  D. worn
  E. youthful

2. In line 3 "Fortune's dearest spite" describes

  A. love
  B. aging
  C. delight
  D. regeneration
  E. currency

3. The subject of the poem might possess all of the following except

    A. affluence
    B. cleverness
    C. ineptitude
    D. attractiveness
    E. lineage

4. Line 6, "Or any of these all, or all, or more," refers to

    A. an excess that undermines
    B. an overabundance that causes wonder
    C. an ambiguity rendering the narrator desolate
    D. an extraction of the suffering old age endures
    E. an abstinence from all indulgence

5. The diction in "Entitled in thy parts, do crowned sit"(line 7) embues in the subject qualities that are

    A. regal and royal
    B. partial and opinionated
    C. bookish and statuesque
    D. obsequious and clairvoyant
    E. lowly and coarse

"Sonnet 37" (continued)
        by William Shakespeare

As a decrepit father takes delight
To see his active child do deeds of youth,
So I, made lame by Fortune's dearest spite,
Take all my comfort of thy worth and truth;
For whether beauty, birth, or wealth, or wit,   5
Or any of these all, or all, or more,
Entitled in thy parts, do crowned sit,
I make my love engrafted to this store:
So then I am not lame, poor, nor despised,
Whilst that this shadow doth such substance give   10
That I in thy abundance am sufficed,
And by a part of all thy glory live.
        Look what is best, that best I wish in thee:
        This wish I have; then ten times happy me!

6. Line 8 "I make my love engrafted this store" indicates that the narrator has

    A. rejected the ways of the young
    B. embraced his old age in all its doddering senility
    C. emerged as a young flower at a nursery
    D. connected himself to the subject's abundant advantages
    E. returned to nature's eternal growth

7. In line 9, the description of "lame, poor . . . despised" most directly contrasts with

   A. line 1
   B. line 5
   C. line 10
   D. line 13
   E. line 14

8. As delineated in lines 10–12, the narrator draws on the subject to gain

   A. financial wealth
   B. a past
   C. parsimony
   D. vitality
   E. sanity

9. For the narrator, the subject of the poem serves as a(n)

   A. obstacle
   B. inspiration
   C. discouragement
   D. initiation
   E. enemy

10. As confirmed by the last two lines of the sonnet, the narrator appears to be living

   A. vicariously
   B. delusionally
   C. clandestinely
   D. forlornly
   E. cruelly

"Sonnet 43"

     by William Shakespeare

       When most I wink, then do mine eyes best see,
       For all the day they view things unrespected;
       But when I sleep, in dreams they look on thee,
       And darkly bright, are bright in dark directed.
       Then thou, whose shadow shadows doth make bright,   5
       How would thy shadow's form form happy show
       To the clear day with thy much clearer light,
       When to unseeing eyes thy shade shines so?
       How would, I say, mine eyes be blessed made
       By looking on thee in the living day,   10
       When in dead night thy fair imperfect shade
       Through heavy sleep on sightless eyes doth stay?
          All days are nights to see till I see thee,
          And nights bright days when dreams do show thee me.

1. In context, "unrespected" (line 2) is best interpreted as

A. abused
B. not noticed
C. not feared
D. despised
E. loved

2. On line 3 "they" refers to

A. women
B. ghosts
C. the dead
D. eyes
E. things

3. In line 4 "darkly bright" is an example of

   A. onomatopoeia
   B. anaphora
   C. oxymoron
   D. symbolism
   E. anaphora

4. Line 4, "And darkly bright, are bright in dark directed," refers to

   A. the effect of moonlight on memory
   B. the visions the narrator sees in his slumbers
   C. the ray of light flashed by an intruder
   D. the narrator noticing the sun peeking through on a cloudy day
   E. the pleasant performances witnessed

5. The "thou" described in line 5

   A. has such a strong presence that even a memory of that individual is illuminating
   B. is now in heaven, as an angel, sprinkling sunshine through the darkness
   C. has suffered such a tragic death that its spirit now fires sparks across shadows
   D. provides a beacon of light for all travelers lost on nocturnal journey
   E. offers up illuminating candle light in the frosty darkness

"Sonnet 43"
by William Shakespeare

The following questions are based on the information you've gathered from the activity for Day 58 and having closely read "Sonnet 43."

6. In lines 6–8, the shadow's light appears to the narrator in

A. daylight
B. dreams
C. nightmares
D. twilight
E. storms

7. In the context of the sonnet, the "unseeing eyes" in line 8 indicate the narrator is

A. blind
B. asleep
C. incoherent
D. resistant
E. ignorant

8. "All days are nights" (line 13) because the narrator

A. misses this individual
B. is unable to sleep
C. has lost his vision
D. has been abandoned by this individual
E. has indulged in nocturnal tendencies

9. What is ironic about the final lines of the poem?

   A. That his beloved visits in the night but always disappears by the morning
   B. That the eclipse allowed the narrator to see better in shadowy visions than in day's clear light
   C. That the best time for the narrator to see his beloved is in the darkness of dreams
   D. That the narrator sees his beloved better in death than in life
   E. That the dreams have disintegrated into nightmares

10. Lines 9–14 of the sonnet

   A. restate the argument but place more emphasis on the narrator's troubled longing
   B. introduce a new theory as to why his beloved will inevitably return
   C. present a series of metaphors about how rebirth offers the narrator newfound hope
   D. undermine the narrator's initial argument by presenting a detailed explanation of daylight's preeminence
   E. establish an inherent relationship between light and dreams

11. Overall, the poet employs night and shadows to demonstrate how the narrator perceives

   A. darkness as the epicenter of fear and misery
   B. ghosts as haunting those afflicted by blindness
   C. light as the sole means for visions to emerge
   D. the natural order as inverted and confounded
   E. twilight as the nexus for visions to be resolved

Form and Content

> **"London, 1802"**
> **by William Wadsworth**
>
> Milton! thou shouldst be living at this hour:
> England hath need of thee: she is a fen
> Of stagnant waters: altar, sword, and pen,
> Fireside, the heroic wealth of hall and bower,
> Have forfeited their ancient English dower   5
> Of inward happiness. We are selfish men;
> Oh! raise us up, return to us again;
> And give us manners, virtue, freedom, power.
> Thy soul was like a Star, and dwelt apart:
> Thou hadst a voice whose sound was like the sea: 10
> Pure as the naked heavens, majestic, free,
> So didst thou travel on life's common way,
> In cheerful godliness; and yet thy heart
> The lowliest duties on herself did lay.
>
> **1.** Considering the rhyme and form, the poem is an example of _____.
>
> **2.** The poem breaks in form and meaning into two sections. The first is called _____.
>
> **3.** The second section is known as _____.
>
> **4.** The organization indicates that the poem is developed by _____.

Metaphor and Meaning

Having carefully deconstructed the prompt as you did on Day 31, it is time to closely read the poem again for meaning and *how* MacLeish develops that meaning.

"The End of the World"
        by Archibald MacLeish

Quite unexpectedly, as Vasserot[1]
The armless ambidextrian[2] was lighting
A match between his great and second toe,
And Ralph the lion was engaged in biting
The neck of Madame Sossman while the drum   5
Pointed, and Teeny was about to cough
In waltz-time swinging Jocko by the thumb
Quite unexpectedly to top blew off:

And there, there overhead, there, there hung over
Those thousands of white faces, those dazed eyes,   10
There in the starless dark, the poise, the hover,
There with vast wings across the cancelled skies,
There in the sudden blackness the black pall
Of nothing, nothing, nothing—nothing at all.

[1] French, 1900 Olympic cyclist
[2] a person who can use both arms equally well

1. What is the central metaphor of the poem?

2. In one sentence state what happens in the poem.

3. What is the actual subject of the poem?

Day 62

Writing the Thesis Statement

"The End of the World"
          by Archibald MacLeish

4. Given your answers to questions 1, 2, and 3, presented in the previous day's activities, what can you infer is the poet's attitude toward the subject?

5. Using the information you've gained in the preceding activities for "The End of the World," compose the first draft of a thesis statement that would address the prompt.

A Different View of a Sonnet

One of the best-known and loved modern poets is Billy Collins, U.S. Poet Laureate 2001–2003. Listen to his reading of one of his poems on YouTube:

https://www.youtube.com/watch?v=s9BEKoTq09w

Listen closely while you follow along with the on-screen wording. If you would like to have a hard copy, you can find it at: **http://www.poetryarchive.org/poem/sonnet**.

1. The given title and subject of this poem is _____.

2. At what points in the reading does the audience laugh?

3. What do you think is the cause of this laughter?

4. What appears to be the poet's attitude toward his subject?

5. What is the comment being made about this subject?

6. Given the diction, tone, and imagery, what can the reader conclude is the intent of this poem?

Day 64

Close Reading of a Poetry Passage

from *Macbeth*
    by William Shakespeare

Me thought I heard a voice cry, "Sleep no
more!..."
Sleep that knits up the raveled sleave of care,
The death of each day's life, sore labor's bath,
Balm of hurt minds, great nature's second course,
Chief nourisher in life's feast.

1. The "death of each day's life" refers directly to _____.

2. The passage includes all of the following except:

A. metaphor
B. personification
C. rhyme
D. alliteration
E. flashback

3. The examples provided in lines 2–5 are best described as:

A. challenging
B. negative
C. confusing
D. contradictory
E. metaphoric

Day 65

Poetic Diction and Meaning

Carefully read the following poem. Then, in a well-constructed essay describe the poet's major point and how he develops it in the poem.

"When God Decided to Invent"
by e.e. cummings

> when god decided to invent
> everything he took one
> breath bigger than a circustent
> and everything began
>
> when man determined to destroy
> himself he picked the was
> of shall and finding only why
> smashed it into because

1. In the first stanza, God is the _____. [line(s) _____] This action is _____ simple and direct _____ complicated. [line(s) _____]

2. In the second stanza, humankind is the _____. [line(s) _____] This is because humankind is always _____ questioning and asking why _____ accepting and complacent. [line(s) _____]

3. Having responded to the questions above, you should now be able to construct the first draft of the thesis statement that addresses the prompt.

Close Reading of a Poem

> **"I Wandered Lonely as a Cloud"**
> **by William Wordsworth**
>
> I wandered lonely as a cloud
> That floats on high o'er vales and hills,
> When all at once I saw a crowd,
> A host, of golden daffodils;
> Beside the lake, beneath the trees,   5
> Fluttering and dancing in the breeze.
>
> Continuous as the stars that shine
> And twinkle on the milky way,
> They stretched in never-ending line
> Along the margin of a bay: 10
> Ten thousand saw I at a glance,
> Tossing their heads in sprightly dance.
>
> The waves beside them danced; but they
> Out-did the sparkling waves in glee:
> A poet could not but be gay,   15
> In such a jocund company:
> I gazed—and gazed—but little thought
> What wealth the show to me had brought:
>
> For oft, when on my couch I lie
> In vacant or in pensive mood,   20
> They flash upon that inward eye
> Which is the bliss of solitude;
> And then my heart with pleasure fills,
> And dances with the daffodils.

1. "I Wandered Lonely as a Cloud" can be classified as what type of poem?

   A. Sonnet
   B. Lyric
   C. Elegy
   D. Epic
   E. Ballad

2. The subject of the central metaphor from lines 3–14 is _____.

3. Following the logic of the central metaphor, lines 13–14 compare _____ to "sparkling waves."

4. Under what circumstances does the narrator experience the central metaphor?

5. Which lines in the poem support your response to question 4?

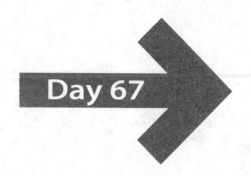

Imagery

"Barter"
        by Sara Teasdale

Life has loveliness to sell
All beautiful and splendid things,
Blue waves whitened on a cliff,
Soaring fire that sways and sings,
And children's faces looking up   **5**
Holding wonder in a cup.

Life has loveliness to sell,
Music like a curve of gold,
Scent of pine trees in the rain,
Eyes that love you, arms that hold,   **10**
And for your spirit's still delight,
Holy thoughts that star the night.

Spend all you have for loveliness,
Buy it and never count the cost;
For one white singing hour of peace   **15**
Count many a year of strife well lost,
And for a breath of ecstasy
Give all you have been, or could be.

1. Cite two examples of imagery (include the lines) that appeal to the sense of sight.

2. Cite two examples of imagery (include the lines) that appeal to the sense of hearing.

3. Cite one example of imagery (include the line) that appeals to the sense of smell.

Day 68

Writing the Introductory Paragraph

Carefully read the following poem. Then in a well-developed essay analyze the different techniques the poet uses to convey her attitude toward her subject

"Love Is Not All"
by Edna St. Vincent Millay

Love is not all: it is not meat nor drink
Nor slumber nor a roof against the rain;
Nor yet a floating spar to men that sink
And rise and sink and rise and sink again;
Love can not fill the thickened lung with breath,   **5**
Nor clean the blood, nor set the fractured bone;
Yet many a man is making friends with death
Even as I speak, for lack of love alone.
It well may be that in a difficult hour,
Pinned down by pain and moaning for release,   **10**
Or nagged by want past resolution's power,
I might be driven to sell your love for peace,
Or trade the memory of this night for food.
It well may be. I do not think I would.

5 Minutes to a 5

You are going to play AP English Literature teacher in this activity. Assume that this is the first paragraph written in response to the prompt.

> In the poem, Millay talks about love. She uses literary terms such as personification, negativity, and incongruence.

1. Would you rate this introduction _____ strong, _____ average, or _____ weak?

2. This introduction _____ does or _____ does not have a real thesis sentence.

3. Using your AP English Literature background, revise this introduction to meet the expectations of an AP English Literature essay.

Irony and Imagery

"Richard Cory"
by Edwin Arlington Robinson

Whenever Richard Cory went down town,
We people on the pavement looked at him:
He was a gentleman from sole to crown,
Clean favored, and imperially slim.

And he was always quietly arrayed,   5
And he was always human when he talked;
But still he fluttered pulses when he said,
"Good-morning," and he glittered when he walked.

And he was rich—yes, richer than a king—
And admirably schooled in every grace: 10
In fine, we thought that he was everything
To make us wish that we were in his place.

So on we worked, and waited for the light,
And went without the meat, and cursed the bread;
And Richard Cory, one calm summer night,   15
Went home and put a bullet through his head.

1. What are the contrasting points of view described in the poem?

2. Highlight a line or image in each stanza that is critical to the meaning or that moves you personally.

5 Minutes to a 5

"Richard Cory" (continued)
        by Edwin Arlington Robinson

The following questions are based on the information you've gathered from the activity for Day 69 and having closely read "Richard Cory."

3. Explain the function of repetition in stanza two.

4. What is the effect of the quotation in stanza two?

5. What is the purpose of the caesura in stanza three?

6. What does the image "one calm summer night" contribute to the poem?

Close Reading and Analysis

**from *Henry VIII*
by William Shakespeare**

The following soliloquy is from Shakespeare's play *Henry VIII*. For purposes of practice exercises, this soliloquy has been broken down for analysis over the course of five days. For each of these five days, you should read the segment of the soliloquy carefully and then turn to the bolded numbers, which serve as touchstones for key elements in the soliloquy. Below, respond to the questions that are associated with each of the bolded numbers as they will aid in developing an argument.

In the soliloquy, Cardinal Wolsey considers his fate after he has been quickly removed from his role as counselor to the king.

> So farewell—[1] to the little good you[2] bear me.
> Farewell? a long farewell[3] to all my greatness[4]!
> This is the state of man:[5] to-day he puts forth
> The tender leaves[6] of hopes, to-morrow blossoms,[7]
> And bears[8] his blushing honors[9] thick upon him;

1. What is the purpose of the long dash?

   The question mark?

   The exclamation point?

2. Who is "you"? What effect would the message have depending on if "you" were the king, the audience, or someone else (or even something abstract or metaphorical)?

3. What is the effect of the repetition of "farewell"?

4. How might "greatness" have multiple meanings? How might the author use the word ironically?

5. Why is Wolsey talking about the state of man rather than directly about himself? What outlook does this approach give him at least momentarily?

6. How is Wolsey setting up this extended metaphor? What can be said about the word "tender"?

7. Why do you think Wolsey has this transformation occur in seemingly a day?

8. What multiple meanings can you draw from "bears"?

9. Why "blushing honors"? What interpretations can you draw?

from *Henry VIII*
by William Shakespeare

Respond to the questions that are associated with each of the bolded superscripted numbers as they will aid in developing an argument.

> The third day[10] comes a frost, a killing frost,[11]
> And when he thinks, good easy[12] man, full surely
> His greatness[13] is a-ripening, nips his root,
> And then he falls as I do.[14] I have ventur'd,

10. What could be an allusion to the third day (remember Wolsey is a Cardinal)?

11. Why the repetition of "frost"?

12. What multiple meanings can you draw from "easy"?

13. What might "greatness" mean this time? Has the tone shifted?

14. How has he completed the connection between the state of man and himself?

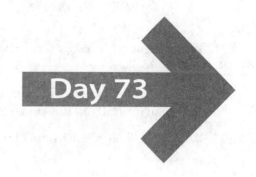
from _Henry VIII_
      by William Shakespeare

Respond to the questions that are associated with each of the bolded superscripted numbers as they will aid in developing an argument.

> Like little wanton boys[15] that swim on bladders,   10
> This many summers[16] in a sea of glory,[17]
> But far beyond my depth.[18] My high-blown[19] pride
> At length broke under me, and now has left me,
> Weary and old with service,[20] to the mercy[21]
> Of a rude stream[22] that must for ever hide[23] me.   15

15. Why do you think he compares himself to "little wanton boys"?

16. What season do you think Wolsey was discussing in the previous section? How does summer serve as a reflection of his former perception of himself and his powers?

17. Compare this conceit (an extended metaphor) to the previous one. What do the two have in common?

18. What is the tone here? Is it different from everything preceding it?

19. How does "high-blown" add another physical element to the soliloquy and play off the previous ones? How does the pride lamented here still remain ingrained in the speaker?

20. What words in this line and the previous line contrast with the language of the earlier conceits? How has Wolsey moved into a new season of his life?

21. What might be Wolsey's tone when he says "mercy" here? And what else might "mercy" imply?

22. Contrast "rude stream" with previous images. What might be the most accurate definition of "rude" in this context?

23. What does "hide" imply simultaneously about Wolsey's predicament and his self-perception?

from *Henry VIII*
   by William Shakespeare

Respond to the questions that are associated with each of the bolded superscripted numbers as they will aid in developing an argument.

> Vain[24] pomp and glory[25] of this world, I hate ye![26]
> I feel my heart new open'd.[27] O[28] how wretched
> Is that poor man[29] that hangs[30] on princes' favors![31]

24. What are the multiple meanings of "vain"?

25. Does Wolsey mean "pomp and glory" in a positive sense? Why or why not?

26. Who is "ye"? Where did this exclamation come from? Has it been building over the course of the soliloquy or was it suppressed only to be released in this outburst?

27. How is this phrase used in an untraditional way?

28. What does "O" do for the narrative?

29. Why does Wolsey talk about "that poor man" instead of himself?

30. What are the multiple meanings for "hangs" here?

31. How could this phrase be considered ironic? How does the exclamation point influence the reader's understanding/interpretation?

from *Henry VIII*
> by William Shakespeare

Respond to the questions that are associated with each of the bolded superscripted numbers as they will aid in developing an argument.

> There is, betwixt that smile we would aspire to,
> That sweet aspect of princes,[32] and their ruin,   20
> More pangs and fears than wars or women have;[33]
> And when he falls, he falls like Lucifer,[34]
> Never to hope again.[35]

32. Again, think tone here and think of the earlier reference to **blossom.**

33. What do you make of these two vastly different points of comparison? Why do you think Wolsey uses such extremes? Do the comparisons serve as flattering or humiliating reflections on him?

34. What is the significance of the comparison to Lucifer? How would such a comparison simultaneously elevate and diminish Wolsey?

35. This last line is also an allusion. Any idea to what work? Why do you think Wolsey ends on such an absolute?

Summative Analysis: Use the space below to synthesize some of your thoughts over the past five days of responding to the soliloquy.

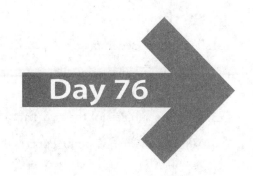

Poetic Structure

from "An Essay on Criticism"
        by Alexander Pope (1711)

'Tis hard to say, if greater want of skill
Appear in writing or in judging ill;
But, of the two, less dang'rous is th' offence
To tire our patience, than mislead our sense.
Some few in that, but numbers err in this,   5
Ten censure wrong for one who writes amiss;
A fool might once himself alone expose,
Now one in verse makes many more in prose

'Tis with our judgments as our watches, none
Go just alike, yet each believes his own.   10
In poets as true genius is but rare,
True taste as seldom is the critic's share;
Both must alike from Heav'n derive their light,
These born to judge, as well as those to write.
Let such teach others who themselves excel,   15
And censure freely who have written well.
Authors are partial to their wit, 'tis true,
But are not critics to their judgment too?

1. The rhyme scheme is _____.

2. The 18 lines are constructed using pairs of rhyming lines of iambic pentameter. This is classified as a(n) _____.

3. The two subjects of the two stanzas are _____.

4. What is the major point Pope makes about the two subjects in this section of his poem?

Rhyme and Structure

"Sonnet 55"
     by William Shakespeare

Not marble nor the gilded monuments
Of princes shall outlive this powerful rhyme;
But you shall shine more bright in these contents
Than unswept stone, besmear'd with sluttish time.
When wasteful war shall statues overturn,   5
And broils root out the work of masonry,
Nor Mars his sword nor war's quick fire shall burn
The living record of your memory.
'Gainst death and all-oblivious enmity
Shall you pace forth; your praise shall still find room,   10
Even in the eyes of all posterity
That wear this world out to the ending doom.
So, till the judgment that yourself arise,
You live in this, and dwell in lovers' eyes.

1. Label the rhyme scheme of the poem.

2. Using the rhyme scheme as a guide, separate and identify the sections of the poem.

3. Based on the above information, this poem can be classified as a _____.

Lyric Poetry

> **"The Darkling Thrush"**
> **by Thomas Hardy (1900)**
>
> I leant upon a coppice gate
> When Frost was spectre-grey,
> And Winter's dregs made desolate
>   The weakening eye of day.
> The tangled bine-stems scored the sky   5
>   Like strings of broken lyres,
> And all mankind that haunted nigh
>   Had sought their household fires.
>
> The land's sharp features seemed to be
>   The Century's corpse outleant,   10
> His crypt the cloudy canopy,
>   The wind his death-lament.
> The ancient pulse of germ and birth
>   Was shrunken hard and dry,
> And every spirit upon earth   15
>   Seemed fervourless as I.
>
> Atonce a voice arose among
>   The bleak twigs overhead
> In a full-hearted evensong
>   Of joy illimited;   20
> An aged thrush, frail, gaunt and small,
>   In blast-beruffled plume,
> Had chosen thus to fling his soul
>   Upon the growing gloom.

So little cause for carolings   25
    Of such ecstatic sound
Was written on terrestrial things
    Afar or nigh around,
That I could think there trembled through
    His happy good-night air   30
Some blessed Hope, whereof he knew
    And I was unaware.

1. In "The Darkling Thrush," the word "eye" in line 4 is best defined as the

    A. sun
    B. pupil
    C. calm
    D. orb
    E. spy

2. Lines 9–12 possess imagery best described as

    A. topographical
    B. psychological
    C. minimal
    D. funereal
    E. theatrical

3. All of the following refer to the thrush's singing except

    A. fullhearted (line 19)
    B. joy (line 20)
    C. frail (line 21)
    D. ecstatic (line 26)
    E. happy (line 30)

4. The thrush can be seen by the narrator as an

    A. annoyance
    B. inspiration
    C. alarm
    D. impossibility
    E. infidel

5. The following shifts dramatically in the work

    I. The weather   II. The mood   III. The thrush

    A. I only
    B. II only
    C. III only
    D. I and II
    E. I, II, and III

Narrative Perspective and Diction

Follow-up on Thomas Hardy's "The Darkling Thrush"

Using the information you've gathered from the activity for Day 78, compare the perspective and the diction of the first two stanzas with the two that follow and conclude "The Darkling Thrush." In your commentary consider the transitional nature of the third stanza.

Close Reading and Analysis of a Poem

---

from "To an Athlete Dying Young"
by A.E. Housman

The time you won your town the race
We chaired you through the market-place;
Man and boy stood cheering by,
And home we brought you shoulder-high.

Today, the road all runners come,   5
Shoulder-high we bring you home,
And set you at your threshold down,
Townsman of a stiller town.

Smart lad, to slip betimes away
From fields where glory does not stay,   10
And early though the laurel grows
It withers quicker than the rose.

1. The word "chaired" in line 2 of "To an Athlete Dying Young" can best be defined as

A. insulted
B. led a meeting
C. led a team
D. lifted
E. cheered

---

2. The first and second stanzas possess which elements?

I. Irony   II. Juxtaposition   III. Hyperbole

A. I only
B. II only
C. III only
D. I and II
E. I, II, and III

3. The central message of stanza three is

A. all men die
B. flowers do not last
C. fame rapidly fades
D. intelligence always triumphs
E. love will find a way

4. Given the context presented, the reader can infer that the narrator is

A. a local resident
B. an athlete
C. the deceased
D. a gardener
E. a farmer

from "To an Althete Dying Young" (continued)
by A.E. Housman

Eyes the shady night has shut
Cannot see the record cut,
And silence sounds no worse than cheers   15
After earth has stopped the ears.

Now you will not swell the rout
Of lads that wore their honours out,
Runners whom renown outran
And the name died before the man.   20

So set, before its echoes fade,
The fleet foot on the sill of shade,
And hold to the low lintel up
The still-defended challenge-cup.

And round that early-laurelled head   25
Will flock to gaze the strengthless dead,
And find unwithered on its curls
The garland briefer than a girl's.

5. According to the central message of stanza 4, the athlete, by dying young, has avoided being

A. eclipsed and ignored
B. insulted and derided
C. manipulated and exploited
D. broken and crushed
E. dropped and distorted

6. In line 16, "stopped" can best be defined as

A. ended
B. clogged
C. deteriorated
D. chopped
E. removed

7. Line 19–"Runners whom renown outran"–is an example of

I. Paradox   II. Consonance   III. Personification

A. I only
B. II only
C. III only
D. I and II
E. I, II, and III

8. According to the poem, the other runners

A. were given heroic farewells
B. found dignity and respect in old age
C. created a new generation of runners
D. also died young
E. were forgotten by the general public

Day 82

Five Activities Analyzing a Poem in Preparation for the Poetry Essay

The following excerpt is from William Wordsworth's long poem *The Prelude*. For purposes of practice exercises, this poetry passage has been broken down for analysis over the course of five days. For each of these five days, you should read the segment of the poem carefully and then turn to the bolded numbers, which serve as touchstones for key elements in the excerpt. Below, respond to the questions that are associated with each of the bolded numbers as they will aid in developing an argument. Since the segments are broken sometimes mid-thought and even mid-line, it is a good idea to return to the previous day's verse before you examine the current day's segment.

In this excerpt, the narrator describes his interaction with the natural world on summer evening.

"The Prelude"
> **by William Wordsworth**

> One summer evening (led by her)[1] I found
> A little[2] boat tied to a willow tree
> Within a rocky cave, its usual home.
> Straight I unloosed her chain,[3] and stepping in
> Pushed from the shore.[4] It was an act of stealth

1. The "her" in this poem is nature. What is the significance of nature being referred to as "her," and why do you think it's identified in lowercase letters?

2. What is the significance of the boat being little?

3. Describe the significance that the narrator "unloosed her chain." From what is the narrator releasing himself?

4. What is the significance of being "Pushed from the shore"? What is the symbolic quality of such a detachment?

5 Minutes to a 5

from "The Prelude"
by William Wordsworth

And troubled pleasure;[5] nor without the voice
Of mountain-echoes did my boat move on;
Leaving behind her still, on either side,
Small circles glittering idly in the moon,
Until they melted all into one track
Of sparkling light. But now, like one who rows,
Proud of his skill, to reach a chosen point
With unswerving line,[6] I fixed my view
Upon the summit of a craggy ride,
The horizon's utmost boundary;[7] far above
Was nothing but the stars and the grey sky.
She was an elfin pinnace, lustily,[8]
I dipped my oars into the silent lake
And, as I rose upon the stroke, my boat
Went heaving through the water like a swan;

5. What do you make of the oxymoronic phrase "trouble pleasure"?

6. What is the importance of the narrator making an "unswerving line"? What does it say about his outlook?

7. What is the significance of the author's choice of language: "horizon's utmost boundary"? What might this phrase symbolize?

8. Why "lustily"? How does such a word reflect on the narrator's outlook?

from "The Prelude"
by William Wordsworth

When, from behind the craggy steep till then
The horizon's bound, a huge peak, black and huge,
As if with voluntary power instinct
Upreared its head. I struck and struck again,[9]
And growing still in stature the grim shape
Towered[10] up between me and the stars, and still,
For so it seemed, with purpose of its own
And measured motion like a living thing,[11]
Stroke after me. With trembling oars I turned,
And through the silent water stole[12] my way
Back to the covert of the willow tree;

9. What do you think are the major reasons for the repetition of "a huge peak, black and huge"? In contrast, what is the purpose of the repetition of "struck and struck again"?

10. What attitude does the word "Towered" reflect in the narrator?

11. What is the significance of the phrase "measured motion like a living thing"? In your analysis, give particular attention to the word "measured."

12. Why are the oars "trembling"? What is the purpose of this metonymy? Why "stole"? What does such a word indicate about the narrator's thought process and behavior?

from "The Prelude"
        by William Wordsworth

There in her mooring place I left my bark* –
And through the meadows homeward went, in grave[13]
And serious mood; but after I had seen
That spectacle, for many days, my brain
Worked with a dim and undermined[14] sense
Of unknown modes of being; o'er my thoughts
There hung a darkness,[15] call it solitude
Or blank[16] desertion. No familiar shapes
Remained, no pleasant images of tree,
Of sea or sky, no colours of green fields;

_____

*bark: a small boat

13. Consider the phrase "in grave/And serious mood." What multiple meanings can you draw from the word "grave"?

14. Consider the phrase "dim and undetermined sense." What is its significance, especially the word "undetermined," which is followed by the prepositional phrase "of unknown sense"?

15. What does the narrator mean by "There hung a darkness"? What are the nuances of the word "hung" in this context?

16. How does the word "blank" set up the parallel phrases that follow, all grounded by the repetition of "no"?

from "The Prelude"
        by William Wordsworth

But huge and mighty forms,[17] that do not live
Like living men, moved slowly[18] through the mind
By day, and were a trouble to my dreams.

17. Are these "huge and mighty forms" positive or negative? What do these forms intimate to the narrator and to the reader?

18. What is the significance of the word "slowly" here? How is that word wedded to the poem's obsessive and haunting qualities?

Summative Analysis: Use the space below to synthesize some of your thoughts over the past five days of responding to the excerpt from *The Prelude*.

The Poetry Essay

You've already completed an activity based on a close reading of "My Parents." Now, let's assume you are given the following essay prompt that has as its subject Spender's poem.

Carefully read "My Parents" by Stephen Spender in which he comments on a situation from his childhood. Then, in a well-constructed essay, analyze how Spender uses poetic devices to develop and convey the complex attitude of the poem's narrator toward his subject.

"My Parents"
by Stephen Spender

My parents kept me from children who were rough
Who threw words like stones and wore torn clothes
Their thighs shown through rags. They ran in the street
And climbed cliffs and stripped by the country streams.

I feared more than tigers their muscles like iron   5
Their jerking hands and their knees tight on my arms
I feared the salt coarse pointing of those boys
Who copied my lisp behind me on the road.

They were lithe, they sprang out behind hedges
Like dogs to bark at my world. They threw mud   10
While I looked the other way, pretending to smile
I longed to forgive them but they never smiled.

Referring to the poem and the previous activity related to "My Parents," compose your preliminary thesis statement in response to the prompt.

1. The subject of the poem is _____.

2. The attitude of the narrator toward his subject(s) is _____.

3. My preliminary thesis statement is _____.

Close Reading and Analysis of "Dover Beach"

Part 1: Multiple Choice for the First Two Stanzas

from "Dover Beach"
      by Matthew Arnold

The sea is calm to-night.
The tide is full, the moon lies fair
Upon the straits; on the French coast the light
Gleams and is gone; the cliffs of England stand;
Glimmering and vast, out in the tranquil bay.   5
Come to the window, sweet is the night-air!
Only, from the long line of spray
Where the sea meets the moon-blanched land,
Listen! you hear the grating roar
Of pebbles which the waves draw back, and fling,   10
At their return, up the high strand,
Begin, and cease, and then again begin,
With tremulous cadence slow, and bring
The eternal note of sadness in.

Sophocles long ago   15
Heard it on the Aegean, and it brought
Into his mind the turbid ebb and flow
Of human misery; we
Find also in the sound a thought,
Hearing it by this distant northern sea.   20

1. The opening physical scene (1ines 1–3) is one of

   A. sadness
   B. turbulence
   C. tranquility
   D. loneliness
   E. struggle

2. What is offered in line 6 is an

   A. interjection
   B. intimation
   C. invitation
   D. inclination
   E. indecision

3. Which word signals a turn in the imagery toward sadness?

   A. lies (line 2)
   B. Come (line 6)
   C. Night (line 6)
   D. Only (line 7)
   E. slow (line 13)

4. Which of the following call(s) for the reader to interact with the narrator?

   I. Come (line 6)   II. Listen (line 9)   III. hear (line 9)

   A. I only
   B. II only
   C. III only
   D. I and II
   E. I, II, and III

5. Lines 15–16 contain

   A. onomatopoeia
   B. allusion
   C. personification
   D. iambic pentameter
   E. metaphor

Part 2: Multiple Choice for the Last Two Stanzas

from "Dover Beach"
          by Matthew Arnold

The Sea of Faith
Was once, too, at the full, and round earth's shore
Lay like the folds of a bright girdle furled.
But now I only hear
Its melancholy, long, withdrawing roar,   25
Retreating, to the breath
Of the night-wind, down the vast edges drear
And naked shingles of the world.

Ah, love, let us be true
To one another! for the world, which seems   30
To lie before us like a land of dreams,
So various, so beautiful, so new,
Hath really neither joy, nor love, nor light,
Nor certitude, nor peace, nor help for pain;
And we are here as on a darkling plain   35
Swept with confused alarms of struggle and flight,
Where ignorant armies clash by night.

6. Lines 21–23 possess all of the following except

A. apostrophe
B. consonance
C. metaphor
D. symbol
E. simile

7. Which word is not in its conventional place syntactically?

    A. hear (line 24)   ·
    B. breath (line 26)
    C. drear (line 27)
    D. naked (line 28)
    E. world (line 28)

8. The antecedent of "Its" in line 25 is

    A. "The sea of faith" (line 21)
    B. "the full" (line 22)
    C. "the folds" (line 23)
    D. "bright girdle furled" (line 23)
    E. "melancholy, long, withdrawing roar" (line 25)

9. The final line of the poem suggests

    A. an affirmation of the poem's opening line
    B. a double sense of error and confusion
    C. a rejection of the statement on lines 30–34
    D. a cry to the reader for help
    E. an embracement of religion

10. "Dover Beach" most clearly and fully depicts

    A. the inspiration gained by looking back on the great writers of the past
    B. the great solace gained by looking out onto soothing bodies of water
    C. the problem of dealing with ignorant armies that control all aspects of society
    D. the anxiety caused by turbulent historical forces and the loss of religious faith in our world
    E. the sadness of knowing about all the negative experiences of the history of religions

Considering Allusion

from "Dover Beach"
by Matthew Arnold

An allusion is a brief and indirect reference to a person, a place, or an idea of literary, historical, or cultural significance. While the connection by the narrator to the Greek playwright Sophocles is direct, the references to Greek civilization are not. Describe how the poet, Matthew Arnold, broadens the meaning of the poem by relating his experience with the sea to that of Sophocles' in the previous stanzas. What implications can be drawn from Arnold making this connection?

A conceit is an extended metaphor, usually comparing two unlike things in an unexpected way. Stanza three compares the sea with faith. Consider how Arnold builds this conceit over the course of the stanza, and describe how the poet connects the scope and motions of the sea with faith. Carefully incorporate specific details from the stanza to present your view.

from "Dover Beach"
       by Matthew Arnold

> The sea is calm to-night.
> The tide is full, the moon lies fair
> Upon the straits; on the French coast the light
> Gleams and is gone; the cliffs of England stand;
> Glimmering and vast, out in the tranquil bay.   **5**
> Come to the window, sweet is the night-air!
> Only, from the long line of spray
> Where the sea meets the moon-blanched land,
> Listen! you hear the grating roar
> Of pebbles which the waves draw back, and fling,   **10**
> At their return, up the high strand,
> Begin, and cease, and then again begin,
> With tremulous cadence slow, and bring
> The eternal note of sadness in.

Sophocles long ago   15
Heard it on the Aegean, and it brought
Into his mind the turbid ebb and flow
Of human misery; we
Find also in the sound a thought,
Hearing it by this distant northern sea.   20

The Sea of Faith
Was once, too, at the full, and round earth's shore
Lay like the folds of a bright girdle furled.
But now I only hear
Its melancholy, long, withdrawing roar,   25
Retreating, to the breath
Of the night-wind, down the vast edges drear
And naked shingles of the world.

Ah, love, let us be true
To one another! for the world, which seems   30
To lie before us like a land of dreams,
So various, so beautiful, so new,
Hath really neither joy, nor love, nor light,
Nor certitude, nor peace, nor help for pain;
And we are here as on a darkling plain   35
Swept with confused alarms of struggle and flight,
Where ignorant armies clash by night.

Writing an AP Literature Essay, A Practice Process

The following set of activities is based on a careful reading of Henry V's soliloquy in Shakespeare's historical play *Henry V*. Each question/activity is specifically related to a close reading of the text and composing a well-developed essay that responds to the prompt. It is best to complete each of these questions/activities in the given order.

Spoken by King Henry V in *Henry V*, Act IV, Scene 1 (the night before the battle of Agincourt with the French)

> Indeed, the French may lay twenty French crowns to
> one, they will beat us; for they bear them on their
> shoulders: but it is no English treason to cut
> French crowns, and to-morrow the king himself will
> be a clipper.   5
>
> *Exeunt soldiers*
>
> Upon the king! let us our lives, our souls,
> Our debts, our careful wives,
> Our children and our sins lay on the king!
> We must bear all. O hard condition,
> Twin-born with greatness, subject to the breath   10
> Of every fool, whose sense no more can feel But
> his own wringing! What infinite heart's-ease
> Must kings neglect, that private men enjoy!
> And what have kings, that privates have not too,

Save ceremony, save general, ceremony?   **15**
And what art thou, thou idle ceremony?
What kind of god art thou, that suffer'st more
Of mortal griefs than do thy worshippers?
What are thy rents? what are thy comings in?   **20**
O ceremony, show me but thy worth!
What is thy soul of adoration?
Art thou aught else but place, degree and form,
Creating awe and fear in other men?
Wherein thou art less happy being fear'd   **25**
Than they in fearing.
What drink'st thou oft, instead of homage sweet,
But poison'd flattery? O, be sick, great greatness,
And bid thy ceremony give thee cure!
Think'st thou the fiery fever will go out   **30**
With titles blown from adulation?
Will it give place to flexure and low bending?
Canst thou, when thou command'st the beggar's knee,
Command the health of it? No, thou proud dream,
That play'st so subtly with a king's repose;   **35**
I am a king that find thee, and I know
'Tis not the balm, the sceptre and the ball,
The sword, the mace, the crown imperial,
The intertissued robe of gold and pearl,
The farced[1] title running 'fore the king,   **40**
The throne he sits on, nor the tide of pomp
That beats upon the high shore of this world,
No, not all these, thrice-gorgeous ceremony,
Not all these, laid in bed majestical,
Can sleep so soundly as the wretched slave,   **45**
Who with a body fill'd and vacant mind
Gets him to rest, cramm'd with distressful bread;
Never sees horrid night, the child of hell,
But, like a lackey[2], from the rise to set
Sweats in the eye of Phoebus[3] and all night   **50**
Sleeps in Elysium[4]; next day after dawn,
Doth rise and help Hyperion[5] to his horse,
And follows so the ever-running year,
With profitable labour, to his grave:
And, but for ceremony, such a wretch,   **55**
Winding up days with toil and nights with sleep,
Had the fore-hand and vantage of a king.
The slave, a member of the country's peace,
Enjoys it; but in gross brain little wots[6]

What watch the king keeps to maintain the peace,
Whose hours the peasant best advantages.   60

---

[1] stuffed
[2] a foot soldier or servant
[3] Greek god Apollo
[4] home of the blessed after they die
[5] Greek god Helios, god of the sun
[6] thoughts

Henry V, Reading the Prompt, 1

Carefully read and annotate the following prompt.

In this scene from *Henry V*, we find King Henry in the English encampment on the night before the battle of Agincourt. Facing an adversary that is in better condition and that outnumbers his, Henry wishes "no other company," and asks to be left alone to "debate" with himself. Read the soliloquy carefully. Then, in a well-developed essay analyze how Shakespeare uses literary techniques/devices to convey Henry's attitude toward leadership/kingship.

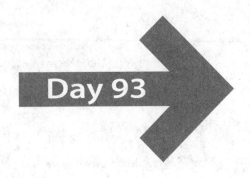

Henry V, Reading the Text

Now that you've carefully read and annotated the prompt, you are ready to read the text with the demands of the prompt in mind:

- Read as if you are reading the text out loud to an audience.

- Read with a pen or pencil ready in hand.

- Now, listen to Samuel West deliver the soliloquy on **YouTube: https://www.youtube.com/watch?v=USQvp7skuTY**

- As you read and listen, remember you are trying to find out what is King Henry's attitude toward kingship.

- When you've completed reading and listening to the text, move on to the next activity.

Henry V, Identifying King Henry's Attitude Toward Leadership/Kingship

Having closely read the soliloquy, what have you determined is Henry's attitude toward kingship?

Henry V, Composing the Thesis Statement

Based on your close reading of the soliloquy in Act IV, Scene 1, and your conclusion(s) about Henry's attitude toward kingship, which of the thesis statements given below *best* addresses the prompt?

_____ **1.** As far as King Henry V is concerned, being a king is a heavy burden that the common citizen does not have to bear.

_____ **2.** King Henry V is a troubled man.

_____ **3.** In his soliloquy in Act IV, Scene 1, King Henry V debates with himself about whether or not to give up his crown.

_____ **4.** In his soliloquy in Act IV, Scene 1, King Henry V sees the pomp, ceremony, and power of a king as much less a privilege than it is a burden that the ordinary citizen will never know.

_____ **5.** In Act IV, Scene 1, King Henry V makes it quite clear that he is not happy being king.

Henry V, Choosing Major Points

> What are the major points you could use in support of your thesis? (Look back at Activity 3 and your inferences/conclusions. Also refer to the prompt again.)

Henry V, Identifying Examples to Support Major Points

Underline/highlight the specific examples/details you will use to illustrate or support your major points. Note in the margins a brief reason for selecting each example/ detail.

Spoken by King Henry V in *Henry V*, Act IV, Scene 1 (The night before the battle of Agincourt with the French)

Indeed, the French may lay twenty French crowns to
one, they will beat us; for they bear them on their
shoulders: but it is no English treason to cut
French crowns, and to-morrow the king himself will
be a clipper.   5

Exeunt soldiers

Upon the king! let us our lives, our souls,
Our debts, our careful wives,
Our children and our sins lay on the king!
We must bear all. O hard condition,
Twin-born with greatness, subject to the breath   10
Of every fool, whose sense no more can feel But
his own wringing! What infinite heart's-ease
Must kings neglect, that private men enjoy! And
what have kings, that privates have not too,

Save ceremony, save general ceremony?   15
And what art thou, thou idle ceremony?
What kind of god art thou, that suffer'st more
Of mortal griefs than do thy worshippers?
What are thy rents? what are thy comings in?
O ceremony, show me but thy worth!   20
What is thy soul of adoration?
Art thou aught else but place, degree and form,
Creating awe and fear in other men?
Wherein thou art less happy being fear'd
Than they in fearing.   25
What drink'st thou oft, instead of homage sweet,
But poison'd flattery? O, be sick, great greatness,
And bid thy ceremony give thee cure!
Think'st thou the fiery fever will go out
With titles blown from adulation?   30
Will it give place to flexure and low bending?
Canst thou, when thou command'st the beggar's knee,
Command the health of it? No, thou proud dream,
That play'st so subtly with a king's repose;
I am a king that find thee, and I know   35
'Tis not the balm, the sceptre and the ball,
The sword, the mace, the crown imperial,
The intertissued robe of gold and pearl,
The farced[1] title running 'fore the king,
The throne he sits on, nor the tide of pomp   40
That beats upon the high shore of this world,
No, not all these, thrice-gorgeous ceremony,
Not all these, laid in bed majestical,
Can sleep so soundly as the wretched slave,
Who with a body fill'd and vacant mind   45
Gets him to rest, cramm'd with distressful bread;
Never sees horrid night, the child of hell,
But, like a lackey[2], from the rise to set
Sweats in the eye of Phoebus[3] and all night
Sleeps in Elysium[4]; next day after dawn,   50
Doth rise and help Hyperion[5] to his horse,
And follows so the ever-running year,
With profitable labour, to his grave:
And, but for ceremony, such a wretch,
Winding up days with toil and nights with sleep,   55

Had the fore-hand and vantage of a king.
The slave, a member of the country's peace,
Enjoys it; but in gross brain little wots[6]
What watch the king keeps to maintain the peace,
Whose hours the peasant best advantages.   **60**

---

[1]stuffed

[2]a foot soldier or servant

[3]Greek god Apollo

[4]home of the blessed after they die

[5]Greek god Helios, god of the sun

[6]thoughts

Henry V, Illustrating Specific Details to Support Major Points

List the specific examples/details you will use to support your major points. Include your notations.

Henry V, Composing the Says/Does or What/Why Sentence

> Which of the following sentences BEST addresses an example/detail from Henry V's soliloquy in Act IV, Scene 1?
>
> _____ **1.** Shakespeare uses personification in lines 15–42.
>
> _____ **2.** The personification of "ceremony" (lines 15–42) allows Henry to internally debate the pros and cons of the power, admiration, and wealth of being king.
>
> _____ **3.** Personification of ceremony can be found in two rhetorical questions (lines 16–18) that ask whether or not "ceremony" is "idle" or a "god" that suffers more than the people who worship it.

PROSE

Deconstructing the Prose Prompt

The following passage is from the novel *A Room with a View*, by E. M. Forster (1908). At the beginning of the first chapter, Lucy Honeychurch and Miss Charlotte Bartlett are traveling together and arrive at their hotel in Florence, Italy.

Read the passage carefully. Then write a well-developed essay in which you analyze how Forster portrays these two characters and their relationship with one another and with the world around them.

You may wish to consider such literary devices as selection of detail, language, and tone.

Deconstruct the above prompt by underlining, highlighting, and/or notating the requirements of the task.

Definition of Terms

Match the term with the correct definition.

_____ **1.** Plot   A. Foreshadowing

_____ **2.** Setting   B. Opinion

_____ **3.** Character   C. Time and place

_____ **4.** Theme   D. Tragic hero

_____ **5.** Point of view   E. Carries out the action of the narrative

                                 F. The main idea

                                 G. Series of episodes

                                 H. How the author tells the story

Ways of Knowing Character

Jot down a list of how characters are revealed to the reader.

(Hint: Think of how you learn about a new person and apply your process to literary characters.)

Understanding Diction and Tone

> **from** *To Kill a Mockingbird*
> **by Harper Lee (1960)**
>
> Maycomb was an old town, but it was a tired old town when I first knew it. . . .
> grass grew on the sidewalks, the courthouse sagged in the square. Somehow, it was
> hotter then: a black dog suffered on a summer's day; bony mules flicked flies in the
> sweltering shade of the live oaks. Men's stiff collars wilted by nine in the morning.
>
> Highlight the adjectives and verbs that the speaker chooses to describe the setting.
>
> Write a sentence that characterizes the tone developed by the diction.

Types of Novels, Forms, and Definitions

Match the novel form with its characteristics.

_____ **1.** Picaresque

_____ **2.** Gothic

_____ **3.** Allegorical

_____ **4.** Epistolary

_____ **5.** Romantic

A. Letter writing, early novel form

B. First person, reader interacts with narrator

C. Macabre, supernatural, exotic

D. Grounded in reality, factual detail

E. Episodic, young rogue, misadventures

F. Idealistic, hero, exotic locales

G. Symbolic, metaphoric, representative

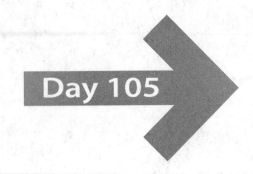

Setting and Theme

Carefully read the following excerpt from the stage directions for *Desire Under the Elms* by Eugene O'Neill (1924).

The action of the entire play takes place in, and immediately outside of, the Cabot farmhouse in New England, in the year 1850. The south end of the house faces front to a stone wall with a wooden gate at center opening on a country road. The house is in good condition but in need of paint. Its walls are a sickly grayish, the green of the shutters faded. Two enormous elms are on each side of the house. They bend their trailing branches down over the roof. They appear to protect and at the same time subdue. There is a sinister maternity in their aspect, a crushing, jealous absorption. . . . They are like exhausted women resting their sagging breasts and hands and hair on its roof, and when it rains their tears trickle down monotonously and rot on the shingles.

1. Reread the passage, this time annotating as you read.

2. What mood is created in this passage?

3. Cite the words and/or phrases that support your response to question 2.

4. Given the answers above, what could you infer about the probable theme of this drama? Will the tensions and theme developed be positive or negative?

Tone and Theme

from the opening of *Heart of Darkness*
by Joseph Conrad

(anchored on the Thames, a sailing ship waits for the tide to rise as the sun sets . . .)

And at last, in its curved and imperceptible fall, the sun sank low, and from
glowing white changed to a dull red without rays and without heat, as if about
to go out suddenly, stricken to death by the touch of that gloom brooding
over a crowd of men.

Forthwith a change came over the waters, and the serenity became less brilliant   5
but more profound. The old river in its broad reach rested unruffled at the
decline of day, after ages of good service done to the race that peopled its banks,
spread out in the tranquil dignity of a waterway leading to the uttermost ends
of the earth. We looked at the venerable stream not in the vivid flush of a short
day that comes and departs for ever, but in the august light of abiding memories.   10
And indeed nothing is easier for a man who has, as the phrase goes, "followed
the sea" with reverence and affection, that to evoke the great spirit of the past
upon the lower reaches of the Thames. The tidal current runs to and fro in its
unceasing service, crowded with memories of men and ships it had borne to
the rest of home or to the battles of the sea. It had known and served all the   15
men of whom the nation is proud, from Sir Francis Drake to Sir John Franklin,
knights all, titled and untitled—the great knights-errant of the sea. It had borne
all the ships whose names are like jewels flashing in the night of time, from the
Golden Hind returning with her rotund flanks full of treasure, to be visited
by the Queen's Highness and thus pass out of the gigantic tale, to the Erebus   20
and Terror, bound on other conquests—and that never returned. It had known
the ships and the men. They had sailed from Deptford, from Greenwich, from
Erith—the adventurers and the settlers; kings' ships and the ships of men on
'Change; captains, admirals, the dark "interlopers" of the Eastern trade, and the
commissioned "generals" of East India fleets. Hunters for gold or pursuers   25

of fame, they all had gone out on that stream, bearing the sword, and often the torch, messengers of the might within the land, bearers of a spark from the sacred fire. What greatness had not floated on the ebb of that river into the mystery of an unknown earth! . . . The dreams of men, the seed of commonwealths, the germs of empires.

30

1. This opening section of the novel introduces the reader to the River Thames. What is the attitude of the narrator toward the river?

2. Highlight the details that led you to your conclusion in question 1.

3. After reading this passage, the reader begins to formulate an idea about what the theme of this novel is. Most likely, the theme will involve which of the following? (Check all that apply.)

_____ a river	_____ Marlowe
_____ exploration	_____ childhood memories
_____ religious practices	_____ man vs. nature
_____ modern warfare	_____ the ends justify the means
_____ good vs. evil	_____ business practices

Mood in Film

Watch the opening sequence of the Israeli film *Waltz with Bashir* (2008) at the following website:

https://www.youtube.com/watch?v=OApxExSkkTw

You will be viewing this film excerpt with mood and tone in mind. There is no need to pay any attention to the foreign language printed on the screen. There is no dialogue, and the meaning and effect will be easily discerned. But, before doing anything else, **watch the film**. You may want to return and watch it again or even a third time as you respond to the questions that follow.

1. What mood has the artist and director of *Waltz with Bashir* created? (*MOOD*: a prevailing feeling that can create a sense of expectation)
   A. Weariness
   B. Sadness
   C. Annoyance
   D. Fear
   E. Excitement

2. Cite three specific details from the opening sequence of *Waltz with Bashir* that support your characterization of the mood.

3. Given your responses to the questions above, what expectations are created in this opening sequence?

Imagery, Foreshadowing

Carefully read the opening lines from *The Kite Runner* by Khaled Hosseini.

I became what I am today at the age of twelve, on a frigid overcast day in the winter of 1975. I remember the precise moment, crouching behind a crumbling mud wall, peeking into the alley near the frozen creek. That was a long time ago, but it's wrong what they say about the past, I've learned, about how you can bury it. Because the past claws its way out. Looking back now, I realize I have been peeking into that deserted alley for the last twenty-six years.

1. This narrative will be told from which point of view?

2. What word or phrase could you use to describe the mood of the opening lines?

3. Underline those words/phrases that support your description of the mood of the opening.

4. Given your answers to the questions above, what does this opening foreshadow?

Narrative Openings

---

from "Outcasts of Poker Flat"
by Hart Crane

As Mr. John Oakhurst, gambler, stepped into the main street of Poker Flat on the morning of the twenty-third of November, 1850, he was conscious of a change in its moral atmosphere since the preceding night. Two of three men, conversing earnestly together, ceased as he approached, and exchanged significant glances. There was a Sabbath[1] lull in the air, which, in a settlement unused to Sabbath influences, looked ominous.

Mr. Oakhurst's calm, handsome face betrayed small concern in these indications. Whether he was conscious of any predisposing cause was another question. "I reckon they're after somebody," he reflected; "likely it's me." He returned to his pocket the handkerchief with which he had been whipping away the red dust of Poker Flat from his neat boots, and quietly discharged his mind of any further conjecture.

---

[1]Sabbath: a religious day of observance

1. This opening passage of a short story accomplishes which of the following?
   A. Presents an original and probing argument about the nature of small Western towns
   B. Establishes a humorous, playful tone about the charming local color of regional provincialism
   C. Offers a first-person account of everyday life in the mid-nineteenth century
   D. Introduces the possibility the central character might be confronting troubling circumstances
   E. Negates any opportunity for the reader to be unclear about what is about to transpire

2. This passage reveals Mr. Oakhurst to be

   A. rash and impetuous
   B. composed and observant
   C. nervous and cowardly
   D. bold and heroic
   E. kind and generous

3. The two of three men conversing appear to be

   A. predatory
   B. oblivious
   C. fearful
   D. insecure
   E. unrefined

4. The mood established in this opening scene is

   A. sentimental
   B. nightmarish
   C. passionate
   D. hopeful
   E. apprehensive

from "An Occurrence at Owl Creek Bridge"
        by Ambrose Pierce

A man stood upon a railroad bridge in northern Alabama, looking down into the swift water twenty feet below. The man's hands were behind his back, the wrists bound with a cord. A rope closely encircled his neck. It was attached to a stout cross-timber above his head and the slack fell to the level of his knees. Some loose boards laid upon the ties supporting the rails of the railway supplied a footing for him and his executioners—two private soldiers of the Federal army, directed by a sergeant who in civil life may have been a deputy sheriff. At a short remove upon the same temporary platform was an officer in the uniform of his rank, armed. He was a captain. A sentinel at each end of the bridge stood with his rifle in the position known as "support," that is to say, vertical in front of the left shoulder, the hammer resting on the forearm thrown straight across the chest—a formal and unnatural position, enforcing an erect carriage of the body. It did not appear to be the duty of these two men to know what was occurring at the center of the bridge; they merely blockaded the two ends of the foot planking that traversed it.

1. This opening passage of a short story accomplishes which of the following?
   A. It presents the thoughts and emotions of a man very likely to die in the next few moments.
   B. It describes the scene in preparation for a hanging.
   C. It establishes the lack of organization and incompetence within a federal army unit.
   D. It introduces a light and joyful mood.
   E. It renders a graphic description of a military battle.

2. The word "stout" indicates to the reader that

    A. the men who built the scaffold were unusually large

    B. that the man's neck was very weak and already pulsed with tension

    C. that the body of the man was much heavier than the average victim

    D. the cross timber is unlikely to snap when the man is hanged

    E. that the sergeant was unusually brave and strong

3. The narrator's comment about the sergeant suggests that

    A. he was a deeply impressive soldier and commander of men

    B. he was uncertain whether he had any right to hang the man

    C. he had abandoned responsibility for the consequences of the act

    D. he was someone who could have great empathy for the victim

    E. he gave the impression that he had experience in these matters

4. The narrator points out the two sentinels on either end of the bridge to

    A. express that there are participants clearly opposed to what is about to transpire

    B. confirm that the bridge is poorly constructed and may not hold for the entire incident

    C. undermine the notion that the captain is truly in charge of the proceedings

    D. underscore the irony of these two participants being oblivious to the event on the bridge

    E. reinforce the use of anaphora as a central rhythmic motif throughout the passage

from *Emma*
> **by Jane Austen**

Emma Woodhouse, handsome, clever, and rich, with a comfortable home and happy disposition, seemed to unite some of the best blessings of existence; and had lived nearly twenty-one years in the world with very little to distress or vex her.

She was the youngest of the two daughters of a most affectionate, indulgent father; and had, in consequence of her sister's marriage, been mistress of his house from a very early period. Her mother had died too long ago for her to have more than an indistinct remembrance of her caresses; and her place had been supplied by an excellent woman as governess, who had fallen little short of a mother in affection.

Sixteen years had Miss Taylor been in Mr. Woodhouse's family, less as a governess than a friend, very fond of both daughters, but particularly of Emma. Between *them* it was more the intimacy of sisters. Even before Miss Taylor had ceased to hold the nominal office of governess, the mildness of her temper had hardly allowed her to impose any restraint; and the shadow of authority being now long passed away, they had been living together as friend and friend very mutually attached, and Emma doing just what she liked; highly esteeming Miss Taylor's judgment, but directed chiefly by her own.

1. This opening passage of the novel *Emma* makes clear that the title character
   A. had a good deal of freedom and had lived a privileged life
   B. felt a huge void in her life due to the loss of her mother
   C. endured the guidance of a controlling governess and a strict father
   D. was joyous despite the many financial strains she encountered
   E. loves her father but has very little affection for Miss Taylor

2. Emma's personality could be characterized as

  A. sullen and inward
  B. lively and cruel
  C. nervous and intense
  D. humorous and hostile
  E. amiable and strong willed

3. Emma's father was all of the following except

  A. generous
  B. restricting
  C. kind
  D. accommodating
  E. caring

4. This opening passage of a novel accomplishes which of the following?

  A. It envelops the Woodhouse family in an aura of mystery.
  B. It establishes the dynamic of Emma's familial environment.
  C. It delineates the fiduciary restraints placed on Emma due to her circumstances.
  D. It carves out a satiric portrait of the wealthy, but eccentric aristocratic Woodhouse family.
  E. It suggests that Emma may be in imminent danger.

**from "Bunner Sisters"
   by Edith Wharton**

In the days when New York's traffic moved at the pace of the drooping horse-car, when society applauded Christine Nilsson at the Academy of Music and basked in the sunsets of the Hudson River School[1] on the walls of the National Academy of Design, an inconspicuous shop with a single show-window was intimately and favourably known to the feminine population of the quarter bordering on Stuyvesant Square.[2]

It was a very small shop, in a shabby basement, in a side-street already doomed to decline; and from the miscellaneous display behind the window-pane, and the brevity of the sign surmounting it (merely "Bunner Sisters" in blotchy gold on a black ground) it would have been difficult for the uninitiated to guess the precise nature of the business carried on within. But that was of little consequence, since its fame was so purely local that the customers on whom its existence depended were almost congenitally aware of the exact range of "goods" to be found at Bunner Sisters'.

———————

[1]Hudson River School: a 19th-century art movement focused on landscape paintings.

[2]Stuyvesant Square: a fairly affluent section of New York City.

1. The opening paragraph of the short story accomplishes which of the following?

A. It provides psychological insight into the protagonist.
B. It undermines notions of business discretion.
C. It establishes a setting and offers context.
D. It develops a haunting and disturbing mood.
E. It conveys a subtle sense of guilt and insecurity.

5 Minutes to a 5

2. The nature of the society described in the first paragraph can be characterized as

    A. impoverished and unrefined
    B. slick and modern
    C. pastoral and traditional
    D. fast paced and celebrity obsessed
    E. cultured and deliberately paced

3. The shop possesses all of the following qualities except

    A. an ostentatious storefront
    B. a discreet location
    C. a modest scale
    D. a showing of disparate goods
    E. a subterranean setting

4. What does the narrator intimate about the Bunner Sisters in these first two paragraphs?

    A. The women are old spinsters who don't understand business.
    B. The shop will soon be moved to more spacious and appropriate quarters.
    C. The shop serves as a metaphor for the cultural institutions of the time.
    D. The contents of the shop belies its outer appearance.
    E. The owners struggle with commercial outreach to the community.

Day 113

---

from "The Yellow Wallpaper"
        by Charlotte Perkins Gilman

It is very seldom that mere ordinary people like John and myself secure ancestral halls for the summer.

A colonial mansion, a hereditary estate, I would say a haunted house, and reach the height of romantic felicity—but that would be asking too much of fate!

Still I will proudly declare that there is something queer about it.

Else, why should it be let so cheaply? And why have stood so long untenanted?

John laughs at me, of course, but one expects that in marriage.

John is practical in the extreme. He has no patience with faith, an intense horror of superstition, and he scoffs openly at any talk of things not to be felt and seen and put down in figures.

John is a physician, and *perhaps*—(I would not say it to a living soul, of course, but this is dead paper and a great relief to my mind)—*perhaps* that is one reason I do not get well faster.

You see he does not believe I am sick!

And what can one do?

If a physician of high standing, and one's own husband, assures friends and relatives that there is really nothing the matter with one but temporary nervous depression—a slight hysterical tendency—what is one to do?

1. The opening paragraph of the short story accomplishes all of the following except

  A. engenders a somber shroud of logical ruminations
  B. establishes an aura of mystery about the mansion
  C. develops the psychological state of the narrator
  D. presents conflicting viewpoints of John and the narrator
  E. offers opposing perspectives of the narrator's reliability

2. John's outlook toward the narrator can be viewed as one of

   A. adoration
   B. condescension
   C. ambivalence
   D. insecurity
   E. repulsion

3. In the seventh paragraph, the author uses parentheses

   A. to offer some non-essential information to the reader
   B. to assure the reader that better prospects are forthcoming
   C. to show that the narrator is indeed calm and collected
   D. to uncover a disturbing prevarication
   E. to expose incidentally an aspect of the narrator's condition

4. The passage reveals the narrator

   A. in preparation for liberation
   B. unable to consider her situation
   C. oblivious to her husband's thoughts
   D. in a heightened state of emotional intensity
   E. comforted by her inner strength

Character and Tone

from Chapter Nine of *Catch-22*
by Joseph Heller (1961)

Major Major had been born too late and too mediocre. Some men are born mediocre, some men achieve mediocrity, and some men have mediocrity thrust upon them. With Major Major it had been all three.

Even among men lacking all distinction he inevitably stood out as a man lacking more distinction than all the rest, and people who met him were always impressed by how unimpressive he was.

1. Identify the speaker's attitude toward his subject.

2. Underline or highlight the details that develop this portrait.

3. After analyzing the details, identify the primary technique employed to describe the subject and to develop the tone of the selection.

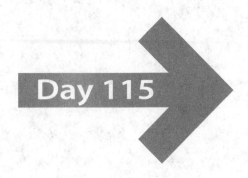

Tone and Character

from "The Boar-Pig"
by Saki (1904)

"There is a back way on to the lawn," said Mrs. Philidore Stossen to her daughter, "through a small grass paddock and then through a walled fruit garden full of gooseberry bushes. I went all over the place last year when the family were away. There is a door that opens from the fruit garden into a shrubbery, and once we emerge from there we can mingle with the guests as if we had come in by the ordinary way. It's much safer than going in by the front entrance and running the risk of coming bang up against the hostess; that would be so awkward when she doesn't happen to have invited us."

1. Identify the tone of the passage.

2. Identify three character traits Mrs. Stossen demonstrates.

Diction and Character

---

from Chapter One of *Little Women*
by Louisa May Alcott

"Christmas won't be Christmas without any presents," grumbled Jo, lying on the rug.

"It's so dreadful to be poor!" sighed Meg, looking down at her old dress.

"I don't think it's fair for some girls to have plenty of pretty things, and other girls nothing at all," added little Amy, with an injured sniff.

"We've got Father and Mother, and each other," said Beth contentedly from her corner.

Identify the specific diction that developed your analysis of each girl.

1. Jo:

2. Meg:

3. Amy:

4. Beth:

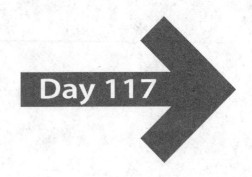
Character Through Dialogue

**from Chapter One of *Little Women*
by Louisa May Alcott**

Using the information you've gathered from the activity for Day 116, indicate an insight about each speaker that you have based upon the character's own words.

1. Jo:

2. Meg:

3. Amy:

4. Beth:

Diction and Tone

---

from "Eveline"
> **by James Joyce**

She sat at the window watching the evening invade the avenue. Her head was leaned against the window curtains and in her nostrils was the odour of dusty cretonne.[1] She was tired.

----

[1] a type of fabric

1. Identify the tone of the passage.

2. Underline the word(s) and phrases that support your identified tone.

Context and Meaning

from *Middlemarch*
by **George Eliot**

And how should Dorothea not marry?—a girl so handsome and with
such prospects?

Nothing could hinder it but her love of extremes, and her insistence
on regulating life according to notions which might cause a wary man
to hesitate before he made her an offer, or even might lead her at last   5
to refuse all offers. A young lady of some birth and fortune, who knelt
suddenly down on a brick floor by the side of a sick laborer and prayed
fervidly as if she thought herself living in the time of the Apostles—who
had strange whims of fasting like a Papist,[1] and of sitting up at night
to read old theological books! Such a wife might awaken you some fine   10
morning with a new scheme for the application of her income which
would interfere with political economy and the keeping of saddle-horses:
a man would naturally think twice before he risked himself in such
fellowship. Women were expected to have weak opinions; but the great
safeguard of society and of domestic life was, that opinions were not acted   15
on. Sane people did what their neighbors did, so that if any lunatics were
at large, one might know and avoid them.

The rural opinion about the new young ladies, even among the
cottagers, was Generally in favor of Celia, as being so amiable and
innocent-looking, while Miss Brooke's [Dorothea] large eyes seemed, like   20
her religion, too unusual and striking. Poor Dorothea! compared with
her, the innocent-looking Celia was knowing and worldly-wise; so much
subtler is a human mind than the outside tissues which make a sort of
blazonry or clock-face for it.

---

[1]Papist: Roman Catholics (those who supported the Pope)

1. This scene presents Dorothea as

A. heretical
B. unpredictable
C. traditional
D. reserved
E. sweet

2. In this passage, the general public view was that women should be

A. assertive and thoughtful
B. demonstrably religious
C. whimsical and capricious
D. meek and passive
E. active and committed

3. In the sensibility of this society, sanity is equated with

A. conventionality
B. financial security
C. strong opinions
D. Christian charity
E. originality

4. Given the diction and tone of the passage, the narrator's opinion of this provincial environment can best be interpreted by the reader as

A. nostalgically affectionate
B. brutally dismissive
C. quietly approving
D. hearty approval
E. subtly critical and satirical

Style

The opening paragraph of *A Tale of Two Cities*
by Charles Dickens (1859)

It was the best of times, it was the worst of times, it was the age of wisdom, it was the age of foolishness, it was the epoch of belief, it was the epoch of incredulity, it was the season of Light, it was the season of Darkness, it was the spring of hope, it was the winter of despair, we had everything before us, we had nothing before us, we were all going direct to Heaven, we were all going direct the other way—in short, the period was so far like the present period, that some of its noisiest authorities . . .

1. Which two major literary devices are used in this opening paragraph?

2. For what purpose does Dickens employ these two literary devices?

Characterization

from *Uncle Tom's Cabin*
by Harriet Beecher Stowe

It is impossible to conceive of a human creature more wholly desolate and forlorn than Eliza, when she turned her footsteps from Uncle Tom's cabin.

Her husband's suffering and dangers, and the danger of her child, all blended in her mind, with a confused and stunning sense of the risk she was running, in leaving the only home she had ever known, and cutting loose from the protection of a friend whom she loved and revered. Then there was the parting from every familiar object,—the place where she had grown up, the trees under which she had played, the groves where she had walked many an evening in happier days, by the side of her young husband,—everything, as it lay in the clear, frosty starlight, seemed to speak reproachfully to her, and ask her whither could she go from a home like that?

But stronger than all was maternal love, wrought into a paroxysm of frenzy by the near approach of a fearful danger. Her boy was old enough to have walked by her side, and, in an indifferent case, she would only have led him by the hand; but now the bare thought of putting him out of her arms made her shudder, and she strained him to her bosom with a convulsive grasp, as she went rapidly forward.

1. This scene captures Eliza at a moment of

A. fear and anxiety

B. triumph and joy

C. hope and enlightenment

D. peace and solace

E. guilt and redemption

2. As she departs, Eliza encounters pangs of

  A. culpability
  B. resentment
  C. nostalgia
  D. elation
  E. repulsion

3. In the context of the passage, the word "bare" in the next to the last line can best be defined as

  A. naked
  B. fundamental
  C. uncovered
  D. simple
  E. harsh

4. This passage can be best characterized as

  A. a subtle exploration of sin
  B. a narrative that tends to extremes
  C. a measured consideration of loss
  D. an exalted expression of joy
  E. a proclamation of liberation

from *Washington Square*
            by Henry James (1880)

Characterization can be developed using even the smallest of details. After carefully reading the following excerpt from Chapter 7 of *Washington Square* by Henry James (1880), respond to the questions that follow.

> After dinner Morris Townsend went and stood before Catherine,
> who was standing before the fire in her red satin gown.
> "He doesn't like me—he doesn't like me at all!" said the young man.
> "Who doesn't like you?" asked Catherine.
> "Your father; extraordinary man!"   5
> "I don't see how you know," said Catherine, blushing.
> "I feel; I am very quick to feel."
> "Perhaps you are mistaken."
> "Ah, well; you ask him and you will see."
> "I would rather not ask him, if there is any danger of his saying what you think."   10
> Morris looked at her with an air of mock melancholy.
> "It wouldn't give you any pleasure to contradict him?"
> "I never contradict him," said Catherine.
> "Will you hear me abused without opening your lips in my defence?"
> "My father won't abuse you. He doesn't know you enough."   15
> Morris Townsend gave a loud laugh, and Catherine began to blush again.
> "I shall never mention you," she said, to take refuge from her confusion.
> "That is very well; but it is not quite what I should have liked you to say.
> I should have liked you to say: 'If my father doesn't think well of you,
> what does it matter?'"   20
> "Ah, but it would matter; I couldn't say that!" the girl exclaimed.

He looked at her for a moment, smiling a little; and the Doctor, if he had been watching him just then, would have seen a gleam of fine impatience in the sociable softness of his eye. But there was no impatience in his rejoinder—none, at least, save what was expressed in a little appealing sigh. "Ah, well, then, I must not give up the hope of bringing him round!"   25

1. After reading the passage, characterize in a word/phrase:

   CATHERINE:

   MORRIS TOWNSEND:

2. Cite specific details from the passage that support your characterization for each.

Characterization Paragraph

> ## Writing the Topic Sentence
>
> **from** *Washington Square*
> **by Henry James (1880)**
>
> Go to the activities presented for Day 122. Review the text and your responses to the questions.
>
> Based on the above information, you are going to compose a single paragraph that addresses the subject of Day 122's activity.
>
> Your first assignment is to write the topic sentence for this paragraph.

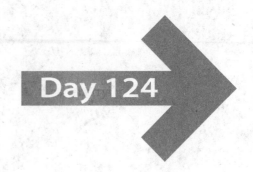
Writing the Body of the Paragraph, 1

from *Washington Square*
by Henry James (1880)

Using the information you've gathered from the activities from Days 122–123, compose three to four sentences that describe Catherine's character.

Writing the Body of the Paragraph, 2

from *Washington Square*
      by Henry James (1880)

Using the information you've gathered from the activities for Days 122–123, compose three to four sentences that describe Morris Townsend's character.

Writing the Complete Paragraph

from *Washington Square*
            by Henry James (1880)

You now have the major parts of your paragraph. You need to

- organize

- provide any needed connecting words/phrases

- write the complete paragraph

from *Emma*
by Jane Austen

Emma Woodhouse, handsome, clever, and rich, with a comfortable home and happy disposition, seemed to unite some of the best blessings of existence; and had lived nearly twenty-one years in the world with very little to distress or vex her.

She was the youngest of the two daughters of a most affectionate, indulgent father; and had, in consequence of her sister's marriage, been mistress of his house from a very early period. Her mother had died too long ago for her to have more than an indistinct remembrance of her caresses; and her place had been supplied by an excellent woman as governess, who had fallen little short of a mother in affection.

Sixteen years had Miss Taylor been in Mr. Woodhouse's family, less as a governess than a friend, very fond of both daughters, but particularly of Emma. Between *them* it was more the intimacy of sisters. Even before Miss Taylor had ceased to hold the nominal office of governess, the mildness of her temper had hardly allowed her to impose any restraint; and the shadow of authority being now long passed away, they had been living together as friend and friend very mutually attached, and Emma doing just what she liked; highly esteeming Miss Taylor's judgment, but directed chiefly by her own.

1. This opening passage of the novel *Emma* makes clear that the title character
   A. had a good deal of freedom and had lived a privileged life
   B. felt a huge void in her life due to the loss of her mother
   C. endured the guidance of a controlling governess and a strict father
   D. was joyous despite the many financial strains she encountered
   E. loves her father but has very little affection for Miss Taylor

5 Minutes to a 5

2. Emma's personality could be characterized as

   A. sullen and inward
   B. lively and cruel
   C. nervous and intense
   D. humorous and hostile
   E. amiable and strong willed

3. Emma's father was all of the following except

   A. generous
   B. restricting
   C. kind
   D. accommodating
   E. caring

4. This opening passage of a novel accomplishes which of the following?

   A. It envelops the Woodhouse family in an aura of mystery.
   B. It establishes the dynamic of Emma's familial environment.
   C. It delineates the fiduciary restraints placed on Emma due to her circumstances.
   D. It carves out a satiric portrait of the wealthy, but eccentric aristocratic Woodhouse family.
   E. It suggests that Emma may be in imminent danger.

Character and Meaning

from "The Rocking Horse Winner"
by D. H. Lawrence

There was a woman who was beautiful, who started with all the advantages, yet she had no luck.

She married for love, and the love turned to dust. She had bonny children, yet she felt they had been thrust upon her, and she could not love them. They looked at her coldly, as if they were finding fault with her. And hurriedly she felt she must cover up some fault in herself. Yet what it was that she must cover up she never knew. Nevertheless, when her children were present, she always felt the centre of her heart go hard. This troubled her, and in her manner she was all the more gentle and anxious for her children, as if she loved them very much. Only she herself knew that at the centre of her heart was a hard little place that could not feel love, no, not for anybody. Everybody else said of her: "She is such a good mother. She adores her children." Only she herself, and her children themselves, knew it was not so. They read it in each other's eyes.

There were a boy and two little girls. They lived in a pleasant house, with a garden, and they had discreet servants, and felt themselves superior to anyone in the neighbourhood.

Although they lived in style, they felt always an anxiety in the house. There was never enough money. The mother had a small income, and the father had a small income, but not nearly enough for the social position which they had to keep up. The father went into town to some office. But though he had good prospects, these prospects never materialised. There was always the grinding sense of the shortage of money, though the style was always kept up.

1. This scene presented the woman as

A. confident and strong
B. reckless and mean
C. cold and humble
D. insecure and discontented
E. graceful and charming

2. The woman perceives that she suffers from a dearth of all of the following except

A. financial resources
B. domestic elegance
C. familial affection
D. good fortune
E. internal serenity

3. In the context of the passage, the word "some" ("The father went into town to some office") in the third from the last line is employed to indicate

A. that the particulars and the nature of the office were not really important
B. that the father has worked in many different offices
C. that the office had the kind of reputation which would guarantee success
D. that the mysteries of the office indicated the father was involved in suspicious behavior
E. that the office probably didn't really exist

4. This passage gives the reader the general understanding

A. that the family has considerably more financial resources than was originally revealed
B. that the father possesses a hidden cruelty masked by his genial public countenance
C. that the mother deep down inside feels tremendous affection for her family
D. that the children were thankfully oblivious to the familial strife
E. that the outward appearances are covering up financial and emotional strains

Making Inferences

Carefully read the following introductory passage from the first chapter of
A Room with a View by E. M. Forster (1908).

THE BERTOLINI

"The Signora had no business to do it," said Miss Bartlett, "no business at
all. She promised us south rooms with a view close together, instead of which
here are north rooms, here are north rooms, looking into a courtyard, and a
long way apart. Oh, Lucy."

"And a Cockney, besides!" said Lucy, who had been further saddened by the   5
Signora's unexpected accent. "It might be London." She looked at the two
rows of English people who were sitting at the table; at the row of white
bottles of water and red bottles of wine that ran between the English people;
at the portraits of the late Queen and the late Poet Laureate that hung behind
the English people, heavily framed; at the notice of the English church (Rev.   10
Cuthbert Eager, M.A. Oxon), that was the only other decoration of the wall.

"Charlotte, don't you feel, too, that we might be in London? I can hardly
believe that all kinds of other things are just outside. I suppose it is one's
being so tired."

"This meat has surely been used for soup," said Miss Bartlett, laying down   15
her fork.

"I wanted so to see the Arno. The rooms the Signora promised us in her letter
would have looked over the Arno. The Signora had no business to do it at
all. Oh, it is a shame I"

"Any nook does for me," Miss Bartlett continued; "but it does seem hard that   20
you shouldn't have a view."

Lucy felt that she had been selfish. "Charlotte, you mustn't spoil me: of
course, you must look over the Arno, too. I meant that. The first vacant room
in the front"

"You must have it," said Miss Bartlett, part of whose travelling expenses were paid by Lucy's mother—a piece of generosity to which she made many a tactful allusion.

"No, no. You must have it."

"I insist on it. Your mother would never forgive me, Lucy."

"She would never forgive me."

The ladies' voices grew animated, and—if the sad truth be owned—a little peevish. They were tired, and under the guise of unselfishness they wrangled. Some of their neighbours interchanged glances, and one of them—one of the ill-bred people whom one does meet abroad—leant forward over the table and actually intruded into their argument. He said:

"I have a view, I have a view."

Miss Bartlett was startled. Generally, at a pension people looked them over for a day or two before speaking, and often did not find out that they would 'do' till they had gone. She knew that the intruder was ill-bred, even before she glanced at him. He was an old man, of heavy build, with a fair, shaven face and large eyes. There was something childish in those eyes, though it was not the childishness of senility. What exactly it was Miss Bartlett did not stop to consider, for her glance passed on to his clothes. These did not attract her. He was probably trying to become acquainted with them before they got into the swim. So she assumed a dazed expression when he spoke to her, and then said:

"A view? Oh, a view! How delightful a view is!"

"This is my son," said the old man; "his name's George. He has a view, too."

"Ah," said Miss Bartlett, repressing Lucy, who was about to speak.

"What I mean," he continued, "is that you can have our rooms, and we'll have yours. We'll change."

The better class of tourist was shocked at this, and sympathized with the new-comers. Miss Bartlett, in reply, opened her mouth as little as possible, and said:

"Thank you very much indeed: that is out of the question."

"Why?" said the old man, with both fists on the table.

"Because it is quite out of the question, thank you."

"You see, we don't like to take," began Lucy.

Her cousin again repressed her.

"But why?" he persisted. "Women like looking at a view; men don't." And he thumped with his fists like a naughty child, and turned to his son, saying, "George, persuade them!"

"It's so obvious they should have the rooms," said the son. "There's nothing else to say."

1. Based on your close reading of this passage, what can you infer (briefly) about the characters?

   Lucy Honeychurch:

   Miss Bartlett:

2. Based only on your reading of this passage, what can you infer will be three areas of conflict/tension as the novel progresses? (briefly)

Inference

> **from _Great Expectations_**
> **by Charles Dickens**
>
> Mr. Pocket said he was glad to see me, and he had hoped I was not sorry to see him. "For, I really am not," he added, with his son's smile, "an alarming personage." He was a young-looking man, in spite of his perplexities and his very grey hair, and his manner seemed quite natural. I use the word natural in the sense of its being unaffected; there was something comic in his distraught way, as though it would have been downright ludicrous but for his own perception that it was very near being so. When he talked with me a little, he said to Mrs. Pocket, with a rather anxious contraction of his eyebrows, which were black and handsome, "Belinda, I hope you welcomed Mr. Pip?" And she looked up from her book, and said "Yes." She then smiled upon me in an absent state of mind, and asked me if I liked the taste of orange-flower water. As the question had no bearing, near or remote, on any foregone or subsequent transaction, I considered it to have been thrown out, like her previous approaches, in General, conversational condescension.

1. Given the entire passage, what can be inferred by Mr. Pocket saying he hoped the narrator was "not sorry to see" him?

   A. That the narrator would be very happy to see Mr. Pocket
   B. That the narrator would have absolutely no pleasure in seeing Mr. Pocket
   C. That Mr. Pocket is a pompous and uncouth individual
   D. That Mr. Pocket is modest and subtle in his manner of speech
   E. That Mr. Pocket is fraught with regret over his relationship with the narrator

2. What can be inferred by saying that Mr. Pocket had his son's smile?

A. That Mr. Pocket's smile cannot be trusted

B. That Mr. Pocket's smile is covering up some deep-seated secrets

C. That Mr. Pocket's son is someone completely unknown to the narrator

D. That the narrator has rarely witnessed a smile such as the one Mr. Pocket flashes

E. That the narrator knows the son and therefore associates Mr. Pocket's smile with him

3. Given subsequent descriptions, the characterization that Mr. Pocket's "manner seemed quite natural" indicates

A. that Mr. Pocket is, utterly and unequivocally, a fraud

B. that Mr. Pocket is exactly how he seems: a man with a truly natural manner

C. that Mr. Pocket has worked hard to cultivate the appearance of being a snob

D. that Mr. Pocket possesses an inner savagery of all men who are quite natural

E. that Mr. Pocket has to make an effort to appear like he is behaving unself-consciously

4. The description of Mrs. Pocket presents her as

A. high-minded and scheming

B. kind and accommodating

C. aloof and distant

D. morose and depressed

E. compassionate and sociable

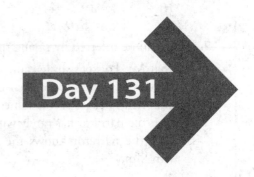

Characterization

Follow-up on the excerpt from *Great Expectations* by Charles Dickens

Characterization is often developed incrementally over the course of a novel as descriptions, comments, and actions accumulate about the nature of an individual. This passage is the reader's introduction to both Mr. and Mrs. Pocket. While the reader in this case does not have the opportunity to gain further understanding with later encounters, this initial scene is very revealing. Charles Dickens has a nuanced prose style in which he expresses much about a character in deceptively few words.

Mr. Pocket said he was glad to see me, and he had hoped I was not
sorry to see him. "For, I really am not," he added, with his son's smile,
"an alarming personage." He was a young-looking man, in spite of his
perplexities and his very grey hair, and his manner seemed quite natural.
I use the word natural in the sense of its being unaffected; there was   5
something comic in his distraught way, as though it would have been
downright ludicrous but for his own perception that it was very near
being so. When he talked with me a little, he said to Mrs. Pocket, with
a rather anxious contraction of his eyebrows, which were black and
handsome, "Belinda, I hope you welcomed Mr. Pip?" And she looked up   10
from her book, and said "Yes." She then smiled upon me in an absent
state of mind, and asked me if I liked the taste of orange-flower water.
As the question had no bearing, near or remote, on any foregone or
subsequent transaction, I considered it to have been thrown out, like her
previous approaches, in General, conversational condescension.   15

Drawing from the passage, write a **brief** character analysis of both Mr. and Mrs. Pocket. In addition, **briefly** describe the dynamics of their relationship.

Mr. Pocket:

Mrs. Pocket

Their Relationship:

Context and Characterization

from *Frankenstein*
    by Mary Shelley

These thoughts supported my spirits, while I pursued my undertaking
with unremitting ardour. My cheek had grown pale with study, and my
person had become emaciated with confinement. Sometimes, on the very
brink of certainty, I failed; yet still I clung to the hope which the next
day or the next hour might realise. One secret which I alone possessed   5
was the hope to which I had dedicated myself; and the moon gazed on
my midnight labours, while, with unrelaxed and breathless eagerness, I
pursued nature to her hiding-places. Who shall conceive the horrors of
my secret toil, as I dabbled among the unhallowed damps of the grave,
or tortured the living animal to animate the lifeless clay? My limbs now   10
tremble and my eyes swim with the remembrance; but then a resistless,
and almost frantic, impulse urged me forward; I seemed to have lost all
soul or sensation but for this one pursuit. It was indeed but a passing
trance that only made me feel with renewed acuteness so soon as, the
unnatural stimulus ceasing to operate, I had returned to my old habits. I   15
collected bones from charnel houses; and disturbed, with profane fingers,
the tremendous secrets of the human frame. In a solitary chamber, or
rather cell, at the top of the house, and separated from all the other
apartments by a gallery and staircase, I kept my workshop of filthy
creation: my eye-balls were starting from their sockets in attending to the   20
details of my employment. The dissecting room and the slaughterhouse
furnished many of my materials; and often did my human nature turn
with loathing from my occupation, whilst, still urged on by an eagerness
which perpetually increased, I brought my work near to a conclusion…

1. The narrator's approach to his pursuit can best be described as

    A. lackadaisical
    B. monomaniacal
    C. distracted
    D. heroic
    E. orderly

2. The sentence in lines 5–6, "and the moon gazed on my midnight labours, while, with unrelaxed and breathless eagerness, I pursued nature to her hiding-places" has all of the following literary techniques except

    A. characterization
    B. symbolism
    C. personification
    D. metaphor
    E. paradox

3. The description "profane fingers" in line 12 is an example of

    A. irony
    B. apostrophe
    C. synecdoche
    D. assonance
    E. off-rhyme

4. The end of the passage reveals that the narrator has become increasingly

    A. conflicted
    B. exuberant
    C. serene
    D. detached
    E. focused

Developing a Response to a Specific Prompt

Assume you are presented with the following prompt in a timed situation of 45 minutes. This is really where you are going to have to "think on your feet."

> Although written in 1949, Arthur Miller's *Death of a Salesman* continues to be a popular and successful theatrical production for professionals and amateurs alike. In a well-written essay examine the specific characteristics of this drama that allow it to appeal to the modern audience.

As with any prompt, you need to carefully read and annotate it so that you are well aware of what the prompt requires you to do. Do that now.

Developing the Thesis Statement

Based on your knowledge of *Death of a Salesman* and having closely read the prompt, compose the first draft of your thesis statement for the essay.

Day 135

Developing the Major Points

Based on the thesis statement, list the major points that will be developed. Cite **two** specific examples from the text that illustrate/support each of the major points. Number the major points in the order that each will be presented in the essay.

Supporting Evidence

Carefully read the following set of sentences from the first body paragraph related to Willy and the prompt.

> Willy is unable to stick with a consistent conception of reality or the truth. He changes interpretations of events as he needs to in order to fit a particular moment. He is self-delusional about himself and his family.

1. Has the writer presented any specific details to illustrate or support the ideas presented?

2. What does the reader expect to follow the first two sentences?

3. Does the third sentence follow logically from the preceding two? Why or why not?

4. Do you consider this to be a successful first paragraph?

5 Minutes to a 5

Revising

Revise the original set of sentences from Day 136. Make certain to consider the weaknesses noted in that activity.

> Willy is unable to stick with a consistent conception of reality or the truth. He changes interpretations of events as he needs to in order to fit a particular moment. He is self-delusional about himself and his family.

Imagery

---

from *The Red Badge of Courage*
       by Stephen Crane (1896)

The trees began softly to sing a hymn of twilight. The sun sank until slanted bronze rays struck the forest. There was a lull in the noises of insects as if they had bowed their beaks and were making a devotional pause. There was silence save for the chanted chorus of the trees.

Following the logic of the extended metaphor developed in this passage, to what is each of the following compared?

_____ **1.** Trees	A. Church
_____ **2.** Forest	B. Stained glass window
_____ **3.** Setting sun	C. Choir
_____ **4.** Insects	D. Hymn
_____ **5.** Sound of the wind	E. Churchgoers praying

5 Minutes to a 5

Setting

Carefully read the following excerpt from the opening of *The Secret Sharer* by Joseph Conrad (1910).

> On my right hand there were lines of fishing stakes resembling a mysterious system of half-submerged bamboo fences, incomprehensible in its division of the domain of tropical fishes, and crazy of aspect as if abandoned forever by some nomad tribe of fishermen now gone to the other end of the ocean; for there was no sign of human habitation as far as the eye could reach. To the left a group of barren islets, suggesting ruins of stone walls, towers, and blockhouses, had its foundations set in a blue sea that itself looked solid, so still and stable did it lie below my feet; even the track of light from the westering sun shone smoothly, without that animated glitter which tells of an imperceptible ripple.

1. If the reader were to infer that this is a dream-like setting, what words/phrases would you underline/highlight that support this inference?

2. The central metaphor being established in this passage is most probably

    A. human survival
    B. sea/land
    C. fishing
    D. sailing
    E. man vs. nature

Linking Detail to Analysis

from *Treasure Island*
    by Robert Louis Stevenson (1915)

I remember him as if it were yesterday, as he came plodding to the inn door, his sea-chest following behind him in a hand-barrow—a tall, strong, heavy, nut-brown man, his tarry pigtail falling over the shoulder of his soiled blue coat, his hands ragged and scarred, with black, broken nails, and the sabre cut across one cheek, a dirty, livid white. I remember him looking round the cover and whistling to himself as he did so, and then breaking out in that old sea-song that he sang so often to.

1. Highlight or underline specific details that are applied to the character being described.

2. Choose at least three details you have highlighted. Responding to the specific information, indicate a prediction, insight, or observation about the character. You may construct a bullet list or map or jot down your ideas. Of course, you may write in sentences or phrases as well.

Context and Meaning

from "The Wife of His Youth"
by Charles Chesnutt

Mr. Ryder was going to give a ball. There were several reasons why this
was an opportune time for such an event.

    Mr. Ryder might aptly be called the dean of the Blue Veins. The
original Blue Veins were a little society of colored persons organized
in a certain Northern city shortly after the war. Its purpose was to   **5**
establish and maintain correct social standards among a people whose
social condition presented almost unlimited room for improvement.
By accident, combined perhaps with some natural affinity, the society
consisted of individuals who were, generally speaking, more white than
black. Some envious outsider made the suggestion that no one was   **10**
eligible for membership who was not white enough to show blue veins.
The suggestion was readily adopted by those who were not of the favored
few, and since that time the society, though possessing a longer and
more pretentious name, had been known far and wide as the "Blue Vein
Society," and its members as the "Blue Veins."   **15**

1. A sentence in lines 5-6 states, "Its purpose was to establish and maintain correct
social standards among a people whose social condition presented almost unlimited
room for improvement." What is inherent in this comment about the Blue Veins?

   A. A desire to elevate all races
   B. A criticism of the plight of colored persons
   C. A plot to attract white members
   D. A rejection of colored persons from this society
   E. An acceptance of white superiority

2. What is a likely description for "some envious outsider"?

   A. A white man
   B. A foreigner
   C. A new Blue Vein member
   D. A man more black than white
   E. A man more white than black

3. How do "those who were not of the favored few" view the name "Blue Vein Society"?

   A. Admiringly
   B. Nostalgically
   C. Inspirationally
   D. Indifferently
   E. Disparagingly

4. Given this passage, Mr. Ryder must be considered

   A. a man excluded from social opportunity
   B. a reformer for all colored people
   C. the impetus for wide-scale racial change
   D. the ultimate insider in a group that used to consist of outsiders
   E. the unfavored, envious outsider

Cataloging

from Book IV of *Gulliver's Travels*
          by Jonathan Swift

Cataloging is the creation of lists, usually presented in some systematic way. Because the readers are used to organizing the entries of these lists in their minds, the approach invites pattern-making. Ultimately, cataloging is a technique used by authors to give the reader a richer, broader understanding in a concise way. In this excerpt from *Gulliver's Travels*, Jonathan Swift presents a great variety of material for readers to absorb and interpret.

In this passage, the main character Gulliver has decided the civilization of horses called the Houyhnhnms is far superior to his own. He shares his thoughts with the reader.

No man could more verify the truth of these two maxims, *That nature is very easily satisfied*; and, *That necessity is the mother of invention*. I enjoyed perfect health of body, and tranquillity of mind; I did not feel the treachery or inconstancy of a friend, nor the injuries of a secret or open enemy. I had no occasion of bribing, flattering, or pimping, to   5
procure the favour of any great man, or of his minion; I wanted no fence against fraud or oppression: here was neither physician to destroy my body, nor lawyer to ruin my fortune; no informer to watch my words and actions, or forge accusations against me for hire: here were no gibers, censurers, backbiters, pickpockets, highwaymen, housebreakers, attorneys,   10
bawds, buffoons, gamesters, politicians, wits, splenetics, tedious talkers, controvertists, ravishers, murderers, robbers, virtuosos; no leaders, or followers, of party and faction; no encouragers to vice, by seducement or examples; no dungeon, axes, gibbets, whipping-posts, or pillories; no cheating shopkeepers or mechanics; no pride, vanity, or affectation;   15

no fops, bullies, drunkards, strolling whores, or poxes; no ranting, lewd, expensive wives; no stupid, proud pedants; no importunate, overbearing, quarrelsome, noisy, roaring, empty, conceited, swearing companions; no scoundrels raised from the dust upon the merit of their vices, or nobility thrown into it on account of their virtues; no lords, fiddlers, judges, or dancing-masters.

20

What are some of the patterns and topics that emerge through Swift's cataloging in the excerpt? Ultimately, draw conclusions on what are the points of this commentary.

Structure and Context

from Book IV of *Gulliver's Travels*
        by Jonathan Swift

In this passage, the main character, Gulliver, has decided the civilization of horses called the Houyhnhnms is far superior to his own. He shares his thoughts with the reader.

No man could more verify the truth of these two maxims, *That nature is very easily satisfied*; and, *That necessity is the mother of invention*. I enjoyed perfect health of body, and tranquillity of mind; I did not feel the treachery or inconstancy of a friend, nor the injuries of a secret or open enemy. I had no occasion of bribing, flattering, or pimping, to procure the favour of any great man, or of his minion; I wanted no fence against fraud or oppression: here was neither physician to destroy my body, nor lawyer to ruin my fortune; no informer to watch my words and actions, or forge accusations against me for hire: here were no gibers, censurers, backbiters, pickpockets, highwaymen, housebreakers, attorneys, bawds, buffoons, gamesters, politicians, wits, splenetics, tedious talkers, controvertists, ravishers, murderers, robbers, virtuosos; no leaders, or followers, of party and faction; no encouragers to vice, by seducement or examples; no dungeon, axes, gibbets, whipping-posts, or pillories; no cheating shopkeepers or mechanics; no pride, vanity, or affectation; no fops, bullies, drunkards, strolling whores, or poxes; no ranting, lewd, expensive wives; no stupid, proud pedants; no importunate, over-bearing, quarrelsome, noisy, roaring, empty, conceited, swearing companions; no scoundrels raised from the dust upon the merit of their vices, or nobility thrown into it on account of their virtues; no lords, fiddlers, judges, or dancing-masters.

1. For most of the passage, the narrator demonstrates how he feels about his current situation by describing

   A. the majesty of the *Houyhnhnm* civilization in great detail
   B. a single incident to represent the civilization as a whole
   C. all the problems of this civilization
   D. the miseries and mistreatments he has not encountered here
   E. the many other places he has visited as points of comparison

2. The narrator's comments about the physician and the lawyer are examples of

   A. personification
   B. apostrophe
   C. onomatopoeia
   D. allusion
   E. irony

3. From the third line to the end of the passage, the narrator regularly employs the technique of

   A. personification
   B. anaphora
   C. understatement
   D. paradox
   E. allusion

4. In the passage the narrator's view of human society appears to be

   A. apathetic
   B. open-minded
   C. misanthropic
   D. undeveloped
   E. optimistic

Close Reading of a Prose Passage

---

from *Villette*
      by Charlotte Bronte

My mistress being dead, and I once more alone, I had to look out for a
new place. About this time I might be a little—a very little—shaken in
nerves. I grant I was not looking well, but, on the contrary, thin, haggard,
and hollow-eyed; like a sitter-up at night, like an overwrought servant,
or a placeless person in debt. In debt, however, I was not; nor quite   **5**
poor; for though Miss Marchmont had not had time to benefit me, as,
on that last night, she said she intended, yet, after the funeral, my wages
were duly paid by her second cousin, the heir, an avaricious-looking
man, with pinched nose and narrow temples, who, indeed, I heard long
afterwards, turned out a thorough miser: a direct contrast to his generous   **10**
kinswoman, and a foil to her memory, blessed to this day by the poor and
needy. The possessor, then, of fifteen pounds; of health, though worn, not
broken, and of a spirit in similar condition; I might still; in comparison
with many people, be regarded as occupying an enviable position. An
embarrassing one it was, however, at the same time; as I felt with some   **15**
acuteness on a certain day, of which the corresponding one in the next
week was to see my departure from my present abode, while with another
I was not provided.

1. From the narrator's description in the opening of the passage, she is clearly

   A. overstating the difficulties of her situation
   B. overjoyed with the possibilities her new opportunities present
   C. filled with much more anxiety than she cares to admit
   D. desolate and sees no positives about her current situation
   E. distracted and unable to consider her challenging plight

5 Minutes to a 5

2. In line 5 of the passage, the word "benefit" most nearly means

    A. help
    B. profit
    C. comfort
    D. ease
    E. give money to

3. Miss Marchmont's second cousin is described

    A. unsympathetically
    B. indifferently
    C. warmly
    D. vaguely
    E. lovingly

4. The last six lines of the excerpt present a narrator who

    A. is determined to succeed no matter what the challenges
    B. tries to have a positive outlook on a bad situation
    C. is secure in knowing her future accommodations
    D. looks to wallow in self-pity after a heart-wrenching loss
    E. rejects society's view about what she should do next

Openings

from *Hard Times*
      by Charles Dickens (1854)

Carefully read the following passage from Chapter One, "The One Thing Needful,"
which has Mr. Thomas Gradgrind instructing the teacher Mr. M'Choakumchild:

> "Now, what I want is, Facts. Teach these boys and girls nothing but Facts.
> Facts alone are wanted in life. Plant nothing else, and root out everything
> else. You can only form the minds of reasoning animals upon Facts:
> nothing else will ever be of any service to them. This is the principle on
> which I bring up my own children, and this is the principle on which I   5
> bring up these children. Stick to Facts, sir!"
>
> The scene was a plain, bare, monotonous vault of a school-room, and the
> speaker's square forefinger emphasized his observations by underscoring
> every sentence with a line on the schoolmaster's sleeve. The emphasis was
> helped by the speaker's square wall of a forehead, which had his eyebrows   10
> for its base, while his eyes found commodious cellarage in two dark caves,
> overshadowed by the wall. The emphasis was helped by the speaker's
> mouth, which was wide, thin, and hard set. The emphasis was helped
> by the speaker's voice, which was inflexible, dry, and dictatorial. The
> emphasis was helped by the speaker's hair, which bristled on the skirts   15
> of his bald head, a plantation of firs to keep the wind from its shining
> surface, all covered with knobs, like the crust of a plum pie, as if the
> head had scarcely warehouse-room for the hard facts stored inside. The
> speaker's obstinate carriage, square coat, square legs, square shoulders,—
> nay, his very neck cloth, trained to take him by the throat with an   20
> unaccommodating grasp, like a stubborn fact, as it was,—all helped the
> emphasis.

'In this life, we want nothing but Facts, sir; nothing but Facts!'
The speaker, and the schoolmaster, and the third grown person present, all backed a little, and swept with their eyes the inclined plane of little **25** vessels then and there arranged in order, ready to have imperial gallons of facts poured into them until they were full to the brim.

1. Using only the passage you just read, what can you infer about the character of Mr. Gradgrind?

2. Cite five specifics from the passage to support your characterization.

3. From only what you've read, do you think this novel will support or criticize Mr. Gradgrind and those who have the same beliefs?

4. On what specifics from the passage are you basing your conclusion?

Setting and Mood

---

from *White Fang*
by Jack London (1906)

The following is the opening paragraph from Jack London's *White Fang*. After carefully reading the passage, complete the activities that follow.

> Dark spruce forest frowned on either side of the frozen waterway. The
> trees had been stripped by a recent wind of their white covering of frost,
> and they seemed to lean toward each other, black and ominous, in the
> fading light. A vast silence reigned over the land. The land itself was a
> desolation, lifeless, without movement, so lone and cold that the spirit of   5
> it was not even that of sadness. There was a hint in it of laughter, but of
> a laughter more terrible than any sadness—a laughter that was mirthless
> as the smile of the Sphinx, a laughter cold as the frost and partaking of
> the grimness of infallibility. It was the masterful and incommunicable
> wisdom of eternity laughing at the futility of life and the effort of life. It   10
> was the Wild, the savage, frozen-hearted Northland Wild.

1. In a word or phrase, what is the general mood that the author creates?

2. In a word or phrase, what is the author's attitude toward his subject?

3. Cite specific details from the text to support your response to question 2. Make certain to cite line numbers.

Inference/Conclusion

---

from *The Importance of Being Earnest*
        by Oscar Wilde (1895)

The following scene takes place early in Act I of *The Importance of Being Earnest*. In it, Algernon speaks with his butler, Lane.

ALG: Why is it that at a bachelor's establishment the servants invariably drink the champagne? I ask merely for information.

LANE: I attribute it to the superior quality of the wine, sir. I have often observed that in married households the champagne is rarely of a first-rate brand.   5

ALG: Good Heavens! Is marriage so demoralising as that?

LANE: I believe it is a very pleasant state, sir. I have had very little experience of it myself up to the present. I have only been married once. That was in consequence of a misunderstanding between myself and a young person.   10

ALG: [Languidly.] I don't know that I am much interested in your family life, Lane.

LANE: No, sir; it is not a very interesting subject. I never think of it myself.

ALG: Very natural, I am sure. That will do, Lane, thank you.

LANE: Thank you, sir.   15
      [Lane goes out.]

ALG: Lane's views on marriage seem somewhat lax. Really, if the lower orders don't set us a good example, what on earth is the use of them? They seem, as a class, to have absolutely no sense of moral responsibility.   20

1. Given only this scene, one may infer that this play is most probably a

    A. serious drama
    B. melodrama
    C. comedy
    D. satire
    E. soap opera

2. Cite three details from the scene to support your inference.

A Close Reading of a Complex Text

from "The Open Boat"
        by Stephen Crane (1897)

Carefully read the following passage from Stephen Crane's "The Open Boat."

A seat in this boat was not unlike a seat upon a jumpy horse, and a
horse is not much smaller. The boat was much like an animal. As each
wave came, and she rose for it, she seemed like a horse leaping over a
high fence. The manner of her ride over these walls of water is a thing of
mystery. Each wave required a new leap, and a leap from the air. Then   5
jumping and slipping and racing and dropping down, she steadied for the
next threat.

A particular danger of the sea is the fact that after successfully getting
through one wave, you discover that there is another behind it. The next
wave is just as nervously anxious and purposeful to overturn boats. In a   10
ten foot boat one can get a good idea of the great force of the sea. As each
gray wall of water approached, it shut all else from the view of the men in
the boat. It was not difficult to imagine that this particular wave was the
final outburst of the ocean, the last effort of the determined water.

1. *A seat in this boat was not unlike a seat upon a jumpy horse, and a horse is not much smaller.* (lines 1–2) contains two examples of

   A. personification
   B. hyperbole
   C. litotes
   D. onomatopoeia
   E. allusion

2. The first paragraph uses an extended metaphor to compare the _____ to a _____.

3. The second paragraph personifies the sea. Cite specific words/phrases that help to construct this analogy.

Anaphora

> **Follow-up Lesson on *"The Yellow Wallpaper"*
> by Charlotte Perkins Gilman**
>
> Anaphora is the repetition of a word or a phrase at the beginning of successive clauses. In "The Yellow Wallpaper" anaphora is used in the following excerpt:
>
> John laughs at me, of course, but one expects that in marriage.
>
> John is practical in the extreme. He has no patience with faith, an intense horror of superstition, and he scoffs openly at any talk of things not to be felt and seen and put down in figures.
>
> John is a physician, and *perhaps*—(I would not say it to a living soul, of course, but this is dead paper and a great relief to my mind)—*perhaps* that is one reason I do not get well faster.
>
> Describe the use of anaphora signaled by the word "John" (and later the word "perhaps"). Why does this structure allow the author to convey additional layers of meaning about both the narrator and her husband?

A Close Reading of a Complex Text

from *The Gay Science*
by Friedrich Nietzsche

The following excerpt from Friedrich Nietzsche's *The Gay Science* describes a madman's thoughts about God.

The madman.—Haven't you heard of that madman who in the bright
morning lit a lantern and ran around the marketplace crying incessantly
"I'm looking for God! I'm looking for God!" Since many of those who
did not believe in God were standing around together just then, he
caused great laughter. Has he been lost, then? asked one. Did he lose   5
his way like a child? asked another. Or is he hiding? Is he afraid of us?
Has he gone to sea? Emigrated?—Thus they shouted and laughed, one
interrupting the other. The madman jumped into their midst and pierced
them with his eyes. "Where is God?" he cried; "I'll tell you! We have
killed him—you and I! We are all his murderers. But how did we do this?   10
How were we able to drink up the sea? Who gave us the sponge to wipe
away the entire horizon? What were we doing when we unchained this
earth from its sun? Where is it moving to now? Where are we moving
to? Away from all suns? Are we not continually falling? And backwards,
sideways, forwards, in all directions? Is there still an up and a down?   15
Aren't we straying as though through an infinite nothing? Isn't empty
space breathing at us? Hasn't it got colder? Isn't night and more night
coming again and again? Don't lanterns have to be lit in the morning? Do
we still hear nothing of the noise of the grave-diggers who are burying
God? Do we still smell nothing of the divine decomposition?—Gods,   20
too, decompose! God is dead! God remains dead! And we have killed
him! How can we console ourselves, the murderers of all murderers! The

holiest and the mightiest thing the world has ever possessed has bled to
death under our knives: who will wipe this blood from us? With what
water could we clean ourselves? What festivals of atonement, what holy   25
games will we have to invent for ourselves? Is the magnitude of this deed
not too great for us? Do we not ourselves have to become gods merely
to appear worthy of it? There was never a greater deed—and whoever is
born after us will on account of this deed belong to a higher history than
all history up to now!" Here the madman fell silent and looked again   30
at his listeners; they too were silent and looked at him disconcertedly.
Finally he threw his lantern on the ground and it broke into pieces and
went out. "I come too early," he then said; "my time is not yet. This
tremendous event is still on its way, wandering; it has not yet reached
the ears of men. Lightning and thunder need time; the light of the stars   35
needs time; deeds need time, even after they are done, in order to be
seen and heard. This deed is still more remote to them than the remotest
stars—and yet they have done it themselves!" It is still recounted how on
the same day the madman forced his way into several churches and there
started singing his *requiem aeternam deo*.[1] Led out and called to account, 40
he is said always to have replied nothing but, "What then are these
churches now if not the tombs and sepulchres of God?"

---

[1]"Grant God eternal rest" (Latin). Nietzsche substitutes "God" for "them" in the traditional passage from
the service for the dead: "Grant them eternal rest"

1. In lines 1–2, the madman carrying the lantern signifies his

    A. optimism
    B. insanity
    C. rationality
    D. magnanimity
    E. brilliance

2. The questions offered by the "many" in lines 3–6 were asked in a tone best characterized as

    A. bewildered
    B. earnest
    C. melancholy
    D. vicious
    E. facetious

3. "They" interrupted each other (line 6) most likely because

    A. they were angry about God's disappearance
    B. they were in disagreement over God's whereabouts
    C. many wanted to toss in mocking comments
    D. they were trying to mollify the madman
    E. they were bewildered by what the madman was saying

4. The tone of the madman is

   A. excited
   B. measured
   C. giddy
   D. inured
   E. solemn

5. The madman in lines 10–12 presents

   A. a series of disorienting metaphors
   B. the personification of death as a titanic figure
   C. a placating series of images to calm the bystanders
   D. a number of questions about love
   E. a stirring defense of gravitational pull

6. The section beginning on line 12 with "Do we still hear nothing . . ." through "Gods, too decompose" on line 14 presents

   A. a cohesive, logical argument for the proceeding discussion
   B. a rebuttal to the madman's previous claims
   C. a transgression away from the madman's essential points
   D. a physical manifestation to what initially appeared to be an abstract claim
   E. an establishment of a wholly different theological argument

from *The Gay Science*
        by Friedrich Nietzsche

The following questions are based on the information you've gathered from the activity for Day 150 and having closely read the excerpt from *The Gay Science*.

7. The madman's comments from line 17 "Do we not ourselves . . ." until they conclude on line 19 are characterized by

A. poised certitude
B. irrelevant mutterings
C. exasperated irony
D. florid complaints
E. mealy-mouthed ambivalence

8. The new mood of the listeners on line 20 can best be explained by

A. a loss of interest in what the madman was saying
B. a newfound understanding of the grave implications of the madman's words
C. a divine vision that has imbued their spirits
D. an abject rejection of the madman's argument
E. an appearance of impenetrable phenomena

9. The extraordinary, unusual, and revolutionary nature of the madman's argument that God is dead is best signified throughout by

A. the bystanders
B. the sea
C. the lantern
D. the blood
E. his eyes

10. "Them" in line 24 refers to

A. the murderers
B. the stars
C. God
D. the deeds
E. the lanterns

11. While the madman says "even after they [the deeds] are done" (line 23), his comments are still presented as

A. diversions
B. prophecies
C. confessions
D. warnings
E. diversions

12. The final sentence of the passage presents

A. a new line of discussion to investigate avarice
B. a meditation on the role of church in society
C. a presentation of a thesis to culminate the argument
D. a paradoxical statement to further the preceding argument
E. a rejection of the previous argument

Seven Activities Analyzing a Prose Passage in Preparation for the Prose Essay

An Excerpt from Jane Austen's *Pride and Prejudice*

This excerpt will be broken up in seven days of short-response questions to demonstrate how a careful reader can gather techniques and build up analysis to develop a free-response essay.

In this scene Mr. Collins proposes to Elizabeth Bennet. Upon her father's death, Elizabeth and her sisters will lose their home as English law at the time passed the house unto a male relation, in this case Mr. Collins. While the accumulated excerpt over the seven days is a bit longer than the traditional AP Literature prose essay passage, it provides the reader with good opportunities to explore analyses central to such responses.

Part 1: Following the Text

"My reasons for marrying are, first, that I think it a right thing for every clergyman in easy circumstances (like myself) to set the example of matrimony in his parish; secondly, that I am convinced that it will add very greatly to my happiness; and thirdly—which perhaps I ought to have mentioned earlier, that it is the particular advice and recommendation of the very noble lady whom I have the honour of calling patroness. Twice has she condescended to give me her opinion (unasked too!) on this subject; and it was but the very Saturday night before I left Hunsford—between our pools at quadrille, while Mrs. Jenkinson was arranging Miss de Bourgh's footstool, that she said, 'Mr. Collins, you must marry.

A clergyman like you must marry. Choose properly, choose a gentlewoman for *my* sake; and for your *own*, let her be an active, useful sort of person, not brought up high, but able to make a small income go a good way. This is my advice. Find such a woman as soon as you can, bring her to Hunsford, and I will visit her.' Allow me, by the way, to observe, my fair cousin, that I do not reckon the notice and kindness of Lady Catherine de Bourgh as among the least of the advantages in my power to offer. You will find her manners beyond anything I can describe; and your wit and vivacity, I think, must be acceptable to her, especially when tempered with the silence and respect which her rank will inevitably excite. . . ."

1. What is revealed by Mr. Collins having a list of reasons for marrying?

2. For most of this proposal Mr. Collins speaks very little to Elizabeth's qualities. What can the reader infer from this approach?

3. Why does Mr. Collins spend so much time talking about Lady Catherine de Bourgh?

4. How is Mr. Collins's final comment in this passage simultaneously contradictory and telling?

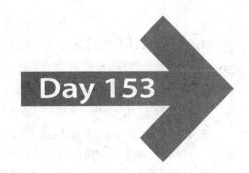

from *Pride and Prejudice*
        by **Jane Austen**

Mr. Collins continues delivering his marriage proposal . . .

"Thus much for my general intention in favour of matrimony; it remains to be told why my views were directed towards Longbourn instead of my own neighbourhood, where I can assure you there are many amiable young women. But the fact is, that being, as I am, to inherit this estate after the death of your honoured father (who, however, may live many years longer), I could not satisfy myself without resolving to choose a wife from among his daughters, that the loss to them might be as little as possible, when the melancholy event takes place—which, however, as I have already said, may not be for several years. This has been my motive, my fair cousin, and I flatter myself it will not sink me in your esteem. And now nothing remains for me but to assure you in the most animated language of the violence of my affection. To fortune I am perfectly indifferent, and shall make no demand of that nature on your father, since I am well aware that it could not be complied with; and that one thousand pounds in the four per cents, which will not be yours till after your mother's decease, is all that you may ever be entitled to. On that head, therefore, I shall be uniformly silent; and you may assure yourself that no ungenerous reproach shall ever pass my lips when we are married."

1. Why does Mr. Collins tell Elizabeth that his own neighborhood has "many amiable young women"?

2. What appears to be the primary reason for Mr. Collins's marrying Elizabeth and how does this motive shed light on an aspect of his character?

3. Mr. Collins tells Elizabeth about his reason: "This has been my motive, my fair cousin, and I flatter myself it will not sink me in your esteem." What does this comment show about his character?

4. Mr. Collins states, "And now nothing remains for me but to assure you in the most animated language of the violence of my affection." What is ironic about the comments that follow?

from *Pride and Prejudice*
       by Jane Austen

After patiently waiting, Elizabeth can hold back no longer.

It was absolutely necessary to interrupt him now.

"You are too hasty, sir," she cried. "You forget that I have made no answer. Let me do it without further loss of time. Accept my thanks for the compliment you are paying me. I am very sensible of the honour of your proposals, but it is impossible for me to do otherwise than to decline them."

"I am not now to learn," replied Mr. Collins, with a formal wave of the hand, "that it is usual with young ladies to reject the addresses of the man whom they secretly mean to accept, when he first applies for their favour; and that sometimes the refusal is repeated a second, or even a third time. I am therefore by no means discouraged by what you have just said, and shall hope to lead you to the altar ere long."

"Upon my word, sir," cried Elizabeth, "your hope is a rather extraordinary one after my declaration. I do assure you that I am not one of those young ladies (if such young ladies there are) who are so daring as to risk their happiness on the chance of being asked a second time. I am perfectly serious in my refusal. You could not make *me* happy, and I am convinced that I am the last woman in the world who could make you so. Nay, were your friend Lady Catherine to know me, I am persuaded she would find me in every respect ill qualified for the situation."

1. In her first comments of this section, how would you characterize Elizabeth's reply to Mr. Collins's proposal?

2. How does Mr. Collins respond to her reply?

3. How does Elizabeth's second response differ from her first?

4. Why does Elizabeth refer to Lady Catherine in her response? How does Elizabeth's diction and tone contribute to the messages she is trying to deliver to Mr. Collins?

from *Pride and Prejudice*
   by **Jane Austen**

Despite Elizabeth's response, Mr. Collins continues his proposal.

"Were it certain that Lady Catherine would think so," said Mr. Collins very gravely—"but I cannot imagine that her ladyship would at all disapprove of you. And you may be certain when I have the honour of seeing her again, I shall speak in the very highest terms of your modesty, economy, and other amiable qualification."

"Indeed, Mr. Collins, all praise of me will be unnecessary. You must give me leave to judge for myself, and pay me the compliment of believing what I say. I wish you very happy and very rich, and by refusing your hand, do all in my power to prevent your being otherwise. In making me the offer, you must have satisfied the delicacy of your feelings with regard to my family, and may take possession of Longbourn estate whenever it falls, without any self-reproach. This matter may be considered, therefore, as finally settled." And rising as she thus spoke, she would have quitted the room, had Mr. Collins not thus addressed her:

1. Describe the diction and syntax of Mr. Collins's comment, "but I cannot imagine that her ladyship would at all disapprove of you"?

2. How does Elizabeth continue to praise Mr. Collins even as she more adamantly rejects him?

3. What is indicated by the final line of this segment: "And rising as she thus spoke, she would have quitted the room, had Mr. Collins not thus addressed her"?

4. With Mr. Collins's dogged and continual efforts to convince Elizabeth, how has the tone of the passage changed?

from *Pride and Prejudice*
by Jane Austen

In which Mr. Collins persists . . .

"When I do myself the honour of speaking to you next on the subject, I shall hope to receive a more favourable answer than you have now given me; though I am far from accusing you of cruelty at present, because I know it to be the established custom of your sex to reject a man on the first application, and perhaps you have even now said as much to encourage my suit as would be consistent with the true delicacy of the female character."

"Really, Mr. Collins," cried Elizabeth with some warmth, "you puzzle me exceedingly. If what I have hitherto said can appear to you in the form of encouragement, I know not how to express my refusal in such a way as to convince you of its being one."

1. At this point in the interaction of Mr. Collins and Elizabeth, what can the reader discern from Mr. Collins's opening clause: "When I do myself the honour of speaking to you next on the subject"?

2. What is Mr. Collins implying with the comment: "I am far from accusing you of cruelty at present"?

3. What could the reader interpret Mr. Collins means when he describes "the true delicacy of the female character"?

4. How can you best characterize Elizabeth's reply?

5 Minutes to a 5

**from *Pride and Prejudice*
by Jane Austen**

In which Mr. Collins continues . . .

"You must give me leave to flatter myself, my dear cousin, that your refusal of my addresses is merely words of course. My reasons for believing it are briefly these: It does not appear to me that my hand is unworthy of your acceptance, or that the establishment I can offer would be any other than highly desirable. My situation in life, my connections with the family of de Bourgh, and my relationship to your own, are circumstances highly in my favour; and you should take it into further consideration, that in spite of your manifold attractions, it is by no means certain that another offer of marriage may ever be made you. Your portion is unhappily so small that it will in all likelihood undo the effects of your loveliness and amiable qualifications. As I must therefore conclude that you are not serious in your rejection of me, I shall choose to attribute it to your wish of increasing my love by suspense, according to the usual practice of elegant females."

"I do assure you, sir, that I have no pretensions whatever to that kind of elegance which consists in tormenting a respectable man. I would rather be paid the compliment of being believed sincere. I thank you again and again for the honour you have done me in your proposals, but to accept them is absolutely impossible. My feelings in every respect forbid it. Can I speak plainer? Do not consider me now as an elegant female, intending to plague you, but as a rational creature, speaking the truth from her heart."

1. What is Mr. Collins providing in the first three sentences of the section? What is not present in that appeal?

2. What can be interpreted from Mr. Collins's comment: "you should take it into further consideration, that in spite of your manifold attractions, it is by no means certain that another offer of marriage may ever be made you"?

3. What is revealed about Elizabeth when she asks Mr. Collins, "Can I speak plainer?"

4. Describe the contrasting interpretations of "elegant female" from Mr. Collins and Elizabeth.

Day 158

---

from *Pride and Prejudice*
        by Jane Austen

In which Mr. Collins concludes . . .

"You are uniformly charming!" cried he, with an air of awkward gallantry; "and I am persuaded that when sanctioned by the express authority of both your excellent parents, my proposals will not fail of being acceptable."

To such perseverance in wilful self-deception Elizabeth would make no reply, and immediately and in silence withdrew; determined, if he persisted in considering her repeate refusals as flattering encouragement, to apply to her father, whose negative might be uttered in such a manner as to be decisive, and whose behaviour at least could not be mistaken for the affectation and coquetry of an elegant female.

1. How does the combination of flattery and threat in the first paragraph serve as a source for comedy?

2. What does Elizabeth come to realize about the role her father has to play in this discussion?

<u>**Summative Comments:**</u> With all of the seven parts of the excerpt in mind, what are your overall perceptions? Consider Elizabeth's thoughts about her situation delivered in the final paragraph of this segment.

Analyzing a Prose Passage in Preparation for the Prose Essay

from *Moby Dick*
        by Herman Melville

This excerpt will be broken up in six days of brief exercises to demonstrate how a careful reader can gather techniques and build up analysis to develop a free-response essay. In this scene Captain Ahab has told his whaling ship crew that they will hunt Moby Dick, a white whale that had previously ripped off Ahab's leg. This demand is extraordinary since the crew should be hunting whales in general, rather than wasting time chasing one specific whale, so they can collect the most oil to sell. Starbuck, Ahab's first mate, questions Ahab's decision.

    "Captain Ahab," said Starbuck, who, with Stubb and Flask, had thus far been eyeing his superior with increasing surprise, but at last seemed struck with a thought which somewhat explained all the wonder. "Captain Ahab, I have heard of Moby Dick—but it was not Moby Dick that took off thy leg?"
    "Who told thee that?" cried Ahab; then pausing, "Aye, Starbuck; aye, my hearties all round; it was Moby Dick that dismasted me; Moby Dick that brought me to this dead stump I stand on now. Aye, aye," he shouted with a terrific, loud, animal sob, like that of a heart-stricken moose; "Aye, aye! it was that accursed white whale that razeed[1] me; made a poor pegging lubber of me for ever and a day!" Then tossing both arms, with measureless imprecations he shouted out: "Aye, aye! and I'll chase him round Good Hope, and round the Horn, and round the Norway Maelstrom, and round perdition's flames before I give him up. And this is what ye have shipped for, men! to chase that white whale on both sides of land, and over all sides of earth, till he spouts black blood and rolls fin out. . . ."

---

[1]A ship is "razeed" when the number of decks is reduced.

How do diction and repetition reveal Ahab's psychological state?

from *Moby Dick*
    by Herman Melville

"What say ye, men, will ye splice hands on it, now? I think ye do look brave."

    "Aye, aye!" shouted the harpooneers and seamen, running closer to the excited old man: "A sharp eye for the white whale; a sharp lance for Moby Dick!"

    "God bless ye," he seemed to half sob and half shout. "God bless ye, men. Steward! go draw the great measure of grog. But what's this long face about, Mr. Starbuck; wilt thou not chase the white whale! art not game for Moby Dick?"

    "I am game for his crooked jaw, and for the jaws of Death too, Captain Ahab, if it fairly comes in the way of the business we follow; but I came here to hunt whales, not my commander's vengeance. How many barrels will thy vengeance yield thee even if thou gettest it, Captain Ahab? it will not fetch thee much in our Nantucket market."

    "Nantucket market! Hoot! But come closer, Starbuck; thou requirest a little lower layer. If money's to be the measurer, man, and the accountants have computed their great counting-house the globe, by girdling it with guineas, one to every three parts of an inch; then, let me tell thee, that my vengeance will fetch a great premium here!"

    "He smites his chest," whispered Stubb, "what's that for? methinks it rings most vast, but hollow."

Compare the arguments of Ahab to those of Starbuck. What are their chief characteristics?

from *Moby Dick*
  by Herman Melville

"Vengeance on a dumb brute!" cried Starbuck, "that simply smote thee from blindest instinct! Madness! To be enraged with a dumb thing, Captain Ahab, seems blasphemous."

  "Hark ye yet again—the little lower layer. All visible objects, man, are but as pasteboard masks. But in each event—in the living act, the undoubted deed—there, some unknown but still reasoning thing puts forth the mouldings of its features from behind the unreasoning mask. If man will strike, strike though the mask! How can the prisoner reach outside except by thrusting through the wall? To me, the white whale is that wall, shoved near to me. Sometimes I think there's naught beyond. But 'tis enough. He tasks me; he heaps me; I see in him outrageous strength, with an inscrutable malice sinewing it. That inscrutable thing is chiefly what I hate; and be the white whale agent, or be the white whale principal, I will wreak that hate upon him. . . ."

Analyze how Starbuck's initial argument leads to Ahab revealing an underlying set of beliefs that intellectualize his need for vengeance. Make certain to include Ahab's use of allegory, metaphor, and diction.

from *Moby Dick*
        by Herman Melville

Here Ahab continues to explain himself to Starbuck who apparently looks at his captain with consternation.

"Talk not to me of blasphemy, man; I'd strike the sun if it insulted me. For could the sun do that, then could I do the other; since there is ever a sort of fair play herein, jealousy presiding over all creations. But not my master, man, is even that fair play. Who's over me? Truth hath no confines. Take off thine eye! more intolerable than fiends' glarings is a doltish stare! So, so; thou reddenest and palest; my heat has melted thee to anger-glow. But look ye, Starbuck, what is said in heat, that thing unsays itself. There are men from whom warm words are small indignity. I meant not to incense thee. Let it go. . . ."

Analyze how through his tone and burgeoning sense of his audience Ahab adapts his language and approach.

from *Moby Dick*
        by Herman Melville

"Look! see yonder Turkish cheeks of spotted tawn—living, breathing pictures painted by the sun. The Pagan leopards—the unrecking and unworshipping things, that live; and seek, and give no reasons for the torrid life they feel! The crew, man, the crew! Are they not one and all with Ahab, in this matter of the whale? See Stubb! he laughs! See yonder Chilian! he snorts to think of it. Stand up amid the general hurricane, thy one tost sapling cannot, Starbuck! And what is it? Reckon it. 'Tis but to help strike a fin; no wondrous feat for Starbuck. What is it more? From this one poor hunt, then, the best lance out of all Nantucket, surely he will not hang back, when every foremast-hand has clutched a whetstone. Ah! constrainings seize thee; I see! the billow lifts thee! Speak, but speak!—Aye, aye! thy silence, then, that voices thee. (*Aside*) Something shot from my dilated nostrils, he has inhaled it in his lungs. Starbuck now is mine; cannot oppose me now, without rebellion."

Analyze how Ahab assesses his situation and manipulates Starbuck to his will. In addition, what is the author's purpose in adding an aside at the end of this speech?

from *Moby Dick*
        by Herman Melville

Consider your five days of analysis to crystallize your understanding of the passage. Write an introduction to a prose essay that characterizes the dynamics between Ahab and Starbuck and delineate the nature of their viewpoints. You may consider literary techniques the author employs in this depiction.

5 Minutes to a 5

FREE RESPONSE

Deconstructing the Prompt

Read the Prompt!

Leo Tolstoy observed that "All happy families are alike; each unhappy family is unhappy in its own way."

Choose a full-length work of literary merit and write a well-developed essay that identifies an unhappy family and its complex effect on character and/or theme.

Deconstruct the above prompt by underlining, highlighting, and/or notating the requirements of the task.

Day 166

The Great Themes

List at least 10 major (universal) themes you have encountered in your literature studies.

The Great Themes, Identification Plus Examples

Refer to your list of great themes.

1. From this list, identify a theme to explore.

2. Identify a full-length work that focuses on your theme.

3. Provide at least three specific examples with details to support the theme you are illustrating. (You may list, bullet, outline, or map your answer.)

Addressing the Free-Response Prompt

Leo Tolstoy observed that "All happy families are alike; each unhappy family is unhappy in its own way."

List five works you have read that would be appropriate to answer this prompt.

Relating Major Works to a Given Quotation

Assume that the following quotation is the basis on which you are to compose an essay in response to a free-response prompt.

"But man is not made for defeat," he said. "A man can be destroyed but not defeated."

—*The Old Man and the Sea* by Ernest Hemingway

1. Quickly list five major works that come to mind that are in some way related to this quotation.

2. Choose the one you feel most comfortable with, and beside it briefly state the major reason you chose it.

Essay Analysis of a Work of Literary Merit: Literary Technique

Literary techniques offer myriad elements to enrich a story line including irony, foreshadowing, satire, allusion, setting, and foil characters. While these approaches are diverse, they share an authorial desire to develop additional layers of a fiction. Below are 19 works of literary merit that employ specific literary techniques. For each work, only one example is provided in order to give you the opportunity to consider other possibilities and alternatives on your own. Further explanation is given where the nature of the literary technique might not be readily apparent. Works are presented in chronological order of their publication.

Oedipus Rex by Sophocles: Irony

Medea by Euripides: Foreshadowing

Monkey (or Journey to the West) by Wu Cheng'En: Dualities and antithesis as the endless desire for growth and destructive impulsivity coexist within Monkey

Macbeth by William Shakespeare: The paradoxes of the witches and others

Gulliver's Travels by Jonathan Swift: Satire

Candide by Voltaire: Satire

Frankenstein by Mary Shelley: Setting as character

The Scarlet Letter by Nathaniel Hawthorne: Foil characters of Dimmesdale and Chillingsworth

Moby Dick by Herman Melville: Allusion, as the novel is rife with Biblical references and religious imagery

Great Expectations by Charles Dickens: Irony in the identity of Pip's benefactor, in Pip only becoming a gentleman when his prospects dim, and in both the lineage and fate of Estella

Crime and Punishment by Fyodor Dostoevsky: Paradox—finding freedom through imprisonment. These paradoxes start right at the beginning of the novel where two drunken men are "abusing and supporting one another" as "Raskolnikov felt giddy and tormented."

The Adventures of Huckleberry Finn by Mark Twain: Satire, particularly in the story of the duke and the king

Hedda Gabler by Henrik Ibsen: Allusion to Greek mythology, particularly in the ironic naming of the local prostitute Diana and the Bacchanalian references to vine leaves

Their Eyes Were Watching God by Zora Neale Hurston: Dialect, specifically rural, Southern black dialects as best demonstrated in the conversation between Sam Watson and Lige Moss in the middle of Chapter 6

Lord of the Flies by William Golding: Irony in the fire, which serves initially as savior, then destroyer and ultimately savior

Things Fall Apart by Chinua Achebe: Irony, particularly in Okonkwo's final act and the district commissioner's closing perception of the Ibo people

Catch-22 by Joseph Heller: Satire, primarily of the military

The Things They Carried by Tim O'Brien: Cataloging as the narrator generates voluminous lists of the items (physical and metaphysical) the soldiers carry

Life of Pi by Yann Martell: Foreshadowing in that the first section centering around the Pondicherry Zoo hints to all that will follow

First Choice: A Major Literary Work for Literary Technique

In the space below, present the nature of the literary technique for a selected work of literary merit. Try to develop specifics of that technique from the text because this commentary will be applicable to the free-response essay that appears on the exam.

An Alternate Work for Literary Technique

In the space below, present the nature of the literary technique for a different work of literary merit. Try to develop specifics of that technique from the text because this commentary will be applicable to the free-response essay that appears on the exam.

Essay Analysis of a Work of Literary Merit: Plot Structures

Plot structures become the frame of a literary work and mold the reader's perceptions of events and characters. The organization of the plot allows for narrative elements to be foreshortened, incidents to be juxtaposed, and elements to be delineated. Below are 15 works of literary merit that employ a specific plot structures. For each work, only one example is provided as to give you the opportunity to consider other possibilities and alternatives on your own. Further explanation is given where the nature of the plot structure might not be readily apparent. Works are presented in chronological order of their publication.

The Odyssey by Homer: Broken into three sections—Telemachus's search, Odysseus's journey, Odysseus's return

Beowulf: Story framed by three battles

Monkey (or Journey to the West) by Wu Cheng'En: The first section presents Monkey's personal growth, albeit selfish and amoral in nature; the longer second part follows Monkey on his arduous journey for redemption

Macbeth by William Shakespeare: The employment of prophecies to drive the plot both early and late in the play

Hamlet by William Shakespeare: Parallel subplots through the actions of Fortinbras and Laertes

Gulliver's Travels by Jonathan Swift: Four episodes traveling to different lands

Candide by Voltaire: Boy finds girl, boy loses girl, boy rediscovers girl, etc.

Jane Eyre by Charlotte Bronte: The episodic structure moves from house to house— Gateshead to Lowood to Thornfield to Moore House to Ferndean

Moby Dick by Herman Melville: On one level, the plot is a quest whaling adventure as the crew chases Moby Dick, but on other levels it is an epistemological exploration for meaning as individuals confront larger, domineering forces.

Their Eyes Were Watching God by Zora Neale Hurston: The novel's structure is generally developed through her relationships with the men in her life—Logan, Jody, and Teacake.

The Stranger by Albert Camus: The novel is framed in two parts—before the shooting in the sun and afterward.

Things Fall Apart by Chinua Achebe: The use of Okonkwo's seven-year exile to condense the story of the white man's incremental takeover

The Color Purple by Alice Walker: The steady rising from abuse to sisterhood to independence

White Noise by Don DeLillo: The Airborne Toxic Event becomes a centerpiece event that informs the behaviors preceding and following.

Life of Pi by Yann Martell: Divided into three parts—in Pondicherry before Pi is trapped on the lifeboat, his time on the lifeboat with a tiger, and his return with the presentation of an alternate story.

First Choice

In the space below, present the nature of the plot structure for a selected work of literary merit. Look to develop specifics from the plot structure for this text because this commentary will be applicable to the essay analysis for a work of literary merit that appears on the exam.

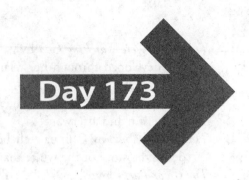
An Alternate Work for Plot Structure

In the space below, present a different work that illustrates plot structure. Try to develop specifics of that technique from the text because this commentary will be applicable to the free-response essay that appears on the exam.

Essay Analysis of a Work of Literary Merit: Narrative Voice

Narrative voice provides the reader with perspective on the storyteller(s) of specific works. Essentially it molds the way the reader understands both the characters and the plot. Below are 23 works of literary merit that employ specific techniques, approaches, and elements. For each work, only one example is provided in order to give students the opportunity to consider other possibilities and alternatives on their own. Further explanation is given where the nature of the narrative voice might not be readily apparent.

Works are presented in chronological order of their publication.

Oedipus Rex by Sophocles: The chorus
Beowulf: The oral tradition
Hamlet by William Shakespeare: Soliloquies
Gulliver's Travels by Jonathan Swift: Gulliver observes societies from perspectives both telescopically (Lilliputians) and microscopically (Brobdingnagians).
Candide by Voltaire: Light, breezy, mocking, unemotional prose, limited character development
Frankenstein by Mary Shelley: A first-person narrative encased in an epistolary opening
Pride and Prejudice by Jane Austen: A limited omniscient third-person narrative, whereby the attention, psychological insight, and activity centers upon Eliza Bennett
Jane Eyre by Charlotte Bronte: A first-person narrative revealing the thoughts and emotions of a highly intelligent, but not beautiful woman from a lower class
The Scarlet Letter by Nathaniel Hawthorne: Told by a third-person author well-versed in America's Puritan past and in the gossip, legends, and conversations of the local folks
Moby Dick by Herman Melville: A first-person narrative that often breaks loose from that structure to develop dramatic theatrical scenes, short fables, essays, soliloquies, and choruses

Great Expectations by Charles Dickens: A first-person narrative told in retrospect, with accompanying self-judgment passed

Crime and Punishment by Fyodor Dostoevsky: The employment of internal and external monologues, particularly Marmeladov's tortured commentary early and Roskolnikov's ruminations throughout

The Adventures of Huckleberry Finn by Mark Twain: A first-person narrative told from the perspective of a poor, quick-thinking, semi-literate orphan

The Great Gatsby by F. Scott Fitzgerald: Told by Nick Carraway who encounters Gatsby during one raucous summer of romance and intrigue, uncovering his past and chronicling his dream

The Sun Also Rises by Ernest Hemingway: Simplicity of writing style and the notion of leaving much of the action below the surface

Their Eyes Were Watching God by Zora Neale Hurston: Although not a first-person narrative, Hurston's text carefully delves into Janie's psychological states and follows her growth.

The Stranger by Albert Camus: A first-person narrative without the self-conscious, psychological explorations, yet with enough careful description of the narrator's (Mersault's) interactions that the reader understands others' perceptions of him

Things Fall Apart by Chinua Achebe: The integration of proverbs, local myths, and rituals into the plot's rhythms

One Flew over the Cuckoo's Nest by Ken Kesey: Chief, the first-person narrator, is considered deaf and dumb, so the characters speak in front of him like he is not even there. In addition, Chief is an unstable narrator, given the damage of the mental institution has wrought upon him.

The Color Purple by Alice Walker: Epistolary novel in which the main letter writer, Celie, grows in articulation and confidence throughout the novel

White Noise by Don DeLillo: Jack Gladney's narrative voice is grounded in late twentieth-century culture: from cinematic descriptions to technological diction and references to dysfunctional family preoccupations.

The Things They Carried by Tim O'Brien: The narrator employs a metafictional approach, where he plays with the true stories and fictional ones.

Life of Pi by Yann Martell: Mainly a first-person narrative from Pi, with occasional short interruptions from his chronicler

First Choice

In the space below, present the nature of the narrative voice for a selected work of literary merit. Try to develop specifics from the narrative because commentary will be applicable to the free-response essay that appears on the exam.

An Alternate Work for Narrative Voice

In the space below, present a different work related to narrative voice. Try to develop specifics of that technique from the text because this commentary will be applicable to the free-response essay that appears on the exam.

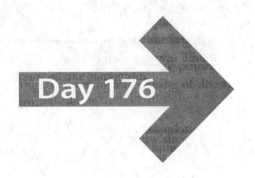

Essay Analysis of a Work of Literary Merit: Motif

A motif is a recurrent image, idea, or symbol that contributes to the meaning of a literary work. These motifs tend to build in power and meaning over the course of a text as later employment of a motif can reverberate or play off of earlier uses. Below are 23 works of literary merit that employ specific motifs. For each work, only one example is provided as to give you the opportunity to consider other possibilities and alternatives on your own. Further explanation is given where the nature of the motif might not be readily apparent. Works are presented in chronological order of their publication.

The Odyssey by Homer: Temptation, from the lotus eaters to the sirens to Calypso

Oedipus Rex by Sophocles: Blindness

Beowulf: Swords as characters

Monkey (or Journey to the West) by Wu Cheng'En: Monkey's protean adaptations

Hamlet by William Shakespeare: Death images from the ghost to Yorick's skull

Macbeth by William Shakespeare: Blood

Gulliver's Travels by Jonathan Swift: The body and bodily functions (scatology)

Candide by Voltaire: The return of characters given up for lost or dead—Cunegonde, Cacambo, the Reverend Father, and especially Pangloss who is apparently killed a couple of times, but resurfaces

The Scarlet Letter by Nathaniel Hawthorne: The wilderness

Moby Dick by Herman Melville: The role of ships as they serve as counterpoints to the *Pequod*'s activities and flesh out the legend of Moby Dick

Great Expectations by Charles Dickens: Imprisonment in its many forms

Crime and Punishment by Fyodor Dostoevsky: Destruction and Regeneration for Raskolnikov, for Dounia, for Sonia. The allusions to Lazarus fortify this motif.

Hedda Gabler by Henrik Ibsen: Pistols—their presence throughout the play, serving purposes from character development to plot advancement to the climax

The Great Gatsby by F. Scott Fitzgerald: The eyes of Dr. TJ Eckleburg

The Sun Also Rises by Ernest Hemingway: Triangular relationships, most of which are centered upon Lady Brett Ashley

Their Eyes Were Watching God by Zora Neale Hurston: The role of nature, specifically in reference to pear trees, life cycles, and a hurricane

The Stranger by Albert Camus: Sky and light, particularly given the Algerian sun, and Mersualt's denial of these phenomena in prison

1984 by George Orwell: Falsehoods as truth, ranging from Winston's job at the Ministry of Truth to his ultimate confession that $2 + 2 = 5$

Things Fall Apart by Chinua Achebe: Proverbs employed as a compendium of Ibo wisdom

Catch-22 by Joseph Heller: Snowden repeated phrase "I'm cold."

The Color Purple by Alice Walker: The strong supportive woman, from Nettie to Miss Sofia to Shug Avery

White Noise by Don DeLillo: Pop culture essays and references

Life of Pi by Yann Martell: Faith in its many incarnations

First Choice

In the space below, present the nature of a motif for a selected work of literary merit. Look to develop specifics of the motif for this text because this commentary will be applicable to the essay analysis for a work of literary merit that appears on the exam.

An Alternative Literary Work for Motif

In the space below, present the nature of motif for a different work of literary merit. Try to develop specifics of that technique from the text because this commentary will be applicable to the free-response essay that appears on the exam.

Essay Analysis of a Work of Literary Merit: Symbols

Symbols are objects or elements that represent a larger, deeper idea in a literary work. Their manifestation in a text provides the readers with concrete touchstones to ground their understanding of the work. Below are 20 works of literary merit that employ specific symbols. For each work, only one example is provided as to give you the opportunity to consider other possibilities and alternatives on your own. Further explanation is given where the nature of the symbol might not be readily apparent. Works are presented in chronological order of their publication.

Monkey (or Journey to the West) by Wu Cheng'En: The cap of discipline

Macbeth by William Shakespeare: Sleep

Pride and Prejudice by Jane Austen: Pemberly as a reflection on Darcy and the changing perceptions of the two central figures

Jane Eyre by Charlotte Bronte: Homes and fires

The Scarlet Letter by Nathaniel Hawthorne: The letter *A*

Moby Dick by Herman Melville: The whiteness of the whale Moby Dick

Great Expectations by Charles Dickens: The forge

The Adventures of Huckleberry Finn by Mark Twain: The river

Hedda Gabler by Henrik Ibsen: Babies, both actual ones and Lovborg's manuscript

The Great Gatsby by F. Scott Fitzgerald: The green light on Daisy's dock

The Sun Also Rises by Ernest Hemingway: Bullfighting and its life-and-death struggles connecting it to World War I

Their Eyes Were Watching God by Zora Neale Hurston: The mule as a beast of burden, bearing heavy loads, but also stubbornly resisting

The Stranger by Albert Camus: Salamano and his dog as a representative of society's violent interactions

1984 by George Orwell: Big Brother

Lord of the Flies by William Golding: The conch

Things Fall Apart by Chinua Achebe: The kola nut and the yam as staples of tribal life

One Flew over the Cuckoo's Nest by Ken Kesey: Fog, used to describe a physical manifestation and the state of the patients at the psychiatric center

The Color Purple by Alice Walker: Pants, representing Celie's independence

White Noise by Don DeLillo: Credit cards and ATMs as symbols of financial security and stability

Life of Pi by Yann Martell: The animals on the boat as representations of specific humans, or at least, archetypes

First Choice

In the space below, present the nature of symbols for a selected work of literary merit. Look to develop specifics from the symbol for this text because this commentary will be applicable to the essay analysis for a work of literary merit that appears on the exam.

An Alternative Literary Work for Symbols

Sample Alternative

For each of the responses, a more developed and specific commentary would be presented in the actual exam essay. For example, the forge in *Great Expectations* represents the low-class, sooty, grimy world into which Pip was born. Even though the kindest and most supportive of men, Joe Gargery, toils at the forge, Pip, as he rises in social class, cannot perceive the forge as anything more than the wincing representation of his embarrassing origins. The hard physical labor of the forge leads to coarse hands and dirty clothes, a far cry from the refined corridors that will usher him toward opportunities for wooing the wealthy Estella. Late in the novel, as Pip comes to terms with his transformation and the shame of his snobbery toward Joe, the humble blacksmith, he learns to better appreciate the forge as being the source of honest industry.

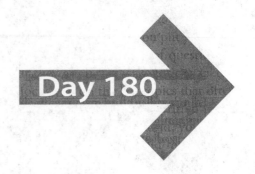
Essay Analysis of a Work of Literary Merit: Theme

A theme can serve simultaneously as the main idea and an underlying concept in a literary work. The theme usually deepens in meaning as the work builds and develops as such a concept becomes intertwined with both the plot and the thoughts and behaviors of individual characters. Below are 24 works of literary merit that employ a specific theme. For each work, only one example is provided in order to give you the opportunity to consider other possibilities and alternatives on your own. Further explanation is given where the nature of the theme might not be readily apparent. Works are presented in chronological order of their publication.

Oedipus Rex by Sophocles: Fate

Medea by Euripides: The plight of the alienated outsider

Beowulf: The warrior ethic

Monkey (or Journey to the West) by Wu Cheng'En: Redemption

Macbeth by William Shakespeare: Ambition

Hamlet by William Shakespeare: Madness

Candide by Voltaire: A philosophical response to "this is the best of all possible worlds," which lands on the understanding that "we must cultivate our own garden."

Frankenstein by Mary Shelley: Creation beyond the creator's control

Pride and Prejudice by Jane Austen: Matrimony and women's role in society

Jane Eyre by Charlotte Bronte: Women's independence

The Scarlet Letter by Nathaniel Hawthorne: Puritan hypocrisy

Moby Dick by Herman Melville: Brotherhood and the interdependence of the crew on the *Pequod*

Great Expectations by Charles Dickens: Social inequities

Crime and Punishment by Fyodor Dostoevsky: Poverty and financial duress

The Adventures of Huckleberry Finn by Mark Twain: Slavery

The Great Gatsby by F. Scott Fitzgerald: The American Dream

The Sun Also Rises by Ernest Hemingway: Rootlessness

Their Eyes Were Watching God by Zora Neale Hurston: Feminism as explored most dramatically through Janie's decision to leave Logan and her relationship with Teacake

The Stranger by Albert Camus: Existentialism

1984 by George Orwell: Totalitarianism

Things Fall Apart by Chinua Achebe: Colonialism

One Flew over the Cuckoo's Nest by Ken Kesey: Power, as wielded by both Nurse Ratched and McMurphy

The Color Purple by Alice Walker: Sisterhood

White Noise by Don DeLillo: Fear of death

First Choice

In the space below, present the nature of the theme for a selected work of literary merit. Look to develop specifics from the theme for this text because this commentary will be applicable to the essay analysis for a work of literary merit that appears on the exam.

A Self-Evaluation

Most probably, you've completed the AP English Literature and Composition course, and you've probably taken the AP English Literature exam. It's worth your while to evaluate how far you've come since the beginning of this course. What is your "take-away" as an AP English Literature student?

- What surprised you most as an AP English Literature student?

- What did you find to be most interesting?

- How is your reading different from where you were at the beginning of the course?

- How is your writing different from where you were at the beginning of the course?

- What one thing covered in this course would you like to learn more about?

- Having taken this course, what is the most important outcome/takeaway for you?

- How has participating in this AP English Literature course prepared you to be a lifelong reader?

Answers

Day 3

1. Alliteration: **The repetition of initial consonant sounds, such as, "the silent snow sifted slowly."**

2. Assonance: The repetition of vowel sounds, such as, "the rain in Spain stays mainly on the plain."

3. Onomatopoeia: **The term for words that sound like the sound they represent, such as, "buzz, hum, slurp, hiss."**

4. Euphony: **The pleasant, harmonious, or sweet sounds in a line or passage.**

5. Cacophony: **The presence of harsh and discordant sounds in a line or passage.**

Day 4

LD 1.		**RS** 6.	
RS 2.		**LD** 7.	
RS 3.		**RS** 8.	
RS 4.		**RS** 9.	
LD 5.		**LD** 10.	

These can be very subtle/minimal differences, but they are ones you need to be aware of as you work your way through a close reading in response to a multiple-choice question or an essay prompt.

Day 5

1. Psychological

2. Social

3. Religious

4. Sexual

5. Political

Day 6

Often, a character's name adds to our understanding of meaning in a work.

The following names should provide an opportunity for you to make predictions, jot down possibilities, examine character or explore insights for interpretation.

Do not be concerned about prior knowledge; just write your thoughts based on the names. Have fun exploring ideas.

1. Abbie and Eben

2. Seymour Glass

3. Ruth Hartwell

4. Holly Golightly

Day 7

Prose.	Poetry
1. Word	1. Syllable
2. Phrase	2. Foot
3. Sentence	3. Line
4. Paragraph	4. Stanza
5. Chapter	5. Canto

Day 8

Here are some familiar words often referred to when analyzing tone.

1. Sarcastic

2. Informal

3. Laudatory

4. Idyllic

5. Maudlin

6. Nostalgic

7. Reverent

8. Ironic

9. Objective

10. Inspiring

Day 9

1. B Dramatic irony

2. A Verbal irony

3. C Situational irony

4. B Dramatic irony

5. A Verbal irony

6. C Situational irony

Day 10

1. C The tone of this scene can best be described as **imperial and provocative**.

2. Here are some details that you could have cited in support of the tone being imperial and provocative:

- dark lighting
- a back-lit figure, wearing a crown and flowing cape, enters into darkness from a brightly lit doorway
- as he walks forward his dark form fills the entire screen
- the music is loud and builds to a crescendo sounding like a huge orchestra is playing
- the over-the-shoulder camera angle from Henry's viewpoint shows each courtier's face looking at the king and bowing his head as Henry passes by

Day 11

1. Keeping the prompt in mind, the organization of the essay should be **Dickinson first** and **Frost** second. (This is a comparison-contrast essay that requires equality and balance.)

2. Change "Though" to **Although**.

3. Include the titles of the poems. (For clarity, it's important to provide needed information for your reader.)

4. Change "gives" to **imposes on**.

5. Change "perspectives" to **perspectives on being alone in the dark**.

Day 12

Here is a sample revised introduction:

> **Although Emily Dickinson's "We Grow Accustomed to the Dark" and Robert Frost's "Acquainted with the Night" share the element of darkness, the poets speak from very different perspectives about being alone in the dark. Dickinson's connotes uncertainty and change, but Frost imposes a far more negative and desolate meaning on the darkness.**

Remember, the purpose of your introduction is to acquaint your reader with YOUR intentions. You want to make it clear to your reader what he or she can expect in the body of your essay.

Day 13

1. **B** Thoughtful

2. **A** Direct

3. **A** Solitary

4. **B** Tense

5. **A** Reportorial

6. **B** Complex

7. **B** Tense

8. **A** Simple

As an AP English Literature student, you should be able to return to the given text and cite specific details that support your conclusions.

- For Hemingway: mainly simple sentences with subject first followed by the simple verb, only one relative clause in the last sentence, brief sentences, does not link sentences
- For Faulkner: complex and compound sentences, links ideas, lengthy sentences

Day 14

The three poems presented in this activity illustrate Emily Dickinson's style, which includes

A. lyrical poems that are short with a single speaker

B. no exact rhyme scheme (Look at the last words of the lines; at times, there is a type of rhyme, but it is not patterned.)

C. Based on these poems, one could conclude that Dickinson's poetry most probably exhibits all of the following characteristics except **blank verse**.

D. lines that are most often common meter with alternating lines of eight syllables and six syllables

E. subject matter, which at first glance, appears to be simple and almost childlike but presents amazing "aha" moments of insight when read more carefully

Day 15

NOTE: Remember that **factual** requires you to go directly to the text and point to the answer. The **technical** stem asks you to locate and/or identify a "tool" that the author employs.

Analytical stems want you to identify how the tools work, what purpose they serve. The **inferential** stem directs you to choose conclusions, implications, or inferences that can be made resulting from a close reading of the text.

1. Technical

2. Factual

3. Inferential

4. Analytical

5. Technical

6. Analytical

7. Inferential

8. Inferential

9. Factual

10. Inferential

Day 16

1. D The antecedent of "Which" in line 2 is **tide**.

2. C Lines 3-4 refer to **flood**.

These two questions require you to go to the text and point to the exact word/phrase/ detail. This is a factual type of multiple-choice question.

Day 17

D Lines 27–29 beginning with "it had sprung up under the footsteps of the sainted Ann Hutchinson" contains an example of **allusion**. The reference to Ann Hutchinson brings up the possibility of past history of this prison, which would be ironic given the circumstances.

Day 18

1. D Metaphor. Every line directly compares flood tide with success and ebb tide with failure.

2. C Cause and effect. The focus is on the result that occurs when one strikes at a high point versus when one cannot act and never moves forward.

Day 19

1. **C** The Universe clearly is detached from the man's statement and indicates its lack of acknowledgment of his life.

2. **B** The key to this answer is the exclamation point, which underscores the man's emphasis and belief.

Day 20

1. **B** All the details of the first two stanzas are negative, violent, and horrible.

2. **D** The images of "beyond this place," "Horror," "shade," and "menace of the years" reinforce the unknown time when we are not of the world but of the afterlife.

Day 21

1. **D** The third-person opening indicates that Mr. Oakhurst has encountered a new mood ("change," "exchanged significant glances," "looked ominous," and "these indications").

2. **B** This is revealed through his demeanor ("calm" and "reflected") and his awareness ("conscious of a change" and he observed the exchange of "significant glances" and "the Sabbath lull in the air").

3. **A** The men ceasing to speak as Mr. Oakhurst approaches is one indication. This outlook is confirmed from Mr. Oakhurst's comment that he reckons they are after somebody.

4. **E** This is determined through diction and descriptions ("change," "ominous," and Mr. Oakhurst's concern that the two men were tense and wary).

Day 22

1. **D** This is a verbal description of a visual scene through detail and poetic techniques. There is nothing predicted in the poem.

2. **C** The author paints the scene with words that echo the actions of the painting. Even though he adds imagined sounds from what he observes, he is not postulating an interpretation of the painting.

Day 23

1. **D** Her quick, bright eyes, her swift looks, her expression, and her engaging manner all point to this alertness and awareness.

2. **B** All of the sentences begin with subject and predicate, with most characterized by having adjectives to flesh out the description.

3. **E** The other answers are all referred to in the passage: watchfulness (quick, bright eyes), pensiveness (thoughtful), openness (frankness of expression), and attractiveness (engaging).

4. **E** In its details and descriptions, the passage is a character study of Mrs. Pontellier.

Day 24

1. **D** The narrator directly addresses memory throughout.

2. **D** The "vain pretence" both flatters the narrator with the thoughts of being remembered and is futile since these thoughts come to no concrete result. While memory could be considered cruel, there is no evidence of the narrator being so.

3. **C** In the first stanza the narrator complains vehemently about the pain memory has wreaked upon her; in the second the narrator, while acknowledging the mockery that accompanies memory, makes clear that she would prefer to be consumed by the intense, torturous bliss of these haunting experiences rather than be left desolate by their absence.

4. **A** The narrator concludes that she "would rather die" than lose the palpably realized memory of a kiss.

Day 25

1. **A** The narrator explains at the end of the first paragraph that he, the avenger, would not succeed unless the victim knows "who has done him wrong."

2. **B** In the second paragraph, the narrator explains that Fortunato did not perceive that his appearance of good will was just the opposite.

3. **D** In the first paragraph the narrator makes clear that his plan must preclude "the idea of risk" and that he must punish "with impunity."

4. **E** The narrator's careful plotting of revenge, his listing of criteria, and his analysis of Fortunato's weak point lead to this characterization.

Day 26

1. **C** The timelessness of soldiers encountering one another both on the battlefield and in everyday life is central to the poem's theme. Naturally, the meeting has relevance (it's the poem's subject) and the appropriateness is marked by the duality of a soldier's life.

2. **D** The narrator is trying to explain why he killed this man, so he hesitates to come up with a reason. There is no evidence in the rest of the poem of a speech impediment.

3. **A** He clearly needs to give himself assurances of why he killed his foe.

4. **E** The understated nature of the phrase points to the ridiculousness of war.

5. **B** The inherent contradictions of war, particularly the role of the soldier, are described here.

6. **D** The narrator's description as "infantry" and his colloquial diction point to this inference.

Day 27

Use the following examples of poetic devices to serve as models illustrating the definition of the terms.

1. Metaphor: **All the world's a stage.**

2. Simile: **Life is like a box of chocolates.**

3. Personification: **My heart dances with the daffodils.**

4. Hyperbole: **And I will love thee still, my dear,**

Till all the seas run dry.

Day 28

1. **Personification**: giving human qualities to inanimate objects

2. **Alliteration**: the repetition of initial consonant sounds

3. **Simile**: an indirect comparison using the word *like* or *as* to create the image

4. **Metaphor**: a direct comparison between different images

5. **Assonance**: the repetition of vowel sounds in a line or phrase

6. **Onomatopoeia**: word (or words) that imitates the sound of the thing to which it refers

Day 29

1. Alliteration: **the repetition of initial consonant sounds, such as "the silent snow sifted slowly"**

2. Assonance: **the repetition of vowel sounds, such as "the rain in Spain stays mainly on the plain"**

3. Onomatopoeia: **The term for words that sound like the sound they represent, such as "buzz, hum, slurp, hiss"**

4. Euphony: **the pleasant, harmonious, or sweet sounds in a line or passage**

5. Cacophony: **the presence of harsh and discordant sounds in a line or passage**

Day 30

1. **A** Frost chooses the diction "should have guessed" as a way of saying he should have believed that the patch was actually a piece of paper. By that form of phrasing, Frost indicates to the reader that a paper on the ground makes much more sense than the presence of snow. That snow is particularly surprising considering the narrator's disbelief and its stubborn presence despite the rainfall he mentions in this first stanza.

2. **D** The assonance (repetition and use of vowel sounds) of the long *A*s in "away paper the rain" is part of the elongation of sound. In addition, many words have stretched-out vowel sounds (patch, snow, corner, should, blow, brought) that slow the pace of the stanza. The narrator has clearly paused to make certain that the patch is indeed snow instead of paper and is taking some time to ruminate about its unexpected presence.

3. **D** Like paper and ink, the dirty snow can be read into for further meaning. In addition, the accumulated diction describing the snow from patch to speckled to grime give this once pure, white substance the impression of being dirtied, sullied, and damaged; it is the hardened, darkened remnant of soft, bright snowfall, one that because it has been sheltered from the sun and chilled in the shadows has clung on even as the Earth reclaims its melting crystals.

4. **A.** The metaphor comparing the snow to the news of a day allows the reader to see the larger possibilities in the poem. The snow and the newsprint have stories to tell, yet they ultimately serve as allegories of not what we hold on to in life, but let pass by. The way the narrator questions whether he has forgotten or ever learned about that "news" signals he seems overwhelmed by the blizzard of information that has blown by him over the years.

Day 31

Here is one example of the prompt deconstructed:

Carefully read the following **post–World War I poem by Archibald MacLeish.** Then in a well-developed essay **analyze** the **different techniques** the poet uses to convey his **attitude toward his subject.** You may want to consider **form, literary devices, and tone.**

Your deconstruction should include the following data:

- post–World War I poem
- Archibald MacLeish
- well-developed essay
- analyze different techniques
- attitude toward subject
- consider form, literary device, and tone

Now, you know that as you closely read the poem you will be looking for (1) the subject; (2) the poet's attitude toward that subject; (3) the literary devices, etc., that MacLeish uses to convey his meaning.

Day 32

1. The central metaphor of this passage is ***All the world's a stage***, found in line 1. This extended metaphor compares the stages of human life to the acts of a play.

2. **E** The only stage not included in the seven stages is **scholar.** Each of the others can be located in the passage: infant (lines 5–6); schoolboy (lines 7–9); lover (lines 9–11); and soldier (lines 11–15).

3. Given the extended metaphor of *All the world's a stage*, the seven stages of a human life is compared to the **acts of a play** (line 5).

4. **A Disillusioned** is the best description of the tone of the passage. Lines 25–28 using "mere oblivion, Sans teeth, sans eyes, sans taste, sans everything" illustrate and support this tone being one of disillusion.

Day 33

1. The controlling/extended metaphor in this poem is a **nation's government compared to a ship**.

2. A. The first, in lines 1–2, exhorts **the state or union to get on with its business**.

   B. The second, in lines 3–5, says **humanity is anxious and hanging on to what will happen to the state/union**.

   C. Lines 6–11 describe **the building of the ship of state**.

   D. The subject of the fourth point (lines 12–18) is **humanity beseeching the ship of state not to be afraid**.

   E. The last lines (19–22) address **the hopes of humanity** and the promise to **continue to support the ship of state**.

Day 34

1. **Mercy** is the antecedent of all references in lines 1–6, where it is defined.

2. Line 9 refers to **his scepter**.

3. Lines 1–2 are an example of **a simile comparing mercy and gentle rain**.

4. Line 8 refers to **the force of temporal power** as exemplified by the scepter.

5. The comparison comes **full circle as line 12 refers to** *the quality of mercy* in **line 1**.

Day 35

1. The antecedent of "these growing feathers . . ." is *the vulgar*, line 3. The term applies to the commoners and populace who may support Caesar.

2. Caesar is compared to **a bird**.

3. The following images extend the basic metaphor:

   growing feathers   (line 5)

   Caesar's wing   (line 5)

   fly an ordinary pitch   (line 6)

   would soar above   (line 7)

Day 36

1. **Line 1**. Direct address to Milton

2. **Line 2:** "Need of thee"

   Line 7: "Oh! Raise us up,"

3. Line 9: "Thy soul"

    Line 10: "Thou hadst"

    Line 12: "So didst thou"

    Line 13: "thy heart"

Day 37

1. a train/locomotive

2. extended metaphor

3. train/locomotive to a horse

Day 38

These five lines are an example of an **allusion**. (An allusion is an indirect reference to a person, place, thing, or idea of historical, cultural, literary, or political significance.) In this epic poem, Milton alludes to the Garden of Eden and the fall of humankind who will be redeemed by a savior.

Day 39

1. B The tone of the poem can best be described as **proud and optimistic**. Because of the positive nature of the poem's diction and imagery, A, C, and E are not applicable to this passage. While D may appear to be a good choice, you must remember that *both* words must apply to the text. *Hopeful* could be stretched to describe the passage, but *sarcastic* is not a supportable choice.

2. Examples of enjambment can be found in lines **3–4 and lines 9–11**. Remember enjambment in poetry means the line flows from one line to another without a terminating punctuation mark. In this passage, Tennyson uses the semicolon to terminate the thought in the middle of a line (lines 4 and 10).

Day 40

1. C While imagery, anaphora, and alliteration are throughout and a simile appears in line 4, litotes are absent from a poem that focuses on direct statements.

2. E "[T]he cage bird beats his wing/Till its blood is red on the cruel bars."

3. B The "old, old scars" indicate the bird has a history of this behavior.

4. D *Invocation* is the closest to the bird's "prayer" or "plea."

Day 41

Here is an example of a response:

The long dash in the third stanza reveals to the reader that the narrator actually does not have an immediate clear reason as to why he killed the man. The dash points to his hesitation and that he has to come up with an answer that hardly seems satisfactory. The dashes in the fourth stanza demonstrate that the narrator is actually thinking about the man he killed, groping for understanding this foe, comparing the foe to himself, and methodically coming to terms with how that soldier had joined the war just as he had. The dashes show a level of rumination and contemplation by the soldier previously unexplored.

Day 42

Here is a possible response:

The variations in the consonance are consistent with the poem's multiplicities. The uses of the *f*s and the *l*s offer a lilting softness often interrupted by the more thudding sounds of the *d*s, *p*s, and *t*s. The density of the consonance allows the sounds and images to pile atop each other (especially with all the compound words), so that they become as overabundant and diverse as nature itself. All the activity of the stanza is buttressed by the sounds from the consonance, as if the words are as much God's creations as the very marvels they describe.

Day 43

1. C Consonance is prominent in Hughes' use of "l."

2. A This world-weary mood is signified by diction such as "drowsy," "mellow," "dull," "lazy sway," "sad raggy," and "melancholy."

3. E While imagery and assonance are throughout the excerpt, repetition occurs with "blues" and "he did lazy sway" and onomatopoeia occurs with "moan."

4. A The last two lines from the poem's excerpt explain this outlook.

Day 44

Here is an example of a response:

The opening phrase, "droning a drowsy" with its long "o" sounds, establishes the deliberate pace of the poem. Words with elongated vowel sounds like "croon," "tune," "blues," and "moan" assure that the lines will continue to mosey along in slow rhythms, especially since many of them land on the rhyme. In addition, Hughes presents lines that practically force the reader to take his time. With its ellipses and its repetition, the line "He did a lazy sway. . . ." encourages the reader to keep time with the performer. Even vowel sounds that are not conventionally long can stretch out pronunciations in lines like, "By the pale dull pallor of an old gas light." Finally, the rhymes preceding the performer's song are particularly drawn out, starting with "stool" and "fool" and concluding with "tone" and "moan." The pacing developed through assonance contributes mightily to the poem's melancholy mood.

Day 45

Here is a sample response:

Frost's comparing the snow to the news of a day allows the reader to see the larger possibilities in the poem. The snow and the newsprint have stories to tell, yet they ultimately serve as allegories of not what we hold on to in life, but let pass by. The way the narrator questions whether he has forgotten or ever learned about that "news" signals he seems overwhelmed by the blizzard of information that has blown by him over the years. The patch of snow comes to represent all those days when the major events of the world have passed and we have hardly noticed. Sure, some days we pay attention better than others, like those days of a war, an economic collapse, a plane crash, or a presidential election. But like the patch of snow that represents the larger snowfall of previous days, we've either hardly noticed or have forgotten what proceeded on those days. Ultimately, the poem becomes about those dirty remnants that are reminders of what has passed across the days of our lives, but will ultimately melt from our memories.

Day 46

Here is one possible response:

Through hyperbole, Coleridge is able to reinforce an emotional tone that almost sounds desperate. The narrator speaks in extremes, signaling her instability and her desire to send a message of urgency to the reader. Hyperbole also contextualizes the narrator's experiences as she has clearly been haunted by her memories for quite some time. Her suffering is continual and leaves her in a frazzled state. The use of hyperbole makes her amended response to memory in the second stanza both surprising and one fitting for her overall outlook. She may be regularly wounded by these memories, but she also indulges in them, which may well be why she cannot rid herself of them.

Day 47

1. **D** The poem is without traditional meter: it has neither blank verse (unrhymed iambic pentameter) nor terza rima (verses arranged in triplets) nor heroic couplets (rhyming pairs of iambic pentameter) nor ballad meter (four-line stanzas, usually with an abcb rhyme scheme).

2. **C** From line 4: "And its look, rude, unbending, lusty, made me think of myself." He contrasts his outlook on companionship with the loneliness of the tree.

3. **B** All of the other verbs refer directly to the tree while "hung" refers to the moss dangling from the branches.

4. **B** The narrator oddly associates the tree with "manly love." This is odd because the tree achieves its joy without companionship. This isolation seems unthinkable in his human interactions.

Day 48

Here is one possible response:

All three stanzas begin and end with the words "I know" and speak of "the caged bird." The repetition of the opening and closing lines (with minor alterations) of each stanza gives the poem a choral refrain to echo the song the caged bird sings in the final stanza. The progression of the bird's outlook through this repetition (from feeling to beating to singing) demonstrates the coping mechanisms of the imprisoned and explains the turn to prayer in the third stanza as a last hope. Finally, the use of exclamation points to punctuate the end of each stanza (and the beginning of stanzas one and three) reveals that singing out functions as both a lamentation and a passionate appeal.

Day 49

1. **C** Cause/effect is the primary organizational pattern of this poem. The first stanza compares the dark thoughts to thunderstorms and the negative results of these thunderstorms. The second stanza, however, describes the opposite results of these thunderstorms. The poem contains no examples of any of the other choices.

2. **B** The imagery in the poem is created primarily with the use of metaphor. Thoughts are compared to thunderstorms (lines 1, 6), rain (line 3–8), flowers (lines 4–9), and birds (line 5, 10). The poem contains no examples of any of the other choices.

Day 50

1. The shift in the development of the poem occurs in **line 6**: "Yet come, dark thunderstorms." Here, the poet no longer describes the dark results, but actually invites these "thunderstorms," these dark thoughts into his mind.

2. Here is one example of a compound sentence using the shift cited in question 1 as the connecting feature:

   My desperate, silent, dark thoughts last for hours, yet I still welcome them because they often lead to positive results.

How does yours compare to the one above? Have you indicated the shift with *yet*, *but*, *however*, or *nevertheless* to indicate moving from negative to positive?

Day 51

1. **D** The opening line signals this dappled nature of I, while II is explored in the colorful, varied, and abundant assortment. The diction in the first stanza does not give the reader any impression of fear.

2. **B** While personification is an incredibly common literary technique, in this passage cataloging (listing), assonance (repetition of vowel sounds), simile (line 2), and consonance (repetition of consonant sounds) reign.

3. **E** All three are literary techniques that mark the poem and enhance its meaning.

4. **A** While in Hopkins's vision God is the creator of these dappled things, he is not described as one.

5. B Wonder is expressed throughout. While prayer is an appropriate answer, the narrator is by no means silent about his praise.

Day 52

1. A. Enjambment can be found in lines 3–4, 9–10.

   B. Similes are located in lines 2 and 5.

   C. Lines 3 and 11 contain examples of caesura.

   D. Alliteration is used in lines 3, 4, 5, 6, 7, 9, and 12.

   E. Line 2 contains an example of internal rhyme.

Note: If this activity caused you trouble, make certain to review these poetic devises in Chapter 9 or the Glossary in the main text.

2. E The narrator of the poem can best be described as **reflective and ambivalent**. One of the major clues is the use of past tense throughout the poem. Another is the last line of the poem: "I longed to forgive them but they never smiled." None of the pairs of describers is supported by the text.

3. However you constructed the statement of the poem's theme, you should have included at least one of the following ideas:
* protective love of parents for their child
* ambivalence toward parents
* bullying

Day 53

1. A conceit is the term for an extended metaphor.

2. "Sauce," "stomach," "digest," and "appetite" develop the conceit about rudeness.

3. The speaker is **perceptive and has great facility with imagery and diction**.

4. The subject is **clever, devious, and manipulative**.

There is always leeway in literary interpretation, but you must be able to support your answers with evidence from the work.

Day 54

1. The poem's rhyme scheme is **a, b, a, a, b, c, b, c, b**.

2. The shift in the poem occurs in line **5** with the word **But**.

3. Frost associates fire with desire in lines **3 and 4**.

4. Frost associates ice with hate in lines **6 and 7**.

5. Here's one way of identifying the position of the poet on the destruction of the world:

Desire and hate both have an equal ability to destroy the world.

Day 55

1. The subject of the sonnet is: Sad remembrances of things lost in the past are forgotten when good friends are remembered.

2. The first cause is indicated in **lines 1–2**.

   Lines 3–4 contain the second cause.

   The first effect is described in **lines 5–8**.

   The second effect is given in **lines 9–12**.

   Line 13 presents the third/final cause.

   The final effect is found in **line 13**.

3. The shift in the poem occurs in line **13** with the word **But**.

4. The narrator is **complimentary** toward the speaker's "**dear friend**."

Day 56

1. **D** The contrast with words like "active" and the connection to words like "lame" offer contextual clues.

2. **B** As opposed to the "youth" described on the previous line

3. **C** From line 5: affluence ("wealth"), cleverness ("wit"), attractiveness ("beauty"), and lineage ("birth")

4. **B** The narrator is taking "all my comfort" (line 4) in the many attributes the youth possesses and is filled with "delight" (line 1) by them.

5. **A** In addition to "crowned," "entitled" suggests the idea of aristocratic titles.

Day 57

6. **D** With the "store" serving as a collection of the youth's fine qualities, the narrator grafts (attaches) himself to these aspects.

7. **B** The "beauty, birth, or wealth, or wit" offers a clear counterweight.

8. **D** The "substance" in line 10 and the "live" in line 12 are central to this interpretation.

9. **B** The diction of "delight" (line 1), "abundance" (line 11), and "glory" (line 12) help form this understanding.

10. **A** The delight the narrator takes in the subject's youthful deeds and drawing on the youth's shadow for substance points to this vicarious indulgence.

Day 58

1. **B** The eyes view "things" of little importance compared with the hours of sleep.

2. **D** The antecedent is "mine eyes" in line 1.

3. **C** Much of the poem's language is characterized by antithesis and paradox.

4. B The narrator sees these images in his dreams.

5. A In the poem "thou" has such a strong presence that the shadow's shadow gives off light.

Day 59

6. B As noted in line 3 and confirmed in the "unseeing eyes" in line 8, and further confirmed in line 12.

7. B The idea is first hinted in line 1 ("when most I wink"), then line 3 ("when I sleep, in dreams . . ."), followed by the discussion of shadows and the contrasts to day.

8. A As indicated by the remainder of line 13 and line 14.

9. C While indicated throughout the sonnet, Shakespeare emphasizes the topsy-turvy quality of day and night reversing themselves.

10. A The first eight lines describe the narrator's bright dreams at night of the individual in contrast to his duller days while the last six lines recapitulate those visions, offering a personal expression of the narrator's hopes.

11. D The contradictory language of lines 4–5, 8, 12, and 13–14 in particular drive home this point.

Day 60

1. Considering the rhyme and form, the poem is an example of a sonnet.

2. The poem breaks in form and meaning into two sections. The first is called an octave.

3. The second section is known as a sestet.

4. The organization indicates that the poem is developed by comparison and contrast.

Day 61

1. The central metaphor of the poem is **the world compared to a circus**.

2. In the middle of its performance, the circus's tent top blows off leaving the audience staring up at nothing but the black sky.

3. One way to state the actual subject of the poem is: **war and the result of war**.

Day 62

4. Given the answers to questions 1, 2, and 3, presented in the previous day's activities, you can infer that the poet's attitude toward the subject is **dark and disillusioned**.

5. Here is an example of a thesis statement that addresses the prompt: **Written directly after World War I, "The End of the World" by Archibald MacLeish presents a dystopian world that is destroyed as its inhabitants look on.**

Day 63

1. The given title and subject of this poem is "**Sonnet**."

2. The audience laughs when Billy Collins reads **lines 1, 6–8, 13, and 14**.

3. The most likely causes of this laughter are the poet's **seemingly casual attitude toward what always appears to be a serious subject; the unexpected comparison/ metaphor; or the unexpected treatment of one of the "fathers" of the sonnet**.

4. The poet's attitude is light-hearted, nonchalant.

5. The comment being made about this subject is: **Don't take this stuff so seriously. Have a little fun with it *and* life**.

6. Given the diction, tone, and imagery, the reader can conclude that the intent of this poem is **satirical**. Collins uses humor to poke fun at the way English experts take poetry and the sonnet in particular so seriously. "Sonnet" is an example of Horatian satire that gently criticizes.

Day 64

1. The antecedent of line 3 is the subject, **sleep**.

2. **C** There is no rhyme scheme in this passage.

3. **E** Sleep is compared to a knitter, death, a bath, balm, and food.

Day 65

1. In the first stanza, God is the **creator/inventor. [lines 1–2]** This action is simple and direct. **[lines 2–4]**

2. In the second stanza, humankind is **the destroyer. [lines 5-6]** This is because humankind is **always questioning and asking why. [lines 6-8]**

3. Here is one example of the first draft of a thesis statement that addresses the prompt:

   In the two brief stanzas of "When God Decided to Invent," e.e. cummings delves deep into the old adage that states, "God creates and man destroys."

It would also be possible to address this prompt with the thought of simplicity versus complexity. The prompt also could have been designed to ask the reader how the poem relates to the world today. There are many possibilities.

Day 66

1. **B** "I Wandered Lonely as a Cloud" can be classified as a **lyric** poem. (Remember, a lyric poem expresses the personal thoughts and feelings of the poet or the poem's narrator.)

2. The subject of the central metaphor from lines 3–14 is **a field of daffodils**.

3. Following the logic of the central metaphor, lines 13–14 compare **grass** to "sparkling waves."

4. The narrator/poet experiences this "vision" of a field of daffodils **when alone and relaxed in a reclining position**.

5. The response to question 4 is supported in **lines 1–2 and the entire last stanza**.

Day 67

1. Two examples of imagery that appeal to the sense of **sight** are:

   - **blue waves whitened on a rock (line 3)**
   - **children's faces looking up and holding wonder like a cup (lines 5–6)**

2. Two examples of imagery that appeal to the sense of **hearing** are:

   - **the soaring fire that sways and sings (line 4)**
   - **music like a curve of gold (line 8)**

3. One example of imagery that appeals to the sense of **smell** is:

   - **the scent of pine trees in the rain (line 9)**

Day 68

1. This introduction would be rated **weak**.

2. The introduction **does not** have real thesis statement. There is no real attempt on the part of the writer to make a claim about the poem. It does not provide the full name of the poet or the title of the poem. It only focuses on the literary devices.

3. Here is one example of a revised introduction:

   In her poem "Love Is Not All," Edna St. Vincent Millay examines her conflicting attitude toward love and the one she loves. She develops this examination in a sonnet using literary devices such as metaphor, anaphora, and irony.

Day 69

1. The contrasting points of view described in the poem are **between the perceived ideal life and the lot of those who do not feel privileged**.

2. Highlighting a line or image in each stanza that is critical to the meaning or that moves you is quite personal, but you should have included some of these details:

   Lines 2 and 3

   Lines 7 and 8

   Lines 9 and 12

   Lines 13, 14, 15, and 16

Day 70

3. **Repetition is a tool for emphasis and to reinforce the reader's understanding of theme and character**. In addition, "always" implies that Richard Cory is infallible.

4. In the second stanza, "Good-morning," gives a voice to Richard Cory and personalizes the poem by making it seem as if the reader is being spoken to directly.

5. In stanza three, the caesura, a break in the flow of a line generally achieved by punctuation, **serves to force the reader to concentrate on the isolated thought or image set apart. Here, it stresses one reason for the speaker's envy.**

6. The image, "one calm summer night" **heightens the irony of the poem by establishing a peaceful and warm setting that contrasts with the unexpected violence to come.**

Day 71

1. Wolsey pauses with this dash; his comment about the little good reveals a bitterness. The question mark indicates he is ruminative and contemplative about his fate. The exclamation mark points to his excited emotional state.

2. For whichever cases of "you," Wolsey reflects a sense of betrayal by those about him.

3. Wolsey might be mocking either himself or the kingdom he helped manage. More likely, he repeats "farewell" because he is struggling to absorb what's happening to him.

4. Wolsey must be wondering how great he was, since he did fall, or whether he was ever great at all. The meaning of "greatness" could be in terms of magnitude (size of his job) or of his ability (how well he functioned in that capacity).

5. By talking about the state of man in general, Wolsey can consider his fate more philosophically, distancing the loss from himself.

6. He compares his growth to vegetation, positioning his rise as a natural occurrence. The word "tender" is often used in vegetation to describe its early/young ripeness; but as the term suggests, "tender" also indicates how delicate and precarious this growth can be.

7. His rise could well have come as quickly as his fall.

8. The word "bears" could be used to mean "to carry or to be a burden"; in addition, its homonym "bares" could be used to mean "to expose or reveal."

9. The honors may have come so quickly that he didn't know how to accept them comfortably, or perhaps, he wasn't sure he deserved them.

Day 72

10. The third day in Christian terms could allude to both Christ's death and his resurrection.

11. "Frost" may have been repeated to specify that the rough conditions were not something either the vegetation or Wolsey could weather—that frost would prove fatal.

12. "Easy" could describe simple and comfortable; it could also describe being in a relaxed state, as in at ease, perhaps being lulled into a false sense of security.

13. "Greatness" here seems to speak to an overconfidence: Wolsey had begun to so believe in his power and position that he was not aware of how vulnerable he really was. In the ruminative tone, intimations of self-criticism emerge.

14. The return to *I* makes clear that any point of comparison or use of metaphor is for the sole purpose of Wolsey making sense of what has happened to him.

Day 73

15. The word *wanton* is generally connected to cruel, impulsive acts, so the simile compares Wolsey to those who commit rash, wayward acts. He seems now to be filled with regret.

16. Those summers hint to Wolsey in his prime and the many pleasures he gained from these experiences.

17. Each conceit draws on nature in the comparison, connecting those primal forces with those inside of Wolsey. The former conceit does not contain the inherent criticism found in this comparison here.

18. As Wolsey continues to ruminate, the tone shifts to one more of rueful regret; his admission (that he was "far beyond my depth") indicates he is only now aware of how in over his head he has been.

19. Through these conceits, Wolsey has come to face that fact that he had inflated his ego to such an extent he had not taken precaution that would have either prevented his downfall or at least protected him more.

20. Wolsey has removed all artifice—all metaphor—from his language. He is now willing to talk directly about his current state. Those conceits seemed to have allowed him to build up the courage to rediscover a clarity of mind so that he can baldly examine his fate.

21. The use of "mercy" could be considered ironic, since there will be no mercy in the rude stream. The term *mercy* has often been used when an individual is begging for his life. The religious aspect of mercy might be only invoked to indicate any better fate than the miserable one awaiting Wolsey would be miraculous.

22. This "rude stream" is the lowest of channels, far removed from the "sea of glory." "Rude" could be defined here as "gross and insulting." The "rude stream" could well be the gutter, straits of running wastes into which chamber pots are emptied.

23. Wolsey seems destined for obscurity. In a secondary meaning of the word, "hide" can also mean "to be beaten up," which certainly relates to Wolsey's present state.

Day 74

24. "Vain" can refer both to the ego (the high-blown of a few lines earlier) and to futility, since all his efforts now will lead to nothing.

25. No, the "pomp and glory" in his new view are shallow, overwrought illusions; something Wolsey chased that truly had no value.

26. The "ye" in this line could be the king, the public, or a specific individual who has brought him down. The absence of his naming the "ye" has the effect of revealing Wolsey's current state as dark and misanthropic. This exclamation appears to have been building up over the course of the soliloquy.

27. Normally, an open heart would indicate a connection either to love or to see the best in others. Here Wolsey's heart newly opened suggests a wound, and a bad one at that.

28. The exclamative "O" serves a lamentation, a howl of pain and suffering, characterizing his intense emotional state.

29. By using "that poor man," Wolsey links himself to a long line of ambitious, clever men who have served princes and then been cast aside.

30. "Hangs" can suggest that a man can be left dangling in his position at the whim of a king; more morosely, it can also mean he's destined for the scaffold with a noose around his neck.

31. The princes' "favors" could mean both their preferences and their regard. In either case, the "poor man" is in quite a precarious position. The exclamation point drives home the harrowing nature of the situation.

Day 75

32. Wolsey now realizes that the sweetness of the prince is ephemeral, like the blossoms before. More disturbingly, that sweetness is quite fickle, less the result of the natural course of growth, than the traps of the capriciousness of royalty.

33. Wolsey sees his fall as a matter of life and death, like those of war, and, like those of love and women, the loss is deeply personal and heart-wrenching. The gamut between a prince's sweet favor and ruin is vexing and the end of its run torments him. These comparisons paradoxically elevate Wolsey's standing while humiliating him in his fall.

34. The comparison to Lucifer raises Wolsey to a formidable state; Lucifer, after all, was God's brightest angel. However, any comparison to Lucifer has its darker side, since the fallen angel was mistaken, misguided, and evil.

35. The sign at the gates of hell in Dante's *Inferno* reads: "Abandon all hope, ye who enter here." Wolsey's allusion to Dante indicates that he is hell bound (as does his reference to Lucifer), and his utter hopelessness reinforces how dramatically he has fallen.

Day 76

1. The rhyme scheme is **aa, bb, cc, dd, ee, ff, gg, hh, ii**.

2. The 18 lines of paired rhyming lines of iambic pentameter are classified as **an heroic couplet**.

3. The two subjects of the two stanzas are **writers and critics**.

4. The major point made about the two subjects in this section of the poem is: **There are pros and cons about each, so who is to say who is the better of the two.**

Day 77

1. The rhyme scheme of the poem is: **abab, cdcd, efef, gg.**

2. The poem comprises **three separate sections of four lines** and **two linked lines**

   Each stanza of four lines is called a quatrain.
   The two linked lines are known as a couplet.

3. The rhyme scheme indicates the poem is a **sonnet.**

Day 78

1. **A** The gray winter day and its sky are depicted.

2. **D** As evidenced by "corpse," "crypt," and "death's lament"

3. **C** Frail describes the nature of the bird rather than its song.

4. **B** The narrator has encountered a hope of which he had previously not known.

5. **A** The weather and the thrush are presented as constants; the thrush's song alters the mood.

Day 79

Here is an example of a response:

   The first two stanzas are fraught with depressing images of dull, dim brokenness that descends by second stanza into a deathly ghostliness. Those images have rendered everyone and everything desolate, including the narrator who is "fervorless." The third stanza contains remnants of the pessimistic vision of the earlier stanzas ("frail, gaunt, and small" and "growing gloom") even as the "joy illimited" of the thrush's song begins to elevate the outlook. The final stanza with the thrush's "ecstatic sound" and his "happy good-night air" summons up such hope that the narrator has been marked by it.

Day 80

1. **D** This definition is confirmed by the line "And home we brought you shoulder-high."

2. **D** While the irony and juxtaposition of the athlete first lifted as a conquering hero and later being hoisted in his coffin are evident, the stanza offers no hint of exaggeration, especially given the poem's moderate tone.

3. **C** The acknowledgment that the laurel, traditionally worn by victors, withers quickly and the line "glory does not stay" drive home this point.

4. **A** The "We" in the second line indicates the narrator is part of the community.

Day 81

5. **A** The athlete does not have to watch his record beaten or hear silence replace cheers.

6. **B** The reference is to the dead body in the ground.

7. E The idea of renown outrunning runners is paradoxical; the multiple uses of "r" and "n" imbue the passage with consonance; and renown is personified as a runner.

8. E This notion is confirmed by the comment "the name died before the man."

Day 82

1. The narrator personalizes nature by calling it "her," and the use of lowercase letters indicates an intimacy and friendliness he has with her. If he capitalized "her," he would be conferring unto nature a God-like distance.

2. The small size of the boat adds to the sense of comfort the narrator seems to have with nature; he follows nature in a vessel designed to leave as small of a trail as possible in nature—it's just a personal extension of himself. He seems to have no concern about having a larger boat for his protection.

3. The narrator is releasing both the boat and himself from the chains of society to enter more deeply and fully into the natural world.

4. The shore represents here a safer place, one on the edges of nature. When the narrator pushes off, he is immersing himself in nature on a profound level.

Day 83

5. The contradictory phrase indicates that while the narrator is enjoying his quest, he is taking a risk and has some unease about entering into unknown territory.

6. The narrator demonstrates his determination and commitment to go on this journey.

7. The narrator has set his sights ambitiously, perhaps well beyond any place he's heretofore ventured.

8. The narrator's actions are shot through with desire. He is excited by the possibilities that are before him and embraces his own animalistic tendencies in the context of nature.

Day 84

9. The repetition of the nature of the peak marks a narrator absorbing its wonder, and the repetition of his response indicates how his mind returns to consider and reconsider what he is encountering.

10. Already awed by nature, the narrator is overwhelmed by scope and scale of "the grim shape."

11. The huge peak appears to have a life of its own, which makes it simultaneously more majestic and menacing. The word "measured" intimates that the peak gives the impression that it is a thoughtful, contemplative creature.

12. The oars appear to be trembling as a reflection of the narrator's newfound anxiety. The description subtly transfers the observer's emotions onto the vessel ushering him through the journey. The narrator is discovering that the risk of his daring journey has reared his head, similar to the way the huge peak has come into view.

Day 85

13. The narrator's playful journey has turned dark and serious. Ultimately, "grave" is a timely reminder that for all the wonders of nature, it is also a scary, deadly environment.

14. The narrator is struggling to figure out how to integrate this phenomenon with his previous understanding of nature. The diction in this passage shows his confusion and how much the experience has shaken his views.

15. The experience has clearly clouded and shrouded the narrator's outlook. The word "hung" would most likely mean "draped over" in this context, but the vision of the narrator feeling constricted (like a noose around a neck) by this new awareness is also applicable.

16. The blankness is confirmed from the subsequent no's, wiping away all of the narrator's usually comforting images of nature.

Day 86

17. While the narrator's view toward the "huge and mighty forms" is conflicted, it is clearly negative compared to how positively predisposed he was to nature as he initiated his journey. These forms present a new and disturbing factor that the narrator must integrate into his perception of nature, and, for the reader, they serve as the impetus behind the narrator's altered viewpoint.

18. Because these "huge and mighty forms" are not easy for the narrator to connect to human life forces, he finds himself turning over their presence repeatedly, so much so that they are lingering and disruptive visions.

Summative Analysis

Sample:

Wordsworth's narrator of the excerpt from *The Prelude* undertakes a risky venture deep into the heart of nature only to discover it is more awe-inspiring, intimidating, and haunting than he had previously imagined. By grabbing a little boat from a cave, the narrator seems to be involved in secretive and illicit activities, considering his "act of stealth and troubled pleasure." Given his rowing with unswerving line, he shows himself determined to penetrate nature's secrets.

However, as he rows farther away from civilization, the diction turns increasingly oppressive, from "heaving" to the huge, black peak to the "grim shape." As he retreats from his explorations, the narrator's contemplations become increasingly somber: his playful impression of colorful, serene nature has been tainted by the realization that more menacing forces lurk there too.

Day 87

There is no one way to respond to the given questions; however, your responses should keep a couple of ideas in mind.

1. The subject of the poem is the **narrator's parents and the boys they tried to keep him away from**.

2. The attitude of the narrator toward his subject(s) is **ambivalent—a mixture of love and possible resentment for the parents plus fear and envy for the "boys."**

3. Here is one example of a preliminary thesis statement that responds to the prompt: **Stephen Spender utilizes a variety of poetic devices to develop the narrator's ambivalence toward his parents and the "rough boys" in "My Parents."**

Day 88

1. C The calm sea, the full tide, and the fair moon signal this tranquility.

2. C The narrator calls another (perhaps the reader, perhaps—as indicated later in the poem—his beloved) to come to the window.

3. D "Only" serves as a transition word to the serpentine sentence that ends with bringing the eternal note of sadness in.

4. D While I and II are direct commands (imperatives), III merely describes.

5. B The allusion to Sophocles explains how the sadness belongs to a larger historical continuum.

Day 89

6. A Apostrophe (a figure of speech in which the poet directly addresses an absent person, an abstract idea, or a thing) is not present.

7. C Conventionally, the word "drear" would immediately precede "edges" and would be in the form "dreary."

8. A The sea of faith is what the narrator describes as withdrawing.

9. B The armies are both ignorant and are fighting at night.

10. D The turbulent forces are signaled by "confused alarms" and "ignorant armies" while the loss of religious faith is delineated in the poem's third stanza (the first stanza of the second half of the poem).

Day 90

Here is one possible response:

The allusion to Greek civilization connects the moment at Dover Beach to a high point in world culture. As such, Arnold indicates that even in the best of times, this eternal note of sadness exists and has been part of mankind throughout his existence. By recognizing that an important artist like Sophocles heard this sadness, the poet indicates that individuals might have to listen carefully to identify it. Furthermore, in relating the Aegean to "this distant northern sea," Arnold has drawn his own British civilization into this loftier context. Such suffering is cyclical ("the turbid ebb and flow of human misery"), but in those rhythms is a confirmation of its role in a larger continuum. This allusion will ultimately be contextualized with the conceit "Sea of Faith," which leads to the next exercise.

Day 91

Here is one possible response:

Like the sea at high tide, faith once dominated the shoreline, serving as a powerful and vital force. The simile inside the conceit ("earth's shore/Lay like the folds of a bright girdle furled") bolsters this view. But the tide is now withdrawing, and the implication is that faith has retreated and its power has ebbed. But the images that close the stanza are more ominous, of "vast edges drear" and "naked shingles." The state of faith has become dire indeed.

Day 92

Here is an example of the annotated prompt:

> In the following scene from *Henry V*, we find **King Henry in the English encampment on the night before the battle of Agincourt. Facing an adversary that is in better condition and that outnumbers his,** Henry wishes "no other company," and **asks to be left alone to "debate" with himself.** Read the soliloquy carefully. Then, in a well-developed essay **analyze how Shakespeare uses literary techniques/devices to convey Henry's attitude toward leadership/kingship.**

This is one of those prompts where almost every section is important. What you should be very aware of is:

- This is Shakespeare.
- Henry V wants to be alone to think about the upcoming battle.
- The writer is required to *analyze* (not describe; not argue for or against his ideas)
- The writer is required to identify Henry's attitude toward being a leader/king.
- The writer needs to locate literary devices/techniques and discuss *how* that leads the reader to conclusions about Henry's attitude.

Day 93

Now that you've carefully read and annotated the prompt, you are ready to read the text with the demands of the prompt in mind:

- Read as if you are reading the text out loud to an audience.
- Read with a pen or pencil ready in hand.
- Now, listen to Samuel West deliver the soliloquy on **YouTube: https://www.youtube.com/watch?v=USQvp7skuTY**
- As you read and listen, remember you are trying to find out what is King Henry's attitude toward kingship.
- When you've completed reading and listening to the text, move on to the next activity.

Day 94

Here are several inferences/conclusions that you could have made about Henry's attitude toward kingship:

- Kingship is a burden. (lines 6–13)
- Kings may have ceremony, but at what cost? (lines 14–25)
- Ceremony's flattery is like a poison. (lines 26–29)
- Ceremony is not what it is cracked up to be. (lines 30–41)
- In all but ceremony, the peasant/ordinary citizen is better off than the king. (lines 43–60)

Day 95

Your best choice is 4.

In his soliloquy in Act IV, Scene 1, King Henry V sees the pomp, ceremony, and power of a king as much less a privilege than it is a burden that the ordinary citizen will never know.

Even though each of the other choices identifies the speaker and an attitude or characteristic, none of these other four statements presents the needed specifics related to the prompt.

- Number 1 only offers the name Henry V and the single idea that kingship is a burden.
- Number 2 does not present an attitude of Henry V toward kingship.
- Number 3 is a misreading of the soliloquy.
- Number 5 mistakenly presents happiness as the subject of the soliloquy.

Day 96

Here are the major points we could develop in support of our thesis: *In his soliloquy in Act IV, Scene 1, King Henry V sees the pomp, ceremony, and power of a king as much less a privilege than it is a burden that the ordinary citizen will never know.*

- Kingship is a burden.
- Ceremony is not all that it seems.
- In almost every aspect, the ordinary citizen is better off than the king.

How does your list compare to ours? Are your major points specifically related to both your thesis statement and the prompt?

Day 97

KING HENRY V, Act IV, Scene 1 (The night before the battle of Agincourt with the French)

Indeed, the French may lay twenty French crowns to
one, they will beat us; for they bear them on their
shoulders: but it is no English treason to cut
French crowns, and to-morrow the king himself will
be a clipper.　　　　　　　　　　　　　　　　　　　　　5

Exeunt soldiers

Upon the king! let us our lives, our souls,
Our debts, our careful wives,
Our children and our sins lay on the king!
We must bear all. O hard condition,
Twin-born with greatness, subject to the breath　　　10
Of every fool, whose sense no more can feel But
his own wringing! What infinite heart's-ease
Must kings neglect, that private men enjoy! And
what have kings, that privates have not too,
Save ceremony, save general ceremony?　　　　　　15
And what art thou, thou idle ceremony?
What kind of god art thou, that suffer'st more
Of mortal griefs than do thy worshippers?
What are thy rents? what are thy comings in?
O ceremony, show me but thy worth!　　　　　　　20
What is thy soul of adoration?
Art thou aught else but place, degree and form,
Creating awe and fear in other men?
Wherein thou art less happy being fear'd
Than they in fearing.　　　　　　　　　　　　　　25
What drink'st thou oft, instead of homage sweet,
But poison'd flattery? O, be sick, great greatness,
And bid thy ceremony give thee cure!
Think'st thou the fiery fever will go out
With titles blown from adulation?　　　　　　　　30
Will it give place to flexure and low bending?
Canst thou, when thou command'st the beggar's knee,
Command the health of it? No, thou proud dream,
That play'st so subtly with a king's repose;
I am a king that find thee, and I know　　　　　35
'Tis not the balm, the sceptre and the ball,
The sword, the mace, the crown imperial,
The intertissued robe of gold and pearl,
The farced[1] title running 'fore the king,
The throne he sits on, nor the tide of pomp　　　40
That beats upon the high shore of this world,
No, not all these, thrice-gorgeous ceremony,

Not all these, laid in bed majestical,
Can sleep so soundly as the wretched slave,
Who with a body fill'd and vacant mind   45
Gets him to rest, cramm'd with distressful bread;
Never sees horrid night, the child of hell,
But, like a lackey², from the rise to set
Sweats in the eye of Phoebus³ and all night
Sleeps in Elysium⁴; next day after dawn,   50
Doth rise and help Hyperion⁵ to his horse,
And follows so the ever-running year,
With profitable labour, to his grave:
And, but for ceremony, such a wretch,
Winding up days with toil and nights with sleep,   55
Had the fore-hand and vantage of a king.
The slave, a member of the country's peace,
Enjoys it; but in gross brain little wots⁶
What watch the king keeps to maintain the peace,
Whose hours the peasant best advantages.   60

---

¹stuffed
²a foot soldier or servant
³Greek god Apollo
⁴home of the blessed after they die
⁵Greek god Helios, god of the sun
⁶thoughts

In the margins of the text, you could also have noted specific literary devices or major points you wanted to use in support of your thesis. Create any shorthand or symbols that make sense to you and make it easy for you to annotate the text.

Day 98

Here are our examples/details that could be used to support the previously listed major points.

Kingship is a burden:

(Lines 6–13) Listing of what is laid on the shoulders of the king (lines 6–9) metaphor "O hard condition" (lines 9–12) That is subject to the breath of every fool. Cannot enjoy what private men enjoy.

Ceremony is not what it seems:

(lines 15–42) personification and accusation, name-calling, questioning, prosecution Metaphor (lines 40–41) tide of pomp

Peasant better off than the king:

(lines 44–60) allusion to Phoebus, Hyperion, Elysium Fields (lines 48–51) Metaphor child of hell re: night (line 47)

For your own listing, have you made it clear to which major point each example/detail refers? Have you cited the line(s) in which the example/detail is found? If needed, have you identified the type of literary device of the example/detail?

Day 99

The sentence that BEST addresses an example/detail from Henry V's soliloquy in Act IV, Scene 1 is:

2. The personification of "ceremony" (lines 15–42) allows Henry to internally debate the pros and cons of the power, admiration, and wealth of being king.

In this sentence, personification of "ceremony" is what Henry *says*. The internal debate that this personification instigates is what it *does*. It is the *what* and the *why*.

Sentence 1 only identifies a specific example of personification. Sentence 3 identifies and describes the personification example. It does not signal the purpose or result of its use.

Day 100

Your deconstruction could look something like this:

> The following passage is from the **novel, *A Room with a View*, by E. M. Forster** (1908). At the beginning of the first chapter, **Lucy Honeychurch and Miss Charlotte Bartlett are traveling together and arrive at their hotel in Florence, Italy**.
>
> Read the passage carefully. Then write a **well-developed essay** in which you **analyze how Forster portrays these two characters** and **their relationship with one another and with the world around them**.
>
> You may wish to consider such literary devices as **selection of detail**, **language**, and **tone**.

If you've allowed yourself three to five minutes to consider the prompt and what it requires, you know that as you read the given text, you will keep the following in mind:

- The title and author
- This is the first chapter of the novel
- The portrayal of the two characters
- How they interact with each other
- How they interact with their surroundings

Day 101

1. G

2. C

3. E

4. F

5. H

Day 102

The following is a general guide to character analysis. Refer to this and your list often and you will always have a starting point to focus your reading and interpretation.

Add to this list throughout your studies.

- What he says when alone or with others
- What he does when alone or with others
- What he thinks when alone or with others
- What others say with, to, or about him
- What others do with, to, or about him
- What others think with, to, or about him
- His physical description
- His environment and setting

Day 103

from *To Kill a Mockingbird*

Maycomb was an **old town**, but it was a **tired old town** when I first knew it. . . . grass **grew through the sidewalks**, the **courthouse sagged** in the square. Somehow, it was **hotter then**: a **black dog suffered** on a summer's day; **bony mules flicked flies** in the **sweltering shade** of the live oaks. Men's stiff **collars wilted** by nine in the morning.

Your highlighting should include many of the details highlighted above.

> The narrator's diction, *old, tired, sagged, suffered, sweltered,* and *wilted,* create a tone of uncomfortable resignation as if awaiting something to relieve the monotony. The emphasis on the heat may foreshadow that the town is on the verge of reaching the boiling point.

Day 104

1. E

2. C

3. G

4. A

5. F

Day 105

1. Here is one example of the annotated passage:

> The **action of the entire play takes place in, and immediately outside of, the Cabot farmhouse in New England, in the year 1850.** The south end of the house faces front to a stone wall with a wooden gate at center opening on a country road. The house is in good condition but in need of paint. Its **walls are a sickly grayish**, the **green of the shutters faded.** Two **enormous elms are on each side of the house.** They bend their trailing branches down over the roof. They appear to

5

protect and at the same time subdue. There is a **sinister maternity in their aspect, a crushing, jealous absorption**. . . . They are like **exhausted women** resting their sagging breasts and hands and hair on its roof, and when it rains their **tears** trickle down **monotonously** and **rot** on the shingles. (Metaphor) 10

2. The mood created in this passage is **somber**, **stifling**, **gloomy**, **decaying**.

3. The words/phrases that support this somber, gloomy mood are **"sickly grayish"** (line 5), **"shutters faded"** (line 6), **"sinister"** (line 8), **"crushing, jealous absorption"** (line 9), **"exhausted"** (line 9), **"tears"** (line 10), **"monotonously, rot"** (line 11).

4. Based on a close reading of the passage and the answers to the given questions, the tensions and theme of this drama will most probably be **negative.**

Day 106

1. The narrator's attitude toward the Thames could best be described as **reverent and proud**.

2. Here is an example of the annotated passage indicating the details that led to the response to question 1.

"And at last, in its curved and imperceptible fall, the sun sank low, and from glowing white changed to a dull red without rays and without heat, as if about to go out suddenly, stricken to death by the touch of that gloom brooding over a crowd of men.

Forthwith a change came over the waters, and the serenity became less brilliant 5 but more profound. The old river in its broad reach rested unruffled at the decline of day, after ages of good service done to the race that peopled its banks, spread out in the tranquil dignity of a waterway leading to the uttermost ends of the earth. We looked at the venerable stream not in the vivid flush of a short day that comes and departs for ever, but in the august light of abiding memories. 10 And indeed nothing is easier for a man who has, as the phrase goes, "followed the sea" with reverence and affection, that to evoke the great spirit of the past upon the lower reaches of the Thames. The tidal current runs to and fro in its unceasing service, crowded with memories of men and ships it had borne to the rest of home or to the battles of the sea. It had known and served all the 15 men of whom the nation is proud, from Sir Francis Drake to Sir John Franklin, knights all, titled and untitled—the great knights-errant of the sea. It had borne all the ships whose names are like jewels flashing in the night of time, from the Golden Hind returning with her rotund flanks full of treasure, to be visited by the Queen's Highness and thus pass out of the gigantic tale, to the Erebus 20 and Terror, bound on other conquests—and that never returned. It had known the ships and the men. They had sailed from Deptford, from Greenwich, from Erith—the adventurers and the settlers; kings' ships and the ships of men on 'Change; captains, admirals, the dark "interlopers" of the Eastern trade, and the commissioned "generals" of East India fleets. Hunters for gold or pursuers 25 of fame, they all had gone out on that stream, bearing the sword, and often the torch, messengers of the might within the land, bearers of a spark from the sacred fire. What greatness had not floated on the ebb of that river into the mystery of an unknown earth! . . . The dreams of men, the seed of commonwealths, the germs of empires."

3. The theme will most probably involve

    X   **a river**

    X   **exploration**

    X   **good vs. evil**

    X   **man vs. nature**

    X   **the ends justify the means**

Although Marlowe, religion, memories, business, and battles are mentioned in the passage, they are specific characters or specific illustrations of a general concept.

Day 107

1. D The mood created by the artist and director of *Waltz with Bashir* is one of **fear**. While examples of the other choices are present, only fear is the constant. Each of the other choices is really contributing to the creation of fear.

2. There are many details to choose from in the creation of the mood of fear. Here are a few specific examples:

- Dark color scheme

- Ominous music

- Large, dark dogs with yellow eyes; snarling, bared teeth; growling barks running wild in a pack

- People huddling together on the street as the dogs run past

- Food carts and carriages being knocked over

- Dog pack stopping and staring up at a window in a building that has a single man starring out

3. The expectations created by this nightmarish opening sequence could include:

- Something sinister will happen.

- The nightmare will continue.

- The man at the window is going to become part of this fearsome situation.

- The film could be about the horrors of war.

Day 108

1. The narrative will be told from the **first-person point of view**.

2. Haunted and cold could be used to describe the mood of the opening lines.

3. Here is an example of the annotated text:

I became what I am today at the age of twelve, on a **<u>frigid overcast day in the winter</u>** of 1975. I remember the precise moment, **<u>crouching behind a crumbling mud wall</u>**, peeking into the alley near the **<u>frozen creek</u>**. That was a long time ago, but it's wrong what they say about the past, I've learned, about **<u>how you can bury it</u>**. Because **<u>the past claws its way out</u>**. Looking back now, I realize **<u>I have been peeking into that deserted alley for the last twenty-six years</u>**.

4. The opening suggests that the story will involve the event that haunts him and how he resolves this tormenting conflict.

Day 109

1. D The third-person opening indicates that Mr. Oakhurst has encountered a new mood ("change," "exchanged significant glances," "looked ominous," and "these indications").

2. B As revealed through his demeanor ("calm" "reflected") and his awareness ("conscious of a change") as well as he observed the exchange of "significant glances" and "the Sabbath lull in the air."

3. A The men ceasing to speak as Mr. Oakhurst approaches is one indication. This outlook is confirmed from Mr. Oakhurst's comment that he reckons they are after somebody.

4. E The diction and descriptions ("change" and "ominous") and Mr. Oakhurst's concern about the two men establish the mood.

Day 110

1. B. All the figures, including the man to be hanged, are delineated, down to the sentries on the two sides of the bridge, as is the setting, from the platform to the swift water to the bridge.

2. D. The description directly applies to the cross timbers, which are central to this edifice of execution.

3. E. The comment that the "sergeant who in civil life may have been a deputy sheriff" intimates to the reader that the sergeant either had past experience in law enforcement or acted like he did.

4. D. That "these two men" don't seem to "know what was occurring at the center of the bridge" allows the narrator to let the reader into the preparation for a hanging even while some of the participants are unaware.

Day 111

1. A The descriptions of Emma ("rich, with a comfortable home and happy disposition") and the lack of authority from either father or governess confirm this view.

2. E Emma's friendliness is described throughout and the last paragraph points to her strong will ("doing just what she liked" and "directed chiefly by her own" judgment).

3. B The description of Mr. Woodhouse ("a most affectionate, indulgent father") fits all the other answers and is the opposite of *restricting*.

4. B Emma's upbringing, her personality, and her relationships with her father and governess are depicted.

Day 112

1. C The location, time period, and local awareness to the shop are incorporated.

2. E The references to the various cultural institutions address the former and the mentions of the "drooping horse-car" and the basking in sunsets point to the latter.

3. A The shop's inconspicuousness is reinforced by references to a "miscellaneous display," its size, and its shabbiness.

4. D The shop's local fame and that it was "intimately and favourably known" fly in the face of the incredibly low profile that the Bunner Sisters maintain.

Day 113

1. A The emotional nature of the passage and the depictions of John and the narrator render A the only possible choice.

2. B As evidenced by John's laughing at the narrator and his scoffing at phenomena the narrator considers valuable

3. E Unlike in most expository writing, parenthetical comments in creative works are often employed to reveal key aspects of a plot and character. Here Gilman indicates that the narrator is writing from an unreachable place.

4. D Beyond the content, the use of two exclamation points, four question marks, and two italics suggests a narrator intensely recounting her initial thoughts about her husband and the mansion.

Day 114

1. The speaker's attitude is **satiric and deprecating**. He presents his information matter-of-factly while ridiculing his subject.

2. Underline or highlight the details that develop this portrait.

> **Major Major** had been born **too late** and **too mediocre. Some men are born mediocre, some men achieve mediocrity,** and **some men have mediocrity thrust upon them**. With Major Major it had been all three. Even **among men lacking all distinction** he inevitably stood out as **a man lacking more distinction than all the rest,** and people who met him were **always impressed** by **how unimpressive he was**.

3. The **repetition of words and phrases creates contrasts** designed to point out Major Major's ridiculousness. In addition, the **unexpected mock-serious presentation reinforces the implied sarcasm**.

Day 115

1. The tone of the passage is **humorous and satiric**.

2. Three character traits of Mrs. Stossen include:

- Mrs. Stossen is **nosy and sneaky**. She deliberately trespassed when the family was absent.

- She is **devious and persistent** as evidenced by her elaborate and challenging route to the event.

- Her **sense of irony and understatement** are revealed in her final sentence.

    There are many other acceptable variations as well.

Day 116

Identify the specific diction that developed your analysis of each girl.

1. Jo: *won't be Christmas, without presents, grumbled*

2. Meg: *dreadful, poor, sighed, looking down, old dress*

3. Amy: *don't think it's fair, some girls have plenty, others nothing, injured sniff*

4. Beth: *got Father and Mother, each other, contentedly*

Day 117

5. Jo: **shallow, dissatisfied, complaining, self-pitying**

6. Meg: **self-pitying, ashamed, resigned**

7. Amy: **angry, jealous, self-absorbed**

8. Beth: **loving, satisfied, content, accepting**

Day 118

1. The passage presents a **tone of detached resignation and isolation**.

2. Words such as *sat, watching, evening invade, was leaned, odour, dusty,* and *tired* support the character's weariness and withdrawal.

Day 119

1. B Dorothea's love of extremes and her tendency to behave in unconventional ways provide support for this view.

2. D As the author notes, "Women were expected to have weak opinions; but the great safeguard of society and of domestic life was, that opinions were not acted on."

3. A As supported by the comment, "Sane people did what their neighbors did, so that if any lunatics were at large, one might know and avoid them."

4. E The nuanced support of Dorothea's individuality and the description of the close-mindedness of the townspeople steer the reader to this view.

Day 120

1. The two major literary devices used in the opening paragraph are **anaphora** (repetition of a beginning phrase) and **paradox** (conflicting ideas).

2. Dickens uses these two literary devices to **introduce one of the novel's primary motifs: contradiction in the form of opposing pairs; the struggle of conflicting ideas and ideals.**

Day 121

1. **A** The description of Eliza consistently fits this characterization.

2. **C** The second paragraph recalls what she treasured from her past experiences.

3. **E** Given the fact that Eliza refuses to let the boy down, the thought is indeed "harsh."

4. **B** The author ("impossible to conceive," "more wholly desolate and forlorn," "only home she had ever known," "loved and revered," "every familiar object," etc.) uses polarized diction liberally.

Day 122

1. After reading the passage, the following could be used to characterize:

   Catherine: an obedient, loving daughter

   Morris Townsend: impatient and concerned about what others think of him

2. Cite specific details from the passage that support your characterization for each.

   • **Morris: impatience** (lines 7, 21)

   • **Catherine: obedient and loving** (lines 10, 13, 20)

   • **Morris: concerned about what others think of him** (lines 14, 24)

Day 123

Here is a sample topic sentence:

   Small details in this brief passage from Chapter 7 of *Washington Square* help to reveal the characters of both Catherine and Morris Townsend.

Notice the use of *this*, which makes it clear to the reader that the paragraph is connected to a larger context. The sentence also provides the paragraph's subject and its organization. The reader will expect Catherine to be first with Morris Townsend second in the presentation of information.

Day 124

Here is a sample set of sentences:

> In this after-dinner confrontation Catherine is portrayed as an obedient, loving daughter. When Morris asks her to confront her father, Catherine makes it clear that she would rather not ask him for an opinion when she says, "I would rather not ask him, if there is any danger of his saying what you think." She confirms this attitude with another pointed response, "I never contradict him." And, the final brushstroke in this portrait is her answer to Morris's hope that it wouldn't matter what her father said: "Ah, but it would matter; I couldn't say that!"

Day 125

Here is a sample set of sentences:

> Obviously in love with Catherine and hoping to make a favorable impression on her father, Morris shows himself to be both impatient and concerned with what others think of him. He is quick to request Catherine to ask her father what he thinks of him: "He doesn't like me—he doesn't like me at all!" . . . "I am very quick to feel." Also, it becomes clear in the last paragraph that he cares about the opinions of others, including her father: "Ah, well, then, I must not give up hope of bringing him around."

Note the use of the colon in the characterization of both Morris and Catherine. The colon is indicating examples are to follow. Notice also that the colon comes at the end of a sentence. This is just one method if incorporating direct quotations into the text.

Day 126

Here is a sample paragraph:

> Small details in this brief passage from Chapter 7 of *Washington Square* help to reveal the characters of both Catherine and Morris Townsend. In this after-dinner confrontational conversation, Catherine is portrayed as an obedient, loving daughter. When Morris asks her to confront her father, Catherine makes it clear that she would rather not ask him for an opinion when she says, "I would rather not ask him, if there is any danger of his saying what you think." She confirms this attitude with another pointed response: "I never contradict him." And, the final brushstroke in this portrait is her answer to Morris's hope that it wouldn't matter what her father said: "Ah, but it would matter; I couldn't say that!" These responses are predicated on Morris's remarks. Obviously in love with Catherine and hoping to make a favorable impression on her father, he shows himself to be both impatient and concerned with what others think of him. Morris is quick to request Catherine to ask her father what he thinks of him: "He doesn't like me—he doesn't like me at all!" . . . "I am very quick to feel." Also, it becomes clear in the last paragraph that he cares about the opinions of others, including her father: "Ah, well, then, I must not give up hope of bringing him around."

This is a 222-word paragraph that addresses how details are used to develop characterizations. The topic sentence is the first sentence of the paragraph. Notice the beginning of the section on Morris: *These responses are predicated on Morris's remarks.* This sentence acts as "connective tissue" between the two parts of the paragraph.

Day 127

1. **A** The descriptions of Emma ("rich, with a comfortable home and happy disposition") and the lack of authority from either father or governess confirm this view.

2. **E** Emma's friendliness is described throughout and the last paragraph points to her strong will ("doing just what she liked" and "directed chiefly by her own" judgment).

3. **B** The description of Mr. Woodhouse ("a most affectionate, indulgent father") fits all of the other answers and is the opposite of "restricting."

4. **B** Emma's upbringing, her personality, and her relationships with her father and governess are depicted.

Day 128

1. **D** The insecurity is revealed in her need to "cover up" and her discontentment with her husband, children, and absence of money are depicted throughout the passage. For C, while cold, the woman lacks humility.

2. **B** The "pleasant house," sense of superiority compared to others in the neighborhood, and the notion that "style was always kept up" support this answer.

3. **A** The use of "some" in this context indicates that wherever the father works and whatever he toils at doesn't matter, since he is not going to bring substantial money to the family.

4. **E** The emphasis of what others say about the woman's relationship with her children and quality of the household appearance hide the family's turmoil.

Day 129

1. One could infer that:

   Lucy Honeychurch is a proper, young British woman who wants to please Miss Bartlett but can be argumentative.

   Miss Bartlett is Lucy's older cousin and chaperone who is a traditional British lady who does not like to have the untraditional or unexpected occur.

2. Based only on a reading of this passage, one could infer the possibility of the following conflicts/tensions as the novel progresses: (Some possibilities)

   • Lucy and Miss Bartlett will clash.

   • Miss Bartlett will be in conflict with George and his father.

   • Lucy will be conflicted with expectations, desires, and reality.

Day 130

1. D Mr. Pocket's use of "not sorry" is more nuanced and less assuming than saying "happy." Furthermore, this interpretation fits with the subsequent descriptions of his behavior.

2. E Given the usual phrasing that would say a son had his father's smile, this reversal indicates the narrator's greater familiarity with the son.

3. E The understanding that Mr. Pocket has to work hard to seem natural is furthered by the complex comment: "there was something comic in his distraught way, as though it would have been downright ludicrous but for his own perception that it was very near being so."

4. C While Mrs. Pocket does ask the narrator a question in the passage, it appears to be one without context or result (the reader does not get the impression that if the narrator said he liked orange-flower water, she would have served him some). In addition, Mr. Pocket's question to her and her monosyllabic, distracted answer speak to these qualities.

Day 131

Mr. Pocket: By the way Mr. Pocket speaks, he is clearly educated and sophisticated. However, he tries very hard with the narrator to behave naturally. His actions reveal that he is a gentleman who is considerate of others. He is aware that sometimes his thoughts and self-consciousness ("his perplexities") prevent him from acting naturally, even though his manners and his genuineness lead him to make great efforts to act unaffectedly.

Mrs. Pocket: The wife reveals herself to be distracted by the book and not very interested in being an attentive hostess of the narrator. Her reply to her husband and her non-sequitur question to the narrator reveal that her efforts are perfunctory at best. Unlike Mr. Pocket, she is perceived by the narrator as being condescending to him.

Their Relationship: Mr. Pocket's "anxious contraction of the eyebrows" indicates he is both accustomed to and horrified by Mrs. Pocket's treatment of guests. Her terse response to Mr. Pocket's question shows her lack of engagement with him and her distance.

Day 132

1. B As the narrator says halfway through the passage, "I seemed to have lost all soul or sensation but for this one pursuit."

2. E The others—characterization (he pursues nature's hidden places with "unrelaxed and breathless eagerness"), symbolism (his hiding places), personification (the "moon gazed"), and metaphor (nature's hiding places)—are all represented.

3. C The "profane fingers" stand in for the narrator's entire being as he is engaged in activity he deems "unnatural."

4. A That view is exhibited by his alternating feelings of loathing and eagerness about his endeavor.

Day 133

Sample annotation:

> Although written in **1949, Arthur Miller's** *Death of a Salesman* continues to be a **popular and successful** theatrical production for **professionals and amateurs alike.** In a well-written essay **examine the specific characteristics** of this drama **that allow it to appeal to the modern audience.**

The date, writer, and title is important to this prompt. It will be necessary to address what specifically makes this a popular and successful play for the modern audience. The key word is *specific*.

Day 134

Sample thesis statement:

> **Arthur Miller's 1949 dramatization of Willy Loman's obsessive and unrealistic desire to succeed and the effects of this obsession on his family are primary factors that allow** *Death of a Salesman* **to appeal to the modern audience.**

This preliminary thesis statement makes clear to the reader the title, author, and date. It also states the two major points that the essay will develop and the reason why these major points are important.

Day 135

Sample list:

- Willy Loman's obsessive and unrealistic desire to succeed (1)
  - unrelenting and delusional belief in the American dream
- effects of this obsession on Willy's family (2)
  - Biff's identity crisis
  - Happy's self-delusion
  - Willy's wife Linda's being the core of the family who acts as a buffer

Day 136

1. The writer **does not** present any specific details to illustrate or support the ideas presented.

2. The reader expects **specifics from the play that illustrate the ideas** presented in the first two sentences.

3. The third sentence **does not** follow logically from the preceding two **because it introduces an entirely new subject.**

4. This is not a successful first paragraph. The ideas are general with no specifics to support them.

Day 137

Sample revision:

Willy is unable to stick with a consistent conception of reality or the truth. He changes interpretations of events as he needs to in order to fit a particular moment. For example, during the first act, in response to his wife asking about the car being damaged, Willy responds that nothing really happened and that he just kept falling into a kind of trance while driving. Again, about the car, Willy, at first, calls it a piece of trash, but he later changes that to it being "the finest car ever built." Also, Willy calls his son Biff a "lazy bum," but he switches that label and characterizes him as anything but lazy. This kind of behavior continues throughout the play.

The revision has gone from 38 words that are general with no support together with the introduction of a new subject to a 121-word brief examination of the general points supported by specifics from the play.

Day 138

1. **Trees** are compared **to a choir**. (lines 1 and 3)

2. The **forest** is compared **to a church**. (the sum of all the images)

3. The **setting sun** is compared **to a stained glass window** and its light. (lines 1 and 2)

4. **Insects** are compared **to churchgoers praying**. (lines 2 and 3)

5. The **sound of the wind** is compared **to a hymn**. (lines 1 and 3)

Day 139

1. Here is an example of the annotated text that would allow for the inference of it being a dream-like setting:

> On my right hand there were lines of fishing stakes **resembling a mysterious system** of half-submerged bamboo fences, **incomprehensible** in its division of the domain of tropical fishes, and **crazy of aspect** as if abandoned forever by some nomad tribe of fishermen now gone to the other end of the ocean; for there was **no sign of human habitation as far as the eye could reach.** To the left a group of **barren islets, suggesting** ruins of stone walls, towers, and blockhouses, had its **foundations set in a blue sea that itself looked solid,** so still and stable did it lie below my feet; even the track of light from the westering sun shone smoothly, without that **animated glitter** which tells of an **imperceptible ripple.**

2. **B** The central metaphor being established in this passage is most probably **sea/land**. The entire passage describes a landscape that has the sea and land interconnected and almost inseparable.

Day 140

1. Here is an example of the annotated text:

I remember him as if it were yesterday, as he came plodding to the inn door, his **sea-chest** following behind him in a hand-barrow--a tall, strong, heavy, nut-brown man, his **tarry pigtail** falling over the shoulder of his **soiled blue coat**, his **hands ragged and scarred**, with **black, broken nails**, and the **sabre cut across one cheek**, a **dirty, livid white**. I remember him looking round the cover and whistling to himself as he did so, and then breaking out in that old sea-song that he sang so often.

2. Here are a few examples of details that can lead to analysis:

- Tarry pigtail. Perhaps poor; possibly away from civilization for a time

- Soiled coat

- Dirty white scar

- Ragged, scarred hands. Might reveal a violent history

- Black, broken nails. Victim or attacker?

- Sabre cut cheek

- Sea chest. Pirate or sailor

Day 141

1. B The second part of the sentence ("among a people whose social condition presented almost unlimited room for improvement") speaks to the poor lives of colored people.

2. D Since the society's members were more white than black, only those more black than white would be considered envious, since they were the excluded parties.

3. E The darker-colored people ("those who were not of the favored few") used the name to make clear they are once again being left out because of their race.

4. D Since he is called "the dean of the Blue Veins," Mr. Ryder is the leader of a group trying to make inroads into society levels that were heretofore blocked.

Day 142

Here is one possible response:

The cataloging provides a grand scope and scale for poor human behavior. The list moves from action ("bribing, flattering, or pimping," etc.) to the actors committing the sins (physicians, lawyers, informers, etc.). The actors are so diverse and voluminous (more than 20 types) that they cover the entire societal spectrum. The catalog then moves on to those instruments used to punish offenders both real and imagined ("dungeon, axes, gibbets," etc.). Ultimately, the narrator returns to the offenders with greater specificity, and more importantly, to figures who have personal roles in individual lives (bullies, wives, companions, etc.). The narrator concludes his catalog tossing out the names of seemingly random offenders. The reader gets the impression that the narrator could continue this miserable catalog for pages, but he does not consider that pursuit worth the effort, since he has already clearly made his point.

Day 143

1. D The narrator's complaints and attacks are about the civilization he used to live in. The absence of these abuses and cruelties is what makes this *Houyhnhnm* civilization superior.

2. E The irony derives from the notions that physicians generally heal bodies, not destroy them, and lawyers generally protect fortunes, not ruin them.

3. B The use of "no" throughout this section establishes a rhythmic and thematic structure.

4. C The narrator presents such a rich and broad attack on seemingly every aspect of civilization that he can leave no other impression but a disgust with humanity.

Day 144

1. C While the narrator grudgingly admits being "shaken in nerves," her physical description and the unflattering comparisons to the condition of others are particularly revealing.

2. E In the context of the words and sentences next to "benefit," the term is connected to her financial state.

3. A The words used to describe the second cousin are overwhelmingly negative.

4. E Even though she has no clear idea of where she will live, the narrator compares her troubled plight to others and describes her position as relatively enviable.

Day 145

1. From the passage, including his name, the most obvious characterization would be that Mr. Gradgrind is just that—a man who is a grind who is only interested in the facts and passing on those facts.

2. Here are some specifics from the passage to support the characterization:

- All of paragraph 1

- Line 6 and its description of the room

- Mr. Gradgrind's description in lines 6–17 (Each part of this section could be cited.)

3. From only what is presented to the reader, this novel **will criticize Mr. Gradgrind and his philosophy**.

4. Specifics from the passage that support this conclusion include:

- The names of the characters: Mr. Gradgrind and Mr. M'Choakumchild

- The description of the classroom (line 6)

- The description of the students (lines 21–22)

Day 146

1. The author creates a general mood of **harshness and desolation**.

2. The author's attitude toward the "**Northland Wild**" is one of **cynicism and futility**.

3. Specific details from the text in support of the attitude of cynicism and futility can be found in the following lines: Lines 5–7 contain the analogy of silence to laughter and this laughter to the smile of the Sphinx; also this laughter is compared to frost and the "grimness of infallibility." Lines 7–9 compare the silence/laughter to "futility of life" and the "effort of life." The last line calls the land "savage" and "frozen-hearted."

Day 147

1. D Given only this scene, one may infer that this play is most probably a **satire**. The dialogue between Algernon and his butler, Lane leads on to infer that this play is going to criticize a particular type of society. There is humor, pointed remarks, and an obvious type of society structure at work in the scene.

2. Three details that could be cited to support the inference that this play is a satire are:

- The nonchalance of attitudes toward marriage

- The trivialization of marriage

- Algernon's relationship with Lane and his attitude toward the lower classes

Day 148

1. C *A seat in this boat was not unlike a seat upon a jumpy horse, and a horse is not much smaller.* (lines 1–2) contains two examples of **litotes**. A litotes is a literary device that uses a negative to affirm a positive: in this instance boat to horse.

2. The first paragraph uses an extended metaphor to compare the **boat** to a **jumpy horse**.

3. Specific words/phrases that help to construct the personification of the sea can be found in the following lines:

- next wave is just as **nervously anxious** and **purposeful** (lines 8–9)

- was the final **outburst** of the ocean (lines 10–11)

- last **effort** of the **determined** water (line 11)

Day 149

The use of anaphora reveals certain rhythms and patterns in the relationship of the couple. By listing a series of behaviors and descriptions of John in such a structured way, the narrator appears to have gone over John's qualities repeatedly. Furthermore, the reader is given the impression that John has expressed his opinions and outlooks to her so many times that she catalogs them matter-of-factly. The additional repetition of "perhaps" in the final paragraph of the passage indicates that while John is certain about both his views and diagnosis, the narrator feels quite differently. For the narrator, the anaphora allows her to reveal John's condescension and a complete lack of sympathy for her thoughts and feelings.

Day 150

1. B He lit a lantern in a bright morning; an act that on the surface does not make sense.

2. E The bystanders are clearly not taking the madman's pronouncements seriously.

3. C The comments amount to a cumulative piling on.

4. A Note the preponderance of exclamation marks.

5. A The only answer that is fully accurate; the disorientation derives from seemingly impossible behaviors.

6. D God's physical corpse, including its odor and decay, is contemplated here.

Day 151

7. C The devastating notion of killing God is juxtaposed with the language of a "greater deed" and a new "higher history" in a demonstration of the madman playing with the absurdities and the aftermath of such an act.

8. B The listeners are no longer joking because some aspect of the madman's speech has resonated with them.

9. C Appearing on lines 1, 12, and 20 (at which point he breaks it), the lantern functions as a ray of understanding obscured by the brightness of day. It appears where it is not traditionally necessary (in daylight) and establishes the distorted and disjointed nature of the madman's message.

10. A The deed referred to here is the killing of God, a deed as line 24 states, "they have done it themselves!"

11. B The madman is telling the listeners what has happened. But since they are unable to understand it now, the comments serve as a prophecy, predicting that they will come to realize their present actions in the future.

12. D The paradox results from church housing tombs as a place where the dead and the living can be closer to God, but in this situation it is God who is dead and the roles of worshipped have reversed. Such inversions have been presented throughout the madman's argument, which at the church has found its final resting place.

Day 152

1. He sees marrying as more of a logical decision rather than an emotional one—his union with a wife being one based more on convenience than love.

2. The marriage proposal to Elizabeth is primarily about getting married; Elizabeth's qualities are secondary and Mr. Collins's phrasing indicates he could just as easily procure a worthwhile replacement.

3. He references Lady Catherine de Bourgh to make clear that he has high class, aristocratic connections, and that the lady's opinions matter much more to Mr. Collins than Elizabeth's.

4. Mr. Collins compliments Elizabeth's wit and vivacity, but then tells Elizabeth that Lady Catherine expects silence, a state that would completely suppress these fine qualities. Mr. Collins is clearly instructing Elizabeth how to behave and sending signals of how he will control the relationship.

Day 153

1. Mr. Collins is making clear to Elizabeth that he is doing her a favor and that he could as easily marry another.

2. Mr. Collins is marrying Elizabeth so that she, as one of the daughters who would have completely lost her inheritance upon her father's death, will remain at the family home with this marriage. This motive does show that Mr. Collins—despite his cold, ridiculous officiousness—possesses at least one noble reason for his proposal.

3. While Mr. Collins is taking a somewhat noble course, his need to point out his actions to Elizabeth and look to extract praise (and perhaps groveling gratitude) soil and sully his initial intentions.

4. Ironically, Mr. Collins does not express his affection; instead, he reminds Elizabeth how poor she is while promising he won't remind her how poor she is.

Day 154

1. While polite and gracious, Elizabeth firmly rejects his proposal.

2. Mr. Collins is not discouraged at all by her refusal, explaining that she is merely doing so out of perverse feminine conventionality, rather than as an expression of her true intentions.

3. Her rejection is more forceful now. Elizabeth is also clearly repulsed by the fact that Mr. Collins would lump her in with teasing and supercilious young women who treat courtship as a frivolous game rather than a serious matter that merits earnest discourse.

4. By mentioning Lady Catherine, Elizabeth is hoping to turn Mr. Collins's attention toward the woman he truly respects and to make clear to her courter that she cannot meet the Lady's standards. In her diction and tone, she attempts to make her intentions clear while trying to remain humble and self-deprecating in her rejection.

Day 155

1. Mr. Collins tends to comment in a backward manner, never really speaking directly, filling his pronouncements with preambles and tangents. The fact that the half-sentence quoted has three different negative words—"but," "cannot," and "disapprove"—to speak positively about Elizabeth indicates his roundabout way of delivering a compliment.

2. She points to the delicacy of feelings he must have had for her family in offering the proposal and makes clear that he would be happier and richer without her. She is showing gratitude for his efforts to keep the estate within the family even as she tells him she wants no part of either the marriage or the estate.

3. That no matter how direct and clear Elizabeth is, Mr. Collins has his mind set on how this proposal will turn out.

4. With each effort, Mr. Collins has demonstrated that he is not really listening to Elizabeth at all and he has become an increasingly comic figure as Austen satirizes this brand of mannered, but ultimately dismissive version of "gentlemanly" behavior.

Day 156

1. While never particularly sincere to begin with, Mr. Collins's indirect compliments seem to be increasingly perfunctory.

2. While Mr. Collins sprinkles his comments to Elizabeth with niceties, albeit condescending in their delivery, he raises the issue of "cruelty" as perhaps an indication of what he really thinks about the initial rejections of brides to marriage proposals they deeply desire and need to accept. The fact that he even raises this issue reinforces how fully he has misinterpreted Elizabeth's replies.

3. If the female character rejects marriage proposals simply so the male will pursue with greater ardor and determination, then the woman is cast as insecure, inane, and imprudent.

4. Elizabeth has become increasingly frustrated, almost to the point of repressed anger ("cried Elizabeth with some warmth"), and she seems to have arrived at an exasperated loss of how to deliver her message about a central matter of her life to someone who has consciously decided to not take her replies seriously.

Day 157

1. He presents confidence that she will marry him because of the myriad advantages he offers her and the logic of their union. The absence of any discussion of love and affection is revealing.

2. Mr. Collins is warning Elizabeth that he will be the best offer she receives, and despite his compliments, that she is not really that attractive of a catch. He is subtly implying that his marriage offer is a bit of an act of charity.

3. Elizabeth is trying to maintain her manners and decorum as she turns increasingly blunt almost to the point of mocking Mr. Collins's obstinate refusal to hear her. Her appeal for him to listen to her as "a rational creature" confirms that she knows he perceives her as mindless and illogical.

4. Mr. Collins uses the term to signal the conventional behavior of young women; while he prefers they would behave differently, he understands their denials as only part of the courting ritual. He uses "elegant female" as a euphemism for a lovely manipulator. In contrast, Elizabeth is horrified by this "elegant female" since it represents the mindless silliness and commoditization of marriage so alien to her nature.

Day 158

1. Mr. Collins, with his "air of awkward gallantry," has become an increasingly absurd figure over the course of these seven segments that make up the longer passage. His compliment, "You are uniformly charming!," can by now be interpreted as "you are behaving in a silly and stupid manner." In practically the same breath, he is threatening to get her parents involved to force her to accept the proposal.

2. Elizabeth now knows that no matter how clear and articulate she is in expressing her views, Mr. Collins will not listen to her denials for he views her as a silly woman; alas, only a man of authority, her father, can make clear her views.

Possible response:

The overall excerpt builds in comedy as the determined and ridiculous Mr. Collins continues to press Elizabeth to marry him even as her refusals become increasingly frank and blunt. The excerpt demonstrates his perceptions of young women as silly, cruel narcissists who deny marriage only to extract greater exclamations of their worthiness. As a woman who is repulsed by such game playing, Elizabeth gives clear, mature, intelligent denials, even as she has the manners to express gratitude for the offers. The excerpt depicts Elizabeth's steady realization that no matter what she says, Mr. Collins will not listen to any denial of his request. She is palpably aware that the very person asking to spend the rest of his life with her has absolutely no understanding of her mind, her thoughts, and her words. Through this scene, author Jane Austen implies that such an absence of perception by males of the woman they court and marry was common.

Day 159

Possible response:

Ahab's diction and that describing him are emotionally charged throughout the passage, whether he connects his suffering to damage of a ship ("dismasted" and "razeed") or to baser creatures ("with terrific, loud, animal sob, like that of a heart-stricken moose"). His obsessive determination is revealed by the geographic breadth and extremes (Good Hope, the Horn, the Norway Maelstrom) he is willing to bear in his search. His resolve to "round perdition's flames" in his quest reveals a man who will transgress moral boundaries as well as physical ones. The final graphic imagining of Moby Dick's death ("till he spouts black blood and rolls fin out") signals the brutish hostility of his outlook. Furthermore, the idea of using the whale's name, Moby Dick, and constantly referring to the whale as "he" rather than "it" reveals how personal his desire for vengeance is. The repetition of "Aye" serves as a lamentation, a feral wailing that speaks to a deep pain that cannot be mollified.

Day 160

Possible response:

Ahab appeals to emotion while Starbuck appeals to logic. Ahab seizes on the crew's desire to embrace a manliness ("I think ye do look brave"), and his demonstrative gratitude ("he seemed to half sob and half shout) marks his passionate investment in this quest. He challenges Starbuck to take up the quest ("are thou not game for

Moby Dick?") as if the decision is the ultimate measurement of his character. Even as he continues to play with emotions, Ahab in his last argument weighs his vengeance against financial considerations, finding his personal quest deeper and more meaningful. Meanwhile, Starbuck focuses on the business of whaling, the reason the crew boarded the ship in the first place. In a nice parallel of physical and metaphysical jaws, he clearly has heard of Moby Dick (he knows of his "crooked jaw") and understands the dangers of the business (he's game for "the jaws of Death too"). For Starbuck, this business is already dangerous enough without adding other factors. He argues that vengeance serves no financial benefit. Ultimately, Starbuck expunges any personal motives for fighting Moby Dick.

Day 161

Possible response:

Starbuck sees Moby Dick as an unthinking animal that simply lashed out at Ahab from instinct. For Ahab, the situation goes much deeper. As with the previous excerpt, Ahab refers to "the little lower layer." For Ahab, Moby Dick is a mere vessel for something bigger and more disturbing: the reason Ahab and all of mankind are confined, restricted, and limited. This greater force (that "inscrutable thing") is what Ahab is attacking. To make his point, Ahab speaks on numerous allegorical and metaphorical levels. He speaks of all visible objects as merely "pasteboard masks" he looks to penetrate. Comparing himself to a prisoner walled in, Ahab looks to force his way free. But in all of this contemplative thinking, the most daring approach Ahab takes in explaining his view is the originality of his complaint about Moby Dick: "He tasks me; he heaps me." By turning the word "task," normally a noun, into a verb, Ahab broadens the weight on his shoulders; and by transforming the word "heap," he piles burden atop of burden onto himself. With all of this philosophical discussion, Ahab returns to attacking that animal Starbuck describes at the beginning of this section, since the only way to strike at the "lower layer" is through the body of Moby Dick.

Day 162

Possible response:

In his opening comment, Ahab makes clear that he will not bow down to any force if he feels he has been disrespected. That he claims "I'd strike the sun if it insulted me" demonstrates that Ahab forms his outlook not on what is possible, but on what he deems right. As Ahab talks about "my master," the reader steadily comes to realize that the figure behind Moby Dick and the forces behind the sun must inevitably be God. Given his expression that Ahab finds so disturbing, Starbuck too must have come to realize that Ahab is engaged in nothing less than a personal battle with God. By his softer subsequent description of Starbuck and his backward apology ("that thing unsays itself"), Ahab understands he has revealed too much of his soul. His mollifying comments concluding this section reveal a man wrestling with the competing needs to express his views and to convince Starbuck of the legitimacy of his quest.

Day 163

Possible response:

Ahab sees the entire crew unified behind his quest, except for Starbuck. By depicting his first mate as "one tost sapling," Ahab is devaluing Starbuck's opposition. After placing so much weight and significance on killing Moby Dick, Ahab now simplifies and diminishes the act: "Tis but to help strike a fin; no wondrous feat for Starbuck." This comment begins Ahab's flattery of his first mate, which concludes with calling him "the best lance out all Nantucket," and is followed by more cajoling. That coaxing is marked by many exclamatory comments, which earlier in Ahab's speech signaled his impassioned fury, but now turns jocular and almost jovial. The aside the author (Melville) inserts allows Ahab to interpret Starbuck's silence. By using the aside, the author further emphasizes the theatricality of this scene, since asides generally appear in plays rather than novels. Just like Ahab, the author is unwilling to be limited by conventions.

Day 164

Possible response:

In his passage Ahab must confront the cold logic of the first mate, Starbuck, as he tries to unite the crew in his quest to hunt Moby Dick. To defend himself against Starbuck's desire to focus on the business of whaling, Ahab presents deeper philosophical motivations for vengeance. In this argument, he employs metaphorical images and unusual diction to connect the whale to the motivations of God. Given the nontraditional and "blasphemous" nature of these beliefs, Ahab must ultimately shift his tactics to flattery and cajoling to quell Starbuck's prospective rebellion.

Day 165

This is an example of a brief prompt in which almost every word/phrase is important in understanding what is required. Here is a sample annotated prompt:

> **Fyodor Dostoyevsky observed that "All happy families are alike; each unhappy family is unhappy in its own way."**
> Choose a **full-length work of literary merit** and write a **well-developed essay** that **identifies an unhappy family and its complex effect on character and/or theme.**

Your deconstruction has made note of these details

- Each unhappy family is unhappy in its own way
- Full-length work
- Literary merit
- Well-developed essay
- Unique nature of the unhappiness
- The complex effect on character and/or theme

Day 166

There are many variations on the great themes. Here are examples of great themes you should be aware of:

Love	Honor
Love lost	Prejudice
Unrequited love	Betrayal
Death	Disobedience
Ambition	Self-sacrifice
Power	Religion
Greed	Guilt
Jealousy	

Day 167

Your answer should be similar to this example.

<u>Theme</u>: betrayal

<u>Work</u>: Hamlet

<u>Examples and details</u>:

Hamlet's uncle Claudius betrays Old Hamlet—initiates the events

Hamlet meets ghost—afraid it may be a betrayer

Hamlet betrays Ophelia—feigns madness, rejects her, precipitates her death

Hamlet betrays Claudius—the play's the thing to catch the conscience of the king

Rosenkrantz and Guildenstern betray Hamlet on the way to Wittenberg

Day 168

The following works would lend themselves to a complex discussion of the prompt-related families. Your list may be very different. The AP Literature exam provides varied lists as suggestions, but you are not required to use their choices.

Hamlet

Oedipus Rex

Death of a Salesman

Hedda Gabler

Desire Under the Elms

A Doll's House

As I Lay Dying

The Color Purple

King Lear

A Streetcar Named Desire

Day 169

1. Here is a sample list of five major works that are in some way related to the quotation.

> *1984*
>
> *Things Fall Apart*
>
> *Their Eyes Were Watching God*
>
> *The Odyssey*
>
> *Catch-22*

Were any of these on your list? A note: You could have also chosen Hemingway's *The Old Man and the Sea*. Don't be afraid to choose the obvious.

2. This is a sample response to choosing *1984*.

> ***1984*: Although living in a totalitarian society, Winston Smith, a rewriter of history, rebels in his own way against those who maintain this dystopian world.**

Notice that this is brief and to the point. It reminds the writer WHY she chose it, and from this short beginning, she will be able to build her essay using specifics from the novel to illustrate the quotation and support her thesis.

Day 170

For each of the responses, a more developed and specific commentary would be presented in the actual exam essay. For example, satire is developed in *Gulliver's Travels* to reveal the absurdities of human behavior. In Lilliput, Swift satirizes the brutal pettiness of human nature as countries fight wars over which side of the populace should crack eggs. In addition, he mocks man's tendency to select its leaders not on qualifications, but on superficialities as officials are picked by their ability to dance on a rope. By having the much larger Gulliver gaze upon the Lilliputian society from a secure and cerebral perspective, Swift is able to demonstrate how man's intellect and efforts are perverted in the service of base causes.

Day 171

Sample response:

For each of the responses, a more developed and specific commentary would be presented in the actual exam essay. For example, satire is developed in *Gulliver's Travels* to reveal the absurdities of human behavior. In Lilliput, Swift satirizes the brutal pettiness of human nature as countries fight wars over which side the populace should crack eggs. In addition, he mocks man's tendency to select its leaders not on qualifications, but on superficialities as officials are picked by their ability to dance on a rope. By having the much larger Gulliver gaze upon the Lilliputian society from a secure and cerebral perspective, Swift is able to demonstrate how man's intellect and efforts are perverted in the service of base causes.

Day 172

Sample response:

For each of the responses, a more developed and specific commentary would be presented in the actual exam essay. For example, the plot structure for *Things Fall Apart* allows the author, Chinua Achebe, to present the effects of colonization on the Igbo tribe both from a deeper personal level and a cerebral distance. The first section of the novel deeply immerses the reader in the Igbo culture from its proverbs to its marriage rituals to its myths. Furthermore, it chronicles the rise of the brutish, yet respected, protagonist Okonkwo. Achebe dramatically alters the narrative structure after Okonkwo accidentally kills a tribal member and is sent into exile. During these seven years away from the tribe, Okonkwo receives secondhand reports of the white man's slow, but steady intrusions on the Igbo culture, from the first missionaries to the interventions of European powers. Through this exile, Achebe is able to foreshorten the colonial progression to heighten the impact on both Okonkwo and the reader. When Okonkwo and the reader return to the Igbo tribe, the society has changed dramatically as its members are divided between the new colonial opportunities and the traditional ways. Ultimately, Okonkwo's subsequent suicide and the usurpation of both the culture and the novel's narrative by the district commission provide more shifts in the plot's structure. These structural elements of the plot illustrate how the cultural subjugation of the Igbo tribe is realized.

Day 173

Possible response:

Don't try to impress the reader of your essay. Make certain to choose a literary work that you feel comfortable with. Remember that it is important to address the prompt. A mere review of the plot is not going to earn more than a 2.

Day 174

Possible response:

For each of the responses, a more developed and specific commentary would be presented in the actual exam essay. For example, the chorus in *Oedipus Rex* may offer the traditional voice of the people, but in the context of this tragedy, it also presents a population conflicted about whom to believe (especially when Tieresias and Oedipus argue) and what to make of the king, who is both a hero and destroyer. The chorus captures a society in turmoil, shocked by revelations of incest, suicide, and self-mutilation, even while acknowledging the noble self-sacrifice of the king.

Day 175

Sample alternate:

As we continually advise, make certain to address the prompt. Mere plot summaries or reviews are not going to earn a passing score. For this prompt, don't pass up the opportunity ties presented by novels like *The Color Purple, Huckleberry Finn, Jane Eyre,* and *The Great Gatsby.*

Day 176

Possible response:

For each of the responses, a more developed and specific commentary would be presented in the actual exam essay. For example, the role of strong, supportive women in *The Color Purple* is synthesized through the stitching of the quilt aptly named Sister's Choice. Very early in the novel, Celie is encouraged by the women in her life. Albert's sister Kate explains that Celie deserves more, and her own sister Nettie builds her sense of self-worth. When the tough and strong Sofia enters her life, Celie comes to see how women do not have to be submissive. More importantly, the companionship of Albert's old love Shug Avery gives Celie the affection and encouragement to become independent. When Shug takes her to Memphis, Celie starts her own business and breaks free of male dominance. In fact, all of the major women characters in *The Color Purple* lean on each other in order to make decisions that release them from the control of men.

Day 177

Possible response:

Don't be afraid to work with the "old stand-bys." Why not choose to develop the obvious motif in *The Scarlet Letter*?

Day 178

Possible response:

For each of the responses, a more developed and specific commentary would be presented in the actual exam essay. For example, the forge in *Great Expectations* represents the low-class, sooty, grimy world into which Pip was born. Even though the kindest and most supportive of men, Joe Gargery, toils at the forge, Pip, as he rises in social class, cannot perceive the forge as anything more than the wincing representation of his embarrassing origins. The hard physical labor of the forge leads to coarse hands and dirty clothes, a far cry from the refined corridors that will usher him toward opportunities for wooing the wealthy Estella. Late in the novel, as Pip comes to terms with his own transformation and the shame of his snobbery toward Joe, the humble blacksmith, he learns to better appreciate the forge as being the source of honest industry.

Day 179

Possible response:

Some other literary works to consider are ones you may have read in 9th or 10th grade, or ones you read on your own. Why not develop the "symbol" essay with novels like *Lord of the Flies*, *1984*, or even *Animal Farm*?

Day 180

Possible response:

For each of the responses, a more developed and specific commentary would be presented in the actual exam essay. For example, the theme of a creation moving beyond the control of the creator is central to the novel *Frankenstein*. Shelley initially presents Victor Frankenstein as obsessed with the idea of the reanimation of life, but when he finally completes the creature, he is so repulsed by the results that he rejects his creation. Since that creature is faster, stronger, and, perhaps, smarter than his creator, it spends the remainder of their lives exacting revenge upon his progenitor. Victor's perception of his inability to exercise any control on his creation builds incrementally from the death of his brother William to that of his best friend Henry to the tragic loss of his new bride Elizabeth. Victor's awareness of this condition is fully realized after the creature calls upon him to create a companion. Even though he knows he will pay a great price for his decision, Victor chooses not to make yet another creation since he now understands how far beyond his control his actions can take him.

A Self-Evaluation

The most important thing you can do for yourself is to be honest with yourself. Have you given the amount of time that you felt you needed to address the work of AP English Literature? No matter what the outcome, remember that you are all the better for having taken this course and allowing yourself to become involved with the important ideas of others and to express and test your own ideas. You have been willing to take risks, and you have grown because of it.

Congratulations.

Appendixes

Suggesting Reading Guide
General Bibliography
Glossary
Websites

SUGGESTED READING GUIDE

As you probably know, a standard curriculum for AP Lit does not exist. Instead, teachers are urged to present material that will be appropriately challenging and enlightening while providing the opportunity for literary analysis. There are several ways of organizing the literature you study in an AP Literature and Composition course. Regardless of specifics, a broad selection of literature, covering many centuries and many styles, should be offered. Be confident that your teacher and course will meet the needs of the AP requirements.

We've developed several ways for you to reflect upon your own background. Once you have a clear overview of what you do know, you will be able to assess your particular strengths and weaknesses. You will also see the interrelationships of the literature you've studied and the commonalities and differences you will draw on to write your essays.

One approach to organizing your studies is chronological. This is the traditional survey of literature from "Beowulf to Virginia Woolf to Thomas Wolfe." This broad-based study provides you with many samples from different time periods and offers a context grounded in history. Another approach is the thematic one. Works are grouped by common ideas and are variations on a theme through time and genre. Often, it is obvious that certain works share a common sensibility. Generally, these characteristics are classified together as a literary movement. By connecting form and function, this type of reflection will broaden your understanding and analysis.

What follows is a bibliographic overview of literary movements.

Classicism

The classical writer generally exhibits or is concerned with the following:

- Universality
- Noble ideas
- Dignified language
- Restraint
- Clarity
- Objectivity
- The importance of structure
- An edifying purpose

Suggested classical works and authors:

Homer	*The Iliad, The Odyssey*
The Bible	"Genesis," "Exodus," "Matthew"
Sophocles	*Antigone, Oedipus Rex*
Euripides	*Medea*
Aristotle	"On the Nature of Tragedy"
Plato	"The Apology," "The Allegory of the Cave"

Molière	*Tartuffe, The Misanthrope*
Racine	*Phaedra*
John Milton	"L'Allegro," "Il Penseroso," "On His Blindness," *Paradise Lost* (excerpts)
Alexander Pope	"An Essay on Man," "An Essay on Criticism," "The Rape of the Lock"
Jonathan Swift	*Gulliver's Travels*
Voltaire	*Candide*

Make a list of classical works you have read: Cite title, author, and major thoughts about each.

_____

_____

_____

_____

Realism

The realistic writer generally exhibits or is concerned with the following:

- Truth and actuality
- Detail
- Character portrayal
- Psychology
- Objectivity
- Lack of sentimentality

Suggested realistic works and authors:

Chaucer	*The Canterbury Tales*
Fyodor Dostoyevsky	*Crime and Punishment*
Leo Tolstoy	*Anna Karenina*
Anton Chekhov	*The Cherry Orchard*
Ernest Hemingway	*The Sun Also Rises*
Henrik Ibsen	*Hedda Gabler, A Doll's House*

Make a list of realistic works you have read: Cite title, author, and major thoughts about each.

_____

_____

_____

_____

Romanticism

The romantic writer generally exhibits or is concerned with the following:

- Emotions and passion
- Imagination and wonder
- The variety and power of Nature
- The individual
- Freedom and revolution
- Dreams and idealism
- Mystery and the supernatural
- Experimentation with form
- Spontaneity

Suggested romantic prose works and authors:

Anonymous	*Beowulf*
Bocaccio	*The Decameron*
Rabelais	*Gargantua*
Cervantes	*Don Quixote*
Shakespeare	*Hamlet, King Lear*
Goethe	*Faust*
Hawthorne	*The Scarlet Letter*
Brontë	*Jane Eyre*
Hugo	*Les Miserables*

Suggested romantic poetic works and authors:

Multiple authors	The Ballads—Scottish and British
Shakespeare	Sonnets
Robert Burns	"To a Mouse," "John Anderson, My Jo," "A Red, Red, Rose"
William Blake	"A Poison Tree," "The Sick Rose," "London," "The Chimney Sweep"
William Wordsworth	"Tintern Abbey," "My Heart Leaps Up," "London, 1802," "The World Is Too Much With Us," "I Wandered Lonely as a Cloud," "Ode on Intimations of Immortality," Preface to the Lyrical Ballads
Samuel Taylor Coleridge	"Kubla Khan," "The Frost at Midnight," "The Rime of the Ancient Mariner"
Lord Byron	"Sonnet on Chillon," "When We Two Parted," "Maid of Athens," "The Isles of Greece," "She Walks in Beauty"
Percy Bysshe Shelley	"Ode to the West Wind," "To a Skylark," "Ozymandias"
John Keats	"On First Looking Into Chapman's Homer," "Ode to a Nightingale," "Ode on a Grecian Urn," "When I Have Fears That I May Cease to Be"
Alfred, Lord Tennyson	"Ulysses"
Robert Browning	"My Last Duchess," "Pippa's Song," "Soliloquy of the Spanish Cloister"

Make a list of romantic works you have read: Cite title, author, and major thoughts about each.

_____

_____

_____

_____

_____

Impressionism

The impressionist writer generally exhibits or is concerned with the following:

- Appeals to the senses
- Mood and effects
- Vagueness and ambiguity
- Momentary insights
- Impressions of setting, plot, and character
- Emphasis on color and light
- Emotions and feelings
- Sensations into words

Suggested impressionistic works and authors:

Henry James	*The American*
Joseph Conrad	*Heart of Darkness, The Secret Sharer,* "The Lagoon"
Katherine Mansfield	"Bliss"
Kate Chopin	"Story of an Hour," *The Awakening*

Make a list of impressionistic works you have read: Cite title, author, and major thoughts about each.

_____

_____

_____

_____

Expressionism

The expressionist writer generally exhibits or is concerned with the following:

- Subjective responses
- Inner reality
- Abstract and mystical ideas

- Symbols and masks
- Man and society in chaos
- Creation of new worlds

Suggested expressionistic works and authors:

James Joyce	*Dubliners*
Eugene O'Neill	*Desire Under the Elms, The Hairy Ape, The Iceman Cometh*
T. S. Eliot	"The Hollow Men," "The Love Song of J. Alfred Prufrock"
Franz Kafka	*Metamorphosis, The Trial*

Make a list of expressionistic works you have read: Cite title, author, and major thoughts about each.

_____

_____

_____

_____

_____

Naturalism

The naturalist writer generally exhibits or is concerned with the following:

- Realism to its extreme
- Fact and detail
- Social awareness and reform
- A broad spectrum of subjects, both positive and negative
- Man as animal in society
- Scientific impartiality

Suggested naturalistic works and authors:

Tennessee Williams	*A Streetcar Named Desire, Cat on a Hot Tin Roof*
Frank Norris	*The Octopus*
Stephen Crane	*Maggie, A Girl of the Streets*
Upton Sinclair	*The Jungle*

Make a list of naturalistic works you have read: Cite title, author, and major thoughts about each.

_____

_____

_____

_____

_____

A note about literary movements: These are the movements you will find emphasized in the Western canon of literature. However, be aware that there are other literary movements that are currently recognized. Among them are the:

- Symbolist—an outgrowth of romanticism
- Existentialist—concern with man's alienation
- Absurdist—takes existentialism one step further into the realm of fractured reality
- Magical realism—modern genre that moves between the objective world and the world of fantasy

Recommended Poets

In addition to those referred to throughout this book, the following poets are representative of the poets you will encounter on the exam.

Matthew Arnold

Fatimah Asghar

W. H. Auden

Jay Bernard

Hera Lindsay Bird

Elizabeth Bishop

Gwendolyn Brooks

Billy Collins

Sophie Collins

e. e. cummings

Tishani Doshi

Rita Dove

T. S. Eliot

Lawrence Ferlinghetti

Robert Francis

Allen Ginsberg

Robert Graves

Donald Hall

Robert Hayden

Seamus Heaney

Luke Kennard

Galway Kinnell

Maxine Kumin

Zaffar Kunial

Hollie McNish

Pablo Neruda

Sharon Olds

Mary Oliver

Wilfred Owen

Linda Pastan

Safiya Sinclair

Edna St. Vincent Millay

Hannah Sullivan

May Swenson

Wislawa Szymborska

Dylan Thomas

Natasha Tretheway

Kevin Young

Recommended Authors

Chinua Achebe: *Things Fall Apart*

Aeschylus: *Oresteia*

Margaret Atwood: *The Handmaid's Tale, Orynx and Crake*

Jane Austen: *Pride and Prejudice, Sense and Sensibility*

James Baldwin: *Go Tell It on the Mountain, Another Country*

Saul Bellow: *The Adventures of Augie March*

Charlotte Brontë: *Jane Eyre*

Emily Brontë: *Wuthering Heights*

Albert Camus: *The Stranger*

Willa Cather: *My Antonia, One of Ours, Death Comes to the Archbishop*

Anton Chekhov: *The Cherry Orchard*

Kate Chopin: *The Awakening*

Sandra Cisneros: *The House on Mango Street*

Joseph Conrad: *Heart of Darkness, Lord Jim, The Secret Sharer*

Stephen Crane: *The Red Badge of Courage*

Don Delillo: *White Noise*
Charles Dickens: *Great Expectations, A Tale of Two Cities*
Juno Diaz: *The Brief Wonderful Life of Oscar Wao*
Isak Dinesen: *Out of Africa*
Fyodor Dostoyevsky: *Crime and Punishment*
Theodore Dreiser: *An American Tragedy, Sister Carrie*
George Eliot: *Silas Marner, Middlemarch, Mill on the Floss*
Ralph Ellison: *Invisible Man*
Euripides: *Medea*
William Faulkner: *As I Lay Dying, The Sound and the Fury*
Henry Fielding: *Tom Jones*
F. Scott Fitzgerald: *The Great Gatsby*
Gustave Flaubert: *Madame Bovary*
E. M. Forster: *A Passage to India*
Thomas Hardy: *Jude the Obscure, Tess of the D'Urbervilles, Mayor of Casterbridge*
Nathaniel Hawthorne: *The Scarlet Letter*
Joseph Heller: *Catch-22*
Ernest Hemingway: *The Sun Also Rises*
Homer: *The Iliad, The Odyssey*
Khaled Hosseini: *The Kite Runner*
Zora Neale Hurston: *Their Eyes Were Watching God*
Aldous Huxley: *Brave New World*
Henrik Ibsen: *A Doll's House, Ghosts, Hedda Gabler*
Kazuo Ishiguro: *The Remains of the Day*
Henry James: *The Turn of the Screw, The American*
James Joyce: *A Portrait of the Artist as a Young Man, Dubliners*
Franz Kafka: *Metamorphosis, The Trial*
Ken Kesey: *One Flew Over the Cuckoo's Nest*
Barbara Kingsolver: *The Poisonwood Bible, Animal Dreams*
Maxine Hong Kingston: *The Woman Warrior*
D. H. Lawrence: *Sons and Lovers*
Chang-Rae Lee: *Native Speaker*
Cormac McCarthy: *The Road, Blood Meridian, All the Pretty Horses*
Gabriel García Márquez: *One Hundred Years of Solitude*
Herman Melville: *Moby-Dick, Billy Budd*
Arthur Miller: *Death of a Salesman, The Crucible*
N. Scott Momaday: *House Made of Dawn, In the Presence of the Sun, In the Bear's House, The Way to Rainy Mountain*
Toni Morrison: *Beloved, Song of Solomon, The Bluest Eyes*
V. S. Naipaul: *A Bend in the River*
Gloria Naylor: *Women of Brewster Place, LindenPlace*
Tim O'Brien: *The Things They Carried*
Eugene O'Neill: *Desire Under the Elms, Long Day's Journey into Night*
George Orwell: *1984*
Alan Paton: *Cry, the Beloved Country*
Jean Rhys: *Wide Sargasso Sea*
Jean Paul Sartre: *No Exit, Nausea*
William Shakespeare: *Hamlet, King Lear, Macbeth, Othello, Twelfth Night*
George Bernard Shaw: *Major Barbara, Man and Superman, Pygmalion*
Mary Shelley: *Frankenstein*

Sophocles: *Antigone, Oedipus Rex*
John Steinbeck: *The Grapes of Wrath, Of Mice and Men, Cannery Row*
Tom Stoppard: *Rosencrantz and Guildenstern Are Dead*
Jonathan Swift: *Gulliver's Travels*
Amy Tan: *The Kitchen God's Wife, The Bonesetter's Daughter*
Leo Tolstoy: *Anna Karenina*
Mark Twain: *Adventures of Huckleberry Finn*
John Updike: *Rabbit Run*
Voltaire: *Candide*
Kurt Vonnegut: *Slaughterhouse-Five*
Alice Walker: *The Color Purple*
Edith Wharton: *Ethan Frome, The House of Mirth*
Oscar Wilde: *The Importance of Being Earnest*
Thornton Wilder: *Our Town*
Tennessee Williams: *A Streetcar Named Desire, The Glass Menagerie*
Virginia Woolf: *To the Lighthouse*
Richard Wright: *Native Son*

allegory A work that functions on a symbolic level.

alliteration The repetition of initial consonant sounds, such as "Peter Piper picked a peck of pickled peppers."

allusion A reference contained in a work.

anapest A metrical pattern of two unaccented syllables followed by an accented syllable (˘ ˘ ´).

antagonist The force or character that opposes the main character, the protagonist.

annotation To make personal notes on a text in order to get a better understanding of the material. These notes can include questions, an argument with the author acknowledging a good point, a clarification of an idea, theme, etc.

apostrophe Direct address in poetry. Yeats's line "Be with me Beauty, for the fire is dying" is a good example.

aside Words spoken by an actor intended to be heard by the audience but not by other characters on stage.

assonance The repetition of vowel sounds in non-rhyming words in close proximity.

aubade A love poem set at dawn which bids farewell to the beloved.

ballad A simple narrative poem, often incorporating dialogue that is written in quatrains, generally with a rhyme scheme of *a b c d*.

blank verse Unrhymed iambic pentameter. Most of Shakespeare's plays are in this form.

cacophony Harsh and discordant sounds in a line or passage of a literary work.

caesura A break or pause within a line of poetry indicated by punctuation and used to emphasize meaning.

catharsis According to Aristotle, the release of emotion that the audience of a tragedy experiences.

character One who carries out the action of the plot in literature. Major, minor, static, and dynamic are types of characters.

climax The turning point of action or character in a literary work, usually the highest moment of tension.

comic relief The inclusion of a humorous character or scene to contrast with the tragic elements of a work, thereby intensifying the next tragic event.

commentary To present an explanation with evidence about a specific text based on the prompt, the audience, and the intended line of reasoning.

complexity The presence of tension, conflict, differences, changes, emotions, and human foibles in a specific text.

conflict A clash between opposing forces in a literary work, such as man vs. man; man vs. nature; man vs. God; man vs. self.

connotation The interpretive level of a word based on its associated images rather than its literal meaning.

convention A traditional aspect of a literary work, such as a soliloquy in a Shakespearean play or a tragic hero in a Greek tragedy.

couplet Two lines of rhyming poetry; often used by Shakespeare to conclude a scene or an important passage.

dactyl A foot of poetry consisting of a stressed syllable followed by two unstressed syllables, (´ ˘ ˘).

denotation The literal or dictionary meaning of a word.

denouement The conclusion or tying up of loose ends in a literary work; the resolution of the conflict and plot.

deus ex machina A Greek invention, literally "the god from the machine" who appears at the last moment and resolves the loose ends of a play. Today, the term refers to anyone, usually of some stature, who untangles, resolves, or reveals the key to the plot of a work. See the conclusion of Euripides's *Medea* for an example or the sheriff at the end of *Desire Under the Elms* by O'Neill.

diction The author's choice of words.

dramatic monologue A type of poem that presents a conversation between a speaker and an implied listener. Browning's "My Last Duchess" is a perfect example.

elegy A poem that laments the dead or a loss. "Elegy for Jane" by Roethke is a specific example. Gray's

"Elegy in a Country Church Yard" is a general example.

enjambment A technique in poetry that involves the running on of a line or stanza. It enables the poem to move and to develop coherence as well as directing the reader with regard to form and meaning. Walt Whitman uses this continually.

epic A lengthy, elevated poem that celebrates the exploits of a hero. *Beowulf* is a prime example.

epigram A brief witty poem. Pope often utilizes this form for satiric commentary.

euphony The pleasant, mellifluous presentation of sounds in a literary work.

exposition Background information presented in a literary work.

fable A simple, symbolic story, usually employing animals as characters. Aesop and La Fontaine are authors who excel at this form.

figurative language The body of devices that enables the writer to operate on levels other than the literal one. It includes metaphor, simile, symbol, motif, hyperbole, and others discussed in Chapter 8.

flashback A device that enables a writer to refer to past thoughts, events, episodes.

foot A metrical unit in poetry; a syllabic measure of a line: iamb, trochee, anapest, dactyl, and spondee.

foreshadowing Hints of future events in a literary work.

form The shape or structure of a literary work.

free verse Poetry without a defined form, meter, or rhyme scheme.

hyperbole Extreme exaggeration. In "My Love is Like a Red, Red Rose," Burns speaks of loving "until all the seas run dry."

iamb A metrical foot consisting of an unaccented syllable followed by an accented one; the most common poetic foot in the English language, (˘ ´).

idyll A type of lyric poem which extols the virtues of an ideal place or time.

image A verbal approximation of a sensory impression, concept, or emotion.

imagery The total effect of related sensory images in a work of literature.

impressionism Writing that reflects a personal image of a character, event, or concept. *The Secret Sharer* is a fine example.

irony An unexpected twist or contrast between what happens and what was intended or expected to happen. It involves dialogue and situation, and it can be intentional or unplanned. Dramatic irony centers around the ignorance of those involved while the audience is aware of the circumstance.

line of reasoning The logical sequencing of claims that present support of a thesis statement. This is accomplished by showing the relationship between and among the thesis and the claim developed in each of the body paragraphs.

lyric poetry A type of poetry characterized by emotion, personal feelings, and brevity; a large and inclusive category of poetry that exhibits rhyme, meter, and reflective thought.

magical realism A type of literature that explores narratives by and about characters who inhabit and experience their reality differently from what we term the objective world. Writers who are frequently placed in this category include Gabriel García Márquez, Günter Grass, and Isabel A llende.

metaphor A direct comparison between dissimilar things. "Your eyes are stars" is an example.

metaphysical poetry Refers to the work of poets like John Donne who explore highly complex, philosophical ideas through extended metaphors and paradox.

meter A pattern of beats in poetry. (Answers to questions in poetry review: 5, 3, 2, 2, 4)

metonymy A figure of speech in which a representative term is used for a larger idea. ("The pen is mightier than the sword.")

monologue A speech given by one character. (Hamlet's "To be or not to be . . . ")

motif The repetition or variations of an image or idea in a work which is used to develop theme or characters.

narrative poem A poem that tells a story.

narrator The speaker of a literary work.

octave An eight-line stanza, usually combined with a sestet in a Petrarchan sonnet.

ode A formal, lengthy poem that celebrates a particular subject.

onomatopoeia Words that sound like the sound they represent (hiss, gurgle, bang).

oxymoron An image of contradictory terms (bittersweet, pretty ugly, giant economy size).

parable A story that operates on more than one level and usually teaches a moral lesson. (*The Pearl* by John Steinbeck is a fine example. See *Allegory*.)

paradox A set of seemingly contradictory elements which nevertheless reflects an underlying truth.

For example, in Shakespeare's *Much Ado About Nothing*, the Friar says to Hero, "Come, Lady, die to live."

parallel plot A secondary story line that mimics and reinforces the main plot. (Hamlet loses his father, as does Ophelia.)

parody A comic imitation of a work that ridicules the original.

pathos The aspects of a literary work that elicit pity from the audience.

personification The assigning of human qualities to inanimate objects or concepts. (Wordsworth personifies "the sea that bares her bosom to the moon" in the poem "London, 1802.")

plot A sequence of events in a literary work.

point of view The method of narration in a work.

protagonist The hero or main character of a literary work, the character the audience sympathizes with.

quatrain A four-line stanza.

resolution The denouement of a literary work.

rhetorical question A question that does not expect an explicit answer. It is used to pose an idea to be considered by the speaker or audience.

rhyme/rime The duplication of final syllable sounds in two or more lines.

rhyme scheme The annotation of the pattern of the rhyme.

rhythm The repetitive pattern of beats in poetry.

romanticism A style or movement of literature that has as its foundation an interest in freedom, adventure, idealism, and escape.

satire A mode of writing based on ridicule, which criticizes the foibles and follies of society without necessarily offering a solution. (Jonathan Swift's *Gulliver's Travels* is a great satire that exposes mankind's condition.)

scansion Analysis of a poem's rhyme and meter.

sestet A six-line stanza, usually paired with an octave to form a Petrarchan sonnet.

sestina A highly structured poetic form of 39 lines, written in iambic pentameter. It depends upon the repetition of six words from the first stanza in each of six stanzas.

setting The time and place of a literary work.

simile An indirect comparison that uses the word, "like" or "as" to link the differing items in the comparison. ("Your eyes are like stars.")

soliloquy A speech in a play which is used to reveal the character's inner thoughts to the audience.

(Hamlet's "To be or not to be . . . " is one of the most famous soliloquies in literature.)

sonnet A 14-line poem with a prescribed rhyme scheme in iambic pentameter. (See Chapter 9 for a comparison between Shakespearean and Petrarchan sonnets.)

sophistication In the support of the thesis and development of the line of reasoning, the writer demonstrates a mature control of language and/or the ability to connect the text and prompt to a broader context, perspective, or argument.

spondee A poetic foot consisting of two accented syllables (′ ′).

stage directions The specific instructions a playwright includes concerning sets, characterization, delivery, etc. (*See Hedda Gabler* by Ibsen.)

stanza A unit of a poem, similar in rhyme, meter, and length to other units in the poem.

structure The organization and form of a work.

style The unique way an author presents his ideas. Diction, syntax, imagery, structure, and content all contribute to a particular style.

subplot A secondary plot that explores ideas different from the main storyline. (In *Hamlet*, the main storyline has Hamlet avenging the death of his father. The subplot has Hamlet dealing with his love for Ophelia.)

subtext Implied meaning of a work or section of a work.

symbol Something in a literary work that stands for something else. (Plato has the light of the sun symbolize truth in "The Allegory of the Cave.")

synecdoche A figure of speech that utilizes a part as representative of the whole. ("All hands on deck" is an example.)

syntax The grammatical structure of prose and poetry.

tercet A three-line stanza.

theme The underlying ideas that the author illustrates through characterization, motifs, language, plot, etc.

tone The author's attitude toward his subject.

tragic hero According to Aristotle, a basically good person of noble birth or exalted position who has a fatal flaw or commits an error in judgment which leads to his downfall. The tragic hero must have a moment of realization and live and suffer.

trochee A single metrical foot consisting of one accented (stressed/long) syllable followed by one unaccented (unstressed/short) syllable (´ ˘).

understatement The opposite of exaggeration. It is a technique for developing irony and/or humor where one writes or says less than intended.

villanelle A highly structured poetic form that comprises six stanzas: five tercets and a quatrain. The poem repeats the first and third lines throughout.

There are literally thousands of sites on the internet that are in some way related to the study of college-level English. We are not attempting to give you a comprehensive list of all of these websites. What we are going to do is to provide you with a list that is most relevant to your preparation and review for the AP Literature and Composition exam. It is up to you to log on to a site that may be of interest to you and to see for yourself just what it can offer and whether or not it will be of specific benefit to you. Don't forget that you have a dedicated AP website from McGraw Hill that can be of great help to you as you work your way through the AP English Literature course and as you prepare for the exam in May. Go to the Cross-Platform Prep Course: www.xplatform.mhprofessional.com and enter your access code printed on the back cover.

> *Note:* These websites were available and online at the time this book was revised. Please be aware that we cannot guarantee that a site you choose to explore will be operating when you go to that URL.

Because this is an Advanced Placement exam for which you are preparing, why not go to the source as your first choice? The College Board's AP site is called AP Central:

- **http://www.collegeboard.com/apc**

Related to British Literature:

- Romanticism: **http://www.uh.edu/engines/romanticism/poets.html**
- British history: **http://www.bbc.co.uk/history**
- Study guide: **http://www.studyguide.org/brit_lit_timeline.htm**
- Ultimate Shakespeare site: **http://playshakespeare.com**

Related to American Literature:

- Authors, timelines, literary movements: **http://public.wsu.edu/~campbelld/amlit/sites .htm**
- Literature: Voice of the Shuttle: **http://vos.ucsb.edu**

Of General Interest:

- Purdue Online Writing Lab: **http://owl.english.purdue.edu**
- For links to other websites for English literature: **http://www.kn.att.com/wired/fil/ pages/listaplitma.html**
- For terms, exercises, tips, and rules from a primate with attitude, go to Grammar Bytes: **http://chompchomp.com**
- For help with rhetorical and literary terms, there are three useful sites: **http://mcl.as.uky .edu/glossary-rhetorical-terms,** **http://andromeda.rutgers.edu/~jlynch/Terms/**, and **http://humanities.byu.edu/rhetoric/**

- For access to the world of arts and letters, including newspapers, literary magazines, and blogs: **http://artsandlettersdaily.com**
- To download free e-books: **www.bartleby.com**
- For a directory to free downloadable e-books as well as articles, reviews, and comments: **www.e-booksdirectory.com**
- For WebNotes, a useful tool that allows you to compile and organize information from multiple web pages and share findings: **www.webnotes.net**

Each of these websites will lead you to many more. You will have to take the time to explore the various sites and to make your own evaluation as to their value to you and your expectations.

We suggest you use your favorite web server or search engine and type in ADVANCED PLACEMENT ENGLISH (AP), or ADVANCED PLACEMENT (AP) LITERATURE. (Our favorite search engine is www.google.com.) From that point on, you can "surf the net" for those sites that suit your particular needs. You will have to take the time to explore these various domains and to make your own evaluation of their value to you and your expectations. Perhaps, you might even decide to set up your own AP Lit website or chat room.

The Cross-Platform Prep Course

McGraw Hill's multi-platform course gives you a variety of tools to help you raise your test scores. Whether you're studying at home, in the library, or on-the-go, you can find practice content in the format you need—print, online, or mobile.

Print Book

This print book gives you the tools you need to ace the test. In its pages you'll find smart test-taking strategies, in-depth reviews of key topics, and ample practice questions and tests. See the Welcome section of your book for a step-by-step guide to its features.

Online Platform

The Cross-Platform Prep Course gives you additional study and practice content that you can access *anytime, anywhere*. You can create a personalized study plan based on your test date that sets daily goals to keep you on track. Integrated lessons provide important review of key topics. Practice questions, exams, and flashcards give you the practice you need to build test-taking confidence. The game center is filled with challenging games that allow you to practice your new skills in a fun and engaging way. And, you can even interact with other test-takers in the discussion section and gain valuable peer support.

Getting Started

To get started, open your account on the online platform:

Go to the URL shown on the inside front cover

↓

Enter your access code

↓

Provide your name and e-mail address to open your account and create a password

↓

Click "Start Studying" to enter the platform

It's as simple as that. You're ready to start studying online.

Your Personalized Study Plan

First, select your test date on the calendar, and you'll be on your way to creating your personalized study plan. Your study plan will help you stay organized and on track and will guide you through the course in the most efficient way. It is tailored to *your* schedule and features daily tasks that are broken down into manageable goals. You can adjust your test date at any time and your daily tasks will be reorganized into an updated plan.

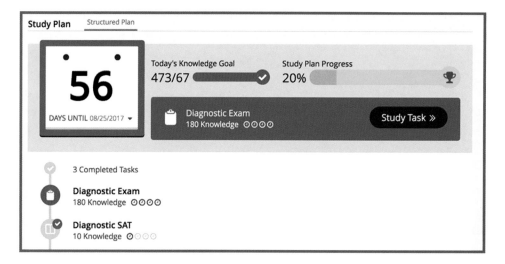

You can track your progress in real time on the Study Plan Dashboard. The "Today's Knowledge Goal" progress bar gives you up-to-the minute feedback on your daily goal. Fulfilling this every time you log on is the most efficient way to work through the entire course. You always get an instant view of where you stand in the entire course with the Study Plan Progress bar.

> *If you need to exit the program before completing a task, you can return to the Study Plan Dashboard at any time. Just click the Study Task icon and you can automatically pick up where you left off.*

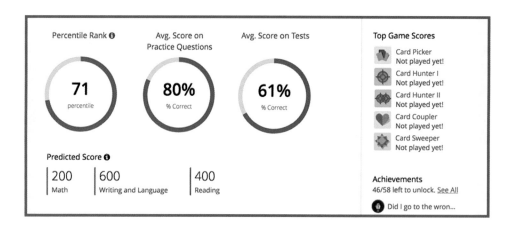

Practice Tests

One of the first tasks in your personalized study plan is to take the Diagnostic Test. At the end of the test, a detailed evaluation of your strengths and weaknesses shows the areas where you need the most focus. You can review your practice test results either by the question category to see broad trends or question-by-question for a more in-depth look.

The full-length tests are designed to simulate the real thing. Try to simulate actual testing conditions and be sure you set aside enough time to complete the full-length test. You'll learn to pace yourself so that you can work toward the best possible score on test day.

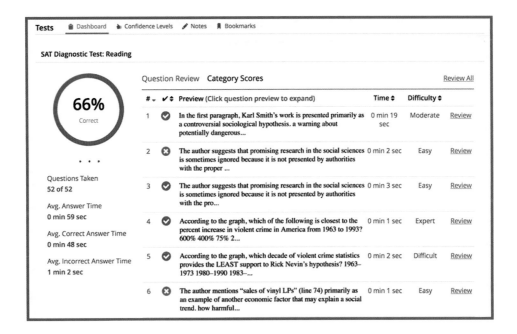

Lessons

The lessons in the online platform are divided into manageable pieces that let you build knowledge and confidence in a progressive way. They cover the full range of topics that you're likely to see on your test.

After you complete a lesson, mark your confidence level. (You must indicate a confidence level in order to count your progress and move on to the next task.) You can also filter the lessons by confidence levels to see the areas you have mastered and those that you might need to revisit.

> *Use the bookmark feature to easily refer back to a concept or leave a note to remember your thoughts or questions about a particular topic.*

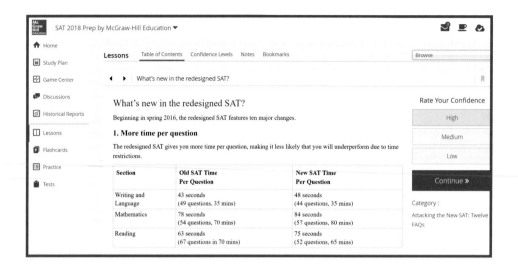

Practice Questions

All of the practice questions are reflective of actual exams and simulate the test-taking experience. The "Review Answer" button gives you immediate feedback on your answer. Each question includes a rationale that explains why the correct answer is right and the others are wrong. To explore any topic further, you can find detailed explanations by clicking the "Help me learn about this topic" link.

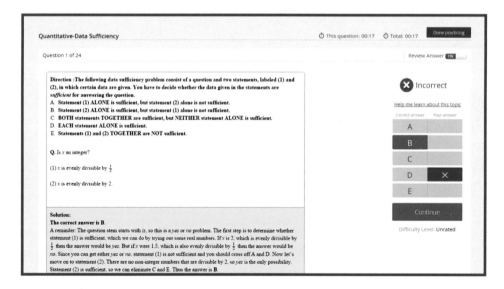

You can go to the Practice Dashboard to find an overview of your performance in the different categories and sub-categories.

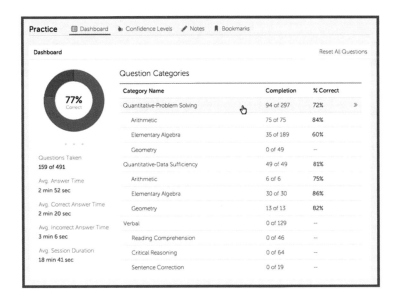

Dashboard

The dashboard is constantly updating to reflect your progress and performance. The Percentile Rank icon shows your position relative to all the other students enrolled in the course. You can also find information on your average scores in practice questions and exams.

A detailed overview of your strengths and weaknesses shows your proficiency in a category based on your answers and difficulty of the questions. By viewing your strengths and weaknesses, you can focus your study on areas where you need the most help.

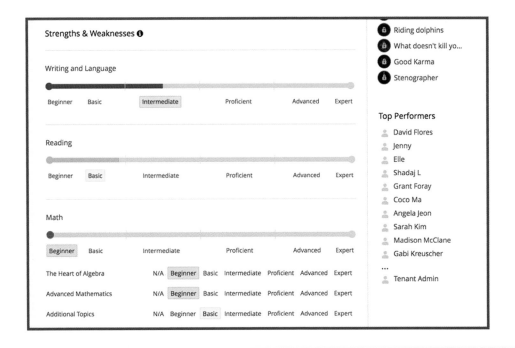

Flashcards

The hundreds of flashcards are perfect for learning key terms quickly, and the interactive format gives you immediate feedback. You can filter the cards by category and confidence level for a more organized approach. Or, you can shuffle them up for a more general challenge.

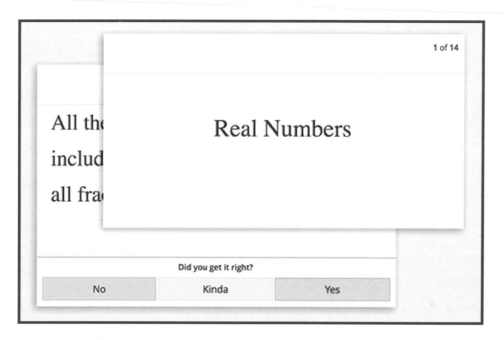

Another way to customize the flashcards is to create your own sets. You can either keep these private or share or them with the public. Subscribe to Community Sets to access sets from other students preparing for the same exam.

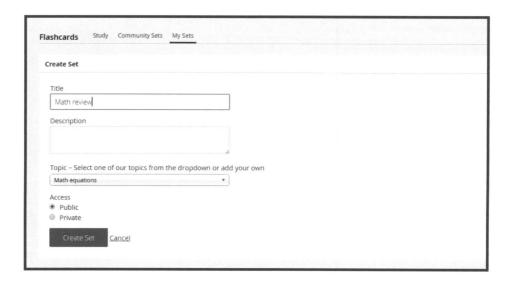